Women, Families, and Communities

READINGS IN AMERICAN HISTORY

Women, Families, and Communities

READINGS IN AMERICAN HISTORY

SECOND EDITION

NANCY HEWITT

KIRSTEN DELEGARD

PEARSON

Longman

New York   San Francisco   Boston
London   Toronto   Sydney   Tokyo   Singapore   Madrid
Mexico City   Munich   Paris   Cape Town   Hong Kong   Montreal

Vice President and Publisher: Priscilla McGeehon
Executive Editor: Michael Boezi
Executive Marketing Manager: Sue Westmoreland
Production Manager: Savoula Amanatidis
Project Coordination and Text Design: Elm Street Publishing Services, Inc.
Electronic Page Makeup: Integra Software Services, Pvt. Ltd.
Cover Design Manager: Wendy Ann Fredericks
Cover Designer: Susan Koski Zucker
Cover Photo: Andreas Larsen Dahl/WHS/Robertstock/Classicstock.com
Photo Researcher: Anita Dickhuth
Manufacturing Buyer: Lucy Hebard
Printer and Binder: Courier Corporation—Stoughton
Cover Printer: Courier Corporation—Stoughton

For permission to use copyrighted material, grateful acknowledgment is made to the
copyright holders on p. 283, which are hereby made part of this copyright page.

Library of Congress Cataloging-in-Publication Data

Women, families, and communities: readings in American history/[edited by] Nancy
   Hewitt, Kirsten Delegard—2nd ed.
      p. cm.
   ISBN-13: 978-0-321-41487-8 (alk. paper)
      1. Women—United States—History.   2. United States—Social Conditions.   I. Hewitt,
Nancy A.   II. Delegard, Kirsten.
   HQ1410.W646 2008
   306.85082'0973—dc22

                                                                    2007019733

Please visit us at www.ablongman.com

ISBN-13: 978-0-321-41487-8
ISBN-10: 0-321-41487-X

1 2 3 4 5 6 7 8 9 10—CRS—10 09 08 07

TO MY BROTHER WILL AND IN MEMORY OF TOM.
— N. H.

TO MY MOTHER, DOROTHY DELEGARD,
WHO TAUGHT ME THE IMPORTANCE OF WOMEN,
FAMILIES, AND COMMUNITIES.
— K. D.

Contents

Good research and good teaching go hand in hand. The first edition of *Women, Families, and Communities: Readings in American History* grew directly out of the connection between these two activities in Nancy Hewitt's own work. As a student of women's history—and more specifically of women's activism and women's work in Rochester, New York, and Tampa, Florida—Hewitt traced the ways that ordinary mothers, wives, and daughters contributed to the development of their families and communities. At the same time, as a teacher of introductory American history, she focused on the ways that the major events in our nation's past—wars, elections, depressions, and technological revolutions—shaped and were shaped by the lives and actions of common women and men.

The articles collected here provide an introduction for students and instructors to the rich historical literature on women, families, and communities as well as a means for integrating the insights of this research into the story of North America's past. Most students come to college with a limited knowledge of the diverse experiences of American women across time and place. Fortunately, many college textbooks in American history now incorporate substantial information on women and family life, but given the vast amount of material to be covered, they can generally offer only brief attention to these topics in any one period. Women's history textbooks provide a much richer array of materials on a more diverse range of women. Still, it is difficult in a textbook or in lectures to cover both the broad sweep of American or women's history and the particular experiences and actions of a wide array of historical actors. By combining the readings from this anthology with texts, lectures, and other monographs, students will learn how ordinary individuals, like themselves, participated in the shaping of America's past.

What is clear in looking at the table of contents in this volume and in works on women's history in general is the diversity of American experiences. Although it is impossible to capture this diversity in a single collection, it is possible to encourage students to think about the range and richness of the American past. How did American Indians respond to European colonization? How did Africans respond to slavery? How did the experiences and meanings of industrialization, World War I, or the Great Depression differ by region, race, class, ethnic background, and gender? How and when did groups generally viewed as oppressed—American Indians,

African Americans, workers, women, immigrants—find the means to organize and protest on their own behalf? How did age shape individual experiences of and responses to colonization, war, industrialization, urbanization, and other historical developments? Each of these questions and the many others raised by the authors of the articles included here challenge us to see how everyday life and the "great events" of history intersect.

It is precisely at such intersections that women's historians most often are struck by the impossibility of separating women's experiences from those of men. In teaching American history, many of us have now integrated research on female activists and female workers into the larger stories of social reform and agricultural and industrial development. Even if we focus on seemingly more masculine historical endeavors such as war, we quickly see how the activities and experiences of women and men are intertwined. We cannot fully understand the causes of wars, their short-term consequences or long-term significance, the means by which one side wins and the other loses, or even the particular strategies and tactics employed, without examining women's as well as men's participation.

In the earliest wars studied in an American history survey course—the French and Indian War, the Revolutionary War, the Civil War—the boundaries between the battlefield and the home front were blurred and always changing. During such conflicts, although women and men were expected to carry out different tasks, either sex might find itself called upon to nurse, cook, sew, spy, or fight. In later periods, when North Americans fought their wars overseas—in Cuba, the Philippines, Europe, and Asia—women's and men's roles were more distinct. Still, as men left for training camp and foreign combat, women expanded their activities on the home front to encompass many traditionally male jobs within the family, community, industries, government, and professions. In the most recent conflicts involving the United States—in Afghanistan and Iraq, for example—women have served in a much wider array of roles within the military and more have joined men on the battlefront. In whichever time period, whether men alone or men and women are serving on the frontlines, and whatever the location or duration of battles, family and community members find their normal relations disrupted and transformed—sometimes temporarily, sometimes forever.

Developing links between women's history and history that has traditionally emphasized men and masculine activities is one of the goals of this work. Thus, the readings included here, most of which were written by women's historians, were selected because they chronicle local as well as national history; social as well as political and economic development; and women's as well as men's experiences and actions.

These articles provide case studies of individuals, families, and communities that illustrate broader historical themes. The introductions to each of the chronological parts, the headnotes to each of the articles, and the Suggested Readings and Web Sites and Questions for Study and Review at the end of each article place the individual essays in a wider context. At the same time, this material suggests how larger historical developments were themselves shaped by the events that occurred in particular families and communities. For each article, the study and review questions require students to relate the material presented to major issues of the time period and to other articles in the reader.

As researchers, scholars generally approach history as a complex process in which a wide range of individuals, experiences, and institutions come into play. As teachers, we often find it difficult to convey such complexities to our students. This volume is an attempt to introduce into the American history and women's history survey course more of the process of studying history. By asking students to connect political events with social forces and great affairs of state with common occurrences such as birth, marriage, housework, childrearing, sex, sharecropping, and washing clothes, we can help students understand what was involved in forming, sustaining, and transforming the people, families, and communities that built our nation.

This second edition of *Women, Families, and Communities* reflects many of the changes in American history and American women's history that have occurred since 1990. It also reflects the insights of the co-editor, Kirsten Delegard, an independent historian whose work focuses on revising understandings of women's activism by examining how conservative women shaped politics in the twentieth century. Thus, this edition not only incorporates an even wider range of racial, ethnic, and regional perspectives than the first edition but also incorporates a wider range of ideological perspectives. This edition also explores more fully the gendered character of the American past. Interactions between women and men—whether in the midst of colonial conquest, plantation households, social activism, or military ventures—are highlighted throughout the volumes. In addition, men's relation to other men is also examined in particular contexts, including the California Gold Rush, post-Civil War politics, and the civil rights movement. Finally, since the first edition was published, studies of sexuality have reshaped understandings of women's and gender history. New work in this field appears in this volume, demonstrating the intimate connections among sexuality, family, and community life and local and regional political and social developments.

The selection of articles and images has been an intense learning experience. We have been constantly amazed, and often frustrated, in making hard choices among the profusion of wonderful books, articles, prints, and photographs. We hope that the revisions and additions to this edition of *Women, Families, and Communities* will make the volumes as intellectually engaging and challenging to students as the work has been to us.

For their thoughtful evaluations and constructive suggestions, we wish to thank our reviewers: Kathryn Abbott, Western Kentucky University; Linda Alkana, California State University–Long Beach; Jacqueline Cavalier, Community College of Allegheny County; Stephanie Cole, University of Texas–Arlington; Kate M. Dierenfield, Canisius College; Christine Erickson, Indiana–Purdue University, Fort Wayne; Laura Fishman, York College; Jackie Flowers, Clackamas Community College; Anne Klejment, University of St. Thomas; Wendy Kline, University of Cincinnati; Peter Levy, York College; Alison M. Parker, State University of New York–Brockport; Linda Pitelka, Maryville University; Lelia Roeckell, Molloy College; Catherine Tobin, Central Michigan University; Shirley Teresa Wajda, Kent State University; and Nancy Zens, Central Oregon Community College.

Nancy Hewitt
Kirsten Delegard

H istory has a dual meaning: It refers both to the events of the past and to interpretations of those events. The events that make up American history involved all kinds of people and took place in every type of setting. Rich, middling, and poor; white, brown, and black; native-born and immigrant; young and old; female and male; in cities and on farms; in metropolitan centers and in small villages; in long-settled communities and on the move; North and South; East and West—all Americans shaped the nation's history. Indians, blacks, and Hispanics as well as Europeans populated the North American continent; immigrant and farm families as well as "first families" produced its citizens; workers and grassroots activists as well as entrepreneurs and political leaders shaped its development.

Yet for a long time, scholars' interpretations of the past concentrated on Western Europeans and their American-born descendants, especially the men who served as business, political, or military leaders. These figures received far more attention than any other group, often more than all other groups combined. Such interpretations directed our eyes to a narrow segment of the continent's rich history. Like viewfinders at the Grand Canyon, they focused our gaze on the most spectacular peaks and valleys but failed to reveal the more mundane materials and processes that helped forge these vistas.

Historians are less like viewfinders than photographers. They actively select the angle of vision and the subject that they think will best reflect or illuminate a particular moment. A photographer covering a presidential campaign rally may stand in the crowd, but he or she will use a telephoto lens to zoom in on the candidate. In the morning paper, then, one will see only blurred, background images of the women and men who will vote in the election but a detailed, larger-than-life portrait of the man or woman who seeks to represent them. If we think of history textbooks as providing snapshots of significant moments in America's past, then this volume is an attempt to bring the blurred backgrounds into focus—indeed, to bring those background figures momentarily to the forefront.

Since the first edition of *Women, Families, and Communities* was published in 1990, much has changed in the world of photography as well as in women's history. Digital cameras, scanners, camera phones, computers, and similar technologies make it easier for ordinary people to capture images and events and to disseminate them electronically to a wide and varied audience. Still, it is important to remember that earlier changes in technology also transformed American society and women's and men's relationships to visual culture. In 1839, for example, Louis Daguerre perfected the first practical method for taking photographs, and daguerreotypes (early photographs) became popular among urban residents who sat for pictures at local studios and rural folk who were introduced to the technique by traveling daguerreotypists. The Civil War greatly increased the demand for daguerreotypes as soldiers sent home pictures of themselves in uniform and commercial photographers like Mathew Brady chronicled the conflict on the battlefield. Such images—or engravings and lithographs based on them—were widely circulated due to advances in print technology in the early and mid-nineteenth century, which led to inexpensive illustrated newspapers and magazines. Some women used the new technology to advance their views on the social issues of the day. Abolitionist and women's rights advocate Sojourner Truth sold portraits of herself, known as *cartes de visite,* to help support herself and her reform activities. A host of later inventions, from the first inexpensive handheld camera (marketed as the kodak) to the movie camera, television, video, computers, and camera phones, continued to democratize the creation and circulation of visual images.

Each of these new technologies transformed the way we see the world and whom we see in the world. Today television stations increasingly employ pictures or videos shot by individuals who happen to be present when a newsworthy event occurs. Indeed, those individuals sometimes help to determine what is newsworthy. Video clips produced by amateurs, for instance, might reveal a grainy underside of life—police beating an unarmed suspect—or a heroic moment—neighbors catching a baby thrown from the window of a burning home—that would otherwise be missed. Such images are no more easily interpreted than those created by professional camera crews, but they do provide a different perspective, and they frequently illuminate shadowy figures that might otherwise have remained hidden from history. At the same time, digital cameras, camera phones, and Web sites offer ordinary women and men new opportunities to shape and circulate their own images and those of others. Our familiarity today with the means by which images can be manipulated, for better or worse, should sensitize us as we examine earlier representations of women, and men, in American history. And the pictures and video clips themselves will provide future generations with new ways to investigate at least some of those background figures in American history.

To focus on a wide range of American experiences, we can draw on the voluminous work produced in the last three decades by social historians. Social history emphasizes the experiences of common women and men, allowing us to hear the voices of those rendered "inarticulate" by traditional interpretations. Viewing the past as a dynamic process in which all Americans participated, these scholars have revealed the ways that American Indians, African Americans, immigrants, workers, and women shaped their worlds and our history. Other types of historians have now embraced the questions raised

by social historians. Political historians investigate the role of race, class, and gender in voting and campaigning. Cultural historians trace the rise of the market economy and consumer culture or the ways African Americans and women shape and are shaped by music, literature, art, and film.

These historians have been especially concerned to discover the ways that those with only limited resources influenced the course of economic, social, and political development. By focusing on individual forms of resistance to exploitation (such as a slave feigning illness or purposely setting a slow pace of work) as well as collective acts of protest (such as boycotts, demonstrations, and organized social movements), historians have illuminated an entirely new historical terrain. This terrain is one on which ordinary women and men, regardless of their wealth, status, or formal political power, become active agents of change, affecting critical historical developments.

To uncover the activities and ideas of less powerful groups, historians often search out evidence on individual families and communities as a means of exploring the occurrences of everyday life. These events are then placed beside those we conventionally think of as important in America's past to illuminate the relations between ordinary people and extraordinary events. The present volume will draw on this rich body of research to bring these background figures into focus.

The purpose of focusing on more common people and their daily routines, of moving apparently peripheral figures to center stage, is not simply to replace one angle of vision with another. While we are examining seemingly unremarkable women and men in their families and communities, we will often discover their remarkable qualities—courage, persistence, strength, ingenuity. We will find that common folk performed uncommon feats when social upheaval, economic crisis, wartime mobilization, or personal necessity demanded that they do so. Yet at the same time, we will find women and men prevented from acting in their own interests or those of their neighbors by poverty, prejudice, and other disabling factors. Finally, we will explore how some members of less powerful groups—wealthy women, for example—used their access to education, financial resources, or political influence to shape (or constrain) the lives and life choices of others.

This volume, then, will examine how ordinary people both shaped and were shaped by the persons and events traditionally considered central to the nation's development. Ultimately, a new vision of our history will appear, one that brings into simultaneous focus national events and leaders and ordinary people in local communities. In this way, relationships between common folk in their everyday lives (people like most of you reading this book) and individual leaders of states, armies, corporations, and social movements will be made clearer.

Photographs are not only selective images of persons and events. They are also often idealized versions, simple images that reflect complex realities. The portrait of a former slave holding a white child (previous page) can carry many captions, none of which will fully capture the intimate and ambiguous relations between black women and their white charges. The look in this unnamed woman's eyes may be resignation or defiance. Her employment as a nanny after the Civil War may be a sign of new opportunities or renewed bondage. The baby may grow up to be a member of the Ku Klux Klan or of the National Association for the Advancement of Colored People.

We all develop images of the kinds of people who make up the population—of women and men, blacks and whites, workers and bosses, rural southerners and cosmopolitan northerners. Our perceptions range from accurate to stereotypical to fanciful. These images emerge from newspapers, television, schoolrooms, novels, films, advertising, Web sites, community and family attitudes, and a host of other sources. In past centuries, sermons, paintings, magazines, lectures, traveling museums, cartoons, folktales, and songs were even more important in shaping Americans' views of the world around them and, perhaps more markedly, of people and places far distant. Such images, regardless of their accuracy, affected the ways that any one group of Americans responded to others—Europeans to American Indians, whites to blacks, country folk to city dwellers, southerners to northerners, women to men.

Depictions of women, families, and communities have changed dramatically over the years, but in each era dominant images have provided ideals to be either emulated or defied. Indian princesses, submissive wives, hardy pioneers, black nannies, Victorian ladies, flamboyant flappers, wartime riveters, happy homemakers, women's libbers—each presented a portrait with which, or against which, women were measured and measured themselves. Since most such figures were based on a single class or race of women, it is only by examining a variety of individuals from a range of families and communities that we can begin to understand how such ideal types arose and what their effects were on women and men of particular times and places.

Family and community are also idealized notions. Leading commentators from every generation of American citizens have lamented the decline of the "traditional" family and the loss of the "close-knit" community. Puritan clergy and born-again Christians, female moral reformers of the mid-nineteenth century and political candidates of the twenty-first, eighteenth-century diarists and contemporary bloggers have all bemoaned the failure of real-life families and communities to live up to the models we carry in our minds. We should not let the similarity of these laments obscure real differences in the changing forms of family and community life over time and across region, race, ethnicity, and class.

Yet commonalities in these laments can tell us something important about people's shared desire for a sense of place and of belonging, regardless of how big or developed or powerful the nation as a whole becomes. Again, only by examining a variety of settings and situations over the course of American history can we begin to understand the multiple forms family and community have taken and their effects on regional, racial, ethnic, and class relations and on national development.

Women's historians have devoted particular attention to these dimensions of our American heritage: common folk, daily life, dominant cultural symbols and images, definitions of family and community, popular forms of protest, and differences in each of these rooted in race, class, ethnicity, and region. Women's historians, focusing initially on the differences in women's and men's experiences in the past, have asked new questions, introduced new sources, offered new interpretations of the roles that women played in America, and suggested new ways of marking major transitions and turning points in our nation's history.

Emerging from the women's movement of the 1960s and 1970s, these scholars initially applied the feminist rubric—"the personal is political"—to examinations of history. Thus, they focused on the relations between public and private spheres, home and work, domesticity and politics. They considered whether changes in household technology and birth control methods might be as important as presidential elections and wars in determining how to divide American history into meaningful units of study. To probe these and other issues, researchers examined diaries and letters, census data and wills, sermons and novels, clothing and advertisements, and other artifacts left by those whose words and actions were not purposely recorded for posterity.

This research provides portraits of women as mothers, daughters, and wives; as servants, slaves, and free women; as wage earners, housewives, and volunteers; as immigrants, migrants, and settlers; and the whole range of roles that formed the female half of society. Some scholars focus on notable women—Abigail Adams, Elizabeth Cady Stanton, Ida B. Wells, Eleanor Roosevelt, Rosa Parks—demonstrating their right to be set alongside their male counterparts in the pantheon of American heroes. Others study all-female organizations and institutions—women's colleges and prisons, suffrage associations, literary societies, or single-sex reform groups—arguing for women's vital contributions to every phase of the nation's development. Some examine women's work, in and outside the family, and analyze its contributions to farming, commerce, slavery, industry, and the ever expanding service sector. Many follow the lives of ordinary women, as individuals and in groups, from birth to death, seeking to understand the parameters of female lives and how they have changed over time and place.

Yet researchers were not interested in looking at women only as a separate group, as important as that dimension of our history is. Rather, they also studied women in relation to men, to communities, and to the larger society. From this dual perspective—women's own experiences as women and their relationships with men—women's historians began rewriting American history to reflect the contributions and activities of the whole population. In doing so, they introduced gender—the cultural prescriptions and social roles assigned to individuals on the basis of their sex—as a critical category of analysis.

Since the 1980s, many scholars of women's and gender history have highlighted differences among women and the conflicts and challenges such differences spark. Scholars in the field have long sought to analyze women's agency, but more of them now recognize the ways that women wield power, and not only for progressive causes and ideals. Some women, for example, express racist beliefs and work to have them enshrined in law or enacted through violence in local communities. Throughout the past, women have disagreed with each other over fundamental political and social issues, and some have had a greater chance than others to put their ideas into practice. Given such disparities, it remains critical to trace the histories of women with few resources who have acted on behalf of themselves and their families and communities, confronting individuals and institutions that have more power and resources. Whether focusing on women with abundant or limited resources, it is also important to analyze women's relations with men as they pursue social and political agendas. When do women organize alongside other women, and when do they ally themselves with men? And how does each choice shape their public efforts and private relationships?

A renewed emphasis on culture has also transformed women's and gender history in recent years. For example, scholars have focused on how cultural differences among Indians, Europeans, and Africans shaped contact and conflict in the Americas during the colonial period and beyond. They have explored images and ideals of women and men from various races, regions, nationalities, religions, classes, and ages, exploring the ways that such representations shape, and distort, their interactions across time and place. Finally, cultural historians have joined with social and political historians to demonstrate the intertwined character of public and private life by examining such topics as the militarization of women and society in wartime; women's use of patriotic, moralistic, or racist rhetoric and icons to advance their own rights; and changes in patterns of consumption and consumer culture.

In expanding the reach of women's and gender history, scholars continue to frame their studies in different ways. Some use a wide-angle lens, emphasizing national or international developments; others focus in more closely on regional developments; and still others hone in on local histories or individual biographies.

This volume highlights the work of those who analyze women in the context of their families and communities. In such studies, the new scholarship on women is integrated with that on men, and the lives of native-born white women and men are set beside those of American Indians, African Americans, and immigrants. The particular communities examined here cover various regions of the country and include members of a wide range of races, classes, and ethnic groups. Using gender as a key category of analysis, each study illuminates some important aspect of our nation's development. Collectively, these readings reveal the changing nature of women's and men's roles and of family and community across the course of American history and analyze how these changes shaped and were shaped by larger social, economic, and political forces.

The articles in this book will provide evidence that can be used in combination with information from other readings, lectures, and discussions to draw a new portrait of our national past. Imagine for a moment what the slave trade, the American Revolution, the Gold Rush, the Great Depression, or the civil rights movement would look like if viewed for the first time through the lens of a video camera held by a woman standing in her local community. Imagine the Pocahontas legend if it had been recorded and embellished by Indian women rather than English men. Think for a moment of the way Sherman's March to the Sea during the Civil War would have been portrayed by a house slave in Atlanta. How might the breaking waves of the Atlantic Ocean or the overland trail to the West have been seen by a young wife with a child in tow and another on the way? Consider what a document listing the advantages of technological progress might contain if it were compiled by a young woman factory worker in the 1840s or the owner of a new wringer washer in the 1920s. Contemplate what Pearl Harbor meant to a black domestic servant in Texas or a Japanese-American girl completing her senior year of high school. Speculate on the way organized black women in Montgomery, Alabama, would remember Martin Luther King, Jr., whom they had to persuade to lead the city's bus boycott in 1955.

How might these portraits of the past vary if in each situation the woman recording or recalling the moment was replaced by her brother? How would they differ if history were recorded not from the perspective of their family and community, but from yours? By combining the rich documentation of ordinary women's and men's lives collected by historians with traditional interpretations of significant events and with our own understanding of how change occurs, we can begin to focus on a more complete picture of the past. This picture brings into view diverse groups of Americans and a wide range of issues, individuals, and events. If we could make it move, we would have something like a videotape of the past, perhaps the closest we could come to making the events of history and our interpretations of them converge. Even then, however, we might not agree with another person's idea of American history, for each person's view of historical events is unique. That uniqueness reflects in part America's heritage of diversity.

From the moment when American Indians, Europeans, and Africans first encountered one another in the New World, diversity characterized the continent's development. In the present, diversity—and the creativity and conflict it nurtures—continues to define the American nation. Differences in race and region, ethnicity and class, wealth and power, sex and social status shaped the nation's history as they shape the lives, culture, economic opportunities, and political choices of those who live in the United States. By capturing that half of history that occurred in local communities, among ordinary families, composed of common women and men, we reveal this diversity and thus more fully illuminate both the past and the present. The readings in this book will remind us that everyone—presidents, generals, corporate leaders, students, wage earners, and housewives—helps to create history.

TO 1900

Women,
Families, and
Communities

READINGS IN
AMERICAN HISTORY

PART I

New World Orders

The discovery of America and the role of Queen Isabella in sponsoring Christopher Columbus' first voyage to America in 1492 remained a popular topic for engravers and painters through the nineteenth century. This print appeared in the mass circulation magazine *Harper's Weekly* in May 1868, as the United States sought to reconstitute itself as a nation following the Civil War.

In the early 1600s, three peoples met on the North American mainland. The first group, long settled, initially welcomed the newcomers, seeing opportunities for trade and perhaps for domination. The second, recently arrived from Europe, found survival difficult and the transplantation of lifestyle and values even more problematic. The third, forcibly removed from African homelands, struggled to adjust to the new environment and to the intense labors demanded by white masters.

None of these groups were homogeneous, however. Among American Indians, differences in the size, location, and economic base of nations ensured not only separation but conflict, which might be intensified or eased upon contact with the new arrivals. Though clearly differentiating themseleves from the Indians, Europeans migrated from different regions for diverse reasons and established distinct political, religious, and social patterns in the colonies they founded. Africans, too, emerged from different regions and, especially during their first years in the New World, confronted a variety of legal and laboring conditions.

In addition to these distinctions, each group was divided by sex. Differences in the roles of women and men were probably most noticeable in the area of work, though the sexual division of labor varied significantly both within and among the three groups. Several of the largest and most powerful Indian nations—such as the Iroquois and the Cherokee—assigned women to agricultural labor and men to hunting and war. The importance of women's economic contribution was recognized by their inclusion in religious ceremonies, in tribal government, and in negotiations over war and trade.

In Chapter One, Camilla Townsend highlights a different but equally important role for Indian women. Native women often served as mediators between nations before Europeans arrived in the Americas. When it became clear that Englishmen planned to establish permanent settlements in North America, Indian leaders decided to include native women as mediators in this situation as well. Pocahontas gained fame for her efforts to negotiate relations between the English and the Powhatan Confederacy, the most powerful group of Indians in what would become the Virginia colony. Although much about the Pocahontas legend has been challenged by women's historians, Townsend makes clear that Pocahontas did play a critical role in the early interactions between America's native peoples and the English newcomers.

Initially, Pocahontas and other natives did not see America as a "New World" the way Europeans did. It had been home to their people for centuries. Still, when Europeans conquered and then settled North and South America, they introduced new plants and animals, new forms of labor and government, and new cultures and languages. This New World Order included Africans as well as Indians and Europeans. Indeed, the number of American Indians declined in the 1600s as European diseases and weapons provided formidable foes. In the same period, the number of African women in the mainland American colonies remained relatively small. In Europe's

Caribbean colonies, however, as in Africa, women's agricultural skills were widely recognized and exploited.

In Chapter Two, Jennifer Morgan traces the process by which African women were enslaved alongside men, held in forts along the African coasts or on ships nearby, and transported to the West Indies or mainland North America. Most of these Africans were sold to planters in the West Indies, where enslaved labor fueled the development of cash crops like sugar that would transform European tastes and economies. Morgan is interested not only in African women's manual labor but also in their efforts to reproduce children and families amid the brutal conditions of slavery and the slave trade. Although it would be well into the eighteenth century before births outstripped deaths among enslaved Africans and African Americans, mothers worked from the beginning to establish new networks of support and new cultural practices to protect their children.

Only European women and their colonial-born descendants multiplied rapidly in mainland North America. Despite alarmingly high death rates in the southern colonies, particularly among infants and among women in labor, the white population grew steadily through a combination of immigration and high birthrates. Bearing an average of eight to nine children, women who survived their childbearing years contributed mightily to peopling the New World with their own kind.

Still, the shortage of European women and workers in the early years of settlement and the death of husbands (who were often several years older than their wives) offered a number of opportunities to healthy, enterprising women. Through brewing, baking, innkeeping, sewing, midwifery, shopkeeping, printing, and a variety of other skilled trades and petty enterprises, some female migrants gained a degree of financial autonomy they would not have attained in Europe. Margaret Brent, already a wealthy woman when she arrived in Maryland in 1638, managed plantations, sued (successfully) in court, acted as a business agent for others, and served as executrix for the estate of Lord Calvert, Maryland's governor. Demonstrating the status that few women could obtain, she nonetheless was denied the political rights that a man of her property and stature would have enjoyed.

Most early immigrants, male or female, faced considerably harsher circumstances. Large numbers of women and men reached the colonies by means of indentured servitude, which involved four to seven years' bound labor in exchange for passage to the New World. Engaged in long years of arduous toil, housed in cramped quarters, provided with minimal food and clothing, offered little privacy, and sometimes subjected to severe punishments, colonial servants hoped only to survive their indenture so that they could take advantage of the opportunities that awaited. For female servants, sexual exploitation and premarital pregnancy posed additional hazards on the path to freedom. Though courts were sometimes sympathetic to women abused by masters, most servants who found themselves pregnant had their children taken away and their contracts extended to forestall such behavior in the future.

Premarital pregnancy and other punishable offenses were probably as prevalent in Puritan New England as in other regions of the Americas. Despite the Puritans' desire to set a righteous example for the rest of the world, sexual and social turmoil characterized Massachusetts Bay from its earliest years. Women, moreover, were often at the center of such controversies. In part, this was because female sexual misconduct was starkly visible when manifested as pregnancy or a child born out of wedlock. In addition, all women, as daughters of Eve, were considered more innately evil than men and more firmly ruled by their passions. Recognizing and accepting female sexuality as long as it was contained within marital bonds, Puritan leaders were nevertheless eager to find in unbridled female lust both the cause and the consequence of social disorder.

The wave of heretical teaching that washed over Massachusetts Bay in the 1630s, especially that offered by Anne Hutchinson, gave Puritan leaders an opportunity to voice these fears under the guise of protecting the colony. Convinced that female intellect was a contradiction in terms, Governor John Winthrop characterized Hutchinson as "a woman of fine and haughty carriage, of a nimble wit and active spirit, and a very voluble tongue, more bold than a man, though in understanding and judgement, inferiour to many women." Upon her banishment from the settlement, Reverend John Cotton articulated the presumed links between religious heresy and sexual deviance. He admonished her, "though I have not herd, nayther do I thinke, you have bine unfaythful to your Husband in his Marriage Covenant, yet that will follow upon it."

Beginning in the mid-seventeenth century, accusations of witchcraft appeared in the North American colonies. There were far fewer accusations in this part of the world than in Europe, and most were confined to the New England colonies. Anxieties caused by fear of the unknown, warfare with Indians, debates over colonial governance, and the presence of independent women without fathers or husbands to control them fueled witch hunts in individual towns and villages. The women accused were sometimes poor, older, marginal members of society, or women who were argumentative and difficult. But many were women who had gained control of land and wealth following the deaths of their husbands, and they, too, were viewed as threatening to the developing social order.

The witch hunt in Salem, Massachusetts, in 1692 was the most cataclysmic in colonial North America. In the midst of social and political upheaval, economic and familial tensions erupted in a frenzy of accusations, trials, and executions. Young women, perhaps inspired by Caribbean religious practices taught to them by a slave woman, accused older women in the community of attacking them physically as well as bringing harm to other villagers. Fourteen accused women and six men were put to death before the witch fever subsided in Salem; another half dozen women died in prison. Despite the horrific events in Salem, witchcraft waned by the end of the seventeenth century in New England and throughout the colonies.

Only a small number of women in the North American colonies were condemned for heresy or witchcraft. Although important for revealing the threat posed by women who were considered spiritually or economically independent, those condemned do not represent the experiences of most colonial women.

In Chapter Three, Laurel Thatcher Ulrich uses household inventories and court records to illuminate the activities of ordinary women, whose lives were shaped by the daily round of domestic chores and the births and deaths of family members. Focusing on three women in three distinct Massachusetts communities, Ulrich paints vivid portraits that reflect a broad spectrum of colonial womanhood, lived largely within the confines of domesticity—though here and there an escape hatch opened into some wider world. These women, like their counterparts throughout the colonies, contributed their physical and intellectual labor as workers and mothers to people the New World, one of the few tasks shared by American Indian, African, and European women.

Suggested Readings and Web Sites

Carol Berkin and Leslie Horowitz, eds., *Women's Voices/Women's Lives: Documents in Early American History* (1998)

Kathleen Brown, *Good Wives, Nasty Wenches and Anxious Patriarchs: Gender, Race, and Power in Colonial Virginia* (1996)

John Demos, *The Tried and the True: Native American Women Confronting Colonization* (1995)

Carol Karlsen, *The Devil in the Shape of a Woman: Witchcraft in Colonial New England* (1987)

Karen Ordahl Kupperman, *Indians and English: Facing Off in Early America* (2000)

Jennifer Morgan, *Laboring Women: Reproduction and Gender in New World Slavery* (2004)

The Salem Witch Trials Documentary Archive and Transcription Project
    http://etext.virginia.edu/salem/witchcraft

Africans in America
    http://www.pbs.org/wgbh/aia

P ocahontas has long been a symbol of the peaceful co-existence of American Indians and European settlers in North America. One might easily conclude from the popular legend that the only role women played in Jamestown was that of saving handsome colonists from hostile Indians. Yet the Powhatan Confederacy, in which Pocahontas was raised, provided women with much more diverse roles. Composed of numerous smaller nations, including the Pamunkey, Paspahegh, Monacan, and Chickahominy, the confederacy was held together in part through marriage alliances. This enhanced women's roles since these nations were matrilineal, meaning that land and political authority passed through the mother's line. Women were also central to agricultural production. Thus, few Indian women were likely to be lured away by undernourished, pale, quarrelsome, and seemingly inept Englishmen.

Most of the Englishmen who arrived in April 1607 to establish a settlement on the Chesapeake hoped to find gold or other precious metals or to enslave native women and men to produce cash crops. They were not prepared for arduous agricultural labor, and they suffered through a severe dry spell that shriveled what few crops they had planted. They also settled in a swampy area that fostered malarial fevers and other diseases. And they had assumed, wrongly, that they could easily conquer the local natives. At the end of three years, the death toll was staggering and the colony was near collapse.

Powhatan, a powerful *werowance* (chief) who ruled over some thirteen thousand Indians, hoped to put an early end to the British invasion. After the English threatened local communities, stole food, and killed a number of natives, Powhatan's warriors captured three Englishmen in December 1607. Two of the men were put to death at once, but John Smith was brought to Powhatan. According to Smith's later account, he was feasted for two weeks and then led to his execution. But at the last minute, Pocahontas rushed out to save him. He then took over leadership of the English, who prospered, multiplied, and eventually dominated their one-time foe.

The legend handed down by John Smith is unlikely on many accounts, not least of which is that Pocahontas was probably only ten years old at the time of the reported rescue. It is more likely that her father, Powhatan, sent Pocahontas to "save" Smith as a gesture of mercy. Powhatan had already proved his power through the capture and mock execution of Smith, and now he sought to use that power to force negotiations with the English leader. Pocahontas was sent to signal Powhatan's mercy because women traditionally had the right to determine the fate of captives. They could consign a captive to death, or they could decide to adopt him into the tribe.

Camilla Townsend follows Pocahontas and Powhatan as they continued their negotiations with John Smith and the English settlers. She captures the moment when the English still had only a fragile foothold in North America. She reveals as well the central role that Indian women played in early encounters between Europeans and Indians in North America. In this case, Pocahontas traveled regularly between Powhatan's main village of Werowocomoco and Jamestown, and she honed her English language skills even as she taught Smith and others phrases in her own language. Eventually, she married an Englishman, John Rolfe, who took her to England on their honeymoon in 1617. There she contracted a fever and died. Rolfe then returned to the Chesapeake region and became a leader in the development of tobacco as a profitable cash crop in Virginia. By that time, all hope of Powhatan driving the English from the Chesapeake had also died, transforming the lives of both Indian and English women and men for generations to come.

Jamestown: Pocahontas, Powhatan and the Struggle for Virginia
CAMILLA TOWNSEND

> Kekaten pokahontas patiaquagh ningh tanks manotyens neer mowchick rawrenock audowgh. (Bid Pokahontas bring hither two little Baskets, and I will give her white beads to make her a chaine.)
> —John Smith, *A Map of Virginia* (1612)

[After John Smith was returned to the English colony at Jamestown,]

Powhatan continued to send the colonists gifts of corn and raccoon tails every few days. He frequently requested that Captain [Christopher] Newport visit him at Werowocomoco. In late February 1608 the visit took place. The English were tense at every step. When their guides asked them to cross a narrow fjord of stakes driven into a creek, they suspected a trap. "I intermingled the Kings sonne, our conductors and his chiefe men amongst ours . . . leaving half [our men] at the one ende to make a guard for the passage of [the others]," remembered [John] Smith. That is, he made it impossible for the Indians to shoot at them from the banks by having each man cross with an Indian in front and behind, and he left half his men on the shore with their guns aimed at the Indians crossing. Then the English who had already crossed turned and trained their weapons to protect those yet to come. For the rest of the visit, a portion of the English always stayed ready to shoot. This was to be a longstanding pattern. Powhatan complained of their lack of trust, but to no avail.

Newport brought Powhatan a red silk outfit, a large hat, and a white greyhound dog. The paramount chief professed to be delighted but also asked after the guns that Smith had promised in exchange for his release. Smith insisted that in offering the immovable cannon, he had fulfilled his part of the bargain—"whereat," said

"Jamestown" from *Pocahontas and the Powhatan Dilemma* (2004) by Camilla Townsend. Reprinted by permission of Hill and Wang, a division of Farrar, Straus and Giroux, LLC.

An engraving of Pocahontas, age twenty, based on a portrait by Simon Van de Passe, made in 1616 during her trip to London. Rather than making her features look European as painters would later do, Van de Passe emphasizes her high cheek bones and black hair and shows her facing directly forward, an unusual pose for a woman.

Smith, "with loud laughter, he desired me to give him some of less burthen." The English were able to dissuade Powhatan from insisting on receiving guns by making an offer—long-planned on their part—to leave a purported "son" of Newport's in Werowocomoco, and to send a "son" of Powhatan's to London. The English hoped the boys might become their interpreters. Powhatan accepted: he stood to get essential information out of them as well, which would be more valuable than two guns. The English apparently thought they were deceiving Powhatan. Young Thomas Savage was probably either an apprentice or an indentured servant; he certainly was not Newport's son. Powhatan, however, most likely figured that out. He also deceived some of the English, for there is no reason to believe that Namontack, whom he sent to England, was really his biological son. Although some of the English believed he was, Smith did not.

Over the course of the next few days in Werowocomoco, the Indians and English traded corn for beads and metal wares. Powhatan extracted a promise of some swords that he later did receive. They discussed the possibility of mounting a joint attack on Powhatan's Monacan neighbors (Siouans, not Algonkians) living just to the west, though the project never came to fruition. The English eventually made an awkward exit: having missed the tide, they found they could not get their barge afloat, and they had to beg another night's lodging, with some of their number nervously standing guard yet again. Either to make a point or to express genuine sympathy, that night Powhatan gave them more food than they could possibly eat.

Watching them pull away from the shore the next morning, Thomas Savage, probably about thirteen or fourteen years old, must have felt a loneliness almost impossible to describe. Even if he had hated his English master, even if he had been having a wonderful time with the fun-loving Powhatan children—and either is more than possible—he stood now in a world where nothing was familiar, not even a word. It is possible that the adults encouraged the children to talk to him, that Pocahontas spoke to him, even taught him to say *netoppew*, "my friend." Two months later she would apparently know some English. Thomas may well have taught her what she knew.

In April Captain Newport returned again to England, carrying the completely isolated Namontack away with him. Back in Jamestown the day-to-day work continued incessantly. There had been a serious fire, requiring some significant rebuilding of the settlement. Though the settlers put time into mending the bulwarks, the structures inside the fort were of the relatively primitive cratchet type: that is, a roof was raised up to ceiling height on four forked poles, and rows of sticks were stuck into the ground to make each wall, bearing no weight. One building was put just outside the fort, apparently so the colonists could trade with the Indians without necessarily giving them access to the inner sanctum. It included a fireplace so as to be functional in winter, and a cool cellar, probably to store food purchased from the Indians in the hot summer. Beneath the door on the side farthest from the fort, where the "devilish" Indians were to come and go, they buried a witch's bottle—a glass vessel containing sharp stones, instead of the nails used in Europe—which they believed would keep evil at bay. Eventually, for added protection, they decided to connect the building to the fort with a fence.

It had not taken long for problems to arise. Apparently in an effort to cow the natives, the colonists began drilling and practicing their firing just outside the fort. Powhatan sent Thomas back to Jamestown with the request that he find out what was going on. According to Smith, they sent back a nonsensical answer, the gist of which was that they were preparing for a trip upriver to look for stones to make ax-heads. Powhatan sent young Thomas back to Jamestown; he did not want lies. Either Powhatan's displeasure was such that he actually issued an official statement that his people were free to harass the strangers, in an attempt to drive them away, or his disgust with them was simply so apparent that his people realized they were not likely to be punished if they stole from the fort. They began to molest stragglers found wandering outside the compound and to steal the much-valued metal tools.

In May, after one incident that the English found particularly egregious, they seized a number of Indian hostages. The next day the nearby Paspaheghs took two English men prisoner. The English wasted no time in retaliating: as darkness fell, well armed and well armored, they drew near to a Paspahegh town in their barge. They torched the nearest buildings and showered the village with shot—meaning not bullets, which must be aimed and can miss, but rather hundreds of tiny bits of lead flying everywhere. They withdrew unscathed. The next day the Paspaheghs sued for peace and released the two hostages. The English released one of theirs but continued to hold a number of others, whom they tortured. Under duress the Indians said that Powhatan planned to ambush them as soon as he had Namontack safely back.

On the third morning of the men's captivity, Powhatan sent Pocahontas to try to secure the prisoners' release. "He sent his Daughter, a child of tenne yeares old, which not only for feature, countenance and proportion, much exceedeth any of the rest of his people, but for wit, and spirit, the only Nonpariel [sic] of his Country," wrote Smith about three weeks later, in the report he sent back to England.

It was Pocahontas's first visit to the fort. She walked in, straight-backed, head up. Like all Powhatan girls, Pocahontas wore her hair cut short in front. A long braid may have hung down her back. Accompanying her was a man whose Algonkian name the English heard as "Rawhunt." An adviser to Powhatan, he was in some way physically deformed and was held by his people to have special wisdom and powers of divination. Pocahontas saw the prisoners but pretended not to, looking straight ahead and maintaining a studied silence. Then Rawhunt began a complicated speech, which someone translated: it was almost certainly Pocahontas herself, possibly working with Thomas Savage, whom her father had sent back to Jamestown many days before. Powhatan, Rawhunt said, had not only affection but also respect for the English, in proof of which, he had trusted them so much as to send his dear child to see them and bring them presents. He asked that Thomas, whom he missed and regretted sending away, might return to him, and he asked that the prisoners be released, among whom were men he valued. Later, when other messengers arrived with gifts to serve as ransom and Pocahontas began to perceive that the English were feeling open to negotiation, she herself began to speak to the colonists and to greet and comfort the prisoners.

Why had Powhatan sent her? There were in fact other occasions on which werowances sent their daughters as emissaries. . . . It may even have been a common tactic: it would have been a clear signal of a desire for mutual trust. What Powhatan's feelings were for this particular daughter we cannot be sure. Smith said Rawhunt called her "his child, which he most esteemed." Was she really the one then closest to Powhatan's heart, and did he believe that Smith would know this from his days of captivity and thus recognize her presence as a white flag? Or was she, as the daughter of a commoner and without claims to political power, among the children he could most afford to lose, and thus the one whose safety he chose to risk? Or did he as a shrewd statesmen simply choose the daughter in whose abilities he had most confidence? She was probably the best translator available. Possibly all of the above were true. In any case, he certainly chose well: Pocahontas secured the prisoners' release. "In the afternoone," said Smith, " . . . we guarded them as before to the Church, and after prayer, gave them to Pocahuntas, the Kings Daughter, in regard of her fathers kindnesse in sending her."

That visit was the first of many that Pocahontas made to the fort over the course of the following year. Having returned home in triumph after her first one, it is small wonder that it became an appealing place for her. With her growing language skills, she became ever more powerful—more welcome at the fort, and more important to her father. She also had fun. William Strachey, who arrived the year after she stopped visiting, was told of "a well featured but wanton young girle Powhatan's daughter, sometimes resorting to our Fort, of the age then of II or 12 years." *Wanton* then meant "frolicsome" or "mischievous." He said she would "get the boyes forth with her into the market place and make them wheele, falling on their handes turning their heeles upwards, whome she would follow, and wheel so her self naked as she was all the Fort over." She was not shy; in fact, she was bossy. She was quite an athlete—more so than the boys were. "We can imagine," writes one historian, "a group of pale-faced Jamestown boys, overdressed in wool, being goaded into turning cartwheels by a brown-skinned Indian girl, scantily clad by European standards, whose acrobatic skills probably put them to shame." Yet they liked her. That is what comes through in all accounts. She was energetic and fun-loving, open and interested, adventuresome and smart. They liked "Mischief" just as much as her own people apparently did.

It is only possible to glimpse her character, impossible to study it thoroughly. Historians would give a great deal to find a letter or diary written by Pocahontas, something in her own words, about her aspirations and opinions. With such crumbling papers in our hands, we could gain new insights into her personality and thoughts. Instead, she is visible only in the comments left by the white men who knew her and wrote down their impressions. What we glean comes from reading between the lines. The colonists make clear how little they cared to find out what the girl who admittedly fascinated them was herself thinking. In the words of one scholar, "The documents written by Englishmen display a remarkable indifference to her opinion of them." This is a classic dynamic, of course: it is always the less powerful who must learn to gauge the thoughts of the more powerful. The servant or slave considers the master's reactions; the subservient wife considers the dominant husband's; the courtier must know the king's mind better than he knows it himself. But the master, the husband, and the king are not in the habit of pondering the thoughts and feelings of those beneath them. So, too, the English colonizers gazed at Pocahontas and judged her, but did not ask her what she thought.

The problem is exacerbated by the fact that Pocahontas's language is largely lost, unlike numerous other American Indian languages. In the case of Malinche, for example, the Aztec woman who translated for Cortés, we may not have her own writings, but we do have those of innumerable other Aztecs who wrote about their traditions as soon as they began to learn the Roman alphabet in the 1530s. Even today there are at least a million speakers of the Nahuatl language in Mexico. The Powhatan language—or perhaps we should say languages—met a very different fate. The Indians in the region spoke closely related dialects that were mutually intelligible, varying from village to village. This is a normal pattern in a world where nation-states have not yet developed. An apt comparison would be to the lands in medieval Europe between Paris and Rome. Walking on foot many centuries ago, one would have passed through territories where people spoke at certain points what we recognize today as French, Catalan, Spanish, and Italian, but the shift would have occurred gradually, the people in any one village understanding perfectly what those in the neighboring villages were saying. Only a few people—Thomas Harriot, William Strachey, and John Smith—recorded lists of Algonkian words or phrases, and they almost never mentioned from which tribes their informants came. What results is a hodgepodge of words from all dialects and almost no sense of the grammar. Thus we cannot even gain insights into Powhatan categories and assumptions by studying texts in their own language.

Pocahontas, interestingly, offers one ray of light in this darkness. Formally or informally, she participated in a course of mutual language instruction with John Smith, and it is probably thanks to her that the only full Powhatan sentences that we have were recorded. "Because many doe desire to knowe the maner of their language, I have inserted here these few words," wrote Smith in 1612. In the midst of his lists of numbers and trade goods, he suddenly included several whole sentences. *Mowchick wayawgh tawgh noerach kaquere mecher.* "I am verie hungrie, what shall I eate?" And then: *Kekaten pokahontas patiaquagh hingh tanks manotyens neer mowchick rawrenock audowgh.* "Bid Pokahontas bring hither two little Baskets, and I will give her white beads to make her a chaine." Smith referred elsewhere to giving Pocahontas presents, so one can imagine them enacting an actual exchange as they taught each other the necessary words. Apparently Pocahontas did not want an English-style trinket as a gift, but rather, white beads—such as all Powhatan noblewomen were privileged to wear once they passed the age of about twelve and attained womanhood. Perhaps the eager child did not want to wait for the luxuries due to adults.

Sometimes the topics of conversation were more serious. "In how many daies will there come hither any more English ships?" was the very first full sentence Smith recorded. *Casa cunnakack, peya quagh acquintan uttasantasough?* This clearly was a very early questions, for the speaker, whoever he or she was, used the word *acquintan*, literally meaning "canoe," though within only a few years the Powhatans widely adopted another word that had apparently existed in certain dialects—*messowt*, indicating a particularly large watercraft. The word *uttasantasough* for "English" was probably something borrowed from the Indians farther south who had contact with the Roanoke colonists, for the word was still in use in North Carolina in 1701. At any rate, that question conveyed what the Indians most wanted to know.

The English had other concerns. Smith recorded a short dialogue, carefully translating each part:

> Where dwells Powwahtan?
> Now he dwells a great way hence, at Orapaks.
> You lie, he stayed ever at Werowocomoco.
> Truly, he is there. I do not lie.

It may well have been Pocahontas who uttered these words. "Truly, he is there. I do not lie." Regardless, she clearly participated in conversations very much like this one, revealing something of her interesting and interested self, and demonstrating the strategies each group was attempting to adopt toward the other.

We have some direct evidence as to what John Smith was thinking while Pocahontas cartwheeled, laughed, posed questions, and gave answers. She was a child, probably ten years old, when she began to visit, and eleven or twelve when she stopped coming—a year older at most. She would be considered marriageable by her own people after she had passed puberty and was at least twelve; in fact menarche probably did not usually occur until at least thirteen. Once she spent her first time apart in the women's menstrual hut just outside the village, she would have stopped cartwheeling and cavorting. So we know that she was only a girl. But John Smith loved the books that represented America as a forthcoming young and naked virgin. In 1612 both Smith and William Strachey, back home in England, represented Pocahontas as nubile and sexy in the books they published, years *before* she became famous to the London public as a beautiful (and adult) Indian princess—after which any market-oriented writer might well have been tempted to make retroactive claims as to her alluring qualities. (Indeed, in the 1624 book, when his audience was primed, and envisioning a grown woman, Smith went so far as to claim that she and thirty other naked young women once virtually attacked him in a dance, demanding sexual favors.) Smith's 1612 reference is thus particularly interesting, as it reveals that he thought in sexual terms about a ten- or eleven-year-old prepubescent child.

The comments appeared in a book of testimony collected from friends of his who had been in Jamestown; some of their contributions were in reality written by him, and all were edited under his hand. A segment purportedly by Richard Pots

This 1814 painting of Pocahontas' 1613 baptism at Jamestown by John Gadsby Chapman offers a more romanticized image of Pocahontas that coincides with a renewed interest in her role as a mediator between Virginia Indians and English settlers.

and William Phettiplace reveals that Smith's relationship with Pocahontas had brought him criticism, in the form of innuendos that he was trying to form close bonds with the Indians in order to dominate the other colonists more effectively:

> Some prophetical spirit calculated hee had the Salvages in such subjection, hee would have made himself a king, by marrying Pocahontas, Powhatan's daughter. It is true she was the very nomperell of his kingdome, and at most not past 13 or 14 years of age. Very oft shee came to our fort, with what she could get for Captaine Smith, that ever loved and used all the Countrie well, but her especially he ever much respected: . . . but her marriage could no way have intitled him by any right to the kingdome, nor was it ever suspected hee had ever such a thought, or more regarded her, or any of them, then in honest reason and discretion he might. If he would, he might have married her, or have done what him listed. For there was none that could have hindered his determination.

There had even been a Virginia Company investigation of Smith's behavior toward the girl, orchestrated by his enemies in the corporation:

> Some that knewe not anything to say, the Councel instructed, and advised what to sweare. So diligent were they in this businesse, that what any could remember, hee had ever done, or said, in mirth, or passion, by some circumstantiall oath, it was applied to their fittest use . . . I have presumed to say this much in his behalfe for that I never heard such foule slanders, so certainly believed, and urged for truthes by many a hundred.

These paragraphs give away a great deal—not just that Smith had made many enemies by the time he was finished in Jamestown. On the one hand, they reveal that Smith was a more attentive student of Powhatan culture than most colonists were: he was conscious of the fact, for example, that in a matrilineal polity, his marrying Pocahontas would in no way make him a king. At the same time, the comments reveal his arrogance toward the Indians—or at least toward Indian women. He claimed that if he had wanted to marry Pocahontas, or to sleep with her, he would have done so, as absolutely no one could have stopped him—including Pocahontas herself, presumably. His own—or his friends'—summary of the council's investigation openly acknowledged that he had made lewd comments about her—or had even done things to her—in jokes ("mirth"), or in moments of sexual arousal ("passion"). Perhaps that is why, even as he reminded the people to whom he was defending himself that she was only a child, not yet fit for marriage, he raised her age by a good three years. Suddenly she was "no more than thirteen or fourteen" at the time, instead of her actual ten or eleven.

Did Pocahontas know that Smith viewed her in a sexual way and recognize his overtures as lascivious? Probably. Hers was not a prudish culture. But we cannot know what it meant in such matters to say that an eleven-year-old knew and was apparently not put off. She might, for instance, have said she found it funny or flattering at the time but been pained by memories later. That, indeed, is the most frequent scenario in such cases, then and now. Or she might have found Smith overbearing and troublesome, a pest in her otherwise happy visits to the fort. It is impossible to know. But to imagine that Smith's thoughts reflected her own would be unthinkably presumptuous.

Smith, in any case, took a more and more prominent role in the colony during the time when Pocahontas frequented Jamestown. In the late summer of 1608, a few months after her first visit, he led two exploratory trips. He met with friendly reception in most places. Once when he did not, in the country of the Nansemond, his men opened fire and began to destroy a village's laboriously constructed dugout canoes; the people sued for peace immediately. In the early fall the council members elected him president. It was a rare tribute to a man of his relatively low social rank.

Then Captain Newport returned once more with supplies. Namontack was onboard. Newport sent a message to Powhatan that he should come to Jamestown to swear loyalty to the British king and receive some presents sent by him, including a crown. Powhatan sent back a disdainful reply that they should come to him—and that he would wait for them in his present location only eight days. Newport went, bringing Namontack with him. The young Algonkian must surely have told the paramount chief something about England. Yet he did not say enough: Powhatan would seem only marginally more versed in English plans and capabilities in his later dealings with them. Unfortunately, the well-traveled Namontack was killed less than two years later, eliminating whatever insights he might have offered.

Namontack convinced Powhatan to accept the gifts of a metal basin and pitcher, a cloak, and a bed. "But a fowle trouble there was to make him kneele to receave his crowne." Smith asserted that this was because the Indian did not know the "meaning of a Crowne," but in fact he probably understood only too well the gesture of kneeling to receive a crown at the hands of another. He himself, after all, liked the practice of anointing tributary werowances who were bound to do his bidding. "At last by leaning hard on his shoulders, he a little stooped, and Newport put the Crowne on his head."

After the ceremony, for the rest of the autumn, President Smith made it his business to collect as much corn as possible from the natives. The Indians, however, were beginning to realize that English demands for corn might well be insatiable.

> Arriving at Chickahamina [the Chickahominy villages], that dogged nation was too wel acquainted with our wants, [therefore] refusing to trade, with as much scorne and insolence as they could expresse. The President perceiving it was Powhatan's policy to starve us, told them he came not so much for their corne, as to revenge his imprisonment, and the death of his men murdered by them, and so landing his men, and ready to charge them, they immediately fled, but then they sent their ambassadours, with corne, fish, fowl, or what they had to make their peace.

Smith said, in effect, that he did not care if they did not want to trade: if they would not give him corn in exchange for the trinkets he chose to give them, he would just take it and call it his revenge for their having allowed him to be captured in their territory the previous year.

The settlers' cold reception proved to be the same everywhere. The harvest had been poor that season, and the Indians did not want to turn over their major source of sustenance. In village after village, muskets and steel convinced them they had no choice. Generally the English congratulated themselves on their own cleverness in taking all that they needed, but occasionally a writer admitted to painful memories: "The people imparted what little they had, with such complaints and tears from the women and children; as he had bin too cruell to be a Christian that would not have bin satisfied [that is, refrained from taking any more] and moved with compassion."

In December 1608 the English went to see Powhatan at Werowocomoco. Powhatan played his hand as well as he could. Knowing the English were hungry, and believing that they would be loath to attack his town as quickly as they had attacked others, he said he would certainly trade with them. But he wanted swords and guns—lots of them: "For 40 swords he would procure us 40 bushels." They showed him other "commodities." "But none he liked without gunnes and swords." Smith complained loudly, and then Powhatan answered, demonstrating that his knowledge of the English had improved somewhat—either through observation, or conversation with Namontack, or both—"Captain Smith, some doubt I have of your comming hither, that makes me not so kindly seeke to relieve you as I would; for many do informe me, your coming is not for trade, but to invade my people and possesse my Country." If he hoped that the English would protest their innocence and give him guns, he hoped in vain.

To end the business, Powhatan gave them ten small units of corn in exchange for a large copper kettle. That was expensive corn, and it was all he would do for them. He made a long speech, in which he warned that if the English continued to attack his people and demand more corn than could be spared, his people would remove themselves from the rivers' edges and retreat deep into the woods, where the English could not find them. "What can you get by war, when we can hide our provision and flie to the woodes, whereby you must famish?" He said that he, too, hoped to avoid this. In essence, he promised an annual tribute, though in the form of unequal trade, not overt offerings: "Let this therefore assure you of our loves and everie yeare our friendly trade shall furnish you with corne, and now also if you would come in friendly manner to see us, and not thus with your gunnes and swords, as [if] to invade your foes."

The English were tense during this visit, fearing that in his frustration and anger, in his sense of having few alternatives left, the paramount chief would order an ambush. Smith and the others later described various incidents they believed were foiled attempts on their lives. Smith even said that at one point Pocahontas warned him of one of the plots, coming alone in the dark and the rain. It is possible that she really did it. It is also very possible that she did not. It was not until 1624, when she was dead and he was embellishing, that Smith specifically connected her warning to this period. In 1612 he did refer to such an event, but not in this segment of the narrative, rather only in a vague subordinate clause in another chapter where he detailed her goodness to the colonists—in the same section, in fact, in which he tried to defend himself against the accusations that he had adopted the lifestyle and manners of the natives. Even supposing for the sake of argument that Pocahontas did want John Smith to escape death more than she wanted her father to gain the upper hand, she would have known that the English did not really need her warning. Their implacable suspicion, combined with their arms and armor, had protected their lives thus far.

In fact, it is unlikely not only that Pocahontas fled through the night to warn her English friends but also that Powhatan seriously intended to kill Smith at this point. He knew his warriors could surprise small groups and pick them off—they had done so before. But he also knew that it would do no good. It would only bring more, angrier coat-wearers. Reading the English accounts of these days spent up the York River from start to finish, it seems apparent that the Indians created skirmishes to prevent the English from finding out, until after the event, that Powhatan was quickly moving his entire town and most of his corn supply. After a brief corn-gathering foray into Pamunkey territory farther upriver, the English returned to Werowocomoco a few days later to find the large town completely abandoned, as Powhatan had threatened might happen. Pocahontas had gone with her people, and John Smith did not see her again—until she came to England years later. There was no tearful good-bye in the dark.

The frustrated English soon kidnapped a Paspahegh werowance whom they believed was working with some newly arrived Dutchmen to plan an ambush. With the help of his people, the werowance escaped from Jamestown under cover of night. In retaliation, Smith sacked a village: "Six or 7 salvages were slaine, as many made prisoners." Their werowance then sent a messenger who drove home the point that Powhatan had already made:

> We perceive and well knowe you intend to destroy us, that are here to intreat and desire your friendship, and [ask] to enjoy our houses and plant our fields, of whose fruit you shall participate, otherwise you will have the worst by our absence, for we can plant any where, though with more labour, and we know you cannot live if you want [i.e., do not have] our harvest, and that reliefe wee bring you; if you promise us peace we will believe you, if you proceed in reveng[e], we will abandon the Countrie.

Smith took the deal. He had learned the hard way that this was as good as he would get. If he pushed these people too far, they would, in Powhatan's words, "fly to the woods." And then there would be no tribute in corn at all. Only when the Indians were clustered around rivers and creeks could the English descend on them and defeat them handily.

These were nothing like the Indians of whom Smith had read in the great epic adventure stories of Hernando Cortés and Francisco Pizarro. Smith, indeed, was among the first of the English—perhaps the very first—to gain a clear understanding of the vast difference between the Aztecs and the Incas on the one side, and the North American Indians on the other.

Most North Americans today have lost sight of this distinction, but it was crucial. The Spanish had found indigenous people who had been farming, although not as long as Europeans, for at least several millennia. They were sedentary; they could not possibly fly to the woods. They lived in permanent villages, with schools and temples. They paid taxes. They had roads and fixed long-distance trade routes. Some of them had causeways, small aqueducts, and running water. They knew no more of life in the woods than most modern urbanites do. When the Spanish came, with their superior arms, it soon became clear to the Aztecs that they had no choice other than to offer allegiance to this new government and pay their taxes in goods and services into new coffers.

The Powhatan Indians, however, were not going to settle for that. They were seminomadic. They had moved before, and they would move again. Under no circumstances would they become serflike tributaries. Smith came to understand this quite clearly, but he refused to accept it gracefully. In explaining the greater difficulties he and the Jamestown settlers had faced in comparison with the Spanish, Smith and his friends found it satisfying to insult the Powhatans, to blame them for the English misfortune in having conquered the "wrong" Indians. Wrote Smith:

> It was the Spaniards good hap to happen in those parts, where were infinite numbers of people, whoe had manured the ground with that providence, that it afforded victual at all times: and time had brought them to that perfection, they had the use of gold and silver, and the most of such commodities, as their countries afforded, so that what the Spaniard got, was only the spoile and pillage of those countrie people, and not the labours of their owne hands. But had those fruitfull Countries beene as Salvage, as barbarous, as ill peopled and little planted, laboured and manured as Virginia, their proper labours (it is likely) would have produced as small profit as ours.

Armed with this new understanding, which had yet to make its way back to the theorists in London, Smith made sure there were no more serious skirmishes with the Indians while he was president. But resentful colonists—especially the well-born—continued to rail against his autocratic style of management. They were mutinous on several occasions, and when he accidentally suffered a serious burn in October of 1609, he used it as an excuse to resign and return to England. Those remaining managed but poorly without him and without Powhatan. They starved.

The new president sent a pinnace up the Pamunkey River carrying, in his words, "Powhatan's son and daughter" to try to convince the Indian king to give them some corn. Was this Pocahontas, who had made a final visit to the fort at a bad time? She certainly had some type of communication with the colonists around then, for someone wrongly told her in this period that Smith was dead. Still, it seems likely that the president writing the report would have called her by her name, as she was well known to him. It was probably a half sister of hers, appearing suddenly in the record and disappearing as quickly. Was the boy in fact Henry Spelman, another English adolescent who had been living with Powhatan as a son? Spelman later

The 1995 Walt Disney film presents Pocahontas as older and more sexually enticing when she met John Smith than historical evidence of her age and appearance supports.

admitted that he was there—though he disclaimed any responsibility for what happened next.

The captain of the pinnace, a man named Ratcliffe, let the girl and boy go once they found Powhatan's new village, and some of the men wandered off in small groups to beg for food. Powhatan wanted to make it clear one last time that he would not give corn on demand and that he had withdrawn his settlement for a reason. He had the men killed: Ratcliffe was captured and tortured to death as an enemy warrior. Only one man managed to escape and make it back to the pinnace to travel back to Jamestown with those who had had the wisdom to remain onboard. That winter other colonists who approached Indians demanding food were also killed. Warriors lost their lives in these skirmishes, but Powhatan's policy had changed. He clearly wanted to convince the English to leave, or at least not to pursue his people inland.

It nearly worked.

That horrible winter eventually gave way to spring, and in May 1610, two ships arrived at the settlement's crude port. They had been built in Bermuda by Englishmen who had wrecked there on the way to Jamestwon. The new arrivals found that only about 100 English people were left alive in Virginia—some 60 in Jamestown, 40 in other camps. This was out of a total of about 550 who had migrated thus far. Of the lost 450, an unknown number had returned to England or fled, but most had perished over the course of three years, more than 100 in the last winter alone. Within days the leaders decided to evacuate the colony and go home. They organized the voyage and boarded the ships. On the crowded vessels, they could make it to Newfoundland, and there they would disperse themselves among the fishing boats that came and went. Jamestown, it seemed, was to be added to the list of failed experiments in the New World. English colonization would have to wait a few more years, until the lessons from this venture had been digested and a new scheme developed. Powhatan's people would have some breathing room. And Powhatan's daughter would live out her days with her people in Virginia.

But as the fleeing colonists made their way down the river, they met a grand flotilla. Lord De La Warr, their new governor, had arrived with a new charter, at least 150 additional people, and substantial provisions meant to last. And so they stayed. English technology was to triumph now, not later. A messenger brought Powhatan the devastating tidings.

Questions for Study and Review

1. Why were women and children in the Powhatan Confederacy and other Indian nations employed as mediators with outside groups, whether other Indian nations or European settlers?

2. What can the myth and history of Pocahontas tell us about relations between the English and other European settlers and the native peoples they eventually conquered?

3. How does the process of colonization look different from the perspective of Pocahontas and Powhatan and that of John Smith and the English? How might Pocahontas' age have affected her perspective?

4. What are the difficulties of using sources written by Englishmen to study the lives of Indians and particularly Indian girls and women?

Suggested Readings and Web Sites

Karen Anderson, *Chain Her by One Foot: The Subjugation of Native Women in Seventeenth-century New France* (1991)

Suzanne Lebsock, *A Share of Honour: Virginia Women, 1600–1945* (1984)

Mary Rowlandson, *The Sovereignty and Goodness of God* (1682) reprinted with related documents and introduction, ed. Neil Salisbury (1997)

Nancy Shoemaker, ed., *Negotiators of Change: Historical Perspectives on Native American Women* (1995)

Virtual Jamestown
  http://www.virtualjamestown.org

Virginia History
  http://www.va400.org

Cultural Encounters in North American Exploration
  http://www. americanjourneys.org

The beginning of slavery on mainland North America is generally dated to 1619, when the first boatload of Africans docked at Jamestown. However, slavery and the slave trade actually began much earlier. English traders and planters first became involved when the British conquered islands in the Caribbean, then called the West Indies, and they expanded the enterprise as they established new colonies on the North American mainland. Although slavery existed in many parts of the world—including Africa—before the colonization of the Americas, the demand for slaves in America transformed both Africa and Europe. By the mid-seventeenth century, the slave trade was a major source of wealth in Europe. At the same time, the growing demand for African laborers shattered families, communities, and economic and political systems in many African nations, especially those in West Africa. Gradually, the importation of Africans to the West Indies and mainland North America transformed households, communities, and economies there as well.

Jennifer Morgan brings the horrors and the consequences of slavery and the slave trade to life by exploring their meaning for individual women and for African women and families more generally. Until recently, most studies of slavery in the United States focused on the decades immediately preceding the Civil War, when plantations had become the centerpiece of the southern economy and cotton production fueled industrial development in the North as well. Moreover, historians long assumed that enslaved people shared a common experience that differed little, whether one was a man or a woman. Recently, however, a growing number of studies have analyzed the slave trade and the development of slavery in the Americas from the sixteenth century on, and a few have focused on the particular experience of enslaved women. Morgan brings these two strands of historical research together by tracing the lives of enslaved women in the slave trade and in England's first colonies.

Morgan demonstrates the importance of African women to the slave trade and to the development of North American slavery. She reminds us that "African women comprised four-fifths of all women to make the Atlantic crossing—either voluntarily or involuntarily—before 1800." And she charts the labor performed by African women, before and after their enslavement. In West Africa, women were the primary agricultural laborers. They were also central in many cases to marketing crops and handmade goods. And everywhere, they were involved in the reproduction of families and the daily chores of households. They continued these forms of labor in America.

Recognizing that African women were ripped away from their native cultures by slave traders, Morgan nonetheless traces the ways that African religious rituals, languages, systems of labor, and attitudes toward motherhood shaped the lives that these women established in North America. Blending elements from diverse

West African societies to create a syncretic African American culture, women were central to passing on this heritage to future generations. Even though she focuses on slavery in the British colonies, Morgan nonetheless suggests patterns that likely applied to enslaved women in Dutch, French, and Spanish colonies as well.

The different experiences of enslaved peoples in the West Indies and on the mainland—particularly the longer life spans and greater chances for reproducing children on the mainland—gradually distinguished women's roles in the two locations. In both, however, African women faced hard labor, brutal treatment, and the constant fear of again being separated from all they knew.

Women and Families in Slavery and the Slave Trade
JENNIFER L. MORGAN

Slave Ships and Forts

On February 12, 1678, English slave traders loaded three recently purchased women and the same number of men on the *Arthur,* a slave ship anchored in the Callaber River, at the area known as the Bight of Biafra, West Africa. The ship's factor, George Hingston, paid the "Kinge of New Callabarr" thirty copper bars for each woman; for each man he paid thirty-six. At most embarkation points, women cost less than men did. The exception was Senegambia, the "only known region where Europeans paid equal prices for males and females." The following day canoes brought eighteen women and fourteen men to the ship. The day after only three canoes approached the *Arthur* and Hingston purchased three men, one woman, and some yams with which to feed them. For the next six and a half weeks this piecemeal loading pattern continued, small numbers of women and men purchased each day from individual canoes. Assuming that the three women who boarded the ship on February 12 survived, they would watch with increasing despair from the cramped cargo bays as more and more women, men, and children joined them in the hold.

Food was scarce, and at times Hingston turned back canoe-men bringing captives "by reason of their remissing in Bringn't us provision." Without food, he would purchase no men or women. Provisioning remained a constant problem throughout the six weeks during which Hingston loaded the *Arthur* with African women and men. For the three women and their compatriots, the "problem" was dire. Fed only yams as they languished in a ship from which they could see the land they would never again set foot on, they began to "grow Leane." Hingston found this perplexing as he believed that "they want fore nothinge haveinge doely as much provision as they

From "Slavery and the Slave Trade," in *A Companion to Women's History*, ed. Nancy A. Hewitt. Copyright © 2002 by Blackwell Publishers, Ltd.

Cann make use of." His confusion must have been matched by their horror as only two weeks after the sale of these three women, the people around them began to die. For the African captives waiting in the rank and stifling hold of the ship, the scarce food, dying men and women, and the three to thirty more people thrown in each day, punctuated the weeks until the *Arthur* finally left the river for the Atlantic Ocean.

Once the *Authur* pulled out to sea, the death rate increased. Not a day passed during the voyage without a dead African woman or man, boy or girl, being tossed overboard. On April 22 Hingston noticed that "the winds [were] nott blowinge so fresh" and allowed the 294 women and men out into the open air. As they emerged from the hold of the ship, a common language might have assisted the men and women in the *Arthur* as they mourned their capture and worried about their future. Although they came in small groups from "Bandy," "Donus," and Callabar, all the points Hingston identified were Ibo-speaking trading centers clustered at the basin of the Niger Delta. But an ability to communicate would not assuage the fears and uncertainties of the captives. Glancing around at the expanse of the Atlantic Ocean, the looks and words of terror exchanged by the three women loaded almost two and a half months before, if they still lived, are difficult to imagine. Returned to their shackles, the survivors would remain below for the remainder of the two-month passage to Barbados. By the end of the voyage, forty-nine men and boys and thirty-three women and girls died. Five more weeks passed before they again breathed fresh air. Having brought the ship to Bridgetown, Barbados during the height of the island's sugar boom, Hingston sold the surviving 144 men, 110 women, nine boys, and nine girls in a mere three days. The island's slaveowners wasted no time relieving Hingston of his cargo and initiating the women and men who had survived the journey aboard the *Arthur* into the demands of sugar cultivation.

In December 1727, Cayoba, a woman enslaved at the Royal African Company's fort on Bence Island at Sierra Leone, escaped from the castle. Cayoba ran with three men, renamed Peter, Dick, and Monday. Five months after their escape the local king, Suphulo, recaptured the runaways and returned them to the Company. Weeks later the Royal African Company agent discovered another escape plot, this time among the men and women destined for transport to the Americas who had, perhaps, been emboldened by Cayoba and her companions. The Royal African Company agent stationed at the castle punished the conspirators publicly. But his authority was demolished five months later when castle slaves and "sale slaves" joined together once again and successfully attacked the whites, drove them out, and burned the castle.

The purchasing method used by George Hingston aboard the *Arthur* was one of two employed by European slave traders. The other—to keep enslaved women and men in forts on the coast waiting the arrival of European ships—was used at Bence Island. African slavers brought men and women to the "holes" of European fortresses up and down the Upper Guinea and Gold coasts. There they languished in "damp Trunks" which caused "great Mortality" as they waited to be loaded aboard slaving vessels. Other men and women were brought to the forts to be permanently enslaved therein. The Royal African Company directed agents at distant forts to exchange men and women with one another when obtaining castle slaves so as to remove individuals from familiar landscapes that beckoned runaways. "We have indeed order'd our Agents at Gambia . . . to pick out . . . ten or twenty of the choicest young healthy men and women slaves and to send them

Between 1700 and 1800, British and European slave traders captured or purchased roughly 6.6 million Africans. Just over 5.8 million survived the transatlantic voyage and were sold into slavery in the Americas. Of these, less than 10 percent were shipped to the North American colonies.

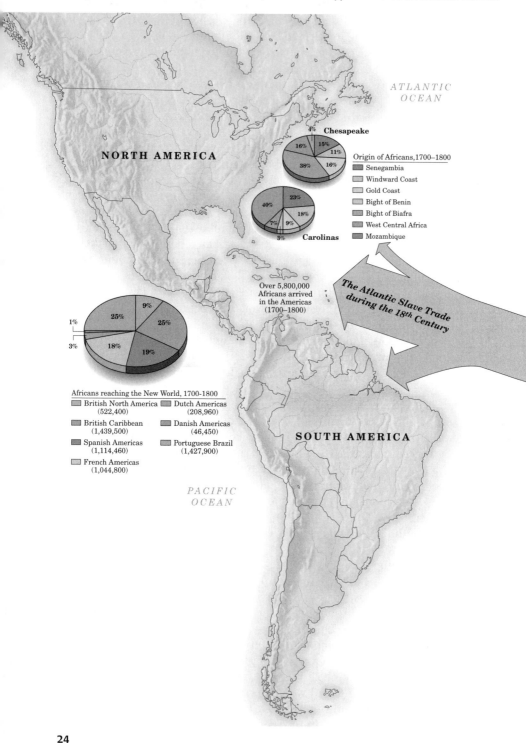

ATLANTIC
OCEAN

NORTH AMERICA

Chesapeake

1%
16%   15%
      11%
38%   16%

Origin of Africans, 1700–1800
- Senegambia
- Windward Coast
- Gold Coast
- Bight of Benin
- Bight of Biafra
- West Central Africa
- Mozambique

40%   23%
      18%
7%   9%
3%   Carolinas

Over 5,800,000 Africans arrived in the Americas (1700–1800)

The Atlantic Slave Trade during the 18th Century

25%   9%
      25%
1%
3%
18%   19%

Africans reaching the New World, 1700-1800
- British North America (522,400)
- British Caribbean (1,439,500)
- Spanish Americas (1,114,460)
- French Americas (1,044,800)
- Dutch Americas (208,960)
- Danish Americas (46,450)
- Portuguese Brazil (1,427,900)

SOUTH AMERICA

PACIFIC
OCEAN

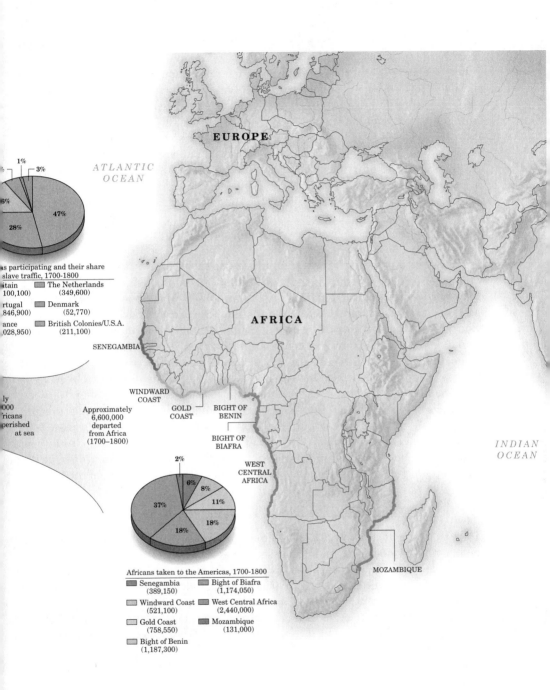

ATLANTIC
OCEAN

1%

3%

47%

28%

...s participating and their share
...slave traffic, 1700-1800

...itain   The Netherlands
100,100)   (349,600)

...rtugal   Denmark
846,900)   (52,770)

...ance   British Colonies/U.S.A.
028,950)   (211,100)

EUROPE

AFRICA

SENEGAMBIA

WINDWARD
COAST

GOLD   BIGHT OF
COAST   BENIN

...ly
000
ricans
perished
   at sea

Approximately
6,600,000
departed
from Africa
(1700–1800)

BIGHT OF
BIAFRA

WEST
CENTRAL
AFRICA

INDIAN
OCEAN

2%

6%   8%

37%   11%

18%   18%

MOZAMBIQUE

Africans taken to the Americas, 1700-1800

Senegambia   Bight of Biafra
(389,150)   (1,174,050)

Windward Coast   West Central Africa
(521,100)   (2,440,000)

Gold Coast   Mozambique
(758,550)   (131,000)

Bight of Benin
(1,187,300)

down to you . . . and to receive from you in return as many young healthy Gold Coast Negroes as they may have occasion for at Gambia."

Like those on board ships awaiting departure, women at slave forts were in the midst of a process of understanding the new terms of their identity. The encounter between far-flung ethnic groups that characterized the experience of enslavement throughout the Americas began on the West African coast. No longer did their place in the world grow out of the particularities of family, region, language, and ethnicity. Rather, it became dependent upon imposed racial sameness. However, the frightening implications of how a woman's reproductive life would be mobilized to support perpetual racial slavery would be a realization slow in coming. In the month following Cayoba's return to the fortress, a woman named Moota, another castle slave, gave birth to her third child. Among the myriad images and expectations which African women brought to their New World enslavement, childbirth among women who answered to a white "owner" and whose children accompanied her as she carried out her labors in an alien land was a painful emblem of their future. Through tiny windows or iron doors, while being "provisioned" or "mustered," women waiting for sale at the forts might catch glimpses of other mothers who labored as slaves. As the weeks and months unfolded before them, those who came aboard the same ships or endured the same fortress walls and who continued to see one another on adjoining plantations or in and around port cities must have truly regarded themselves as kin—connected by an unfathomable ordeal of transportation, deprivation, and loss. If their paths crossed, they must have shared a rare and poignant moment of recognition, one full of a tangible past. Months or years later, as African women were led from the holes of ships and into New World plantations, the stories of Moota and Cayoba—the enslaved mother and resistant woman—continued to resonate. As a newly enslaved African woman contemplated the frightening prospect of sustaining herself in the New World, Moota and the children she bore but did not "own" would stand as powerful portents of all that enslavement in the Americas could mean.

The Parameters of the Trans-Atlantic Slave Trade

In many respects the men and women on board the *Arthur* experienced a demographically normative middle passage. It was far more common for a seventeenth-century slave ship leaving the West or West Central African coast to arrive in the Caribbean or Latin America than in North America. Indeed, those forcibly transported to North America comprised a mere 5 percent of the total number of persons ensnared in the trans-Atlantic slave trade. Between 9.6 and 10.8 million persons survived the middle passage over the course of the 300-year-long trade, of which 481,000 were transported to British North America. Mortality rates were between 10 and 20 percent, bringing the total number of men and women forcibly transported to the Americas to at least 12 million. During the entire period, ships brought a total of some 353,000 Africans to Barbados alone—while close to 4,700,000 enslaved Africans were transported to the British, French, Dutch, and Danish Caribbean.

The proportionally tiny number of Africans transported to British North America seems to conflict with what we know about the economic dependence of the region on slavery and on the enduring social, cultural, and economic impact of African Americans on the American landscape. The situation is clarified by a single crucial factor that differentiated North America from most other slave societies in the hemisphere. Enslaved women and men in North America had children. These children were born and survived in numbers high enough to offset the numbingly high mortality rates; their presence meant a slave society no longer dependent upon African imports to maintain population after the turn of the nineteenth century; and their sale as youngsters and adults to the "deep South" occasioned an ongoing tragedy of familial disruption and instability among enslaved North Americans.

Prior to the 1807 ban on the slave trade to the United States, slaveowners' demand for labor fueled a steady stream of forced migrants to North America. European and American slavers traded up and down the African coast. Enslaved persons embarked from points all along the Western African coast and Southeastern Africa:

> There are seven general regions from which slaves were imported. The first, Senegambia, encompasses that stretch of coast extending from the Senegal River to the Casamance, to which captives from as far away as the upper and middle Niger valleys were transported. The second, Sierra Leone, includes the territory from the Casamance to Assini, or what is now Guinea-Bissau, Guinea, Sierra Leone, Liberia, and the Ivory Coast. Adjoining Sierra Leone is the Gold Coast, occupying what is essentially contemporary Ghana. Further east lay the fourth region, the Bight of Benin, stretching from the Volta to the Benin River and corresponding to what is now Togo, contemporary Benin, and southwestern Nigeria. The Bight of Biafra, in turn, comprised contemporary southeastern Nigeria, Cameroon, and Gabon. West Central Africa includes Congo (formerly Zaire) and Angola, and the seventh region, Mozambique-Madagascar, refers to southeastern Africa, including what is now Mozambique, parts of Tanzania, and the island of Madagascar.

Fully one quarter of all exported persons originated from the Bright of Biafra and another quarter came from West Central Africa. Approximately 15 percent each came from Senegambia, Sierra Leone, and the Gold Coast while only 3 percent came from the Bight of Benin and 2 percent from Mozambique-Madagascar.

Adult men, while the largest group of persons transported, comprised less than half of the total number of people brought to the Americas. Women, boys, and girls combined outnumbered them in the trade. In the last four decades of the seventeenth century, overall, women comprised almost 40 percent of those who crossed the Atlantic, men comprised 50 percent, and children made up the remainder. During the eighteenth century, the proportion of children (those thought by slave traders to be under the age of fifteen) rose to 20 percent, women fell to 30 percent, and men maintained their previous proportion. Not until the nineteenth century would women's numbers fall to almost 15 percent, while men and children equally constituted the remainder. Moreover, African women comprised four-fifths of all women to make the Atlantic crossing—either voluntarily or involuntarily—prior to 1800. It is thus essential that, when examining the contours of early American slave societies, the perspective of enslaved women occupy a central place. Women entered the trans-Atlantic slave trade in significant numbers and comprised an essential part of the workforce on American plantations.

The connections between ethnicity and gender are fundamental. Regional origins did much to influence the sex ratios for the Africans who comprised the cargoes of slave ships. In the seventeenth century, ships leaving the Upper Guinea Coast or West Central Africa carried 20 to 25 percent more men than those leaving the Bight of Biafra. Although as time passed the disparity between the regions

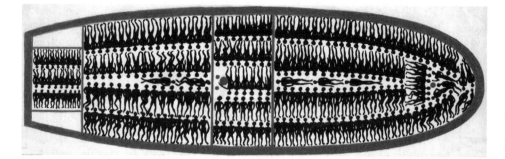

This diagram from an 1808 report on the slave trade prepared for the British Parliament provides a diagram of a slave ship. The largest number of African men, women, and children were packed into the smallest possible space and then chained below decks, creating horrid conditions during the middle passage.

diminished somewhat, in the eighteenth century both the Bight of Biafra and the Bight of Benin continued to supply the highest ratios of women to men, while the Gold Coast, West Central Africa, and the Upper Guinea coast supplied the lowest.

As they oversaw the workings of the slave trade, officials of the Royal African Company in London consistently sent slave ship captains to the West African coast under orders to "view well the Negroes that they may be sound and merchantable[,] between the ages of 15 & 40 [,] and that the major part be male." The injunctions of the Royal African Company have been understood as simply formulaic orders carried out with little difficulty, the conclusion being that European slavers purchased twice as many men as women for labor in the Americas. Yet they occasionally reveal a tone of entreaty rather than authority. "If you are carefull you may have two men for one female," or "endeavour all you can to have your Number of Males exceed the females," or "the number of women Exceeding [men] doeth much disparayes the whole Cargoe." In an attempt to explain to Royal African Company officials the large numbers of women he purchased, George Hingston wrote that "as yett wee find ye women generally Better than the men." Their instructions, then, often reflected the Company's inability to dictate the terms of trade.

The causes of shifting sex ratios are still being explored, but it is now clear that we must look to African sociopolitical relations rather than to European demands in analyzing the issue. For example, patrilineal societies appear to have exported more women than societies ordered along matrilineal lines. The value of women in regional African slave trades (to Northern Africa or Asia) affected the willingness of local slavers to make women available to the Atlantic trade where slave traders paid lower prices for women than men. Regions affected by consistent warfare or military upheaval exported fewer women. In rare cases, gendered prohibitions on the trading of slaves worked in the opposite direction. German trader David Van Nyendael wrote at the turn of the seventeenth century "[that in the city of Benin it is not] allow'd to export any Male slaves that are sold in this Country for they must stay there; But females may be dealt with at anyone's pleasure." Van Nyendael referred here to a state policy in place since 1560 whose enforcement only began to dissipate after the second decade of the eighteenth century. This prohibition against trading in men may well be a key to the reluctance of European traders to stop there. While arguments have been made that African women's value as agricultural producers kept them out of the trans-Atlantic trade, women performed agricultural work throughout West Africa, regardless of the ratio at which they were made available to the Atlantic slave trade. Thus neither European interest in male laborers nor African interest in female laborers satisfactorily explains the pattern of sex ratios. Rather, regional issues, rhythms of supply and demand, of warfare and conquest, and of competing markets for slaves worked together to increase the likelihood that those adult men exposed to capture and slavery would be transported to the Americas.

The Life Left Behind: Sketches of West African Cultures

By the time they were purchased by Hingston, the women on the *Arthur* could not have been ignorant of enslavement at the hands of Europeans. Europe's slaving vessels had been visiting the Bights since before the seventeenth century. Economic upheavals and the desire for trade goods cast a wide web of capture and sale for African women, men, and children. As wars and slave raiders disrupted the rhythms of daily life, people would have heard word of their vulnerability to the white man's ships. Women and men on the Upper Guinea Coast too were well aware of the dangers of capture and sale. From the sixteenth century, the invading *Mane* pressed toward the coast creating a cycle of capture and sale to European traders that endured for centuries. As prisoners of war, men—exported at a rate three times that of women—were particularly vulnerable to European slavers. But, as we know from the examples of Cayoba and Moota, women were not invulnerable.

In all regions of West Africa, internal factors could alter sex ratios from year to year. These large demographic patterns should not be seen as static. In response to high demand, for example, slavers sold equal numbers of women and men to European slave ships from the Gold Coast in 1688. Women captured by the European slave trade that year must have found their capture particularly shocking, it being a fate more often befalling men. Traveling to Allada at the Gold Coast, William Snelgrave carefully negotiated sex ratios such that "I should have three Males to one Female, and take none but what I like." He realized he was in a position to set the terms of trade shortly after viewing the devastation at Whydah in the aftermath of Dahomey's successful military campaign against Whydah and Allada on the coast. "People being in a starving condition [are] obliged to sell their servants and children for money and goods." Snelgrave's vocation—slave trader and apologist for the slave trade—calls into question the veracity of his claim that people sold their own children. However, the aftermath of Dahomean expansion did cause increased numbers of dependent women, and men, from the immediate area to be offered into the trade. Thus, in the late 1720s and 1730s, more females were likely exported from Whydah than at other periods. Internal factors here, and all down the coast, altered sex ratios from year to year.

The women who found their futures so unthinkably changed must have been beset by fears and uncertainties that built as ships languished on the Callabar River or "holes" filled up at Elmina. As they contemplated the unpredictability of their lives, their thoughts must have turned to the children and families left behind. Perhaps they thought of crops untended and children unfed. As night fell, daily evening markets predominated by women up and down the coast, where they had exchanged wares, gossip, food, or friendship, may have crept into their thoughts of an imminently receding past. If they had been members of polygamous households [in which men married multiple wives], perhaps the understanding that they would never again see their relatives would be tempered by the knowledge that another woman would step in to care for their children—a bittersweet confidence indeed. The habits and events that had been so common as to be invisible would be suddenly thrown into sharp relief as the portability of some and the irretrivability of others completely altered their worlds.

By all accounts, Ibo women captured upon the *Arthur* and myriad other slave ships came from communities in which they shouldered important responsibilities. Slave traders watched the way women worked in West and West Central Africa and called these women "slaves" to African men—no doubt an accusation that went some way toward exonerating their own role in the slave trade. All along the area south of Sierra Leone and West of Togo agricultural work fell within the purview of women. While European observers denigrated this essential sphere of women's activity, all members of society depended upon women's agricultural work and compensated for it at the markets.

Agricultural work brought with it particular kinds of social and cultural spaces. The nature of agricultural work on the Upper Guinea Coast required large-scale collective effort, effectively pulling all members of the society into the agricultural sphere. The huge dikes built to accommodate the draining and flooding of fields required the cooperation of hundreds of people. During construction and planting, both men and women moved from their homes to the fields to better tend the crop and manage the waters. Surrounded by numerous rivers and dense mangrove swamps, the peoples who lived in this part of West Africa utilized the waterways for transport and for food. They navigated canoes with as few as one person or as many as sixty people aboard and devised systems of dikes, sometimes miles long, to flood and drain rice fields. Enormous markets took place every eight days bringing thousands to buy and sell, some coming from as far as 60 miles away. In the process they created enduring social networks and utilized canoes and riverways as transport to participate in social, religious, and political gatherings.

At the Gold Coast, prior to European contact, women produced agricultural exports essential to the regional economy. Wilhelm Muller, a German minister who lived at the Gold Coast between 1662 and 1669, noted that "apart from the peasants who bring palm-wine and sugar-cane to market every day, there are no men who stand in public markets to trade, but only women. It is remarkable to see how the market is filled every day with . . . women selling [food]." Samuel Brun commented upon the division of labor concerning cultivated crops at the beginning of the seventeenth century. He noted that, at Cape Palmas (Liberia), men traded Malaguetta pepper for money, and traded beads for rice "because the rice is the ware of women, while Malaguetta is that of the men." The marketplace was a central place for women to meet and trade; and they did not exchange only goods. Muller wrote: "they strengthen their momories by zealously repeating the old stories . . . young people and children listen to such discourse with avid ears and absorb it in their hearts." One wonders how long after their transport to the Americas men and women gathered to "strengthen their memories." While doing so, they might evoke their memories of the marketplace, of their homes, of the physical landscapes of their former lives. Women here decorated their "clean and tidy [homes] . . . with white or red earth which they consider . . . particularly beautiful." What beauty did they unearth from American soil?

On the Upper Guinea Coast, the frequent movement of peoples from place to place no doubt influenced their patterns of cultural and economic acquisitions. Women covered themselves with elaborate scarification, an adornment wholly perplexing to Europeans, but certainly an essential component to girl's coming of age, both physically and spirituallly. *Grigri* prayer amulets were worn all along the coast. Women and men carried their belief systems on their persons, offering food and thanks and requesting blessings from a pantheon of gods before eating, stepping into a boat, or going to sleep. As women moved through the work that defined their day, the protective divine would accompany them.

Much has been made of the "matriarchal" origins of West African families. Perhaps more significant for women transported from the Slave Coast would be the experience of having lived, or served, in households headed by male/female pairs who ruled, in tandem, over their lineage. Such was the case for the Fon. Known as the *Taninon*, the female head's responsibilities came from her role as intermediary between the living and the ancestors of each Fon lineage. Even a woman "enslaved" by a Slave Coast family could have no doubt as to the potential authority and responsibility of women in Fon society. Linkages between powerful women and men were inherent to Fon cosmology. Among the Igbo the Creater was *Chineke*— who represented both male (*Chi*) and female (*Eke*) and whose unity and complementarity formed the crux of Igbo cosmology. In the mid-seventeenth century, Allada had been the focus of Christian missionary efforts. African catechisms prepared by the Capuchins allowed "Lisa" to refer to Jesus Christ. In Allada cosmology Lisa, a white man, and Mawa, a black woman, form a paired deity. As agricultural producers, conduits to the ancestors, complements to Jesus Christ, even as armed guards at the king's palace, the memory of women's multiple and pivotal role at all levels of society would travel with both men and women across the Atlantic.

The particularities of how girls' and women's place in the world had been demarcated varied from region to region. In relation to matters of spirit, perhaps the tangibles of home and public space receded. Thinking back on her life before enslavement a woman from the Gold Coast might remember being a child, of seven or eight, called upon to witness a marriage. Apparently a small girl was compelled to "sleep in between [the bride and groom] and watch out that they do not touch each other for seven days" as part of a wedding ritual. There is no telling what insights a young girl might carry with her, or how her sense of her own importance might be shaped, as a result of her role at the inception of a marriage. Women would carry many different such childhood memories. For many, their girlhood would have been marked by circumcision. Among other things, the rite of circumcision initiáted female children into a sisterhood, creating a bond of shared secrets and pain. In modern accounts the rite is deeply laden with traditional imagery that imparts a longstanding connection between girls, their mothers, grandmothers, and ancestors. Once these women found themselves in American slave societies, slaveowners wrenched this most essential site of commonality between mothers and daughters from them. Enslaved mothers would be forced to devise new ritual spaces as substitutes.

Motherhood was a social role carefully prepared for in Africa, as elsewhere. On the Gold Coast after a marriage announcement, the bride's friends ritually prepared her for conception. Once pregnant she would be "brought to the sea-shore in order to be washed," after being ritually dirtied by "a great number of boys and girls" on her way to the water. As they had since their first trips to West Africa, Europeans believed childbirth came easily to African women. "In the second or third day [after childbirth] they already go among people and do their housework and business," exclaimed Muller. His awe at the speed of women's recovery on the Gold Coast is perhaps contextualized by the length of time that elite European women spent recuperating from childbirth—the German word for childbed in fact meant "six-week bed."

During pregnancy, women and men initiated a sexual distance that extended at least a year and a half after a birth. "Not allowed even the Matrimonial caresses of her husband" from the moment of a discovered pregnancy, men and women cooperated to protect unborn children and to space childbirth. Abstinence reflected an understanding of the relationship between intercourse and pregnancy as well as a mutual desire to spare women's energy and health from too frequent pregnancies. Men as well as women, then, acknowledged and understood the physical demands of childbirth and nursing in ways lost on European observers. As they often did, European observers misconstrued birth spacing in their haste to denounce all African women as either enslaved by their men or "inclined to Wantonness." They associated what they saw as sexual freedom with "an absolute sterility [or] . . . a seldom pregnancy." Thus they believed that the woman who mothered only "two or three [children] in their whole lives" did so as a consequence of sexual promiscuity, not of conscious efforts at birth spacing. Some European observers believed the post-delivery period of abstinence lasted three months; others commented upon a two- to three-year period of breastfeeding. Contemporary studies note the evidence that prolonged breastfeeding in tandem with postpartum sexual abstinence was an essential factor in African women and men's ability to regulate fertility. Modern anthropological studies focused on the area of West Africa from Sierra Leone to the Bight of Biafra calculated the average duration of postpartum taboo a year or longer. By abstaining from sexual contact, or practicing coitus interruptus during breastfeeding, parents were able to assure manageable birth spacing and thereby increase the probability that their children would survive infancy.

At the Gold Coast, parents protected newly born children by anointing them with palm-wine, adorning them with safeguarding fetishes, and strapping them to a mother's back until they could walk. At the Upper Guinea Coast, as throughout West Africa, women were accompanied by the infants they carried upon their backs for "as long as they are breast-feeding them." At the Sierra Leone estuary and the Sess River at Cape Palmas, women carried infants "as long as they have them at the breast . . . in a kind of leather box, in which the little one is sat. They also tie it to their body to prevent accident." In many places, protection also took the form of circumcision. Once in America, however, parents would contend with an inability to carry through essential practices associated with birth and childrearing. Faced with permanent exile, women and men left behind much of what defined them as members of specific sociocultural entities. The inability to provide a child "with all kinds of exquisite beads and with elegantly fashioned gold . . . through whose strength the tender child is to be protected against *summan*, the Devil, and against illness, injury and accident" must have cut deep into the hearts of men and women who became parents in the Americas. It may have been comparable to the inability to circumcise so as to properly initiate boys and girls into their adulthood. The loss of this rite constituted an unbelievable violence to family, ethnic, and religious traditions. The memories and belief systems that dictated female circumcision, or polygamous households, or sexual abstinence as birth control, would live on in the Americas even as men and women's ability to actualize such aspects of their past would be lost and mourned. Over time, these cultural traditions were renegotiated as Africans made sexual connections and gave birth to children whom they guided into an adulthood categorically at odds with their own past.

African Women in the Americas

The traditional beliefs and behaviors that European observers identified as encompassing the worlds of men and women from the Gold Coast, or the Bights of Benin and Biafra, should be seen only as suggestive. It is difficult to know how close these white men, whose reasons for noting black women's lives were heavily laden with their own agendas and fortunes in the slave trade, could come to the heart of women's experiences. Nevertheless, their observations are one means of approaching a more detailed sense of the lives left behind by men and women transported to the Americas. African women who found themselves in the Americas would struggle as the terms and conditions under which they performed agricultural work and tried to maintain traditions of family were drastically and violently altered. Yet they continued to perform agricultural labor and to bring children into the world even as they developed a radically altered vision of the cultural meanings of their pasts and their futures.

Throughout the plantation societies that dominated the seventeenth- and eighteenth-century European colonies in the Americas, women labored in the fields. Despite images of domestic service—cooking, cleaning, and taking care of slaveowners' children—the vast majority of African and African American women spent their entire lives engaged in fieldwork. In some cases, the crops they grew may have tied them to their lives before enslavement. In the early eighteenth century in South Carolina, for example, plantation owners appropriated essential rice cultivation skills from the men and women they enslaved. Indeed, as long as rice was the colony's staple export crop, planters preferred to purchase and enslave persons from the Upper Guinea Coast over any other West African region. Any sense of continutiy for those women from the Upper Guinea Coast would, however, be thwarted in the malaria-infested rice fields of South Carolina. For others, however, surviving the regime of the American colonies included learning to grow less familiar crops. Nonetheless, whether on coffee plantations in Santo Domingo, rice plantations in South Carolina, or sugar plantations in Jamaica, wherever staple crops were grown, women were forced to cultivate them. When we bear in mind that artisanal positions were all but closed to female laborers, women's preponderance in the backbreaking work of the fields begins to make sense. Drivers, boilers, coopers, sailors, blacksmiths, carpenters, herdsmen—all these occupations excluded women. The modicum of increased autonomy, mobility, and release from the violence and violation of slavery that these positions offered was available only to enslaved men. Women who hoped to escape fieldwork had to be resigned to the close confines of domestic work—a space open to only a tiny few and arguably more difficult than fieldwork with the relentless supervision, sexual violation, and retaliatory violence that swirled around women caught up in the immediacy of slaveowners' intimate familial contestations.

Physical and emotional spaces did exist where enslaved women could momentarily escape the violence and drudgery of fieldwork. None was so widely customary as their participation in colonial markets. In many American societies, slaveowners assigned provision grounds to the enslaved. These were small plots of land on which one had to grow food to feed oneself and one's family. Women often were responsible for tending these plots and, subsequently, for selling surplus wares at weekend markets in Charleston, Richmond, Cape Hat, Bridgetown, or St. John's. Even in those colonies where there were no formalized provision grounds, many enslaved women manged to participate in the weekend markets. Outraged at their dependence on black women for produce like eggs and vegetables and the opportunities for covert gatherings that markets and travel to markets provided, but unwilling to shoulder the responsibility for provisioning the labor force themselves, colonial legislators complained bitterly about black women's behavior in the markets. For their part, the women who made the weekly trip to market their goods must have felt fiercely protective of their ability to do so; the market after all was a place for all manner of exchange—financial, informational, and emotional.

Markets were particularly visible places for women to collectively bolster one another against the outrages of enslavement. But marketplaces were not the only sites for subversion. Enslaved women articulated their opposition in many ways to the labor and social system so brutally forced upon them: running away, sometimes with children in tow; establishing Maroon communities; poisoning slaveowners; participating in revolts; feigning illness, pregnancy, or ignorance; breaking tools; working slowly; ministering to the sick; or spitting in the soup. But perhaps the most important opposition to the system of enslavement was the ability and desire to build communities. The regime of plantation work wreaked havoc on the health of all enslaved persons. Although birthrates began to outstrip death rates in North American slave societies in the second half of the eighteenth century, they did not do so until after nineteenth-century emancipations elsewhere in the Americas. Overworked and underfed, enslaved laborers were extremely vulnerable to disease and malnutrition. Infant mortality rates were extremely high. Disease either destoryed women's reproductive ability, or consigned children to early death. Mortality rates were so high in seventeenth-century Barbados, for example, that a typical slaveowner interested in simply maintaining a constant number of laborers over the course of a decade would have to purchase a third again the total number of persons he enslaved. At least some portion of women who had no children while enslaved must have been engaging in an act of withholding this most intimate and emotional form of labor. As an institution, slavery did nothing better than to emphasize the commodification and disposability of a woman and the children she might bear. To have children under slavery was to open oneself up to the inevitability of loss—through sale or death—and to line the pockets of the very person who violated you. On the other hand, to have children was to stake a claim of ownership. It was to stare down the grim future of enslavement and to imagine something different. In the face of a daily existence marked by death, disease, and despair, it is remarkable that among the many legacies of enslavement are enduring traditions of political culture, religion, healing, and arts.

Creating and protecting the spaces in which community could grow was curtailed not only by the physicalities of health and labor. Slaveowners engaged in a constant—albeit fundamentally unsuccessful—struggle to limit women and men's lives to the narrowest of confines. But with or without childbirth, the men and women who crossed the Atlantic became immediately enmeshed in families. Whether the formation of real or fictive family ties was bolstered by shared ethnic antecedents or hindered by the vast cultural divides between far-flung African ethnicities, enslaved women and men created new cultural institutions almost from the moment of their forced arrival. A sense of family emerged from displacement—many persons who shared the middle passage referred to one another as brother or site. As their own expectations about religion, family formation, or healing intersected with those of other enslaved African or Native American persons, women created communities. These communities, these sites of culture formation, took on meaning in relation to the materialities of work, the market, disease, death, and finally birth.

Cayoba's decision to throw her lot in with "fort slaves" and "sale slaves" was both brave and prophetic. She could have no idea how the kind of cross-status and cross-ethnic alliance she was about to participate in would become the essential component in her descendents' lives in the New World. Nor could she possibly imagine the ways in which her extraordinarily visible expression of revolt might actually be connected to Moota's seeming complacency. As Moota appeared to go about her work oblivious to the rebelliousness percolating around her, her children embodied other possibilities for rebellion and other manifestations of subjugation. They were in complicated relationship to the emerging social power that was personified by the slave fort and the Europeans who inhabited it. As Moota negotiated her status as slave she created culture. Her children personified the irretrievability of her past and the unimaginable trajectory of her future.

Questions for Study and Review

1. How does the experience of women change our understandings of slavery and the slave trade?

2. Which aspects of African culture were incorporated into enslaved cultures in North America, and how were they transformed in the process?

3. Compare the lives of enslaved women in the West Indies and on the North American mainland.

4. How might the arrival of enslaved Africans in Jamestown in 1619 have changed relations between the English colonists and the Powhatan Indians?

Suggested Readings and Web Sites

Barry Gaspar and Darlene Clark Hine, eds., *More than Chattel: Black Women and Slavery in the Americas* (1996)
Michael Gomez, *Changing Our Country Marks: The Transformation of African Identities in the Colonial and Antebellum South* (1998)
Kim F. Hall, *Things of Darkness: Economies of Race and Gender in Early Modern England* (1995)
Graham Russell Hodges, *Root & Branch: African Americans in New York and East Jersey, 1613–1863* (1999)
Martin Klein and Claire Robertson, eds. *Women and Slavery in Africa* (1983)
Atlantic Slave Trade and Slave Life in the Americas: A Visual Record
    http://hitchcock.itc.virginia.edu/slavery
African American Migration Experience
    http://www.inmotionaame.org/home.cfm?
PBS's Africans in America
    http://www.pbs.org/wgbh/aia

Chapter 3

Most white women and men in seventeenth-century New England spent their days in the necessary but mundane tasks of providing for families, rearing children, and surviving personal and communal crises. The family was the center of life for these colonists. Women contributed to the family's well-being by assisting men in their labors, managing the household in their absence, and performing the bulk of domestic chores, which included everything from hauling water and planting gardens to making clothes, preparing food, and educating children. Men also helped their wives, of course, and some, such as ships' captains, depended on them for financial and legal as well as domestic activities during long absences from home.

Still, the tightness of family bonds did not mean that sisters, wives, and mothers shared fully in the same experiences as brothers, husbands, and fathers. For instance, while death was an omnipresent reality for all colonists, women of childbearing age lived with a special sense of foreboding. War, which was also omnipresent, affected women and men differently as well. The frequent wars with Indians, for example, called men away to battle, left women behind to fend for their families and themselves, increased the numbers of widows and children, and increased the likelihood that women would be left destitute.

Yet as Laurel Thatcher Ulrich shows, in seventeenth-century New England differences existed not only between women and men but also among women. Some of these differences were stark, such as that between the wife of a colony's governor and the servant who labored in her household. Many women, however, lived as wives and mothers in their own families, without the advantages of great wealth or the leisure time provided by full-time servants. Still, the daily labors of such women varied significantly depending on the amount of land a family owned, whether they lived on the frontier or in a town along the coast, the size of the house in which they resided, and the number of children and other relatives living with them.

Women in New England lived relatively long lives in the seventeenth century, at least if they survived the birth of their children. But even if they learned to read and write when young, most had little time to keep diaries or write letters once they became wives and mothers. Thus, Ulrich depends on two kinds of records kept by men—household inventories and court papers—to re-create the lives of New England women. Household inventories were compiled upon the death of a free male adult or a widow. Because a person needed to have some assets for the court to compile such a list, inventories were not done for the poorest members of society, even if they lived independently, or for slaves or servants. Still, as Ulrich demonstrates, they provide a window into the experiences of a wide range of property-owning families. Individual women or married couples sometimes ended up in court, and the resulting records add further insights into the lives of ordinary colonists.

The following portraits of Beatrice Plummer, Hannah Grafton, and Magdalen Wear illustrate both the particular hardships faced by women and the opportunities open to some as settlements grew and consumer goods became more widely available. They also suggest the ways that ideals of womanhood converged with and diverged from the experiences of real women in their everyday lives.

The Ways of Her Household: Three New England Women
LAUREL THATCHER ULRICH

By English tradition, a woman's environment was the family dwelling and the yard or yards surrounding it. Though the exact composition of her setting obviously depended upon the occupation and economic status of her husband, its general outlines were surprisingly similar regardless of where it was located. The difference between an urban "houselot" and a rural "homelot" was not as dramatic as one might suppose.

If we were to draw a line around the housewife's domain, it would extend from the kitchen and its appendages, the cellars, pantries, brewhouses, milkhouses, washhouses, and butteries which appear in various combinations in household inventories, to the exterior of the house, where, even in the city, a mélange of animal and vegetable life flourished among the straw, husks, clutter, and muck. Encircling the pigpen, such a line would surround the garden, the milkyard, the well, the henhouse, and perhaps the orchard itself—though husbands pruned and planted trees and eventually supervised the making of cider, good housewives strung their wash between the trees and in season harvested fruit for pies and conserves.

The line demarking the housewife's realm would not cross the fences which defined outlying fields of Indian corn or barley, nor would it stretch to fishing stages, mills, or wharves, but in berry or mushroom season it would extend into nearby woods or marsh and in spells of dearth or leisure reach to the shore. Of necessity, the boundaries of each woman's world would also extend into the houses of neighbors and into the cartways of a village or town. Housewives commanded a limited domain. But they were neither isolated nor self-sufficient. Even in farming settlements, families found it essential to bargain for needed goods and services. For prosperous and socially prominent women, interdependence took on another meaning as well. Prosperity meant charity, and in early New England charity meant personal responsibility for nearby neighbors.

None of this was unique to New England. In fact, each aspect of female life described here can be found in idealized form in the Bible in the description of the

Although this 1681 drawing was published in a proposal for the employment of the poor in London, the image illustrates as well the proper role for an industrious goodwife in the British colonies.

"virtuous woman" of Proverbs, chapter 31. The Puritans called this paragon "Bathsheba," assuming rather logically that Solomon could only have learned such an appreciation for huswifery from his mother. Forgotten in their encomia to female virtue was the rooftop bather whose beauty brought King David to grief. In English and American sermons Bathsheba was remembered as a virtuous house-wife, a godly woman whose industrious labors gave mythical significance to the ordinary tasks assigned to her sex.

As described in Proverbs, Bathsheba is a willing servant to her family: "She riseth also while it is yet night, and giveth meat to her household."

She is a skilled manufacturer: "She seeketh wool, and flax, and worketh willingly with her hands."

She is a hard-working agriculturist: "With the fruit of her hands she planteth a vineyard."

She is a resourceful trader: "She is like the merchants' ships; she bringeth her food from afar."

Because her realm includes servants as well as young children, her ability to direct, to inspire, and to nurture others is as important to her success as hard work. "She openeth her mouth with wisdom; and in her tongue is the law of kindness." Her industry and her charity give legitimacy to her wealth. Though dressed in silk and purple, "strength and honour are her clothing" and "she stretcheth out her hand to the poor." Her goal is not public distinction but private competence.

Although her husband is "known in the gates," her greatest reward is in looking well to "the ways of her household." In doing so, she earns the devotion of her children, the praise of her husband, and the commendation of God.

To describe this virtuous Bathsheba is to outline the major components of the housekeeping role in early America. Some of these activities have received greater attention in the literature than others. For most historians, as for almost all antiquarians, the quintessential early American woman has been a churner of cream and a spinner of wool. Because home manufacturing has all but disappeared from modern housekeeping, many scholars have assumed that the key change in female economic life has been a shift from "production" to "consumption," a shift precipitated by the industrial revolution. This is far too simple, obscuring the variety which existed even in the pre-industrial world.

Setting aside for the moment the social skills involved in housekeeping—the nurturing, managing, and charitable responsibilities described in the myth of Bathsheba—we can see how relatively subtle shifts in emphasis among the economic skills—service, manufacturing, agriculture, and trade—might create pronounced differences in patterns of daily work. Evidence derived from 401 household inventories from Essex and York counties (Table 1) sketches the major economic variations in the region.

Predictably, home manufacturing, as measured by ownership of dairying and textile-processing equipment, was more widespread in the farming settlements of Essex County in 1670 than in the more remote fishing and sawmill villages of frontier Maine. With few fences and little hay, frontier planters let their scraggly cows browse in the woods, killing them for meat in winter but expecting little milk in any season. In such a setting, few families bothered with sheep, which were easy prey for wolves. By 1700, however, the dairying statistics for the two counties had almost reversed themselves. Flax appeared almost as often in York County as in Essex, and sheep even more frequently. The hinterland was becoming agricultural. The proportionate decline in cows and churns in Essex County is explained by the increasing diversity of the Massachusetts economy as commercial centers like Salem began to diverge from their agricultural surroundings.

Extracting urban Salem inventories from the larger 1700 sample makes this shift obvious (see Table 2). Although the wives of Salem shopkeepers, craftsmen, and mariners still kept a pig or two "at the door," agriculture had become a less pronounced theme in their daily work. Many farm wives in Essex County continued to milk cows, but most women in the region's largest town did not. At the same time, luxury items like looking glasses, framed pictures, or quilts, which were still rare in the country, had become quite visible. Thus, rather straightforward contrasts between frontier, farming, and commercial communities explain many of the variations in the inventory data.

To more fully understand the diverse ways in which the Bathsheba model was reflected in daily life, we must turn from the general to the particular. Beatrice Plummer, Hannah Grafton, and Magdalen Wear lived and died in New England in the years before 1750. One of them lived on the frontier, another on a farm, and a third in town. Because they were real women, however, and not hypothetical example, the ways of their households were shaped by personal as well as geographic factors. A careful examination of the contents of their kitchens and chambers suggests the varied complexity as well as the underlying unity in the lives of early American women.

TABLE 1 SOME INDICATORS OF AGRICULTURE AND HOME MANUFACTURING
IN HOUSEHOLD INVENTORIES, ESSEX AND YORK COUNTIES, 1670, 1700, 1730

TOTAL INVETORIES	1670[1]	1700[2]	1730[3]
Essex County	97	95	92
York County	39	41	37
DAIRYING			
Cows			
Essex County	77%	64%	57%
York County	73%	79%	84%
Processing Equipment			
Essex County	30%	14%	10%
York County	18%	25%	10%
TEXTILES			
Sheep			
Essex County	43%	45%	39%
York County	18%	64%	46%
Spinning Wheels			
Essex County	38%	46%	38%
York County	21%	46%	40%
Looms			
Essex County	4%	6%	13%
York County	0%	2%	3%
Flax			
Essex County	8%	12%	18%
York County	0%	10%	13%
PROVISIONS (any type of food, any quantity)			
Essex County	56%	26%	32%
York County	37%	53%	30%

[1] Taken from *The Probate Records of Essex County* (Salem, Mass., 1916–1920), II, 237–432, and *Maine Province and Court Records* (Portland, Me., 1931), II.

[2] Book 307, manuscript probate records, Essex County Court House, Salem, Mass. Books I, II, manuscript probate records, York County Court House, Alfred, Me.

[3] Book 321, manuscript probate records, Essex County. Book IV, manuscript probate records, York County.

Let us begin with Beatrice Plummer of Newbury, Massachusetts. Forgetting that death brought her neighbors into the house on January 24, 1672, we can use the probate inventory which they prepared to reconstruct the normal pattern of her work.

With a clear estate of £343, Francis Plummer had belonged to the "middling sort" who were the church members and freeholders of the Puritan settlement of Newbury. As an immigrant of 1653, he had listed himself as a "linnen weaver," but he soon became a farmer as well. At his death, his loom and tackling stood in the "shop" with his pitchforks, his hoes, and his tools for smithing and carpentry. Plummer had integrated four smaller plots to form one continuous sixteen-acre farm. An additional twenty acres of salt marsh and meadow provided hay and forage for his small

TABLE 2 COMPARISON OF SELECTED ITEMS: URBAN SALEM AND OVERALL ESSEX COUNTY INVENTORIES, 1700[1]

	SALEM (N = 12)	ESSEX (N = 83)
Cows	33%	71%
Dairy Tools	0%	17%
Sheep	16%	51%
Spinning Wheels	50%	47%
Swine	41%	51%
Looking Glasses	75%	31%
Pictures	25%	0%
Quilts	15%	2%

[1] The overall Essex County sample was taken from Book 307, manuscript probate records, Essex County Court House, Salem, Mass. The twelve urban inventories drawn from that same source can all be placed on James Duncan Phillips' reconstructed map of the center of Salem, 1700 (*Salem in the Seventeenth Century*, Boston, 1937). In 1700 the town of Salem was still very large geographically and included rural as well as urban neighborhoods. The twelve decedents in this subsample obviously belonged to the commercial world of mercantile Salem. They included three mariners, one innkeeper, a tailor, a cooper, a joiner, and two cordwainers. Sidney Perley, *History of Salem* (Salem, 1924) I, 306, 435, 441; II, 38, 82, 178, 268, 386, 387; III. 29, 51, 52.

herd of cows and sheep. His farm provided a comfortable living for his family, which at this stage of his life included only his second wife, Beatrice, and her grandchild by a previous marriage. Had not death prevented him, he might have filled this January day in a number of productive ways, moving the loom into the sparsely furnished hall, for example, or taking his yoke of oxen to the wood lot "near the little river" to cut wood for the large fireplace that was the center of Beatrice's working world.

The house over which Beatrice presided must have looked much like surviving dwellings from seventeenth-century New England, with its "Hall" and "Parlor" on the ground floor and two "chambers" above. A space designated in the inventory only as "another Roome" held the family's collection of pots, kettles, dripping pans, trays, buckets, and earthenware. Perhaps this kitchen had been added to the original house as a lean-to, as was frequently the case in New England. The upstairs chambers were not bedrooms but storage rooms for foodstuffs and out-of-season equipment. The best bed with its bolster, pillows, blanket, and coverlet stood in the parlor; a second bed occupied one corner of the kitchen, while a cupboard, a "great chest," a table, and a backless bench called a "form" furnished the hall. More food was found in the "cellar" and in the "dairy house," a room which may have stood at the coolest end of the kitchen lean-to.

The Plummer house was devoid of ornament, but its contents bespeak such comforts as conscientious yeomanry and good huswifery afforded. On this winter morning the dairy house held four and a half "flitches" or sides of bacon, a quarter of a barrel of salt pork, twenty-eight pounds of cheese, and four pounds of butter. Upstairs in a chamber were more than twenty-five bushels of "English" grain—barley, oats, wheat, and rye. (The Plummers apparently reserved their Indian corn, stored in another location, for their animals.) When made into malt by a village specialist, barley would become the basis for beer. Two bushels of malt were already stored in the house. The oats might appear in a variety of dishes, from plain breakfast porridge to "flummery," a gelatinous dish flavored with spices and dried fruit. But the wheat and rye were almost certainly reserved for bread and pies. The fine hair sieves stored with the grain in the hall chamber suggest that Beatrice Plummer was particular about her baking, preferring a finer flour than came directly from the miller. A "bushell of pease & beans" found near the grain and a full barrel of cider in the cellar are the only vegetables and fruits listed in the inventory, though small quantities of pickles, preserves, or dried herbs might have escaped notice. Perhaps the Plummers added variety to their diet by trading some of their abundant supply of grain for cabbages, turnips, sugar, molasses, and spices.

Even without additions they had the basic components of the yeoman diet described in English agricultural literature of the seventeenth century. Although the eighteenth century would add a little chocolate or tea as well as increasing quantities of tiny "petators" to the New England farmer's diet, the bread, cider, and boiled meat which fed Francis and Beatrice Plummer also fed their counterparts a century later.

Since wives were involved with early-morning milking, breakfast of necessity featured prepared foods or leftovers—toasted bread, cheese, and perhaps meat and turnips kept from the day before, any of this washed down with cider or beer in winter, with milk in summer. Only on special occasions would there be pie or doughnuts. Dinner was the main meal of the day. Here a housewife with culinary aspirations and an ample larder could display her specialties. After harvest Beatrice Plummer might have served roast pork or goose with apples, in spring an eel pie flavored with parsley and winter savory, and in summer a leek soup or gooseberry cream; but for ordinary days the most common menu was boiled meat with whatever "sauce" the season provided—dried peas or beans, parsnips, turnips, onions, cabbage, or garden greens. A heavy pudding stuffed into a cloth bag could steam atop the vegetables and meat. The broth from this boiled dinner might reappear at supper as "pottage" with the addition of minced herbs and some oatmeal or barley for thickening. Supper, like breakfast, was a simple meal. Bread, cheese, and beer were as welcome at the end of a winter day as at the beginning. In summer, egg dishes and fruit tarts provided more varied nutrition.

Preparing the simplest of these meals required both judgment and skill. As Gervase Markham, an English writer of the seventeenth century, quipped, a woman who was "utterly ignorant" of cookery could "then but perform half her vow; for she may love and obey, but she cannot cherish, serve, and keep him with that true duty which is ever expected." The most basic of the housewife's skills was building and regulating fires—a task so fundamental that it must have appeared more as habit than craft. Summer and winter, day and night, she kept a few brands smoldering, ready to stir into flame as needed. The cavernous fireplaces of early New England were but a century removed from the open fires of medieval houses, and they retained some of the characteristics of the latter. Standing inside one of these huge openings today, a person can see the sky above. Seventeenth-century housewives *did* stand in their fireplaces, which were conceived less as enclosed spaces for a single blaze than as accessible working surfaces upon which a number of small fires might be built. Preparing several dishes simultaneously, a cook could move from one fire to another, turning a spit, checking the state of the embers under a skillet, adjusting the height of a pot hung from the lugpole by its adjustable trammel. The complexity of fire-tending, as much as anything else, encouraged the one-pot meal.

The contents of her inventory suggest that Beatrice Plummer was adept not only at roasting, frying, and boiling but also at baking, the most difficult branch of cookery. Judging from the grain in the upstairs chamber, the bread which she baked was "maslin," a common type made from a mixture of wheat and other grains, usually rye. She began with the sieves stored nearby, carefully sifting out the coarser pieces of grain and bran. Soon after supper she could have mixed the "sponge," a thin dough made from warm water, yeast, and flour. Her yeast might have come from the foamy "barm" found on top of fermenting ale or beer, from a piece of dough saved from an earlier baking, or even from the crevices in an unwashed kneading trough. Like fire-building, bread-making was based upon a self-perpetuating chain, an organic sequence which if once interrupted was difficult to begin again. Warmth from the banked fire would raise the sponge by morning, when Beatrice could work in more flour, knead the finished dough, and shape the loaves, leaving them to rise again.

Even in twentieth-century kitchens with standardized yeast and thermostatically controlled temperatures, bread dough is subject to wide variations in consistency and behavior. In a drafty house with an uncertain supply of yeast, bread-making was indeed "an art, craft, and mystery." Not the least of the problem was regulating the fire so that the oven was ready at the same time as the risen loaves. Small cakes or biscuits could be baked in a skillet or directly on the hearth under an upside-down pot covered with coals. But to produce bread in any quantity required an oven. Before 1650 these were frequently constructed in dooryards, but in the last decades of the century they were built into the rear of the kitchen fireplace, as Beatrice Plummer's must have been. Since her oven would have had no flue, she would have left the door open once she kindled a fire inside, allowing the smoke to escape through the fireplace chimney. Moving about her kitchen, she would have kept an eye on this fire, occasionally raking the coals to distribute the heat evenly, testing periodically with her hand to see if the oven had reached the right temperature. When she determined that it had, she would have scraped out the coals and inserted the bread—assuming that it had risen enough by this time or had not risen too much and collapsed waiting for the oven to heat.

Cooking and baking were year-round tasks. Inserted into these day-by-day routines were seasonal specialties which allowed a housewife to bridge the dearth of one period with the bounty of another. In the preservation calendar, dairying came first, begining with the first calves of early spring. In colonial New England cows were all-purpose creatures, raised for meat as well as for milk. Even in new settlements they could survive by browsing on rough land; their meat was a hedge against famine. But only in areas with abundant meadow (and even there only in certain months) would they produce milk with sufficient butterfat for serious dairying. Newbury was such a place.

We can imagine Beatrice Plummer some morning in early summer processing the milk which would appear as cheese in a January breakfast. Slowly she heated several gallons with rennet dried and saved from the autumn's slaughtering. Within an hour or two the curd had formed. She broke it, drained off the whey, then worked in a little of her own fresh butter. Packing this rich mixture into a mold, she turned it in her wooden press for an hour or more, changing and washing the cheesecloth frequently as the whey dripped out. Repacking it in dry cloth, she left it in the press for another thirty to forty hours before washing it once more with whey, drying it, and placing it in the cellar or dairy house to age. As a young girl she would have learned from her mother or a mistress the importance of thorough pressing and the virtues of cleanliness. She may also have acquired some of the many English proverbs associated with dairying. Taking her finished mound to the powdering tub for a light dusting, she perhaps recalled that "much slatness in white meat is ill for the stone."

The Plummer inventory gives little evidence of the second stage of preservation in the housewife's year, the season of gardening and gathering which followed quickly upon the dairy months. But there is ample evidence of the autumn slaughtering. Beatrice could well have killed the smaller pigs herself, holding their "hinder parts between her legs," as one observer described the process, "and taking the snout in her left hand" while she stuck the animal through the heart with a long knife. Once the bleeding stopped, she would have submerged the pig in boiling water for a few minutes, then rubbed it with rosin, stripped off the hair, and disemboweled it. Nothing was lost. She reserved the organ meats for immediate use, then cleaned the intestines for later service as sausage casings. Stuffed with meat scraps and herbs and smoked, these "links" were a treasured delicacy. The larger cuts could be roasted at once or preserved in several ways. With wine, ginger, mace, and nutmeg, pork could be rolled into a cloth and pickled as "souse." But this was an expensive—and risky—method. Beatrice relied on more common techniques. She submerged some of her pork in brine, trusting the high salt concentration and the low temperature in the dairy house to keep it untainted. She processed the rest as bacon. Each "flitch" stood in salt for two or three weeks before she hung it from the lugpole of her chimney for smoking. In the Plummer house "hanging bacon" must have been a recurring ritual of early winter.

Fall was also the season for cider-making. The mildly alcoholic beverage produced by natural fermentation of apple juice was a staple of the New England diet and was practically the only method of preserving the fruit harvest. With the addition of sugar, the alcoholic content could be raised from five to about seven percent, as it usually was in taverns and for export. The cider in the Plummer house was probably the common farm variety. In early winter the amber juice of autumn sat hissing and bubbling in the cellar in the most active stage of fermentation, a process which came to be described poetically as the "singing of the cider."

Prosaic beer was even more important to the Plummer diet. Although some housewives brewed a winter's supply of strong beer in October, storing it in the cellar, Beatrice seems to have been content with "small beer," a mild beverage usually brewed weekly or bi-weekly and used almost at once. Malting—the process of sprouting and drying barley to increase its sugar content—was wisely left to the village expert. Beatrice started with cracked malt or grist, processing her beer in three stages. "Mashing" required slow steeping at just below the boiling point, a sensitive and smelly process which largely determined the success of the beverage. Experienced brewers knew by taste whether the enzymes were working. If it was too hot, acetic acid developed which would sour the finished product. The next stage, "brewing," was relatively simple. Herbs and hops were boiled with the malted liquid. In the final step this liquor was cooled and mixed with yeast saved from last week's beer or bread. Within twenty-four hours—if all had gone well—the beer was bubbling actively.

All that we know of Beatrice Plummer of Newbury reveals her as a woman who took pride in huswifery. A wife who knew how to manage the ticklish chemical processes which changed milk into cheese, meal into bread, malt into beer, and flesh into bacon was a valuable asset to a man, as Francis Plummer knew. But not long after his death Beatrice married a man who did not appreciate her skills. To put it bluntly, he seems to have preferred her property. Like Francis Plummer before him, Edmund Berry had signed a prenuptial contract allowing Beatrice to retain ownership of the estate she had inherited from her previous husband. Subsequently, however, Edmund regretted his decision and began to hound Beatrice to tear up the paper.

The strategy which Edmund used was wonderfully calculated. Not only did he refuse to provide Beatrice with provisions, he denied her the right to perform her housewifely magic upon them. "Forr such was & still is his absurd manner in eating his victualls, as takeing his meat out of ye pickle: & broyleing it upon ye coales, & this he would tell me I must eate or else I must fast," she told the Salem Quarterly Court in June of 1677. Beatrice had lived peacefully with two husbands, as one neighbor testified, but in old age she had wedded a man who preferred her estate to her cooking. He said she should have nothing of him because he had nothing of hers, and he told one neighbor he did not care if "there were a fire in the south field and she in the middle of it." Berry was fined for his "abusive carriages and speeches."

What is really interesting about this case is not the ill-temper of the husband but the humiliation of the wife, who obviously found herself in a situation for which she was unprepared, despite the experience of two previous marriages. Legally, Beatrice had every right to hold fast to her dower, as Edmund Berry knew. The real issue, however, was not law but custom. Berry simply refused to play by the rules as his wife understood them. She offered to help him "wind his quills" (like his predecessor, he was a weaver), and she brought him "a cup of my owne Sugar & beare" and drank to him, saying, "Come husband lett all former differences be buried & trod under Foote." But he only replied, "Thou old cheating Rogue." Neither the services of a deputy husband nor the ministrations of a wife could salve his distemper. Beatrice's loss is history's gain. The tumult which thrust her into court gives life to the assemblage of objects found in her Newbury kitchen, and it helps to document the central position of huswifery in the self-definition of one northern New England woman.

Beatrice Plummer represents one type of early American housewife. Hannah Grafton represents another. Chronology, geography, and personal biography created differences between the household inventories of the two women, but there are obvious similarities as well. Like Beatrice Plummer, Hannah Grafton lived in a house with two major rooms on the ground floor and two chambers above. At various locations near the ground-floor rooms were service areas—a washhouse with its own loft or chamber, a shop, a lean-to, and two cellars. The central rooms in the Grafton house were the "parlour," with the expected featherbed, and the "kitchen," which included much the same collection of utensils and iron pots which appeared in the Plummer house. Standing in the corner of the kitchen were a spade and a hoe, two implements useful only for chipping away ice and snow on the December day on which the inventory was taken, though apparently destined for another purpose come spring. With a garden, a cow, and three pigs, Hannah Grafton clearly had agricultural responsibilities, but these were performed in a strikingly different context than on the Plummer farm. The Grafton homelot was a single acre of land standing just a few feet from shoreline in the urban center of Salem.

Joshua Grafton was a mariner like his father before him. His estate of £236 was modest, but he was still a young man and he had firm connections with the seafaring elite who were transforming the economy of Salem. When he died late in 1699, Hannah had three living children—Hannah, eight; Joshua, six; and Priscilla, who was just ten months. This young family used their space quite differently than had the Plummers. The upstairs chambers which served as storage areas in the Newbury farmhouse were sleeping quarters here. In addition to the bed in the parlor and the cradle in the kitchen, there were two beds in each of the upstairs rooms. One of these, designated as "smaller," may have been used by young Joshua. It would be interesting to know whether the mother carried the two chamber pots kept in the parlor upstairs to the bedrooms at night or whether the children found their way in the dark to their parents' sides as necessity demanded. But adults were probably never far away. Because there are more bedsteads in the Grafton house than members of the immediate family, they may have shared their living quarters with unmarried relatives or servants.

Ten chairs and two stools furnished the kitchen, while no fewer than fifteen chairs, in two separate sets, crowded the parlor with its curtained bed. The presence of a punch bowl on a square table in the parlor reinforces the notion that sociability was an important value in this Salem household. Thirteen ounces of plate, a pair of gold buttons, and a silver-headed cane suggest a measure of luxury as well—all of this in stark contrast to the Plummers, who had only two chairs and a backless bench and no discernible ornamentation at all. Yet the Grafton house was only slightly more specialized than the Newbury farmhouse. It had no servants' quarters, no sharp segregation of public and private spaces, no real separation of sleeping, eating, and work. A cradle in the kitchen and a go-cart kept with the spinning wheels in the upstairs chamber show that little Priscilla was very much a part of this workaday world.

How then might the pattern of Hannah Grafton's work have differed from that of Beatrice Plummer? Certainly cooking remained central. Hannah's menus probably varied only slightly from those prepared in the Plummer kitchen, and her cooking techniques must have been identical. But one dramatic difference is apparent in the two inventories. The Grafton house contained no provisions worth listing on that December day when Isaac Foot and Samuel Willard appeared to take inventory. Hannah had brewing vessels, but no malt; sieves and a meal trough, but no grain; and a cow, but no cheese. What little milk her cow gave in winter probably went directly into the children's mugs. Perhaps she would continue to breast-feed Priscilla until spring brought a more secure supply. In summer she might make a little cottage cheese or at harvest curdle some rich milk with wine or ale for a "posset," but she would have no surplus to process as butter or cheese. Her orchard would produce fresh apples for pie or puffs for autumn supper, but little extra for the cellar. Her three pigs might eventually appear, salted, in the empty barrels stored in the house, but as yet they represented only the hope of bacon. Trade, rather than manufacturing or agriculture, was the dominant motif in her meal preparations.

In colonial New England most food went directly from processer or producer to consumer. Joshua may have purchased grain or flour from the mill near the shipbuilding center called Knocker's Hole, about a mile away from their house. Or Hannah may have eschewed bread-making altogether, walking or sending a servant the half-mile to Elizabeth Haskett's bakery near the North River. Fresh meat for the spits in her washhouse may have come from John Cromwell's slaughterhouse on

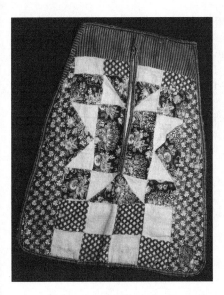

A woman's "pocket" from the colonial era usually did not survive its daily use. This rare pocket, made from scraps of cloth and then embroidered, indicates the anonymous owner's sewing skills as well as her thriftiness.

Main Street near the congregational meetinghouse, and soap for her washtubs from the soap-boiler farther up the street near the Quaker meeting house. Salem, like other colonial towns, was laid out helter-skelter, with the residences of the wealthy interspersed with the small houses of carpenters or fishermen. Because there was no center of retail trade, assembling the ingredients of a dinner involved many transactions. Sugar, wine, and spices came by sea; fresh lamb, veal, eggs, butter, gooseberries, and parsnips came by land. Merchants retailed their goods in shops or warehouses near their wharves and houses. Farmers or their wives often hawked their produce door to door. Salem had a charter for a fair, remarked one English traveler, "but it begins like Ingerstone Market, half an Hour after eleven a Clock, and Ends half an Hour before Twelve."

In such a setting, trading for food might require as much energy and skill as manufacturing or growing it. One key to success was simply knowing where to go. Keeping abreast of the arrival of ships in the harbor or establishing personal contact with just the right farmwife from nearby Salem village required time and attention. Equally important was the ability to evaluate the variety of unstandardized goods offered. An apparently sound cheese might teem with maggots when cut. Since cash was scarce, a third necessity was the establishment of credit, a problem which ultimately devolved upon husbands. But petty haggling over direct exchanges was also a feature of this barter economy.

Hannah Grafton was involved in trade on more than one level. The "shop" attached to her house was not the all-purpose storage shed and workroom it seems to have been for Francis Plummer. It was a retail store, offering door locks, nails, hammers, gimlets, and other hardware as well as English cloth, pins, needles, and thread. As a mariner, Joshua Grafton may well have sailed the ship which brought these goods to Salem. In his absence, Hannah was not only a mother and a housewife but, like many other Salem women, a shopkeeper as well.

There is another highly visible activity in the Grafton inventory which was not immediately apparent in the Plummers'—care of clothing. Presumably, Beatrice Plummer washed occasionally, but she did not have a "washhouse." Hannah did. The arrangement of this unusual room is far from clear. On December 2, 1699, it contained two spits, two "bouldishes," a gridiron, and "other things." Whether those other things included washtubs, soap, or a beating staff is impossible to determine. In a seaport town a building with a fire for heating rinse water, boiling laundry, and drying clothes could have been the base for a thriving home industry. But there is no evidence of this in the Grafton inventory. Like the "butteries" and "dairies" which appear in other New England houses, this room may have retained a specialized English name while actually functioning as a multipurpose storage and service room. With its spits and gridiron Hannah Grafton's "washhouse" may have served as an extra cooking space, perhaps on occasions when all fifteen chairs in the parlor were filled.

But on any morning in December it could also have been hung with the family wash. Dark woolen jackets and petticoats went from year to year without seeing a kettle of suds, but linen shifts, aprons, shirts, and handkerchiefs required washing. Laundering might not have been a weekly affair in most colonial households, but it was a well-defined if infrequent necessity even for transient seamen and laborers. One can only speculate on its frequency in a house with a child under a year. When her baby was only a few months old, Hannah may have learned to hold little Priscilla over the chamber pot at frequent intervals, but in early infancy, tightly wrapped in her cradle, the baby could easily have used five dozen "clouts" and almost as many "belly bands" from one washing to another. Even with the use of a "pilch," a thick square of flannel securely bound over the diaper, blankets and coverlets occasionally needed sudsing as well.

Joshua's shirts and Hannah's own aprons and shifts would require careful ironing. Hannah's "smoothing irons" fitted into their own heaters, which she filled with coals from the fire. As the embers waned and the irons cooled, she would have made frequent trips from her table to the hearth to the fire and back to the table again. At least two of these heavy instruments were essential. A dampened apron could dry and wrinkle while a single flatiron replenished its heat.

As frequent a task as washing was sewing. Joshua's coats and breeches went to a tailor, but his shirts were probably made at home. Certainly Hannah stitched and unstitched the tucks which altered Priscilla's simple gowns and petticoats as she grew. The little dresses which the baby trailed in her go-cart had once clothed her brother. Gender identity in childhood was less important in this society than economy of effort. It was not that boys were seen as identical to girls, only that all-purpose garments could be handed from one child to another regardless of sex, and dresses were more easily altered than breeches and more adaptable to diapering and toileting. At eight years of age little Hannah had probably begun to imitate her mother's even stitches, helping with the continual mending, altering, and knitting which kept this growing family clothed.

In some ways the most interesting items in the Grafton inventory are the two spinning wheels kept in the upstairs chamber. Beatrice Plummer's wheel and reel had been key components in an intricate production chain. The Plummers had twenty-five sheep in the fold and a loom in the shed. The Graftons had neither. Children—not sheep—put wheels in Hannah's house. The mechanical nature of spinning made it a perfect occupation for women whose attention was engrossed by young children. This is one reason why the ownership of wheels in both York and Essex counties had a constancy over time unrelated to the ownership of sheep or looms. In the dozen inventories taken in urban Salem about the time of Joshua Grafton's death, the six non-spinners averaged one minor child each, the six spinners had almost four. Instruction at the wheel was part of the almost ritualistic preparation mothers offered their daughters. Spinning was a useful craft, easily picked up, easily put down, and even small quantities of yarn could be knitted into caps, stockings, dishcloths, and mittens.

Unfortunately, there is no documented event in Hannah Grafton's life corresponding to Beatrice Plummer's colorful appearance in court. But a cluster of objects in the chamber over her kitchen suggests a fanciful but by no means improbable vignette. Imagine her gathered with her two daughters in this upstairs room on a New England winter's day. Little Priscilla navigates around the end of the bedstead in her go-cart while her mother sits at one spinning wheel and her sister at the other. Young Hannah is spinning "oakum," the coarsest and least expensive part of the flax. As her mother leans over to help her wind the uneven thread on the bobbin, she catches a troublesome scent from downstairs. Have the turnips caught on the bottom of the pot? Has the maid scorched Joshua's best shirt? Or has a family servant returned from the wharf and spread his wet cothes by the fire? Hastening down the narrow stairs to the kitchen, Hannah hears the shop bell ring. Just then little Priscilla, left upstairs with her sister, begins to cry. In such pivotal but unrecorded moments much of the history of women lies hidden.

The third inventory can be more quickly described. Elias Wear of York, Maine, left an estate totaling £92, of which less than £7 was in household goods—including some old pewter, a pot, two bedsteads, bedding, one chest, and a box. Wear also owned a saddle, three guns, and a river craft called a gundalow. But his wealth, such as it was, consisted of land (£40) and livestock (£36). It is not just relative poverty which distinguished Elias Wear's inventory from that of Joshua Grafton or Francis Plummer. Every settlement in northern New England had men who owned only a pot, a bed, and a chest. Their children crowded in with them or slept on straw. These men and their sons provided some of the labor which harvested barley for farmers like Francis Plummer or stepped masts for mariners like Joshua Grafton. Their wives and their daughters carded wool or kneaded bread in other women's kitchens. No, Elias Wear was distinguished by a special sort of frontier poverty.

His father had come to northern New England in the 1640s, exploring and trading for furs as far inland in New Hampshire as Lake Winnipesaukee. By 1650 he had settled in York, a then hopeful site for establishing a patrimony. Forty years later he died in the York Massacre, an assault by French and Indians which virtually destroyed the town, bringing death or captivity to fully half of the inhabitants. Almost continuous warfare between 1689 and 1713 created prosperity for the merchant community of

Portsmouth and Kittery, but it kept most of the inhabitants of outlying settlements in a state of impecunious insecurity.

In 1696, established on a small homestead in the same neighborhood in which his father had been killed, Elias Wear married a young widow with the fitting name of Magdalen. When their first child was born "too soon," the couple found themselves in York County Court owning a presentment for fornication [Sex outside of marriage]. Although New England courts were still sentencing couples in similar circumstances to "nine stripes a piece upon the Naked back," most of the defendants, like the Wears, managed to pay the not inconsequential fine. The fifty-nine shillings which Elias and Magdalen pledged the court amounted to almost half of the total value of two steers. A presentment for fornication was expensive as well as inconvenient, but it did not carry a permanent onus. Within seven years of their conviction Elias was himself serving on the "Jury of Tryalls" for the county, while Magdalen had proved herself a dutiful and productive wife.

Every other winter she gave birth, producing four sons—Elias, Jeremiah, John, and Joseph—in addition to the untimely Ruth. A sixth child, Mary, was just five months old when her father met his own death by Indians in August of 1707 while traveling between their Cape Neddick home and the more densely settled York village. Without the benefits of a cradle, a go-cart, a spinning wheel, or even a secure supply of grain, Magdalen raised these six children. Unfortunately, there is little in her inventory and nothing in any other record to document the specific strategies which she used, though the general circumstances of her life can be imagined.

Chopping and hauling for a local timber merchant, Elias could have filled Magdalen's porridge pot with grain shipped from the port of Salem or Boston. During the spring corn famine, an almost yearly occurrence on the Maine frontier, she might have gone herself with other wives of her settlement to dig on the clam flats hedging against the day when relief would come by sea. Like Beatrice Plummer and Hannah Grafton, she would have spent some hours cooking, washing, hoeing cabbages, bargaining with neighbors, and, in season, herding and milking a cow. But poverty, short summers, and rough land also made gathering an essential part of her work. We may imagine her cutting pine splinters for light and "cattails" and "silkgrass" for beds. Long before her small garden began to produce, she would have searched out a wild "sallet" in the nearby woods, in summer turning to streams and barrens for other delicacies congenial to English taste—eels, salmon, berries, and plums. She would have embarked on such excursions with caution, however, remembering the wives of nearby Exeter who took their children into the woods for strawberries "without any Guard" and narrowly avoided capture.

Frontier danger drew scattered families together, sometimes compressing an entire neighborhood into a designated "garrison" for days at a time. Near sawmills, these structures were in some cases true garrisons—fortified houses constructed of machine-smoothed timbers laid edge to edge; just as often they were simply the largest or most substantial dwellings in each settlement. Women like Magdalen Wear went to the doors of these same houses in times of peace, asking to borrow malt or offering to spin for a day.

Only the most prosperous families of Maine and New Hampshire built according to the parlor-hall houseplan which was becoming typical of Essex County by the end of the seventeenth century. The Wears probably lived in a single-story cottage which may or may not have been subdivided into more than one room. A loft above provided extra space for storage or sleeping. With the addition of a lean-to, this house could have sheltered animals as well as humans, especially in harsh weather or in periods of Indian alarm. Housing a pig or a calf in the next room would have simplified Magdalen's chores in the winter. If she managed to raise a few chickens, these too would have thrived better near the kitchen fire.

Thus, penury erased the elaborate demarcation of "houses" and "yards" evident in yeoman inventories. It also blurred distinctions between the work of a husbandman and the work of his wife. At planting time and at harvest Magdalen Wear undoubtedly went into the fields to help Elias, taking her babies with her or leaving Ruth to watch them as best she could. A century later an elderly Maine woman bragged that she "had dropped corn many a day with two governors: a judge in her arms and a general on her back." None of the Wear children grew up to such prominence, but all six of them survived to adulthood and four married and founded families of their own. Six children did not prevent Magdalen Wear from remarrying within two years of her husband's death. Whatever her assets—a pleasant face, a strong back, or lifetime possession of £40 in land—she was soon wed to the unmarried son of a neighboring millowner.

Magdalen Wear, Hannah Grafton, and Beatrice Plummer were all "typical" New England housewives of the period 1650–1750. Magdalen's iron pot represents the housekeeping minimum which often characterized frontier life. Hannah's punch bowl and her hardware shop exemplify both the commerce and the self-conscious civilization of coastal towns. Beatrice's brewing tubs and churn epitomize home manufacturing and agrarian self-sufficiency as they existed in established villages. Each type of housekeeping could be found somewhere in northern New England in any decade of the century. Yet these three women should not be placed in rigidly separate categories. Wealth, geography, occupation, and age determined that some women in any decade would be more heavily involved in one aspect of housekeeping than another, yet all three women shared a common vocation. Each understood the rhythms of the seasons, the technology of firebuilding, the persistence of the daily demands of cooking, the complexity of home production, and the dexterity demanded from the often conflicting roles of housekeeper, mother, and wife.

The thing which distinguished these women from their counterparts in modern America was not, as some historians have suggested, that their work was essential to survival. "Survival," after all, is a minimal concept. Individual men and women have never needed each other for mere survival but for far more complex reasons, and women were *essential* in the seventeenth century for the very same reasons they are essential today—for the perpetuation of the race. As the Indians and Edmund Berry knew, English husbands could live without cheese and beer. Nor was it the monotony of these women's lives or the narrowness of their choices which really set them apart. Women in industrial cities have lived monotonous and confining lives, and they may have worked even harder than early American women. The really striking differences are social.

In this brief exploration of work we have merely hinted at the social setting in which work occurred. We have noted the intervention of Beatrice Plummer's neighbors in her conflicts with her husband, the importance of children in the household of Hannah Grafton, and the blurring of gender boundaries in the frontier environment of Magdalen Wear. [T]he lives of early American housewives were distinguished less by the tasks they performed than by forms of social organization which linked economic responsibilities to family responsibilities and which tied each woman's household to the larger world of her village or town.

For centuries the industrious Bathsheba has been pictured sitting at a spinning wheel—"She layeth her hands to the spindle, and her hands hold the distaff." Perhaps it is time to suggest a new icon for women's history. Certainly spinning was an important female craft in northern New England, linked not only to housework but to mothering, but it was one enterprise among many. Spinning wheels are such intriguing and picturesque objects, so resonant with antiquity, that they tend to obscure rather than clarify the nature of female economic life, making home production the essential element in early American huswifery and the era of industrialization the period of crucial change. Challenging the symbolism of the wheel not only undermines the popular stereotype, it questions a prevailing emphasis in women's history.

An alternate symbol might be the pocket. In early America a woman's pocket was not attached to her clothing, but tied around her waist with a string or tape. (When "Lucy Locket lost her pocket, Kitty Fisher found it.") Much better than a spinning wheel, this homely object symbolizes the obscurity, the versatility, and the personal nature of the housekeeping role. A woman sat at a wheel, but she carried her pocket with her from room to room, from house to yard, from yard to street. The items which it contained would shift from day to day and from year to year, but they would of necessity be small, easily lost, yet precious. A pocket could be a mended and patched pouch of plain homespun or a rich personal ornament boldly embroidered in crewel. It reflected the status as well as the skills of its owner. Whether it contained cellar keys or a paper of pins, a packet of seeds or a baby's bib, a hank of yarn or a Testament, it characterized the social complexity as well as the demanding diversity of women's work.

Questions for Study and Review

1. Describe women's most important contributions to the family in seventeenth-century New England.

2. What are the benefits and limits of household inventories and court records for illuminating the lives of colonial women?

3. Compare the lives of the three women analyzed by Ulrich to the ideals of womanhood described at the beginning of her article.

4. How might the presence of significant numbers of Englishwomen in the New England colonies have influenced the development of that region in contrast to Virginia and other southern colonies where Englishwomen were relatively scarce?

Suggested Readings and Web Sites

Lois G. Carr and Lorena S. Walsh, "The Planter's Wife: The Experience of White Women in Seventeenth-century Maryland," *William and Mary Quarterly* 34 (1974)

John Demos, *A Little Commonwealth: Family Life in Plymouth Colony* (1970)

Jane Kamensky, *Governing the Tongue: The Politics of Speech in Early New England* (1997)

Lyle Koehler, *A Search for Power: The "Weaker Sex" in Seventeenth-century New England* (1980)

Colonial Williamsburg
    http://www.history.org/History/teaching/Dayseries/webactivities/

Colonial House from PBS
    http://www.pbs.org/wnet/colonialhouse/history/

Memorial Hall Museum Online at Pocumtuck Valley Memorial Association, Deerfield, Massachusetts
    http://memorialhall.mass.edu/

Plymouth Colony Archive Project
    http://etext.lib.virginia.edu/users/deetz/

PART II

Negotiating Sex and Gender in the Eighteenth Century

This engraving of an 1816 painting by Louis Choris offers a European view of Indian men dancing at the California mission while Franciscan missionaries and Indian women look on.

By the early 1700s, many areas of North America had been transformed by European conquest and colonization. Along the Atlantic seaboard and well inland in some areas, English settlers had carved out farms, established villages, constructed roads, built forts, and gathered believers into churches. Most of the original inhabitants of these lands had perished of European-borne diseases to which they had no immunities or been driven further west to find new hunting and fishing grounds or to plant crops in areas shared with other Indian nations. At the same time, the population of Africans increased throughout the English colonies, growing most rapidly in the southern colonies and seaport cities.

In long-settled regions from New England to the Chesapeake, women and workers were no longer scarce, Indians were no longer a threat to colonists' safety, and heretics and witches no longer challenged the authority of settled ministers and colonial officials. Yet economic development and population growth coincided to nurture new regional and class divisions. These divisions were aggravated by the repeated eruption of war among European competitors who sought control of American land and the profits to be made from furs, fish, lumber, tobacco, and other cash crops. American Indians took advantage of these imperial rivalries to gain leverage for themselves. For a time, some of the largest nations and confederations—the Cherokee and Creek in the South and the Iroquois in the North—did forge alliances with one European power or another in exchange for goods, guns, and the right to establish new homelands. Still, the expansion and consolidation of European settlements continued. When the British finally defeated the French and their Indian allies in 1763 after nine long years of war, only a few Indian nations residing east of the Mississippi River were strong enough to maintain their independent status.

Wars changed the lives of English and African residents of North America as well. For Africans and their American-born children, the westward march of English settlement ensured the expansion of slavery into the interior of the Carolinas and Virginia and southward into Georgia. This increased the profits of slave traders in New York City, Boston, Baltimore, and other seaport cities where slavery also flourished. Colonies had passed the first slave codes in the late seventeenth century, enshrining in law the right of whites to buy and sell Africans and their American-born children. Fearing confusion if white men fathered the children of African women, these laws defied the patriarchal logic of English common law and insisted that a slave's status follow the mother rather than the father. During the eighteenth century, colonial assemblies passed more laws regulating the status and activities of Africans and African Americans, and the percentage of free blacks in the population gradually declined, especially in the southern colonies.

For white Americans, the conflicts among European nations generally boosted the profits of merchants, shipbuilders, and military provisioners, and temporarily drove up the wages of seamen and skilled laborers. But wars also drove up prices, left large numbers of widows and orphans in their wake, and induced seaboard cities to establish poorhouses to care for those left without family or friends to support them. Between 1740 and 1755, for example, the number of poor people needing assistance in Philadephia grew ten times faster than the population of the city. In Boston, a spinning factory was opened in 1748 in response to the large numbers of women left to fend for themselves. Indeed, women now outnumbered men in many seacoast settlements and thus lost some of the leverage they had gained in the previous century as a result of their scarcity.

Families faced new challenges and responded in varied ways to the upheavals of the eighteenth century. In areas like New England where churches and families had formed the building blocks of communities in the seventeenth century, these institutions no longer wielded the same authority over individual behavior. As Cornelia Hughes Dayton suggests in Chapter Four, women often paid a higher price for this freedom from social constraints than did men. Church and civil courts had once reinforced the power of families to ensure that men who promised marriage made good on their pledge. But by the early eighteenth century, courts "gave up on enjoining sexually active couples to marry," and men were rarely prosecuted for premarital sex, or fornication as it was then called, with single women. However, women who became pregnant faced prosecution, fines, and social ostracism for bearing illegitimate children. Dayton uses a rare case in which a botched abortion led to legal prosecution in Connecticut in the 1740s to explore the implications of this emerging sexual double standard for young women and men.

The consequences of the new social and economic order were quite different for well-to-do Englishwomen in the Chesapeake. In examining planter families in the Chesapeake region, Allan Kulikoff suggests in Chapter Five that "domestic patriarchy," that is, the authority of the father over his family and household, increased in the early to mid-eighteenth century. As the ratio of women to men became more balanced in Virginia and Maryland and as men lived longer, husbands asserted more control over their wives and children. Fathers could use the promise of inheritance to sustain their authority even over adult children. Clearly, such patriarchal power could be wielded most successfully in families with abundant resources. The families of poor whites, free blacks, dispossessed Indians, and enslaved women and men had few such resources to distribute, which could subvert patriarchal authority in their own households and sometimes among the planter elite as well.

In long-established settlements, European Americans recast gender relations and generational authority, often to the detriment of women. There were, however, regions of North America in which the conquest of native peoples was just beginning. In these regions, sexual and gender relations often served as flash points for conflict. The English, for example, confronted new Indian nations as they pushed west, and frontier raids led to the deaths of women and children as well as men in both European settlements and native villages. Similarly, the Spanish moved north from Mexico and the Baja peninsula in the 1770s, hoping to subdue and convert small bands of Indians in Alta (that is, upper) California. Both Catholic missionaries and soldiers took part in this conquest, and in this case, the native women and men had few means to fend off religious and physical domination. In Chapter Six, Antonia Castañeda recounts the violence committed against California natives, especially native women, as Spaniards moved north. She also analyzes the debates among church leaders, military authorities, and officials in Mexico and Spain over the consequences of such violence on Spanish plans for long-term settlement. Here, authority wielded by priests and soldiers, the absence of European women, and the lack of military resources on the part of California natives ensured the brutal subordination of local Indians and the sexual abuse of Indian women.

In English colonies on the eastern seaboard, women, especially servants and slaves, were also sexually abused, and the sexual double standard intensified over the course of the eighteenth century. Still, the existence of established governments and courts and the presence of large numbers of women of all races and nationalities placed some constraints on men's power. Not all women were protected, of course. And many women traded subordination for economic support and physical protection, though not always by choice. Moreover, as Cornelia Hughes Dayton shows, not even wealth and family connections promised women a safe journey through the eighteenth century.

Suggested Readings and Web Sites

Virginia Bouvier, *Women and the Conquest of California, 1542–1840* (2001)
Catherine Clinton and Michele Gillespie, eds., *The Devil's Lane: Sex and Race in the Early South* (1997)
Nancy Cott et al., eds., *Root of Bitterness: Documents of the Social History of American Women* (1996)
Martha Hodes, ed., *Sex, Love, Race: Crossing Boundaries in North American History* (1999)
Capital and the Bay: Narratives of Washington and the Chesapeake Bay Region, c. 1600–1925
    http://memory.loc.gov/ammem/lhcbhtml\
Digital History
    http://www.digitalhistory.uh.edu/

Chapter 4

In colonial North America as in Great Britain in the same period, abortion was not illegal. A pregnancy was generally confirmed at the time by "quickening," which was the moment when the mother first felt the fetus move. This occurs usually about three months after conception. Since pregnancy before quickening could not be confirmed, there was no proof that an abortion had taken place if a fetus was lost in the first trimester. Moreover, a mother might delay reporting fetal movement if she considered using pennyroyal, savin, or another herbal means to induce a miscarriage. Abortions by instruments, that is, by a physician attempting to remove the fetus mechanically, were extremely rare. Indeed, the case discussed in this chapter is likely the first time that a New England court prosecuted a physician or any other individual for carrying out an abortion. And even in this case, it was the fact that Sarah Grosvenor died as a result of the abortion, rather than the abortion itself, that led to prosecution.

The history of abortion is also framed in colonial America and early modern England and Europe by changes in childbirth. Before the mid-eighteenth century, midwives usually oversaw labor and birth. Midwives were often women well-known in their communities who developed a reputation for their birthing skills. Moreover, childbirth was a communal event. Attendants included not only a midwife but also female family members and friends, who offered comfort, support, stories, and perhaps rum or whiskey to those in labor. Beginning among affluent mothers in urban areas in the 1760s, male physicians began attending some births. They had one crucial advantage over midwives. They were trained to use instruments, most notably forceps, to speed delivery. Although instruments could damage an infant, so could a prolonged labor. By law, midwives were not allowed to use instruments since they were not trained to do so. The debate over the training of midwives and the presence of male physicians in the birthing chamber continued for decades, but gradually communal birth experiences directed by a female midwife gave way among many Americans to more private experiences of labor directed by a male physician.

The shift toward privacy was also a result of changes in domestic architecture that accompanied increased affluence among some Americans. Families who had the means no longer lived in houses that had only two rooms downstairs and a sleeping loft above. They began building larger homes with more bedrooms, which allowed the separation of parents from children and boys from girls. This separation ensured greater privacy and often led to closer relations among siblings, but it also meant that children could more easily avoid parental scrutiny. In the case of Sarah Grosvenor, such privacy allowed her to engage in sexual relations, hide her pregnancy from her father and stepmother, and enlist her sister and cousin in an attempt to cover up an abortion. It also ensured that the man who impregnated her, Amasa Sessions, and the doctor who performed the abortion, John Hallowell, had some chance of avoiding detection. The women who assisted Sarah, however, were left wracked with guilt and fearing for their souls. Although the Connecticut court eventually indicted Sessions, Hallowell, and two of Sarah's female relatives, much remains a mystery in this case. Still, Dayton uses the testimony that survives to explore the changing relations among women and men, parents and children, gender and religion, and courts and sexual regulation.

Taking the Trade: Abortion and Gender Relations in an Eighteenth-Century New England Village
CORNELIA HUGHES DAYTON

In 1742 in the village of Pomfret, perched in the hills of northeastern Connecticut, nineteen-year-old Sarah Grosvenor and twenty-seven-year-old Amasa Sessions became involved in a liaison that led to pregnancy, abortion, and death. Both were from prominent yeoman families, and neither a marriage between them nor an arrangement for the support of their illegitimate child would have been an unusual event for mid-eighteenth-century New England. Amasa Sessions chose a different course; in consultation with John Hallowell, a self-proclaimed "practitioner of physick," he coerced his lover into taking an abortifacient. Within two months, Sarah fell ill. Unbeknownst to all but Amasa, Sarah, Sarah's sister Zerviah, and her cousin Hannah, Hallowell made an attempt to "Remove her Conseption" by a "manual opperation." Two days later Sarah miscarried, and her two young relatives secretly buried the fetus in the woods. Over the next month, Sarah struggled against a "Malignant fever" and was attended by several physicians, but on September 14, 1742, she died.

Most accounts of induced abortions among seventeenth- and eighteenth-century whites in the Old and New Worlds consist of only a few lines in a private letter or court record book; these typically refer to the taking of savin or pennyroyal—two common herbal abortifacients. While men and women in diverse cultures have known how to perform abortions by inserting an instrument into the uterus, actual descriptions of such operations are extremely rare for any time period. Few accounts of abortions by instrument have yet been uncovered for early modern England, and I know of no other for colonial North America. Thus the historical fragments recording events in a small New England town in 1742 take on an

From *William & Mary Quarterly*, 3rd series, vol. 48, January 1991. Copyright © by Omohundro Institute of Early American History and Culture.

The death of infants and of mothers in childbirth was a common occurrence in colonial America. Zerviah Allis' gravestone—pictured here—gives a terse account of one of these sad episodes. The Connecticut mother and her newborn twins died in late 1758. Childbirth experiences were shifting in the latter half of the eighteenth century as male physicians replaced female midwives, who had traditionally been responsible for supervising births. Physicians had the ability to ease births by the use of instruments and later anesthetics. But the maternal mortality rate did not decline significantly and mothers were deprived of the emotional support of women in the delivery room.

unusual power to illustrate how an abortion was conducted, how it was talked about, and how it was punished.

We know about the Grosvenor-Sessions case because in 1745 two prominent Windham Country magistrates opened an investigation into Sarah's death. Why there was a three-year gap between that event and legal proceedings, and why justices from outside Pomfret initiated the legal process, remain a mystery. In November 1745 the investigating magistrates offered their preliminary opinion that Hallowell, Amasa Sessions, Zerviah Grosvenor, and Hannah Grosvenor were guilty of Sarah's murder, the last three as accessories. From the outset, Connecticut legal officials concentrated not on the act of abortion per se, but on the fact that an abortion attempt had led to a young woman's death.

The case went next to Joseph Fowler, king's attorney for Windham Country. He dropped charges against the two Grosvenor women, probably because he needed them as key witnesses and because they had played cover-up roles rather than originating the scheme. A year and a half passed as Fowler's first attempts to get convictions against Hallowell and Sessions failed either before grand juries or before the Superior Court on technical grounds. Finally, in March 1747, Fowler presented Hallowell and Sessions separately for the "highhanded Misdemeanour" of attempting to destroy both Sarah Grosvenor's health and "the fruit of her womb." A grand jury endorsed the bill against Hallowell but rejected a similarly worded presentment against Sessions. At Hallowell's trial before the Superior Court in Windham, the jury brought in a guilty verdict and the chief judge sentenced the physician to twenty-nine lashes and two hours of public humilation standing at the town gallows. Before the sentence could be executed, Hallowell managed to break jail. He fled to Rhode

Island; as far as records indicate, he never returned to Connecticut. Thus, in the end, both Amasa Sessions and John Hallowell escaped legal punishment for their actions, whereas Sarah Grosvenor paid for her sexual transgression with her life.

Nearly two years of hearings and trials before the Superior Court produced a file of ten depositions and twenty-four other legal documents. This cache of papers is extraordinarily rich, not alone for its unusual chronicle of an abortion attempt, but for its illumination of the fault lines in Pomfret dividing parents from grown children, men from women, and mid-eighteenth-century colonial culture from its seventeenth-century counterpart.

The depositions reveal that in 1742 the elders of Pomfret, men and women alike, failed to act as vigilant monitors of Sarah Grosvenor's courtship and illness. Instead, young, married householders—kin of Sarah and Amasa—pledged themselves in a conspiracy of silence to allow the abortion plot to unfold undetected. The one person who had the opportunity to play middleman between the generations was Hallowell. A man in his forties, dogged by a shady past and yet adept at acquiring respectable connections, Hallowell provides an intriguing and rare portrait of a socially ambitious, rural medical practitioner. By siding with the young people of Pomfret and keeping their secret, Hallowell betrayed his peers and elders and thereby opened himself to severe censure and expulsion from the community.

Beyond depicting generational conflict, the Grosvenor-Sessions case dramatically highlights key changes in gender relations that reverberated through New England society in the eighteenth century. One of these changes involved the emergence of a marked sexual double standard. In the mid-seventeenth century, a young man like Amasa Sessions would have been pressured by parents, friends, or the courts to marry his lover. Had he resisted, he would most likely have been whipped or fined for the crime of fornication. By the late seventeenth century, New England judges gave up on enjoining sexually active couples to marry. In the 1740s, amid shifting standards of sexual behavior and growing concern over the evidentiary impossibility of establishing paternity, prosecutions of young men for premarital sex ceased. Thus fornication was decriminalized for men, but not for women. Many of Sarah Grosvenor's female peers continued to be prosecuted and fined for bearing illegitimate children. Through private arrangements, and occasionally through civil lawsuits, their male partners were sometimes cajoled or coerced into contributing to the child's upkeep.

What is most striking about the Grosvenor-Sessions case is that an entire community apparently forgave Sessions for the extreme measures he took to avoid accountability for his bastard child. Although he initiated the actions that led to his lover's death, all charges against him were dropped. Moreover, the tragedy did not spur Sessions to leave town; instead, he spent the rest of his life in Pomfret as a respected citizen. Even more dramatically than excusing young men from the crime of fornication, the treatment of Amasa Sessions confirmed that the sexually irresponsible activities of men in their youth would not be held against them as they reached for repute and prosperity in their prime.

The documents allow us to listen in on the quite different responses of young men and women to the drama unfolding in Pomfret. Sarah Grosvenor's female kin and friends, as we shall see, became preoccupied with their guilt and with the inevitability of God's vengeance. Her male kin, on the other hand, reacted cautiously and legalistically, ferreting out information in order to assess how best to protect the Grosvenor family name. . . .

Finally, the Grosvenor case raises more questions than it answers about New Englanders' access to and attitudes toward abortion. If Sarah had not died after miscarriage, it is doubtful that any word of Sessions's providing her with an abortifacient or Hallowell's operation would have survived into the twentieth century. Because it nearly went unrecorded and because it reveals that many Pomfret residents were familiar with the idea of abortion, the case supports historians' assumptions that abortion attempts were far from rare in colonial America. We can also infer from the case that the most dangerous abortions before 1800 may have been those instigated by men and performed by surgeons with instruments. But both abortion's frequency and the lineaments of its social context remain obscure. Did cases in which older women helped younger women to abort unwanted pregnancies far outnumber cases such as this one in which men initiated the process? Under what circumstances did family members and neighbors help married and unmarried women to hide abortion attempts?

Perhaps the most intriguing question centers on why women and men in early America acted *covertly* to effect abortions when abortion before quickening was legal. The Grosvenor case highlights the answer that applies to most known incidents from the period: abortion was understood as blameworthy because it was an extreme action designed to hide a prior sin, sex outside of marriage. Reading the depositions, it is nearly impossible to disentangle the players' attitudes toward abortion itself from their expressions of censure or anxiety over failed courtship, illegitimacy, and the dangers posed for a young woman by a secret abortion. Strikingly absent from these eighteenth-century documents, however, is either outrage over the destruction of a fetus or denunciations of those who would arrest "nature's proper course." Those absences are a telling measure of how the discourse about abortion would change dramatically in later centuries.

The Narrative

. . . The following paragraphs, based on the depositions, offer a reconstruction of the events of 1742. A few caveats are in order. First, precise dating of crucial incidents is impossible, since deponents did not remember events in terms of days of the week (except for the Sabbath) but rather used phrases like "sometime in August." Second, the testimony concentrated almost exclusively on events in the two months preceding Sarah's death on September 14. Thus, we know very little about Sarah and Amasa's courtship before July 1742. Third, while the depositions often indicate the motivations and feelings of the principals, these will be discussed in subsequent sections of this article, where the characters' attitudes can be set in the context of their social backgrounds, families, and community. This section essentially lays out a medical file for Sarah Grosvenor, a file that unfolds in four parts: the taking of the abortifacient, Hallowell's operation, the miscarriage, and Sarah's final illness.

The case reveals more about the use of an abortifacient than most colonial court records in which abortion attempts are mentioned. Here we learn not only the form in which Sarah received the dose but also the special word that Pomfret residents applied to it. What the documents do not disclose are either its ingredients or the number of times Sarah ingested it.

The chronicle opens in late July 1742 when Zerviah Grosvenor, aged twenty-one, finally prevailed upon her younger sister to admit that she was pregnant. In tears, Sarah explained that she had not told Zerviah sooner because "she had been taking [the] trade to remove it." "Trade" was used in this period to signify stuff or goods, often in the deprecatory sense of rubbish and trash. The *Oxford English Dictionary* confirms that in some parts of England and New England the word was used to refer to medicine. In Pomfret trade meant a particular type of medicine, an abortifacient, thus a substance that might be regarded as "bad" medicine, as rubbish, unsafe and associated with destruction. What is notable is that Sarah and Zerviah, and neighboring young people who also used the word, had no need to explain to one another the meaning of "taking the trade." Perhaps only a few New Englanders knew how to prepare an abortifacient or knew of books that would give them recipes, but many more, especially young women who lived with the fear of becoming pregnant before marriage, were familiar with at least the *idea* of taking an abortifacient.

Sarah probably began taking the trade in mid-May when she was already three-and-a-half-months pregnant. It was brought to her in the form of a powder by Amasa. Sarah understood clearly that her lover had obtained the concoction "from docter hollowel," who conveyed "directions" for her doses through Amasa. Zerviah deposed later that Sarah had been "loath to Take" the drug and "Thot it an Evil," probably because at three and a half months she anticipated quickening, the time from which she knew the law counted abortion an "unlawful measure." At the outset, Sarah argued in vain with Amasa against his proposed "Method." Later, during June and July, she sometimes "neglected" to take the doses he left for her, but, with mounting urgency, Amasa and the doctor pressed her to comply. "It was necessary," Amasa explained in late July, that she take "more, or [else] they were afraid She would be greatly hurt by what was already done." To calm her worries, he assured her that "there was no life [left] in the Child" and that the potion "would not hurt her." Apparently, the men hoped that a few more doses would provoke a miscarriage, thereby expelling the dead fetus and restoring Sarah's body to its natural balance of humors.

Presumably, Hallowell decided to operate in early August because Sarah's pregnancy was increasingly visible, and he guessed that she was not going to miscarry. An operation in which the fetus would be removed or punctured was now the only certain way to terminate the pregnancy secretly. To avoid the scrutiny of Sarah's parents, Hallowell resorted to a plan he had used once before in arranging a private examination of Sarah. Early one afternoon he arrived at the house of John Grosvenor and begged for a room as "he was weary and wanted Rest." John, Sarah's thirty-one-year-old first cousin, lived with his wife, Hannah, and their young children in a homestead only a short walk down the hill but out of sight of Sarah's father's house. While John and Hannah were busy, the physician sent one of the little children to fetch Sarah.

The narrative of Sarah's fateful meeting with Hallowell that August afternoon is best told in the words of one of the deponents. Abigail Nightingale had married and moved to Pomfret two years earlier, and by 1742 she had become Sarah's close friend. Several weeks after the operation, Sarah attempted to relieve her own "Distress of mind" by confiding the details of her shocking experience to Abigail.

Unconnected to the Grosvenor or Sessions families by kinship, and without any other apparent stake in the legal uses of her testimony, Abigail can probably be trusted as a fairly accurate paraphraser of Sarah's words. If so, we have here an unparalleled eyewitness account of an eighteenth-century abortion attempt.

This is how Abigail recollected Sarah's deathbed story:

> On [Sarah's] going down [to her cousin John's], [Hallowell] said he wanted to Speake with her alone; and then they two went into a Room together; and then sd. Hallowell told her it was necessary that something more should be done or else she would Certainly die; to which she replyed that she was afraid they had done too much already, and then he told her that there was one thing more that could easily be done, and she asking him what it was; he said he could easily deliver her. but she said she was afraid there was life in the Child, then he asked her how long she had felt it; and she replyed about a fortnight; then he said that was impossible or could not be or ever would; for that the trade she had taken had or would prevent it: and that the alteration she felt Was owing to what she had taken. And he farther told her that he verily thought that the Child grew to her body to the Bigness of his hand, or else it would have Come away before that time. and that it would never Come away, but Certainly Kill her, unless other Means were used. On which she yielded to his making an Attempt to take it away; charging him that if he could percieve that there was life in it he would not proceed on any Account. And then the Doctor openning his portmantua took an Instrument out of it and Laid it on the Bed, and she asking him what it was for, he replyed that it was to make way; and that then he tryed to remove the Child for Some time in vain putting her to the Utmost Distress, and that at Last she observed he trembled and immediately perceived a Strange alteration in her body and thought a bone of the Child was broken; on which she desired him (as she said) to Call in some body, for that she feared she was a dying, and instantly swooned away.

With Sarah's faint, Abigail's account broke off, but within minutes others, who would testify later, stepped into the room. Hallowell reacted to Sarah's swoon by unfastening the door and calling in Hannah, the young mistress of the house, and Zerviah, who had followed her sister there. Cold water and "a bottle of drops" were brought to keep Sarah from fainting again, while Hallowell explained to the "much Surprized" women that "he had been making an Attempt" to deliver Sarah. Despite their protests, he then "used a further force upon her" but did not succeed in "Tak[ing] the Child . . . away." Some days later Hallowell told a Pomfret man that in this effort "to distroy hir conception" he had "either knipt or Squeisd the head of the Conception." At the time of the attempt, Hallowell explained to the women that he "had done so much to her, as would Cause the Birth of the Child in a Little time." Just before sunset, he packed up his portmanteau and went to a nearby tavern, where Amasa was waiting "to hear [the outcome of] the event." Meanwhile, Sarah, weak-kneed and in pain, leaned on the arm of her sister as the young women managed to make their way home in the twilight.

After his attempted "force," Hallowell fades from the scene, while Zerviah and Hannah Grosvenor become the key figures. About two days after enduring the operation, Sarah began to experience contractions. Zerviah ran to get Hannah, telling her "she Tho't . . . Sarah would be quickly delivered." They returned to find Sarah, who was alone "in her Father's Chamber," just delivered and rising from the chamber pot. In the pot was "an Untimely birth"—a "Child [that] did not Appear to have any Life In it." To Hannah, it "Seemed by The Scent . . . That it had been hurt and was decaying," while Zerviah later remembered it as "a perfect Child," even "a pritty child." Determined to keep the event "as private as they Could," the two women helped Sarah back to bed, and then "wr[ap]ed . . . up" the fetus, carried it to the woods on the edge of the farmstead, and there "Buried it in the Bushes."

On learning that Sarah had finally miscarried and that the event had evidently been kept hidden from Sarah's parents, Amasa and Hallowell may have congratulated themselves on the success of their operation. However, about ten days after the miscarriage, Sarah grew feverish and weak. Her parents consulted two college-educated physicians who hailed from outside the Pomfret area. Their visits did little good, nor were Sarah's symptoms—fever, delirium, convulsions—relieved by a visit from Hallowell, whom Amasa "fetcht" to Sarah's bedside. In the end, Hallowell, who had decided to move from nearby Killingly to more distant Providence, washed his hands of the case. A few days before Sarah died, her cousin John "went after" Hallowell, whether to bring him back or to express his rage, we do not know. Hallowell predicted "that She woul[d] not live."

Silence seems to have settled on the Grosvenor house and its neighborhood after Sarah's death on September 14. It was two and a half years later that rumors about a murderous abortion spread through and beyond Pomfret village, prompting legal investigation. The silence, the gap between event and prosecution, the passivity of Sarah's parents—all lend mystery to the narrative. But despite its ellipses, the Grosvenor case provides us with an unusual set of details about one young couple's extreme response to the common problem of failed courtship and illegitimacy. . . . Our abortion tale, it turns out, holds beneath its surface a complex trail of evidence about generational conflict and troubled relations between men and women.

The Pomfret Players

In 1742 the town of Pomfret had been settled for just over forty years. Within its central neighborhood and in homesteads scattered over rugged, wooded hillsides lived probably no more than 270 men, women, and children. During the founding decades, the fathers of Sarah and Amasa ranked among the ten leading householders; Leicester Grosvenor and Nathaniel Sessions were chosen often to fill important local offices.

Grosvenor, the older of the two by seven years, had inherited standing and a choice farmstead from his father, one of the original six purchasers of the Pomfret territory. When the town was incorporated in 1714, he was elected a militia officer and one of the first selectmen. He was returned to the latter post nineteen times and eventually rose to the highest elective position—that of captain—in the local trainband. Concurrently, he was appointed many times throughout the 1710s and 1720s to ad hoc town committees, often alongside Nathaniel Sessions. But unlike Sessions, Grosvenor went on to serve at the colony level. Pomfret freemen chose him to represent them at ten General Assembly sessions between 1726 and 1744. Finally, in the 1730s, when he was in his late fifties, the legislature appointed him a justice of the peace for Windham County. Thus, until his retirement in 1748 at age seventy-four, his house would have served as the venue for petty trials, hearings, and recordings of documents. After retiring from public office, Grosvenor lived another eleven years, leaving behind in 1759 an estate worth over £600.

Nathaniel Sessions managed a sizable farm and ran one of Pomfret's taverns at the family homestead. Town meetings were sometimes held there. Sessions was chosen constable in 1714 and rose from ensign to lieutenant in the militia—always a step behind Leicester Grosvenor. He could take pride in one exceptional distinction redounding to the family honor: in 1737 his son Darius became only the second Pomfret resident to graduate from Yale College, and before Sessions died at ninety-one he saw Darius elected assistant and then deputy governor of Rhode Island.

The records are silent as to whether Sessions and his family resented the Grosvenors, who must have been perceived in town as more prominent, or whether the two families—who sat in adjoining private pews in the meetinghouse—enjoyed a close relationship that went sour for some reason *before* the affair between Sarah and Amasa. Instead, the signs (such as the cooperative public work of the two fathers, the visits back and forth between the Grosvenor and Sessions girls) point to a long-standing friendship and dense web of interchanges between the families. Indeed, courtship and marriage between a Sessions son and a Grosvenor daughter would hardly have been surprising.

What went wrong in the affair between Sarah and Amasa is not clear. Sarah's sisters and cousins knew that "Amasy" "made Sute to" Sarah, and they gave no indication of disapproving. The few who guessed at Sarah's condition in the summer of 1742 were not so much surprised that she was pregnant as that the couple "did not marry." It was evidently routine in this New England village, as in others, for courting couples to post banns for their nuptials [announce their engagement] soon after the woman discovered that she was pregnant.

Amasa offered different answers among his Pomfret peers to explain his failure to marry his lover. When Zerviah Grosvenor told Amasa that he and Sarah "had better Marry," he responded, "That would not do," for "he was afraid of his Parents . . . [who would] always make their lives [at home] uncomfortable." Later, Abigail Nightingale heard rumors that Amasa was resorting to the standard excuse of men wishing to avoid a shotgun marriage—denying that the child was his. Hallowell, with whom Amasa may have been honest, claimed "the Reason that they did not marry" was "that Sessions Did not Love her well a nough for [he] saith he did not believe it was his son and if he Could Cause her to gitt Red of it he would not Go near her again." Showing yet another face to a Grosvenor kinsman after Sarah's death, Amasa repented his actions and extravagantly claimed he would "give All he had" to "bring Sarah . . . To life again . . . and have her as his wife."

The unusual feature of Amasa's behavior was not his unwillingness to marry Sarah, but his determination to terminate her pregnancy before it showed. Increasing numbers of young men in eighteenth-century New England weathered the temporary obloquy of abandoning a pregnant lover in order to prolong their bachelorhood or marry someone else. What drove Amasa, and an ostensibly reluctant Sarah, to resort to abortion? Was it fear of their fathers? Nathaniel Sessions had chosen Amasa as the son who would remain on the family farm and care for his parents in their old age. An ill-timed marriage could have disrupted these plans and threatened Amasa's inheritance. For his part, Leicester Grosvenor may have made it clear to his daughter that he would be greatly displeased at her marrying before she reached a certain age or until her older sister wed. Rigid piety, an authoritarian nature, an intense concern with being seen as a good household governor—any of these traits in Leicester Grosvenor or Nathaniel Sessions could have colored Amasa's decisions.

Perhaps it was not family relations that proved the catalyst but Amasa's acquaintance with a medical man who boasted about a powder more effective than the herbal remedies that were part of women's lore. Hallowell himself had fathered an illegitimate child fifteen years earlier, and he may have encouraged a rakish attitude in Amasa, beguiling the younger man with the promise of dissociating sex from its possible consequences. Or the explanation may have been that classic one: another woman. Two years after Sarah's death, Amasa married Hannah Miller of Rehoboth, Massachusetts. Perhaps in early 1742 he was already making trips to the town just east of Providence to see his future wife.

What should we make of Sarah's role in the scheme? It is possible that she no longer loved Amasa and was as eager as he to forestall external pressures toward a quick marriage. However, Zerviah swore that on one occasion before the operation Amasa reluctantly agreed to post banns for their nuptials and that Sarah did not object. *If* Sarah was a willing and active participant in the abortion plot all along, then by 1745 her female kin and friends had fabricated and rehearsed a careful and seamless story to preserve the memory of the dead girl untarnished.

In the portrait drawn by her friends, Sarah reacted to her pregnancy and to Amasa's plan first by arguing and finally by doing her utmost to protect her lover. She may have wished to marry Amasa, yet she did not insist on it or bring in older family members to negotiate with him and his parents. Abigail Nightingale insisted that Sarah accepted Amasa's recalcitrance and only pleaded with him that they not "go on to add sin to sin." Privately, she urged Amasa that there was an alternative to taking the trade—a way that would enable him to keep his role hidden and prevent the couple from committing a "Last transgression [that] would be worse then the first." Sarah told him that "she was willing to take the sin and shame to her self, and to be obliged never to tell whose Child it was, and that she did not doubt but that if she humbled her self on her Knees to her Father he would take her and her Child home." Her lover, afraid that his identity would become known, vetoed her proposal.

According to the Pomfret women's reconstruction, abortion was not a freely chosen and defiant act for Sarah. Against her own desires, she reluctantly consented in taking the trade only because Amasa "So very earnestly perswaided her." In fact, she had claimed to her friends that she was coerced; he "would take no denyal." Sarah's confidantes presented her as being aware of her options, shrinking from abortion as an unnatural and immoral deed, and yet finally choosing the strategy consistent with her lover's vision of what would best protect their futures. Thus, if Amasa's hubris was extreme, so too was Sarah's internalization of those strains of thought in her culture that taught women to make themselves pleasing and obedient to men.

While we cannot be sure that the deponents' picture of Sarah's initial recoil and reluctant submission to the abortion plot was entirely accurate, it is clear that once she was caught up in the plan she extracted a pledge of silence from all her confidantes.

Near her death, before telling Abigail about the operation, she "insist[ed] on . . . [her friend's] never discovering the Matter" to anyone. Clearly, she had earlier bound Zerviah and Hannah on their honor not to tell their elders. Reluctant when faced with the abortionist's powder, Sarah became a leading co-conspirator when alone with her female friends.

One of the most remarkable aspects of the Grosvenor-Sessions case is Sarah and Amasa's success in keeping their parents in the dark, at least until her final illness. If by July Sarah's sisters grew suspicious that Sarah was "with child," what explains the failure of her parents to observe her pregnancy and to intervene and uncover the abortion scheme? Were they negligent, preoccupied with other matters, or willfully blind? Most mysterious is the role of forty-eight-year-old Rebecca Grosvenor, Grosvenor's second wife and Sarah's stepmother since 1729. Rebecca is mentioned only once in the depositions, and she was not summoned as a witness in the 1745–1747 investigations into Sarah's death. Even if some extraordinary circumstance—an invalid condition or an implacable hatred between Sarah and her stepmother—explains Rebecca's abdication of her role as guardian, Sarah had two widowed aunts living in or near her household. These matrons, experienced in childbirth matters and concerned for the family reputation, were just the sort of older women who traditionally watched and advised young women entering courtship.

In terms of who knew what, the events of summer 1742 in Pomfret apparently unfolded in two stages. The first stretched from Sarah's discovery of her pregnancy by early May to some point in late August after her miscarriage. In this period a determined, collective effort by Sarah and Amasa and their friends kept their elders in the dark. When Sarah fell seriously ill from the aftereffects of the abortion attempt and miscarriage, rumors of the young people's secret activities reached Leicester Grosvenor's neighbors and even one of the doctors he had called in. It is difficult to escape the conclusion that by Sarah's death in mid-September her father and stepmother had learned of the steps that had precipitated her mortal condition and kept silent for reasons of their own.

Except for Hallowell, the circle of intimates entrusted by Amasa and Sarah with their scheme consisted of young adults ranging in age from nineteen to thirty-three. Born between about 1710 and 1725, these young people had grown up just as the town attracted enough settlers to support a church, militia, and local market. They were second-generation Pomfret residents who shared the generational identity that came with sitting side by side through long worship services, attending school, playing, and working together at children's tasks. By 1740, these sisters, brothers, cousins, courting couples, and neighbors, in their visits from house to house—sometimes in their own households, sometimes at their parents'—had managed to create a world of talk and socializing that was largely exempt from parental supervision. In Pomfret in 1742 it was this group of young people in their twenties and early thirties, *not* the cluster of Grosvenor matrons over forty-five, who monitored Sarah's courtship, attempted to get Amasa to marry his lover, privately investigated the activities and motives of Amasa and Hallowell, and, belatedly, spoke out publicly to help Connecticut juries decide who should be blamed for Sarah's death.

That Leicester Grosvenor made no public move to punish those around him and that he avoided giving testimony when legal proceedings commenced are intriguing clues to social changes underway in New England villages in the mid-eighteenth century. Local leaders like Grosvenor, along with the respectable yeomen [farmers] whom he represented in public office, were increasingly withdrawing delicate family problems from the purview of their communities. Slander, illegitimacy, and feuds among neighbors came infrequently to local courts by mid-century, indicating male householders' growing preference for handling such matters privately. Wealthy and ambitious families adopted this ethic of privacy at the same time that they became caught up in elaborating their material worlds by adding rooms and acquiring luxury goods. The "good feather bed" with all of its furniture that Grosvenor bequeathed to his one unmarried daughter was but one of many marks of status by which the Grosvenors differentiated themselves from their Pomfret neighbors. But all the fine accoutrements in the world would not excuse Justice Grosvenor from his obligation to govern his household effectively. Mortified no doubt at his inability to monitor the young people in his extended family, he responded, ironically, by extending their conspiracy of silence. The best way for him to shield the family name from scandal and protect his political reputation in the county and colony was to keep the story of Sarah's abortion out of the courts.

The Doctor

John Hallowell's status as an outsider in Pomfret and his dangerous, secret alliance with the town's young adults may have shaped his destiny as the one conspirator sentenced to suffer at the whipping post. Although the physician had been involved in shady dealings before 1742, he had managed to win the trust of many patients and a respectable social standing. Tracking down his history in northeastern Connecticut tells us something of the uncertainty surrounding personal and professional identity before the advent of police records and medical licensing boards. It also gives us an all-too-rare glimpse into the fashion in which an eighteenth-century country doctor tried to make his way in the world.

Hallowell's earliest brushes with the law came in the 1720s. In 1725 he purchased land in Killingly, a Connecticut town just north of Pomfret and bordering both Massachusetts and Rhode Island. Newly married, he was probably in his twenties at the time. Seven months before his wife gave birth to their first child, a sixteen-year-old Killingly woman charged Hallowell with fathering her illegitimate child. Using the alias Nicholas Hallaway, he fled to southeastern Connecticut, where he lived as a "transient" for three months. He was arrested and settled the case by admitting to paternity and agreeing to contribute to the child's maintenance for four years.

Hallowell resumed his life in Killingly. Two years later, now referred to as "Dr.," he was arrested again; this time the charge was counterfeiting. Hallowell and several confederates were hauled before the governor and council for questioning and then put on trial before the Superior Court. Although many Killingly witnesses testified to the team's suspect activities in a woodland shelter, the charges against Hallowell were dropped when a key informer failed to appear in court.

Hallowell thus escaped conviction on a serious felony charge, but he had been tainted by stories linking him to the criminal subculture of transient, disorderly, greedy, and manually skilled men who typically made up gangs of counterfeiters in eighteenth-century New England. After 1727 Hallowell may have given up dabbling in money-making schemes and turned to earning his livelihood chiefly from his medical practice. Like two-thirds of the male medical practitioners in colonial New England, he probably did not have college or apprentice training, but his skill, or charm, was not therefore necessarily less than that of any one of his peers who might have inherited a library of books and a fund of knowledge from a physician father. All colonial practitioners . . . mixed learned practices with home or folk remedies, and no doctor had access to safe, reliable pharmacological preparations or antiseptic surgical procedures.

In the years immediately following the counterfeiting charge, Hallowell appears to have made several deliberate moves to portray himself as a sober neighbor and reliable physican. At about the time of his second marriage, in 1729, he became a more frequent attendant at the Killingly meetinghouse, where he renewed his covenant and presented his first two children for baptism. He also threw himself into the land and credit markets of northeastern Connecticut, establishing himself as a physician who was also an enterprising yeoman and a frequent litigant.

These activities had dual implications. On the one hand, they suggest that Hallowell epitomized the eighteenth-century Yankee citizen—a man as confortable in the courtroom and countinghouse as at a patient's bedside; a man of restless energy, not content to limit his scope to his fields and village; a practical, ambitious man with a shrewd eye for a good deal. On the other hand, Hallowell's losses to Boston creditors, his constant efforts to collect debts, and his farflung practice raise questions about the nature of his activities and medical practice. He evidently had clients not just in towns across northeastern Connecticut but also in neighboring Massachusetts and Rhode Island. Perhaps rural practitioners normally traveled extensively, spending many nights away from their wives and children. It is also possible, however, either that Hallowell was forced to travel because established doctors from leading families had monopolized the local practice or that he chose to recruit patients in Providence and other towns as a cover for illicit activities. Despite his land speculations and his frequent resort to litigation, Hallowell was losing money. . . . The disjunction between his ambition and actual material gains may have led Hallowell in middle age to renew his illicit money-making schemes. . . .

What is most intriguing about Hallowell was his ability to ingratiate himself throughout his life with elite men whose reputations were unblemished by scandal. Despite the rumors that must have circulated about his early sexual dalliance, counterfeiting activities, suspect medical remedies, heavy debts, and shady business transactions, leading ministers, merchants, and magistrates welcomed him into their houses. In Pomfret such acceptance took its most dramatic form in September 1739 when Hallowell was admitted along with thirty-five other original covenanters to the first private library association in eastern Connecticut. Gathering in the house of Pomfret's respected, conservative minister, Ebenezer Williams, the members pledged sums for the purchase of "useful and profitable English books." In the company of the region's scholars, clergy, and "gentlemen," along with a few yeomen—all "warm friends of learning and literature"—Hallowell marked himself off from the more modest subscribers by joining with thirteen prominent and wealthy signers to pledge a sum exceeding £15.

Lacking college degree and family pedigree, Hallowell traded on his profession and his charm to gain acceptability with the elite. In August 1742 he shrewdly removed himself from the Pomfret scene, just before Sarah Grosvenor's death. In that month he moved, possibly without his wife and children, to Providence, where he had many connections. Within five years, Hallowell had so insinuated himself with town leaders such as Stephen Hopkins that fourteen of them petitioned for mitigation of what they saw as the misguided sentence imposed on him in the Grosvenor case.

Hallowell's capacity for landing on his feet, despite persistent brushes with scandal, debt, and the law, suggests that we should look at the fluidity of New England's eighteenth-century elite in new ways. What bound sons of old New England families, learned men, and upwardly mobile merchants and professionals in an expanded elite may partly have been a reshaped, largely unspoken set of values shared by men. We know that the archetype for white New England women as sexual beings was changing from carnal Eve to resisting Pamela and that the calculus of accountability for seduction was shifting blame solely to women. But the simultaneous metamorphosis in cultural images and values defining manhood in the early and mid-eighteenth century has not been studied. The scattered evidence we do have suggests that, increasingly, for men in the more secular and anglicized culture of New England, the lines between legitimate and illegitimate sexuality, between sanctioned and shady business dealings, and between speaking the truth and protecting family honor blurred. Hallowell's acceptability to men like minister Ebenezer Williams and merchant Stephen Hopkins hints at how changing sexual and moral standards shaped the economic and social alliances made by New England's male leadership in the 1700s.

Women's Talk and Men's Talk

If age played a major role in determining who knew the truth about Sarah Grosvenor's illness, gender affected how the conspiring young adults responded to Sarah's impending death and how they weighed the issue of blame. Our last glimpse into the social world of eighteenth-century Pomfret looks at the different ways in which women and men reconstructed their roles in the events of 1742.

An inward gaze, a strong consciousness of sin and guilt, a desire to avoid conflict and achieve reconciliation, a need to confess—these are the impulses expressed in women's intimate talk in the weeks before Sarah died. The central female characters in the plot, Sarah and Zerviah Grosvenor, lived for six weeks with the daily fear that their parents or aunts might detect Sarah's condition or their covert comings and goings. Deposing three years later, Zerviah represented the sisters as suffering under an intensifying sense of complicity as they had passed through two stages of involvement in the concealment plant. At first, they were passive players, submitting to the hands of men. But once Hallowell declared that he had done all he could, they were left to salvage the conspiracy by enduring the terrors of a first delivery alone, knowing that their failure to call in the older women of the family resembled the decision made by women who committed infanticide. While the pain and shock of miscarrying a five-and-one-half-month fetus through a possibly lacerated vagina may have been the experience that later most grieved Sarah, Zerviah would be haunted particularly by her stealthy venture into the woods with Hannah to bury the shorouded evidence of miscarriage.

The Gosvenor sisters later recalled that they had regarded the first stage of the scheme—taking the trade—as "a Sin" and "an Evil" not so much because it was intended to end the life of a fetus as because it entailed a protracted set of actions, worse than a single lie, to cover up an initial transgression: fornication. According to their religion and the traditions of their New England culture, Sarah and Zerviah knew that the proper response to the sin of "uncleanness" (especially when it led to its visible manifestation, pregancy) was to confess, seeking to allay God's wrath and cleanse oneself and one's community. Dire were the consequences of hiding a grave sin, so the logic and folklore of religion warned. Having piled one covert act upon another, all in defiance of her parents, each sister wondered if she had not ventured beyond the pale, forsaking God and in turn being forsaken.

Within hours after the burial, Zerviah ran in a frenzy to Alexander Session's house and blurted out an account of her sister's "Untimely birth" and the burying of the fetus. While Alexander and Silence Sessions wondered if Zerivah was "in her right mind" and supposed she was having "a very bad fit," we might judge that she was in shock—horrified and confused by what she had done, fearful of retribution, and torn between the pragmatic strategy of silence and an intense spiritual longing to confess. Silence took her aside and demanded, "how could you did it?—I could not!" Zerviah, in despair, replied, "I don't Know; the Devil was in us." Hers was the characteristic refuge of the defiant sinner: Satan made her do it.

Sarah's descent into despondency, according to the protrait drawn in the women's depositions, was not so immediate. In the week following the miscarriage she recovered enough to be up and about the house. Then the fever came on. Bedridden for weeks, yet still lucid, she exhibited such "great Concern of mind" that Abigail, alone with her, felt compelled to ask her "what was the Matter." "Full of Sorrow" and "in a very affectionate Manner," Sarah replied by asking her friend "whether [she] thought her Sins would ever be pardoned?" Abigail's answer blended a reassuringly familiar exhortation to repent with an awareness that Sarah might have stepped beyond the possibility of salvation. "I answered that I hoped she had not Sinned the unpardonable Sin [that of renouncing Christ], but with true and hearty repentance hoped she would find forgiveness." On this occasion, and at least once more, Sarah responded to the call for repentance by pouring out her troubled heart to Abigail—as we have seen—confessing her version of the story in a torrent of words.

Thus, visions of judgment and of their personal accountability to God haunted Sarah and Zerviah during the waning days of summer—or so their female friends later contended. Caught between the traditional religious ethic of confession, recently renewed in revivals across New England, and the newer, status-driven cultural pressure to keep moral missteps private, the Grosvenor women declined to take up roles as accusers. By focusing on their own actions, they rejected a portrait of themselves as helpless victims, yet they also ceded to their male kin responsibility for assessing blame and mediating between the public interest in seeing justice done and the private interests of the Grosvcenor family. Finally, by trying to keep the conspiracy of silence intact and by allowing Amasa frequent visits to her bedside to lament his role and his delusion by Hallowell, Sarah at once endorsed a policy of private repentance and forgiveness *and* indicated that she wished her lover to be spared eventual public retribution for her death.

Talk among the men of Pomfret in the weeks preceding and following Sarah's death centered on more secular concerns than the preoccupation with sin and God's anger that ran through the women's conversations. Neither Hallowell nor Sessions expressed any guilt or sense of sin, as far as the record shows, *until* Sarah was diagnosed as mortally ill. Indeed, their initial accounts of the plot took the form of braggadocio, with Amasa (according to Hallowell) casting himself as the rake who could "gitt Red" of his child and look elsewhere for female companionship, and Hallowell boasting of his abortionist's surgical technique to Sarah's cousin Ebenezer. Later, anticipating popular censure and possible prosecution, each man "Tried to Cast it" on the other. The physician insisted that "He did not do any thing but What Sessions Importuned him to Do," while Amasa exclamied "That he could freely be Strip[p]ed naked provided he could bring Sarah . . . To life again . . . , but Doct Hollowell had Deluded him, and Destroyed her." While this sort of denial and buck-passing seems very human, it was the antithesis of the New England way—a religious way of life that made confession its central motif. The Grosvenor-Sessions case is one illustration among many of how New England women continued to measure themselves by "the moral allegory of repentance and confession" while men, at least when presenting themselves before legal authorities, adopted secular voices and learned self-interested strategies.

For the Grosvenor men—at least the cluster of Sarah's cousins living near her—the key issue was not exposing sin but protecting the family's reputation. In the weeks before Sarah died, her cousins John and Ebenezer each attempted to investigate and sort out the roles and motives of Amasa Sessions and John Hallowell in the scheme to conceal Sarah's pregnancy. Grilled in August by Ebenezer about Sarah's condition, Hallowell revealed that "Sessions had bin Interseeding with him to Remove her Consepcion." On another occasion, when John Grosvenor demanded that he justify his actions, Hallowell was more specific. He "[did] with her [Sarah] as he did . . . because Sessions Came to him and was So very earnest . . . and offered him five pounds if he would do it." "But," Hallowell boasted, "he would have twenty of[f] of him before he had done." John persisted: did Amasa know that Hallowell was attempting a manual abortion at John's house on that day in early August? Hallowell replied that Amasa "knew before he did anything and was at Mr. Waldo's [a Pomfret tavernkeeper] to hear the event."

John and Ebenezer, deposing three or four years after these events, did not mention having thrown questions at Amasa Sessions at the time, nor did they explain why they did not act immediately to have charges brought against the two conspirators. Perhaps these young householders were loath to move against a male peer and childhood friend. More likely, they kept their information to themselves to protect John's wife, Hannah, and their cousin Zerviah from prosecution as accessories. They may also have acted, in league with their uncle Leicester, out of a larger concern for keeping the family name out of the courts. Finally, it is probable that the male cousins, partly because of their own complicity and partly because they may have believed that Sarah had consented to the abortion, simply did not think that Amasa's and Hallowell's actions added up to the murder of their relative.

Three years later, yet another Grosvenor cousin intervened, expressing himself much more vehemently than John or Ebenezer even had. In 1742, John Shaw at age thirty-eight may have been perceived by the younger Grosvenors as too old—too close to the age when men took public office and served as grand jurors—to be trusted with their secret. Shaw seems to have known nothing of Sarah's taking the trade or having a miscarriage until 1745 when "the Storys" suddenly surfaced. Then Hannah and Zerviah gave him a truncated account. Shaw reacted with rage, realizing that Sarah had died not of natural causes but from "what Hollowell had done," and he set out to wring the truth from the doctor. Several times he sought out Hallowell in Rhode Island to tell him that "I could not look upon him otherwise Than [as] a Bad man Since he had Destroyed my Kinswoman." When Hallowell countered that "Amasa Sessions . . . was the Occassion of it," Shaw's fury grew. "I Told him he was like old Mother Eve When She said The Serpent beguild her; . . . [and] I Told him in my Mind he Deserved to dye for it."

Questioning Amasa, Shaw was quick to accept his protestations of sincere regret and his insistence that Hallowell had "Deluded" him. Shaw concluded that Amasa had never "Importuned [Hallowell] . . . to lay hands on her" (that is, to perform the manual abortion). Forged in the men's talk about the Grosvenor-Sessions case in 1745 and 1746 appears to have been a consensus that, while Amasa Sessions was somewhat blameworthy "as concerned in it," it was only Hallowell—the outsider, the man easily labeled a quack—who deserved to be branded "a Man of Death." Nevertheless, it was the stories of *both* men and women that ensured the fulfillment of a doctor's warning to Hallowell in the Leicester Grosvenor house just before Sarah died: "The Hand of Justice [will] Take hold of [you] sooner or Later."

The Law

The hand of justice reached out to catch John Hallowell in November 1745. The warrants issued for the apprehension and examination of suspects that autumn gave no indication of a single informer or highly placed magistrate who had triggered the prosecution so long after the events. Witnesses referred to "those Stories Concerning Amasa Sessions and Sarah Grosvenor" that had begun to circulate beyond the inner circle of Pomfret initiates in the summer of 1745. *Something* had caused Zerviah and Hannah Grosvenor to break their silence. Zerviah provided the key to the puzzle, as she alone had been present at the crucial series of incidents leading to Sarah's death. The only surviving account of Zerviah's belated conversion from silence to public confession comes from the stories told by Pomfret residents into the nineteenth century. In Ellen Larned's melodramatic prose, the "whispered" tale recounted Zerviah's increasing discomfort thus: "Night after night, in her solitary chamber, the surviving sister was awakened by the rattling of the rings on which her bed-curtains were suspended, a ghostly knell continuing and intensifying till she was convinced of its preternatural origin; and at length, in response to her agonized entreaties, the spirit of her dead sister made known to her, 'That she could not rest in her grave till her crime was made public.' "

Embellished as this tale undoubtedly is, we should not dismiss it out of hand as a Victorian ghost story. In early modern English culture, belief persisted in both apparitions and the supernatural power of the guiltless victim to return and expose

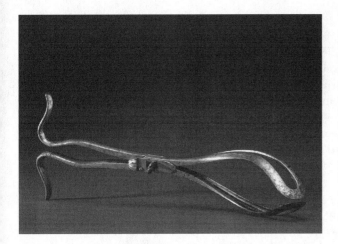

The forceps shown here were developed in the mid-eighteenth century and used initially by "man midwives" to deliver babies. Male physicians, who controlled professional training in medicine, quickly monopolized the use of forceps. Used well, these instruments could save the lives of women and babies; but used poorly, they could cause even greater damage by perforating the uterus or crushing an infant's skull.

her murderer. Zerviah in 1742 already fretted over her sin as an accomplice, yet she kept her pledge of silence to her sister. It is certainly conceivable that, after a lapse of three years, she could no longer bear the pressure of hiding the acts that she increasingly believed amounted to the murder of her sister and an unborn child. Whether Zerviah's sudden outburst of talk in 1745 came about at the urging of some Pomfret confidante, or perhaps under the influence of the revivals then sweeping Windham County churches, or indeed because of her belief in nightly visitations by her dead sister's spirit, we simply cannot know.

The Pomfret meetinghouse was the site of the first public legal hearing into the facts behind Sarah Grosvenor's death. We can imagine that townsfolk crowded the pews over the course of two November days to watch two prominent county magistrates examine a string of witnesses before pronouncing their preliminary judgment. The evidence, they concluded, was sufficient to bind four people over for trail at the Superior Court: Hallowell, who in their opinion was "Guilty of murdering Sarah," along with Amasa Sessions, Zerviah Grosvenor, and Hannah Grosvenor as accessories to that murder. The inclusion of Zerviah and Hannah may have been a ploy to pressure these crucial, possibly still reluctant, witnesses to testify for the crown. When Joseph Fowler, the king's attorney, prepared a formal indictment in the case eleven months later, he dropped all charges against Zerviah and Hannah. Rather than stand trial, the two women taveled frequently during 1746 and 1747 to the county seat to give evidence against Sessions and Hallowell.

The criminal process recommenced in September 1746. A grand jury empaneled by the Superior Court at its Windham session first rejected a presentment against Hallowell for murdering Sarah "by his Wicked and Diabolical practice." Fowler, recognizing that the capital charges of murder and accessory to murder against Hallowell and Sessions were going to fail before jurors, changed his tack. He presented the grand jury with a joint indictment against the two men not for outright murder but for endangering Sarah's health by trying to "procure an Abortion" with medicines and "a violent manual opperation"; this time the jurors endorsed the bill. When the Superior Court trial opened in November, two attorneys for the defendants managed to persuade the judges that the indictment was faulty on technical grounds. However, upon the advice of the king's attorney that there "appear reasons vehemently to suspect" the two men "Guilty of Sundry Heinous Offenses" at Pomfret four years earlier, the justices agreed to bind them over to answer charges in March 1747.

Fowler next moved to bring separate indictments against Hallowell and Sessions for the "highhanded misdemeanour" of endeavoring to destroy Sarah's health "and the fruit of her womb." This wording echoed the English common law designation of abortion as a misdemeanor, not a felony or capital crime. A newly empaneled grand jury of eighteen county yeomen made what turned out to be the pivotal decision in getting a conviction: they returned a true bill against Hallowell and rejected a similarly worded bill against Sessions. Only Hallowell, "the notorious physician," would go to trial.

On March 20, 1747, John Hallowell stepped before the bar for the final time to answer for the death of Sarah Grosvenor. He maintained his innocence, the case went to a trial jury of twelve men, and they returned with a guilty verdict. The Superior Court judges, who had discretion to choose any penalty less than death, pronounced a severe sentence of public shaming and corporal punishment. Hallowell was to be paraded to the town gallows, made to stand there before the public for two hours "with a rope visibly hanging about his neck," and then endure a public whipping of twenty-nine lashes "on the naked back."

Before the authorities could carry out this sentence, Hallowell escaped and fled to Rhode Island. From Providence seven months after his trail, he audaciously petitioned the Connecticut General Assembly for a mitigated sentence, presenting himself as a destitute "Exile." As previoulsy noted, fourteen respected male citizens of Providence took up his cause, arguing that this valued doctor had been convicted by prejudiced witnesses and hearsay evidence and asserting that corporal punishment was unwarranted in a misdemeanor case. While the Connecticut legislators rejected these petitions, the language used by Hallowell and his Rhode Island patrons is yet another marker of the distance separating many educated New England men at mid-century from their more God-fearing predecessors. Never mentioning the words "sin" or "repentance," the Providence men wrote that Hallowell was justified in escaping the lash since "every Person is prompted [by the natural Law of Self-Preservation] to avoid Pain and Misery."

In the series of indictments against Hallowell and Sessions, the central legal question became who had directly caused Sarah's death. To the farmers in their forties and fifties who sat as jurors, Hallowell clearly deserved punishment. By recklessly endangering Sarah's life he had abused the trust that heads of household placed in him as a physician. Moreover, he had conspired with the younger generation to keep their dangerous activities secret from their parents and elders.

Several rationales could have been behind the Windham jurors' conclusion that Amasa Sessions ought to be spared the lash. Legally, they could distinguish him from Hallowell as not being *directly* responsible for Sarah's death. Along with Sarah's male kin, they dismissed the evidence that Amasa had instigated the scheme, employed Hallowell, and monitored all of his activities. Perhaps they saw him as a native son who deserved the chance to prove himself mature and responsible. They may have excused his actions as nothing more than a misguided effort to cast off an unwanted lover. Rather than acknowledge that a culture that excused male sexual irresponsibility was responsible for Sarah's death, the Grosvenor family, the Pomfret community, and the jury men of the county persuaded themselves that Sessions had been ignorant of the potentially deadly consequences of his actions.

Memory and History

No family feud, no endless round of recriminations followed the many months of deposing and attending trials that engaged the Grosvenor and Sessions clans in 1746 and 1747. Indeed, as Sarah and Amasa's generation matured, the ties between the two families thickened. In 1748 Zerviah married a man whose family homestead adjoined the farm of Amasa's father. Twenty years later, when the aging Sessions patriarch wrote his will, Zerviah and her husband were at his elbow to witness the solemn document. Amasa, who would inherit "the Whole of the Farm," was doubtless present also. Within another decade, the third generation came of age, and despite the painful memories of Sarah's death that must have lingered in the minds of her now middle-aged siblings, a marriage directly joining the two families finally took place. In 1775 Amasa's third son, and namesake, married sixteen-year-old Esther Grosvenor, daughter of Sarah's brother, Leicester, Jr.

It is clear that the Grosvenor clan was not willing to break ranks with their respectable yeoman neighbors and heap blame on the Sessions family for Sarah's death. It would, however, be fascinating to know what women in Pomfret and other Windham County towns had to say about the outcome of the legal proceedings in 1747. Did they concur with the jurors that Hallowell was the prime culprit, or did they, unlike Sarah Grosvenor, direct their ire more concertedly at Amasa, insisting that he too was "a Bad man"? Several decades later, middle-class New England women would organize against the sexual double standard. However, Amasa's future career tells us that female piety in the 1740s did not instruct Windham County women to expel the newly married, thirty-two-year-old man from their homes.

Amasa, as he grew into middle age in Pomfret, easily replicated his father's status. He served as militia captain in the Seven Year's War, prospered in farming, fathered ten children, and lived fifty-seven years beyond Sarah Grosvenor. His handsome gravestone, inscribed with a long verse, stands but twenty-five feet from the simpler stone erected in 1742 for Sarah.

After his death, male kin remembered Amasa fondly; nephews and grandsons recalled him as a "favorite" relative, "remarakble capable" in his prime and "very corpulent" in old age. Moreover, local story-telling tradition and the published history of the region, which made such a spectacular ghost story out of Sarah's abortion and death, preserved Amasa Sessions's reputation unsullied: the *name* of Sarah's lover was left out of the tale.

If Sarah Grosvenor's life is a cautionary tale in any sense for us in the late twentieth century, it is as a reminder of the historically distinctive ways in which socialized gender roles, community and class solidarity, and legal culture combine in each set of generations to excuse or make invisible certain abuses and crimes against women. The form in which Sarah Grosvenor's death became local history reminds us of how the excuses and erasures of one generation not unwittingly become embedded in the narratives and memories of the next cultural era.

Questions for Study and Review

1. What were the legal, religious, and social sanctions related to abortion in eighteenth-century New England?

2. How did the women and men involved in Sarah Grosvenor's abortion respond to Sarah's death and that of her fetus?

3. What does the trial in the Grosvenor-Sessions case tell us about gender and generational relations in early eighteenth-century Connecticut?

4. How would you compare the Grosvenor household in Pomfret, Connecticut, with the households described by Laurel Thatcher Ulrich in Chapter Three?

Suggested Readings and Web Sites

Amanda Carson Banks, *Birth Chairs, Midwives, and Medicine* (1999)
Judith Walzer Leavitt, ed., *Women and Health in America: Historical Readings* (1999)
Angus McLaren, *Reproductive Rituals: The Perception of Fertility in England from the Sixteenth Century to the Nineteenth Century* (1984)
Merril D. Smith, ed., *Sex and Sexuality in Early America* (1998)
The Grosvenor-Sessions Abortion Case
    http://oncampus.richmond.edu/~aholton/Dayton/index. html
A Midwife's Tale
    http://www.pbs.org/wgbh/amex/midwife/

Chapter 5

The Chesapeake region of Maryland and Virginia was home to the first permanent English settlers on the North American mainland. The first shipload of enslaved Africans to reach the mainland landed there in 1619, and some of the earliest contact and conflict with American Indians also took place in the Chesapeake. In the seventeenth century, this was a region in which men dramatically outnumbered women among English immigrants. Although such an abundance of men fueled instability and violence in early Virginia, it did have some advantages for the women who made their homes in the colony.

Many women arrived in the Chesapeake as indentured servants who owed four to seven years' labor in return for their passage to America. Still, if a servant survived her term of service, she might marry a prosperous farmer desperate to find a wife. The scarcity of women also meant that most wives were considerably younger than their husbands. Given the high mortality rates in the region, wives generally outlived their husbands, and many became executors of their husbands' wills. That is, they were in charge of the distribution of their husbands' property. Many remarried soon after being widowed, and some inherited property from more than one deceased spouse.

Legally, married women in the Chesapeake, as in England and other British colonies, were defined as *feme coverte,* which meant that once a woman married, her legal identity merged with that of her husband. (Women were thus literally hidden behind their husbands when it came to legal and economic transactions.) Nonetheless, the shortage of women in the seventeenth-century Chesapeake ensured that many wives wielded some economic and legal authority. This authority was enhanced when they became widows since their children were generally too young to gain legal or economic independence. Still, the improved status of women and wives came at a high price: husbands died young and infant mortality rates were staggering. In addition, since religious institutions in the Chesapeake were less developed than those in New England and extended families were nearly nonexistent, women had little protection from abusive husbands (or masters, fathers, and other men).

Allan Kulikoff begins this chapter by showing that the ratio of women to men became more equal in the eighteenth century and that families became more stable. Husbands lived longer, married women closer to their own age, and remained in control of their households and property until their children reached adulthood. These developments, although a blessing to wives in good marriages, increased the authority of the male head of household. He became the family patriarch. Throughout the English colonies, men ruled over wives, children, servants, and slaves. In New England, however, wives and mothers were increasingly lauded for their roles in raising children and maintaining the household.

In the Chesapeake, the domination of the father, or patriarch, was more complete and more firmly entrenched in law, in the economy, and in custom.

Domestic patriarchy was most significant among the planter class, that group of tobacco growers who owned significant amounts of land and enough enslaved workers to make it profitable. But the system of slavery also complicated patriarchal ambitions. In many societies where land was tied to wealth, a father bequeathed all or most of the land to his eldest son to keep the homestead intact and maintain the family's economic and political stature. Slaveholders, however, hoped to make every son a master and were also expected to provide daughters with "movable goods," such as slaves. As a result, plantations were frequently subdivided among several sons, and enslaved women and men were distributed among all the children. Some children moved from the tidewater region along the coast to the piedmont farther west in hopes of gaining sufficient land. The dispersal of planters' children and of the enslaved women and men they took with them disrupted family ties among both blacks and whites, though African Americans, who had no choice in the matter, suffered more severe consequences. Thus domestic patriarchy, though it flourished among elite families in the eighteenth-century Chesapeake, contained the seeds of its own demise.

The Origins of Domestic Patriarchy: White Families in the Eighteenth Century Chesapeake

ALLAN KULIKOFF

In March 1729 Ann Thomas urged the Prince George's County court in Maryland to permit her "to tend such a Quantity of Tobacco for herself, her labouring girls and her [sickly] slave as may be Sufficient for a maintenance for herself and them." Her request ran counter to current law—meant to improve tobacco prices—which permitted slaves and white men and boys to tend tobacco plants but forbade white women to tend them. In support of her petition to waive the law, Thomas recounted her attempts to provide for her family. Her husband's "Several Mismanagements and ill Conduct" had "reduced [her] to so great want and necessity that for some time she had relief by a pension from the Court." About ten years before, her husband left her, but she was "a Constant hard Labourer in Tobacco" and had "made an honest shift to Maintain herself and family of Several Small children without putting the County to charge of a pension." She purchased a slave, but

This painting of the Edward Lloyd family by Charles Wilson Peale (1771) is typical of eighteenth-century family portraits. The family patriarch is generally standing, overseeing his wife and children, who were most often seated. While the father and husband looks directly into the viewer's eyes, women and children gaze off to the side.

he was too sick to work and drained her resources. Despite her husband's departure, she "had frequently done the part of wife by him in his Sickness and been at great expense on his account and never has had any benefit of his Labour for many years." The new law, however, prevented her from making a crop and supporting her three daughters, ages eleven, thirteen, and fifteen, and she would soon require county assistance again.

The justices refused Thomas's request. They probably investigated her claim and discovered that the family had greater resources than Thomas admitted. In the first place, she owned a healthy slave woman who could work in the ground. Two sons, both in their late teens, worked as laborers on nearby plantations and could assist their mother, and a married son resided with his family nearby and might take in his mother and sister. Families as poor as Thomas's survived on similar allotments of tobacco plants, the justices may have reasoned, and there was little reason that Thomas could not emulate them.

Although Thomas and the justices agreed in principle about the fundamentals of family government—that women should nurture children and comfort their husbands in sickness and health while men supported their families by growing tobacco for the market—Thomas's independence challenged the subservient behavior that the justices expected of women. While Thomas explained that her husband's incompetence and departure from the home and her slave's illness forced her into the fields, the justices wanted her husband and sons to return home and fulfill their obligations. . . .

This case suggests the acceptance of a kind of partriarchalism as the ideal form of family government by some early eighteenth-century Chesapeake planters. Although these planters rejected the connection between male supremacy in the family and royal absolutism in government that lay at the heart of European patriarchal theory, they sought to retain patriarchal control over their families. This *domestic patriarchalism* was both a set of beliefs about power relations within families and households and a description of behavior within the family. The ideology of domestic patriarchalism placed husbands over wives within the family, asserted that women were legally inferior to men, and separated the economic roles of men and women into distinct spheres, with men responsible for the economic well-being of the family and for civic participation outside it and women responsible for child nurture and household management. In a patriarchal family system, one would expect to find husbands controlling the distribution of family assets (and preferring sons over daughters), the separation of public and private roles, distinctive economic roles for men, women, and children, and paternal control of their children's marriage decisions. Children and wives willing to accept their place could expect affectionate and even companionate fathers and husbands, especially in wealthy families where servants and slaves lightened the workload of both women and men. This domestic patriarchy was very different from the kind of bourgeois family government that slowly developed in England and the American North. Although both systems of family government ensured male supremacy by keeping women out of public life and by enforcing a sexual division of labor, the equality of husbands and wives in domestic relations and the elevation of women's roles of child nurture and family management to a position of great ideological importance never occurred in the eighteenth-century Chesapeake region.

Although some white immigrants brought patriarchal ideals with them when they came to the Chesapeake, they found the practice of domestic patriarchalism difficult. Since adult life expectancy was quite low in the Chesapeake colonies during the seventeenth century and generational continuity was difficult to maintain, few men lived long enough to impose their will upon their children. Planters' wives, moreover, often had to work in the fields beside their husbands because of the growing shortage of labor during the middle and late seventeenth century, a practice that reduced the economic differentiation of men and women at the heart of patriarchal theory.

When demographic conditions improved at the end of the seventeenth century and the growing slave trade eased the labor shortage, many more families took on patriarchal characteristics. Since men lived longer, they could more readily impose their will upon their wives and children, and the acquisition of slaves permitted them to take their wives out of the tobacco fields and set them to domestic tasks. Men who owned slaves not only could afford this division of labor but knew they should not debase their wives by setting them to do slaves' work. Poor families, in contrast, still needed the wives' labor and probably continued the system of family labor common in the seventeenth century throughout the succeeding generations.

The Demographic Basis of Domestic Patriarchy

Immigrant men and women, who constituted a majority of the white adult population until the end of the seventeenth century, married late, died young, and left numerous orphans to the care of their heirs and the community at large. After English men and women left home, about age twenty, and came to the Chesapeake, they worked four or five years as servants; and those who survived their seasoning could expect to live only about twenty and after completion of their term. Since at least two men migrated for every woman, men had to postpone marriage until nearly age thirty, well after they had become freedmen, and they often married women ten or more years younger than themselves.

In such a demographic environment, a woman could anticipate little long-term support from her first husband, nor could a husband expect to maintain lengthy patriarchal authority over his wife. Very few immigrant marriages were long: in two Maryland counties, for instance, marriages lasted, on average, only eleven to thirteen years before one spouse died. . . . Since widows and widowers soon remarried, several husbands exercised authority sequentially over a woman who lived to age fifty. Because men married much younger women, a wife was likely to become a widow; she probably learned the tobacco business while her husband was alive so she could take over once he died. During the interval between marriages, a widow gained some independent power and sometimes retained control over her first husband's property even after she remarried.

The high ratios of men to women among immigrants and the shortage of labor in the region after 1660 accelerated the development of more egalitarian relations between husbands and wives than were common in rural English families. With so many men clamoring for wives among the few women in the region, women could choose their spouses. Women and men, moreover performed similar tasks and worked together growing tobacco because there was insufficient labor on most plantations to meet European demand for tobacco.

Although women on the tobacco coast thus had some advantages over their English counterparts, they lost the paternal protection common in the mother country. Native-born women commonly married in their middle to late teens during the seventeenth century, often as soon as they reached menarche. Some of these girls may have been forced into marriage by fathers or guardians before they were willing to begin their own families, and they had to bear the risk of reduced immunity to disease that each pregnancy brought. Setting up a household with a new husband did not offer a woman any remission of exploitation. Not only was she expected to work in the fields, but she had to maintain the cabins, bear and nurse infants, and take care of children.

Short marriages and frequent parental death meant great uncertainty for children. Children born in the Chesapeake region during the seventeenth century could anticipate that one or both parents would die before they could fend for themselves. Step-parents, siblings, uncles, and neighbors often succeeded to parental authority before children reached adolescence: the proportion of children in seventeenth-century Middlesex County, Virginia, who lost at least one parent rose from a quarter of the five-year-olds to more than half of the thirteen-year-olds. . . . Guardians on occasion despoiled the estates of orphans (in law, those without fathers), deprived their charges of necessities, or even physically abused them. Children who lost one or both of their parents must have matured early and learned to accept responsibility for their own sustenance at an early age. . . .

The demographic conditions that prevented the development of patriarchal family government disappeared at the end of the seventeenth century. As white immigration declined, the proportion of native-born adults in the white population rose, reaching half by 1700. These natives lived longer and married at younger ages than their immigrant parents. Family life in the eighteenth century therefore became more secure than it had been previously. Women could expect economic support for many years, since the marriages that natives contracted lasted longer than those of immigrants. Fathers could more readily control the economic destiny of their children because they more often lived to see them married. And children could expect more sustained parental care and were less likely to live in families with step-parents and step-siblings than their ancestors.

Marriages celebrated by native-born couples often lasted twice as long as those of immigrants. In Somerset County, Maryland, for instance, marriages between two native-born spouses lasted twenty-six years on average, nearly twice as long as those between two immigrants and a third longer than those between an immigrant and a native. In Prince George's County during the eighteenth century, these longer marriages became typical, lasting, on average, from twenty-two to twenty-five years, with first marriages probably continuing another ten years. One in three recorded marriages was extraordinarily long, lasting more than thirty years—forty-one years on average.

The increased duration of marriage substantially altered the lives of women. A husband could, if he desired, establish and maintain continuous authority over his wife and children, and his wife could count on his economic support for many years. Many wives died before their husbands, and women who lost their husbands tended to be older than forty and, since the surplus of men had disappeared, found remarriage increasingly difficult. Although widows in their twenties and thirties who lived in Prince George's in the 1770s remarried as frequently as widowers of the same age, widowers in their forties and fifties remarried four to seven times more frequently than widows.

When the duration of marriages rose during the first third of the eighteenth century, the probability that children would lose their parents declined substantially. There were both fewer orphans and more children with both parents alive at every age in eighteenth-century Prince George's than in seventeenth-century Middlesex. . . . The proportion of fathers who lived to see their sons reach twenty-one increased from less than half in seventeenth-century Middlesex to nearly two-thirds in Prince George's during the eighteenth century.

Children of native-born parents lived more secure lives than earlier generations in the Chesapeake region. Even though a child still usually lost a parent before maturity, he was older when that event occurred than his ancestors had been, and he probably had adult siblings willing to protect his interests. . . . Parents relied less on the courts and more on informal arrangements with kin and neighbors to care for their orphaned children, and mothers uniformly retained custody of children when their husbands died. The orphans'court became a last resort to adjudicate disputes rather than a pervasive influence over orphan children.

Not only did parents live longer, but fathers retained control over both land and slaves, valuable property that their children needed to prosper. During the seventeenth century, life expectancy was so low that most sons of freeholders inherited land in their early twenties, but as life expectancy rose in the eighteenth century, sons waited longer for their portions. . . . Though fathers often set up their sons on family land when they married, older sons of long-lived fathers usually waited ten or fifteen years after marriage before gaining title to their farms: Fewer than a fifth of fathers under seventy gave any land to their sons, and only half of those over seventy began to distribute it. Older planters held on to their land to support their families, to ensure their maintenance if they fell ill, and to strengthen paternal authority over their sons. . . . The increase in slaveholding added to the power planters held over their children, for slaveholders could added to the power planters held over their children, for slaveholders could offer their offspring (both sons and daughters) the added capital and prosperity that title to slaves would yield, in return for good behavior.

The increased length of marriage, with the reduction in the number of remarriages it brought, helped streamline authority in plantation households. Conflicts within families, between step-children and step-parents, or between guardians and their charges may have been common in the seventeenth century, when most households contained a wide variety of kin, including step-parents, step-siblings, and half-siblings. These conflicts probably diminished, and the authority of fathers probably increased during the eighteenth century because most planter households contained only parents and their own children. The composition of households in Prince George's County in 1776 may have been representative. Although about half the planters owned slaves, these chattels rarely lived in the master's house. Only one-seventh of all householders owned servants, hired laborers, or boarded guests. Nearly half of all county households included only husband, wife, and their own children, and another tenth were headed by widows or widowers and housed the surviving spouse and the children. A third of the households included people other than parents and children, but even these were not particularly complex, with most adding a laborer or two, step-children, or an orphan assigned to the family by the county. Only a tenth of the families were extended generationally or laterally, mostly by widowed mothers of the husband or wife.

Husbands and Wives in the Domestic Economy

Although many unmarried men started households in the Chesapeake region during the seventeenth century, married couples were the center of plantation businesses and of family government during the eighteenth century. . . . Once a new couple married, they set up a plantation almost immediately, only rarely living with the bride's or groom's family. Husbands increasingly ran these domestic commonwealths in ways consistent with the principles of domestic partriarchalism, sometimes responding violently when wives challenged their authority.

Planters and their wives realized that a prosperous farm business and a successful marriage supported each other. "Two young persons who marry without a reasonable prospect of an income to support them and their family," a Virginia essayist wrote in 1770, "are in a condition as wretched as any I know of." As soon as a couple decided to wed, negotiations between their fathers ensued to ensure that the couple would have a good chance to succeed. These negotiations were the most protracted among the gentry class, where parents wished to be certain that bride and groom would bring equal wealth into the marriage, but yeoman families also insisted that portions and dowries be paid to the new couple. Ignatious Doyne of Calvert County followed this custom in 1749 when James Brooke asked for one of Doyne's "Daughters in Marriage." Since he had no objection to the match, he "went to Madame [Sarah] Brooke to know what she would give her Son." Widow Brooke insisted that she did not have "anything in the world," but Doyne persisted and complained that James Brooke had "but one Negro." "I hope you will contrive to give him one at least." She refused and even asked to use the Negro girl she had given to James as her servant. Joseph Wheat of Montgomery County had better luck when his daughter married Zephaniah Prather, son of William, in 1761. After the wedding, Wheat visited Prather and told him "what he intended to give his said Daughter." Prather "appeared well Satisfied" and in turn took Wheat to a "small plantation" near his home, "and said this place I intend to give unto my son Zephaniah Prather Together with my Negro Boy Tobey."

A man and a woman should not contemplate marriage unless they loved and respected each other, for "mutual love and esteem" were "the very cement of matrimonial happiness." This writer would have approved the 1759 marriage of Sarah Lee and Philip Fendall, both members of the Maryland gentry, for they not only possessed "every natural Endowment, and needful Accomplishment to . . . promise them Happiness in private Life," but they were sure to reap "the Benefit of their early and Constant Affection for each other."

Since men and women possessed different sensibilities and performed different roles within marriage, they brought contrasting social qualities into their new homes. Men should enjoy the esteem of other men of their station, possess an upright character and be fair and honest in all their economic dealings, be careful and industrious in their daily tasks, and bhe courteous in their relationships with both men and women. The *Maryland Gazette* eulogized Robert Boone of Anne Arundel County when he died in 1759, for instance, because he was "an honest and industrious Planter, who Died on the same Plantation where he was Born in 1680, . . . and has left a Widow, to whom he was married 57 Years." While men were expected to possess qualities that prepared them for the marketplace, wives were encouraged to practice submissiveness to authority. A well-accomplished woman should above all be agreeable, affable, amenable, and amiable, she should practice charity and benevolence to her neighbors and the poor; and she should always behave virtuously. A woman who possessed these attributes was "endow'd with every Qualification to render a man happy in the Conjugal State."

Gentlemen insisted that wives be submissive to their husbands, and women tolerated, and even on occasion supported, a subordinate role within the family because that was the only way they could gain status as an adult. Marriage reduced the legal rights a single woman enjoyed but, at the same time, made her mistress over her husband's home, permitted her to bear legitimate children, and entitled her to economic support from her husband. An essay published in the *Virginia*

Gazette in 1738 urged a wife to be "a faithful Friend, one who has no Views or Interest different from his, and makes his Joys and Sorrows all her own." Edith Cobb, the wife of the county clerk of Amelia County, Virginia, followed this advice during her long marriage, and her husband Samuel showed his appreciation by bequeathing her most of his estate in 1757. He gave "a very considerable Power" to her because "she has been my Wife near Forty Years during which Time hath always been kind, loving, and obedient to me without affection." . . .

English common law and the statute law of Maryland and Virginia legitimated the subservience of wives by granting husbands legal dominion over them. They controlled their wives' property (unless a premarital agreement was signed), and the wife could rarely sell property, buy goods, sign contracts, or make a will while her husband lived. Even though wives—to protect their dower rights to a third of the family land—had to give their consent before their husbands could sell land, husbands often informed their wives of land sales only after the transaction was completed. In Louisa County, Virginia, between 1765 and 1812, for instance, women gave their consent to land transfers more than seven days after the sale in half of the transactions. Women in Louisa had few choices and always agreed to the sale. One wife, when presented with a completed deed, wished that "land . . . mentioned not be sold, but since it is the case she is entirely willing that the conveyance . . . should be recorded."

Ideally, the division of labor within marriage was supposed to sustain the authority of men in the family. A husband's most important responsibility was to provide food, clothing, and other necessities for his wife and children to the limit of his ability and economic station. That Chesapeake planters considered this task the very essence of manhood is suggested by the sad case of John Jackson. He had rented "a plantation at a very dear rate" in Prince George's County from 1724 to 1731 and had used "his honest Endeavours to maintain himself his Wife and a small Child now but eight years old" despite an illness that had left his wife lame and "altogether helpless" since 1727. Now, in 1731, Jackson found himself and his family destitute, and his "Endeavours fruitless," and begged of the county court to grant him "such relief as your Worships Compassion and charity shall think fit." If Jackson—a tenant who owned no slaves and hired no labor—was ashamed of his predicament, the court was hostile and rejected his petition and waited three years before it granted him a pension.

Not only did planters cultivate tobacco to support their families, but they sold the crop, did all the shopping and marketing, and kept the plantation's books. Husbands, who could expect long marriages in the eighteenth century, refused to share responsibility for plantation management with their wives. From time to time, husbands therefore tried to instruct their wives about plantation work in their wills. In 1758 Thomas Bowie, a wealthy planter with three small children, bequeathed land to his wife "Provided she does not Clear or Cutt down above twenty thousand Tobacco Hills in any one year"; similarly, in 1740 Capt. Charles Beall told his wife "not to Sel or Destroy any timber of . . . moor than what may bee for the Plantations Use and the Mill."

Planters usually worked in the ground as well as directed the labor of their mature sons, slaves, and white hired men in the cultivation of tobacco and in the maintenance of the farm. Although most planters could muster two or three work-ers to help them, many newly married men, tenants, and small freeholders relied only on their own efforts to support their families. A small proportion of planters owned or hired enough workers to stand back and oversee farm operations, and only the richest gentlemen could afford to hire overseers and manage their planta-tions from afar. . . .

While the great majority of men living in counties like Prince George's continued to labor in their fields throughout the eighteenth century, the economic position of planters slowly improved as more of them used slaves to increase the standard of liv-ing of their families. The proportion of planters in Prince George's who toiled alone declined from two-fifths in 1733 to a third in 1776. At the same time, the number of householders who could direct a gang of five to nine workers rose from a tenth to a seventh, and the proportion of men who worked ten or more laborers grew from one in twenty-five to one in fourteen.

While men managed the plantation, women took care of their homes. They pre-pared the family's food, washed clothes, tended gardens, made clothes, spun thread, wove cloth, milked cows, and churned butter. Though a few wives of wealthy gentlemen directed a retinue of slave women in these tasks, most planters kept slave women in the field, leaving their wives to complete household chores by themselves until their daughters were old enough to help them. Each of these tasks had to be repeated week after week, and wives sometimes envied the more varied jobs their husbands performed.

Cloth and clothes production was the wife's most important economic contribu-tion to the household economy. Although women infrequently spun thread, carded wool, or wove cloth from fiber during the seventeenth century, planters responded to recurring depressions in the tobacco trade by purchasing sheep, cards, and spin-ning wheels for their wives, and clothmaking became a very important domestic activity during the first half of the eighteenth century. Women universally made clothes from imported cloth, knitted bulky items, and repaired damaged wearing apparel, thereby saving the household from the great expense of importing ready-made clothing. Cloth production from scratch or, more commonly, local trade of wool, flax, thread, and cloth among farms possessing one part of the production process further added to the value of the wife's production.

Seventeenth-century wives served their families and occasional guests at crude tables or barrels, and the family ate from wooden (or sometimes earthen) bowls with fingers or spoons and knives. Housewives added more formal meal prepara-tion and service to their numerous chores during the eighteenth century, when meals became far more ceremonial and hospitality more common. This change is most clearly documented in St. Mary's County, the poorest county on Maryland's tobacco coast. Planters there began purchasing earthenware plates and bowls and table linen during the seventeenth century, and all but the poorest householders owned all of those items by the 1720s. Knives and forks reached a majority of sub-stantial planters in the 1720s and 1730s and less prosperous folk by the 1750s and 1760s. Finally, county families increasingly livened their meals with spices and tea. Though none but the wealthiest families added spices to their food early in the cen-tury, a majority of middling planters and a third of poorer freeholders used them by the 1750s and 1760s. And while fewer than a tenth of the planters' wives served tea before 1740, the proportion who used it thereafter rose steadily, reaching nearly three-quarters of the households by the 1770s.

Child care was the most time-consuming task assigned to Chesapeake wives. A woman could expect to give birth once every two to three years from marriage to menopause, and she assumed the burdens of childbearing, nursing, weaning, and child care with little assistance from her husband. This division of labor tied younger women to their homes, although it freed men to work in the fields or visit neighbors and nearby villages without concern for the safety or care of their offspring.

No Chesapeake family could possibly attain the harmony and complete separation of tasks that the domestic patriarchal ideal demanded. Husbands and wives bickered, argued, and occasionally even separated. From time to time, husbands and wives brought their difficulties to local or provincial courts. The two cases examined below paint a vivid picture of marital expectations and roles and suggest the limits of patriarchal domestic economy.

When John Abington, a wealthy Prince George's merchant, died in 1739, he left his widow Mary and their six children an estate of two thousand pounds sterling and several thousand acres of land. Unable to manage this fortune, she soon married Dr. Andrew Scott, a man of high status but small fortune. The couple paid almost all of Abington's personal estate to his creditors but collected few debts owed to him. They soon began bickering, and in 1746 Mary Scott sued her husband in Maryland's chancery court for separate maintenance. She claimed that she had behaved properly toward her husband; when he "prevailed upon" her to "joyne in a Deed" to break entail on some of Abington's land and have it assigned to him, she "had in all things . . . Complyed with the Request . . . and had thereby put every thing out of her Power." After he received the land, he treated her "with so much Cruilty and Inhumanity" that she "could not live or Cohabit with him without running a Manifest hazard of her Life." Finally, he turned her "out of Doors almost naked and quite Destitute of all the Necessaries of Life," forced her to turn to neighbors, and refused to give her the thirty pounds he promised her for her support.

Dr. Scott painted a far different picture. While he admitted taking the land, he claimed the estate was otherwise too small to support her and added that he had given Abington's children the land bequeathed to them. He denied treating her "with any Cruelty" but claimed he had suffered from her "indecent, Disorderly, Abusefull and Turbulent" behavior caused by her "common and frequent Drunkedness" until he had to leave the house and stay with neighbors. They urged him to "Seperate from her," but he "was Resolved to bear with her as Long as he could and to endeavour by all easy and Moderate means to Reclaim and reform her." When he learned that "she had been guilty of the worst and most Scandalous of Crimes which a Wife could be guilty of to a husband," of bringing "a Disease upon him which for Decency and the Shamefullness of it he forbears to give a name," he finally forced her from the house. After listening to both sides, the court ordered Scott to pay his wife thirty pounds as long as she lived apart from him.

A decade before the Scotts separated, Jane Pattison of Calvert County sued her second husband, Jeremiah, a middling planter, for separate maintenance in chancery court. From the start of her marriage, she had "behaved herself in a virtuous and respectful manner toward" him despite his appropriation of "a considerable Estate" left by her first husband to her and her children. Notwithstanding her good behavior, within a year of the wedding he "conceived so very great Dislike and Aversion to" her that "not only he used her very cruelly by beating her with Tongs . . . without any just or reasonable provocation . . . but also turned her out of Doors about Six years ago destitute of Cloaths and almost naked" and cut off her credit when she tried to replace them. Friends witnessed repeated beatings before the couple separated and later helped find her clothing, but Pattison still refused to support her "suitable to what he could afford." And Mrs. Pattison therefore sued for an annual allowance.

Jeremiah Pattison vehemently disagreed with his estranged wife. While he "was not wealthy" when he married her, he lived "in a comfortable and decent manner." After he paid her first husband's debts and distributed part of the remainder of the estate to her children, little was left. Mrs. Pattison "treated him not only with the greatest . . . Contempt" but even threw firebrands and iron candlesticks at him, all the while shouting "the most horrid and shocking Imprecations" at him. He responded with "the most gentle and persuasive Means he could think of to reclaim" her, and when that did not work, he "corrected her in a very moderate Manner." She abandoned him voluntarily, despite his attempts to "prevail on her to stay at home and manage her household Affairs which she absolutely refused to do." After she left home a second time, he urged her to return, writing: "My Dear I am Sorry that you should be so ill advised to desert your Habitation and send this to desire you would return home and behave Yourself as a loving Wife ought if you'l do that you shall always by me be used Lovingly. I am your Loving Husband." Mrs. Pattison refused to return, and the court ordered him to pay her thirty pounds a year.

Disagreement over the financial operation of the plantation lay at the root of Pattison's unhappiness. Samuel Abbot, her first husband, left a small personal estate with no taxable slaves but farmed four hundred acres of excellent land. Pattison lived on the edge of respectability, working as an itinerant carpenter before his marriage in 1724, but he too owned land. After the marriage, Pattison supported his family on his wife's land and rented his property to tenants, netting about two thousand pounds of tobacco each year. He used the profits from his two estates to buy five adult slaves by 1733. Mrs. Pattison, who wanted this bounty for her children, asked him to "dispose of all that he had at his Death to her Children" and was "much dissatisfied" when he refused. The couple argued repeatedly over this, calling each other vile names and usually concluding with Mrs. Pattison's throwing household implements at him and Pattison's beating his wife so severely that she left home to recover. Finally, since he would not bequeath his property to her children or stop beating her, she resolved to "take no Care of his Affairs but would make all she Could for her Children." She made good on her threat, forcing him to "put out" his linen "to be washed, his Stockings to be knit and his Negroes Cloaths to be made," and refused to serve him when he "asked for victuals," insisting that if he "was above taking it himself he might go without" and at the same time feeding "some very good meat" to a male neighbor.

Although the behavior reported by these two cases may have become increasingly unrepresentative as the number of second marriages diminished, the cross section of ordinary and wealthier planters and their wives who testified in court agreed about the principles of family government. They agreed, for instance, that wives owed their husbands obedience and smooth operation of the household in return for the financial support needed to purchase the necessities of life. The litigants claimed to follow these norms. While Scott and Pattison insisted that they properly supported their wives, their wives claimed fidelity and obedience. . . . Since the husband ruled the household, he had the right to correct his wife moderately when she went astray and punish her more harshly if necessary. Even the wives agreed with this idea, insisting that they gave their husbands no provocation but implying that clear reason would justify punishment.

Landed families generally accepted these principles of family government and the power relations they entailed throughout the eighteenth century. The emotional sensibilities of relations between gentry husbands and wives, however, probably began to soften during the last quarter of the eighteenth century. The slaves owned by these wealthy families performed all the plantation's heavy labor, thus freeing gentlemen and their wives from much of the work of ordinary white women and men. Freed from servile labor, these wealthy women and men increasingly emphasized emotion, love, individual feelings, and companionship within their marriages. Child rearing took on a heightened importance, especially for women. A new and highly charged emotional and possessive language began to appear in family correspondence. These new sensibilities were incorporated into patriarchal family government. Plantations remained units of production. Gentry women did not create a new, semiautonomous sphere dominated by child nurture for themselves. Even the wealthiest women retained important productive functions, for they directed and participated in gardening, cloth production, and candlemaking.

The Family Life Cycle in the Domestic Economy, 1720–1800

Unlike the Scotts and Pattisons, nearly every Chesapeake couple had children soon after marriage, who modified relations between husbands and wives, gave each spouse added responsibilities, and created new layers of authority in the household. Since women bore children regularly until menopause, some children remained at home throughout their parents' lives. Variations within family government probably hinged upon the ages of spouses and their children: Young parents with small children, middle-aged couples with adolescents, and widows and widowers with their unmarried children faced varying problems. This life-cycle approach sheds light on the economy of the family and the changing nature of domestic patriarchy within it.

The birth of children during the early years of marriage increased the work load wives sustained. A woman, age thirty-three, who had married when she was twenty-one, would probably be pregnant with her sixth child. She had spent 4 of her first 12 years of marriage pregnant and perhaps another 4.5 years nursing the surviving children, a task which sometimes made her ill. Each new child, moreover, forced her to make more clothing for her growing family. Few women could call on any help in these tasks in the early years of marriage. Daughters were too young to help with child care and sewing, and only the wealthiest planters owned enough slaves to put one or two to work as domestics. Even the wealthiest wives, furthermore, nursed their own children, sometimes refusing to send them out to wet nurse, even if in delicate health themselves.

The work of all but the wealthiest slaveholders intensified when children began to arrive. Whatever help their wives had provided in the fields was reduced when their domestic duties increased, and infants had to be fed and clothed without providing compensating field work. Poorer men struggled to maintain their standard of living, but might fail during the periodic depressions that hit the tobacco trade. Men who owned slaves possessed greater resources, but unless their labor force grew when their children were born, they probably had to push their slaves harder to sustain the same standard of living.

While women in their thirties and early forties continued to bear and nurse children, their maturing daughters assumed some responsibilities for child care and domestic industry. Parents sometimes left young children with older siblings when they went out. John Hatherly and his wife, for instance, allowed their fourteen-year-old daughter to watch her nine-year-old brother while they attended a funeral in Anne Arundel County in 1751. Daughters copied their mothers' household chores even before they learned the necessary skills. In 1773 Philip Fithian saw little girls—daughters of gentlemen— "imitating what they see in the great House; sometimes tying a String to a Chair and then run buzzing back to imitate the Girls spinning." Adolescent girls, even the daughters of wealthy gentlemen, spent much of their day making clothes. Frances Hill may have been typical of gentlemen's daughters. Throughout 1797 this adolescent girl sewed, knitted, or made clothes nearly every day but Sunday. In January, for example, she knit a stocking for herself, darned her stockings, hemmed a handkerchief for a friend, lined her brother's coat sleeves, mended her brother's breeches and her father's drawers, and made her mother an apron.

Sons joined their fathers in cultivating tobacco and grain at the age of ten to twelve. When the Virginia and Maryland assemblies wished to limit the production of tobacco by permitting only certain groups to tend plants, they allowed white boys over ten (in Virginia) or over twelve (in Maryland) to tend half the number of a full taxable laborer over sixteen. Sons of ordinary planters, age ten or twelve, often joined their fathers in the fields. . . .

Parents enjoyed their children's help on the plantation until the children left home to marry, set up a household, or work on a nearby farm. Few adolescents lived with or worked for neighbors or kin; in Prince George's in 1733, for instance, three-quarters of sons whose fathers were alive lived at home, and nearly every youth waited until he reached his majority at twenty-one before leaving home. Similar numbers of son remained at home in southside Virginia in the 1750s and 1760s, and the proportion of sons living at home until marriage in Prince George's probably increased in the 1770s.

The birth of children modified the distribution of authority in the household. Fathers expected sons and daughters to obey them while at home, insisted upon the right to approve marriage partners they chose, and demanded their respect even after they matured. Mothers shared parental authority with their husbands and gained sole authority over minor children if their husbands died. Siblings also sustained mutual obligations to each other. Peter Dent, a gentleman and justice, suggested the power of this family hierarchy when he wrote his will in Prince George's County in 1757. He urged of his "Dear Children that they be Dutifull to their Mother During her Life and Loving and Obligeing to Each other the youngest always Submitting to the Eldest in reason and the Eldest bearing with the Infirmitys of the youngest and advising them in the best manner they can that they may Live in Concord all their Lives." . . .

Children's obligations to parents and siblings sometimes dictated financial sacrifice. Fathers often insisted that sons allow their mothers full use of the land they would ultimately inherit. Francis Waring, a gentleman of great wealth who died in Prince George's in 1769, bequeathed his home farm to his son Leonard, "provided he Suffers his Mother to Enjoy the Land which I have Alloted her." Similarly, Thomas Wilson gave son Josiah the home plantation only if he did not interrupt "his Mother during her Life for making use of the Land as she shall think proper." Reciprocal obligations between siblings became especially important after both parents died. Edward Willett, a pewterer, gave all his pewterer's molds and tools to his son William when he died in Prince George's in 1744, "provided he Doth make what necessary pewter the rest of my Children shall want." William Young especially wanted to ensure that his son William find a home after he died. He knew that William was "not Capable of himself to Act soe in the world as to Gitt a Liveing," and accordingly he gave William's part of the estate to his son John in his 1760 will, with the request that John "Assist the Said William," his brother.

Fathers held a potent lever over their children. They rarely turned over ownership of land or slaves to their children before they died, even if they permitted use of this capital during their lifetime. If children failed to obey their fathers, they might find themselves cut out of the parental estate. Robert White, of Prince George's County, refused to bequeath land to his son James in 1768 that he had let him farm for thirty years, because the two argued about religion. James had converted to Anglicanism from Catholicism and served as a vestryman and considered his father an "Ignorant Illerate man wholy Biggotted to all the Follies and Superstitions of the Roman Church." Thirteen years earlier John Anderson of Charles County told his daughter Mary Burch that "his Son James and Daughter Caty were running about and took no Care of him," and though "they expected a great Deal when he died, . . . they should find little of it."

Although couples farmed their land together as long as the marriage lasted, the number of children remaining at home diminished greatly when the couple grew older. In Prince George's in 1776, fewer than two children lived at home with mothers over sixty years old, and between two and three children lived with fathers (who had more often remarried) of the same age. Most of the children in these households were adolescents and young adults, well able to take care of themselves and help provide their parents with a comfortable living in their old age.

Married men and widowers, even those of advanced ages, maintained a household and continued working the ground. Only one of every seven men above sixty in Prince George's in 1776 lived as a dependent in the home of kin or neighbors. Two-thirds resided with their wives, and the rest, only a seventh of the total, were widowers. These proud men usually refused to seek aid from loved ones. Ninian Beall of Thomas, a widower of eighty, headed a household on a small plantation near Bladensburg town but worked no slaves. Two children still lived with him, including a daughter and her husband, but whatever help they provided for him was under his direction as the master of the family. . . .

Women faced far greater problems when their husbands died, because of their inferior social status and lack of experience in operating a plantation. Though widows possessed the legal right of the feme sole [single woman] to buy and sell property and act for themselves, most widows in their twenties and thirties probably remarried, thereby losing their legal rights. Older women, whose numbers increased as the century progressed, usually did not remarry but remained widows the rest of their lives. However long a widow stayed single, she needed more than legal rights to support her children. Husbands recognized the economic problems their widows would have and tried to ease their burdens in two ways. First, they often appointed their wives executors of their estate, thereby guaranteeing that they would control all the familial property while the estate passed through probate. And, second, they bequeathed their wives sufficient property to ensure that profitable farming would continue.

Although planters almost always named wives as executors of their estates during the first half of the eighteenth century, they began to question their wives' ability to administer their property as the century progressed. Between 1710 and 1760, planters in tidewater York, St. Mary's, and Prince George's counties sometimes appointed a mature son or, less frequently, another kinsman or friend as coexecutor, but men excluded widows from executorships in only a tenth of the wills in the three counties. In the 1760s and 1770s, however, the proportion of planters in St. Mary's County who appointed adult sons or kinsmen to help wives administer their estates doubled. . . . Frontiersmen used their wills to assert an authority over their wives that might have been more contested in the less-settled piedmont, and sought to protect their children from second husbands. Though two-thirds of these men named wives as executors in the 1750s and 1760s and nearly half continued this practice through the 1790s, they usually appointed a son or friend to help administer the estate. As the county developed and more older men with adult sons died, fathers turned to their sons rather than to their wives and named them sole executors twice as often in the 1790s as in the 1750s.

Eighteenth-century tidewater planters usually gave their wives sufficient property to support their children and live comfortably after the children left home. Despite the increasing age of widows (and the growing number of adult sons), there was remarkable continuity in the powers tidewater planters gave their widows throughout the colonial era. Widows, by law, were entitled to a third of the husband's estate, and they could reject any smaller bequest and demand to reveive their thirds. Only about a third of the planters in tidewater Maryland during the colonial period limited their wives to their dower rights or attempted to have them accept less, and only a tenth granted them property on the condition that they remained widows. . . . Though widows could operate the farms as they saw fit, their husbands often limited their control by bequeathing the property to a particular child or children after the death of their mother. . . .

Although widows usually possessed legal authority over the husband's estate, any widow's actual power depended more upon the age of her sons than on the legal terms of her husband's will. As long as all the children remained minors, the widow as executor controlled most of her husband's estate, but as sons came of age, they took their portions with them or stayed at home uneasily waiting for their mothers to die so they could inherit the home plantation. Tensions between widows and their adult sons over the use of property occurred because of unresolved tensions within domestic patriarchalism between the authority of mothers (whom sons were bound to obey) and the dominance of adult men over women.

Wealthy planters in Prince George's County sometimes tried to prevent this discord between widows and sons by provisions in their wills. In 1751 Daniel Carroll, a wealthy merchant and gentleman planter, urged his wife and children to consult several neighboring kinsmen and friends "In case any Difference or Dispute shou'd hereafter unfortunately happen Between my said loving Wife and any of my Dear Children, either about the management or Division of any part of the Estate." Other planters admonished widows and sons to allow each other to live peaceably on their allotted plantations. In 1744 William Tannehill of Prince George's ordered his wife not to "hinder my son James to get all upon the back branch if he is so minded." Similarly, Charles Walker granted his wife her dower rights in land in 1730 if she permitted their son Joseph, age fifteen, "to have Liberty to live on some part of" it "and theron Work and have the benefit of his Labour, He no ways Interrupting . . . his Mother." . . .

As sons took their portions and daughters married and depleted the estate yet further, widows found themselves unable to earn a subsistence and dependent upon their children for their bread. Only a quarter of the widows in the county in 1776 over the age of fifty-seven maintained their own households. The rest lived with sons or neighbors. Widows frequently lost control even over their own plantation when the son who would inherit the property came of age. Unmarried sons as young as twenty or twenty-one who lived at home assumed the position of head of household from their widowed mothers nearly two-thirds of the time.

Some women, ill prepared to operate plantations, gladly turned over the farm to their sons in return for support. When Thomas Richardson of Prince George's came "of age to receive his fortune by his Fathers Will," his mother Susannah said "that she did not care to put herself to the Trouble of paying him his Fortune" but "had agreed to go Equally halfs in every thing." She was apparently satisfied with the arrangement: Not only did Thomas reopen the family tavern, but his mother felt that "her son Thomas Richardson was very Carefull and that if he continued to be so and took care of the House, she would take care in the House and would not begrudge him the half of every thing that should be made and raised on the plantation."

A son's assertion of authority might, however, leave his mother resentful and force her to find ways to maintain some autonomy. Sarah Brook widow of John of Calvert County, lived with her son Roger in the 1740s and 1750s, when she was in her fifties and sixties. Though Roger operated the plantation, his mother still nominally owned much of it. When he complained that "she did not give his two Negroes Meat enough," she replied that he should "kill Meat of his own as he had Hoggs and then he might give them what he pleased as he was not contented with what She gave them." She wanted "to keep the Staff in her own Hand better her Children should come to her than she to go to them," but her attempts at autonomy were not very successful. She distrubuted all her property to her sons James and Roger, and Roger "made use of all the crops every Year . . . without any Division and disposed of it as he thought proper for his own use" despite the desires of his mother. She depended upon him for subsistence, and without him would have to "beg my Bread from Door to Door," yet even this minimal care was given only grudgingly, for she complained that she had "no Body to do anything for me not so much as to bring me a Coal of Fire to light my Pipe."

Morality, Virtue, and the Family Economy

Parents in the eighteenth-century Chesapeake were responsible for training their children to take their proper place in adult society and teaching them the reciprocal responsibilities of parents and children, husbands and wives, masters and slaves, and magistrates and citizens. All education in the region, whether formal literacy training in schools or informal instruction in the home, aimed at this end. Sons who learned proper behavior in this society were ultimately rewarded with sufficient property from their fathers' estates to permit them to start their own patriarchal families.

Although tidewater planters infrequently expressed emotional religious commitments, they understood the necessity of strong moral education. The Reverend Thomas Craddock of Baltimore County probably expressed the common Anglican view on moral training in a sermon in 1752 on a murder in his parish. The murderers both ignored moral education *and* deprived the victim's children of that training by killing a nurturing parent. If the murderers had "been trained up in the ways of religion and virtue, they wou'd never have been guilty of this wickedness," Cradock told his congregation. But the deed was done, and "a young, defenseless tribe of children" lost "the care and assistance of their father or mother," the adults responsible "for their *spiritual,* as well as temporal interest," and reduced them "to a state of indigence, who, had their parents liv'd, might have had a sufficient competency." To prevent similar acts in the future, masters and fathers ought to be "conspicuous in the worship of God, in acts of justice and charity to man; in a *Spiritual* care of your families . . . ; and such a conduct, with the blessing of God, may have a happy influence o'er many of them."

Planters and their wives shared and on occasion expressed this concern. The *Maryland Gazette* eulogized Rebeccah Sanders, when she died at seventy-five in 1752 in Anne Arundel County, not only because she had "a just Sense of Religion herself" but also because "she instilled the Principles of it thro' her numerous Family; and having educated her Children in the Paths of Virtue and Piety, had the inexpressible satisfaction . . . to reflect that they were each an Honour to her." Several planters in Prince George's County admonished their wives in similar tones in their wills. In 1734, Archibald Edmonston asked his widow and son James to "inspect into the behavior and deportment of my Son Thomas Edmonston," who was to be under their control during his minority. When James Adams, a middling planter, died in 1750, he asked that his son John "be bound till he arrive at the Age of twenty-one years to Some good honest Man, that will Endeavour to Instruct him in his Duty to God, himself, and his Neighbour[s]."

In an ideal society, each person knows how to behave in the presence of social inferiors and superiors. The children of slaveholders—a majority of the white populace—saw their parents deprive slaves of freedom, expropriate their labor, and barter them from hand to hand and learned thereby that they could treat black people with contempt they should never use on their white peers. Thomas Jefferson best captured the consequences of this training in a well-known passage: "The whole commerce between master and slave is a perpetual exercise in the most boisterous passions, the most unremitting despotism on the one part, and degrading submissions, on the other." As "the parent storms," Jefferson insisted, "the child looks on, catches the lineaments of wrath, puts on the same airs in the circle of smaller slaves, gives a loose to the worst of passions, and thus . . . educated and daily exercised in tyranny, cannot but be stamped by it."

Parents instructed their children to take their proper place in white society by training them to perform tasks appropriate to their sex. Fathers took their sons with them when they went abroad from the plantation and sent them on errands to nearby farms or to the general store as soon as they could ride horses and accept responsibilities. Most important, they introduced them to the world of male work by teaching them how to cultivate tobacco and grains and instilled in them the male ethic of aggressive behavior by taking them hunting.

Daughters stayed closer to home and learned both housewifery and their inferior place in the family order from their mothers. The daughters of Robert Carter of Nomini Hall, one of Virginia's richest gentlemen, imitated woman's work at a young age, and Philip Fithian, their tutor, even discovered them one day "stuffing rags and other Lumber under their Gowns just below their Apron-Strings, . . . prodigiously charmed at their resemblance to Pregnant Women!" Mothers were particularly responsible for training their daughters to sew, knit, and spin so they could engage in necessary plantation labor. When Margaret Gough of Calvert County charged her guardians with improperly maintaining her, she considered the fact that she "never was taught to sew and would not have known how to make her own Shifts had her [step-]sister not taught her" to be potent evidence of neglect.

White children learned to identify themselves not only by race and gender but by their position in the social hierarchy. Devereux Jarratt, the son of a prosperous carpenter and slaveholder, grew up in New Kent County, Virginia, in the 1730s and 1740s. He learned as a child that his place was inferior to that of a gentleman's son, and he soon could identify gentlemen both by their demeanor and by the wigs they wore and the coffee and tea they drank, goods not used by his own, somewhat poorer family. "We were accustomed to look upon, what were called *gentle folks*, as beings of a superior order," he wrote in his autobiography. "For my part," he added, "I was quite shy of *them*, and kept off at a humble distance."

Children learned to read and write in order to understand their moral obligations and to help them perform the work demanded of them. Substantial planters sometimes reflected upon these twin goals of formal education. Samuel Pottinger, who died in Prince George's in 1742, directed that his son "be taught to Read write and cast Accompts and my Daughter to Read." Before he died in 1730, Thomas Brooke, a gentleman with many children, similarly requested that his "two youngest Sons . . . be well educated in reading writing and arithmetick and That they shall be brought up in the doctrine and principles of the Church of England."

Since most Chesapeake planters and their wives were barely literate, they had to send their children to school to learn how to read, write, and cipher. Before the middle of the eighteenth century, there were few free schools in Virginia, and private schoolmasters, paid by parents, were in short supply. There was but one schoolteacher for every hundred white families in eight tidewater Virginia parishes in 1724, a figure that implies that each child might attend one short school term. At the same time, only four teachers, each responsible for more than four hundred families, ran schools in two piedmont parishes, and at best they reached a quarter of the children entrusted to their care.

As areas developed, more schools sprang up. In Elizabeth City County, one of Virginia's original shires, the number of schoolmasters grew from two in 1670, to three in 1724, and five in 1782; and at the same time, the number of families each teacher had to serve declined from about eighty-five to sixty-five. The parish schools, furthermore, included an academy where boys might study Latin as well as English. Though Prince George's County was not founded until 1697, there were already several private schools within its borders in 1724, and a free parish school joined them in the 1740s. By 1755, there were between ten and fourteen schoolmasters in the county, each responsible for eighty-five to a hundred families. County schools at that date attracted various kinds of students: although most teachers ran reading schools, one operated a Latin school, another taught practical and advanced mathematics as well as reading and writing, and two women instructed girls in French, sewing, and knitting. . . .

Schools in colonial Virginia did teach their more privileged male students to read and write. About two-thirds of the men born in three tidewater Virginia counties and three-fifths born in five piedmont counties during the first half of the eighteenth century could sign their names as adults. Men with wealthy parents were more likely to learn to sign. Although literacy was nearly universal among planters who owned land and slaves, only two of every five poor tenants could read and write.

Once children learned to read, they had access to a few books. Nearly six of every ten householders living in Prince George's between 1730 and 1769 owned at least one book. Literate parents not only sent their children to school more frequently than their less wealthy, illiterate neighbors, but they also owned books with far greater regularity. Although only a third of the tenant nonslaveholders and about half of the planters who owned land or slaves possessed books, three-quarters of freeholders who worked slaves on their own land owned a book or two.

A majority of literate parents owned a few edifying or practical volumes that they used to teach morality and farm management to their children. Anglican parents used the Bible and the Book of Common Prayer, supplemented by such patriarchal tomes as Richard Allestree's seventeenth-century *Whole Duty of Man* as guides for proper behavior. The Bible was the most important book in most plantation libraries; nearly all literate families owned one, and sometimes they possessed no other book. Parents and schoolmasters commonly taught children to read "distinctly in the Bible," because the Bible was God's literal word and, moreover, no other book contained so many edifying stories and moral principles or had such a prominent role (along with the prayer book and psalter) in divine services.

Planter families commonly counted an almanac among their small bundle of books. Nearly two-thirds of the ten thousand volumes sold in the 1750s and 1760s at the *Virginia Gazette* office in Williamsburg were almanacs. Almanacs contained a broad collection of information useful to planters, including monthly calendars,

The wealthiest planters in the Chesapeake region built more sumptuous homes in the eighteenth century, displaying the profits from tobacco production in the size and opulence of their households. Sabine Hall, pictured here, was the homestead of Landon Carter, one of the largest and wealthiest slaveholders in the eighteenth-century Chesapeake.

data on the time of sunrise and sunset, weather predictions, the distance between the colony's villages and towns, and essays on scientific and medical topics. Moreover, planters could jot down their thoughts or farm accounts in the volume's margins and blank pages. And finally, a Virginia almanac cost only 7.5 pennies each year—a cheap price every planter could afford!

Since most boys received only a brief introduction to literacy, and girls often none, few people in the Chesapeake region read for pleasure or intellectual stimulation. Only sons of the wealthy gentlemen, many of whom attended Latin schools or the College of William and Mary, could participate in a high literary culture or understand the political and philosophical articles found in the region's two newspapers. (Less-educated men, of course, read almanacs, Bibles, and newspaper advertisements.) This lack of childhood training and the subsequent minimal adult interest were reflected in planters' libraries: only magistrates owned law books, and only one literate planter in six possessed a Latin classic, political tract, or volume of history.

White children in the Chesapeake were trained to take their place in society through repeated instruction by adults. Parents taught their children patriarchal principles at home and sent them to school and church to reinforce the lesson. When preachers alluded to biblical passages to sustain a moral principle, parish children understood what they meant; when parents wished to explain the social hierarchy of the Chesapeake to their offspring, they chose to read the Bible or the *Whole Duty of Man*. Children observed and learned to emulate the fundamentals of proper deportment every day at home, in the tobacco fields, at school and church, and in visiting kindred.

Children needed property as well as moral lessons to be able to take their appropriate place in white society. The ownership of land and slaves buttressed the moral order of the region by making the perpetuation of domestic patriarchy possible. Parents therefore tried to ensure that all their children possessed enough property to replicate the family government of their childhood, a goal that led some planters to reject primogeniture (still a part of the law of intestacy) in their wills. In societies where patriarchy and political order were strongly connected, primogeniture maintained the social and political hierarchy that linked king and father, but chattel slavery helped sever that link by making each person a potential master as well as parent. Since servile work and dependence were identified with slaves, all men ideally should have owned land, the hallmark of independence. Planters who lived in frontier areas could readily distribute land to all their sons, and sometimes to their daughters. Wealthy planters gave each of their sons a fully stocked plantation, thereby maximizing the number of men able to behave like patriarchs in their own families. Poorer men favored one or two of their sons, hoping thereby that at least one son could emulate his father, but, of course, thereby reducing the total number of men who could play patriarchal roles in the future. Increased population density reduced the size of landholdings so much that primogeniture began to rise even among middling yeomen. This increased favoritism in the redistribution of resources to eldest sons created a gap between the expectation that all children ought to form their own domestic patriarchies and their ability to do so. . . .

As population density increased in tidewater during the eighteenth century, the typical size of landholdings diminished, and more and more planters excluded one or more of their sons from land distribution in order to give working plantations to the remaining sons. Only one testator in seven in Prince George's County favored one or two sons or practiced primogeniture during the 1730s, when frontier land was still avaiable; but after 1740, nearly all the lands were soon taken, and the proportion of men who favored older sons doubled. Planters who gave all their land to their oldest son owned an average of only 180 acres; and if they had divided their land equally among all their sons, each son would have received only 54 acres, about half the minimum needed to make tobacco. Similarly, planters who gave land to their two or three oldest sons, excluding the rest, bequeathed an average of only 101 acres to each favored son. If they had given all their sons an equal share, each son would have farmed 57 acres. Since the price of land increased more rapidly than any other commodity during the 1760s and 1770s, sons of a small freeholder who inherited land enjoyed a great advantage over their landless brothers, no matter how equitably the rest of their father's assets were disbursed.

Fathers gave each daughter and son a portion of their personal estate sufficient to set up housekeeping, sometimes specifically granting each some livestock, kitchen utensils, bedding, and slaves. While sons received a stocked plantation, daughters took personal goods bequeathed to them as a dowry. Most testators in Prince George's County attempted an equitable distribution of their personal goods: more than half of them divided their movable property equally among all their children, including those who inherited land; another quarter granted landless children a larger share than children with land; and the remaining planters favored some sons at the expense of other children. An equal distribution of movable goods often favored older sons over their siblings because much of the personal property, but not the land, could be used to pay debts the decedent owed. Parents in neighboring Charles County, Maryland, attempted to equalilze bequests by granting land almost exclusively to sons, but gave somewhat greater numbers of slaves to daughters. Fathers bequeathed most male field hands to sons and most female slaves to daughters. These slaves, of course, became the personal property of the daughters' husbands when they married, but fathers apparently expected that some of the female slaves, bequeathed to daughters would remain with them as personal servants. . . .

Domestic Patriarchy within Chesapeake Society

Although seventeenth-century immigrants to the Chesapeake colonies found the practice of domestic patriarchy difficult, by the early eighteenth century landed families in the tidewater region had developed a distinctive patriarchal form of family government and refined it as the century progressed. In these landed and slave-holding families, women obeyed their husbands and kept to their proper place, and children deferred to both parents, but especially to their fathers. Planters educated their children to behave respectfully and used their control of property that adult children wanted to reinforce this lesson.

Even though patriarchal behavior was limited to the family, it did restrain the competitive way that men behaved in informal groups and in political discourse. Although political relations between gentlemen and yeomen were based upon principles of reciprocity rather than upon any analogies with paternal power in the family, when men associated, they replicated the hierarchy of the family by dividing themselves into groups based upon wealth, status, and education. Yeomen learned the habit of deference in their own families and therefore understood the superior place of gentlemen in the political order.

The influence of domestic patriarchy was most strongly felt by freeholding families in tidewater, where resources were becoming scarce. Tidewater slaveholders, whose families stayed on the land for generations, wielded a substantial influence over the behavior of wives and children. But men needed land and slaves in order to follow patriarchal norms. Poor tenants had too few resources to hold their children to the ancestral home and needed all the labor they could muster, including that of their wives, to survive economically, and the poorest freeholders were not much better situated. Migrants to piedmont Virginia, in contrast, lived in a raw society with abundant resources, where a son could always find cheap land just beyond his father's plantation, and he therefore had less incentive to defer to his father.

Since patriarchal norms were not always clear, conflicts between members of partriarchal families sometimes occurred. Three kinds of conflict may have been particularly commen. Because patriarchalism only weakly proscribed violence against wives, husbands sometimes tried to whip their wives into submission, a practice that eventually could lead even the most deferential wife to run away from home. Second, fathers who wanted to hold on to their land may have fought with sons who wished to be fully independent. And third, partiarchal norms did not rank the authority of widowed mothers and adult sons in the family—and once the patriarch had died, the struggle for authority that ensured sometimes led to conflict between mothers and sons.

Patriarchalism, finally, weakened the bonds between slave and master. Fathers distributed slaves among all their children when they died, much like other kinds of personal property. Since few men owned enough slaves to bequeath entire families to each child, they inevitably separated black husbands from wives and parents from children. Those masters who separated families broke one of the primary rules of a paternalistic relationship by arbitrarily breaking up families and thereby lost some of the power they had over the personal lives of their slaves.

Questions for Study and Review

1. How important were sex ratios—the number of women in a society for every one hundred men—in determining women's life chances and choices in the American colonies?

2. How might a domestic patriarch in a Chesapeake community have responded to the Grosvenor-Sessions abortion case?

3. In what ways would relations among husbands and wives and parents and children in African American communities have differed from those in white communities in the Chesapeake?

4. Drawing on the articles read thus far, in what ways did economic status and race shape family relations among women and men who resided in New England and Chesapeake colonies in the seventeenth and eighteenth centuries?

Suggested Readings and Web Sites

Kirsten Fischer, *Suspect Relations: Sex, Race and Resistance in Colonial North Carolina* (2002)
Cynthia A. Kierner, *Beyond the Household: Women's Place in the Early South* (1998)
Daniel Blake Smith, *Inside the Great House: Planter Family Life in Eighteenth-century Chesapeake Society* (1980)
Steven M. Stowe, *Intimacy and Power in the Old South: Ritual in the Lives of the Planters* (1987)
North American Women's Diaries
  http://www.lib.virginia.edu/diaries.html
The Geography of Slavery in Virginia
  http://www.vcdh.virginia.edu/gos
Probing the Past, Probate Inventory
  http://chnm.gmu.edu/probateinventory/

The Spanish had claimed vast lands in the West Indies and South America long before the English began their colonial quest. Yet it was English and French explorers, traders, soldiers, and settlers who controlled the Atlantic coast of North America into the mid-eighteenth century. Then the British victory in the French and Indian War in 1763 secured British control of the area that comprises present-day Canada and much of the upper Midwest in the United States. Spain, meanwhile, decided to extend its reach northward, from Mexico and the Baja peninsula into Alta (or upper) California. In all these areas, European diseases, to which native peoples had no immunities, decimated Indian populations.

The Spanish conquest of Alta California differed from the British or French efforts farther east. The English focused on settlement rather than conquest, bringing large numbers of families to North America from the seventeenth century on. The French sent far fewer people to North America, mainly Catholic missionaries and fur traders. Still, the fur traders developed close ties with native peoples. Although the Spanish also sought to establish a Catholic stronghold in North America, they depended more heavily on military force to subordinate local Indians. Moreover, without valuable trade goods like furs, California natives had little hope of bargaining for better treatment.

Relations between Europeans and Indians were also shaped, of course, by the native peoples who lived in the areas being conquered and colonized. The British, for instance, confronted large and powerful native societies on the Atlantic coast, including the Powhatan and Iroquois Confederacies and the Pequot and Yamasee Nations. The Spanish, on the other hand, faced relatively small and scattered bands of Indians in Alta California, which made resistance to conquest far more difficult.

These different patterns of colonization and conquest had distinct effects on the relations between European colonizers and native women. In French North America, early efforts by the Jesuits to convert native women and men were often brutal. Still, in the long run, fur traders had far more contact with Indians than did the Catholic Church. Anxious to establish working relations with those villages that could supply beaver pelts and other trade items, Frenchmen (and nearly all fur traders were men) developed close ties to Indian women. Indeed, some Frenchmen married native women according to the "custom of the country," that is, according to Indian custom rather than French law or Catholic ceremony. This does not mean that French fur traders never abused Indian women, but rather that their economic interests encouraged them to establish domestic and commercial relations with particular women and, through them, with their families and communities.

Among the English, we have already explored the slow process of contact, conflict, and negotiation that characterized the settlement of Virginia. Throughout the seventeenth century in New England and the Chesapeake, English colonists

and soldiers confronted native peoples with guns and swords. Protestant missionaries also joined British efforts along the eastern seaboard, but Indian converts
were relatively rare. Overall, however, British colonization depended largely on
the settlement of families. By the late seventeenth century, most English colonies
in North America were comprised of families, rather than single men. The presence of European women often curtailed the sexual abuse of native women, but
it also ensured the rapid growth of English settlements and fed the colonists' thirst
for more land.

Antonia Castañeda shows how different life was for California Indians than
for their counterparts on the Atlantic coast. She paints a vivid portrait of the
Spanish conquest of Alta California, revealing the brutality faced by Amerindian
women and men throughout the late 1700s. Although Catholic leaders
protested the sexual violence committed by soldiers, Castañeda makes clear
that it was the Spanish policy of subduing native peoples and the distance of
Spanish authorities from California outposts that minimized the effects of even
the most forceful protests. The Spanish conquest thus had devastating effects
on Amerindians in California for generations to come.

In her analysis, Castañeda explores the interplay between sexual conquest, the
subordination of women, and the racial conquest of Amerindians (the term she
uses to denote California Indians). She uses the phrase "sex/gender" to highlight the
ways that Spanish ideas about the racial inferiority of Amerindians and the sexual
immorality and vulnerability of Amerindian women lead to institutionalized sexual
violence as a weapon of conquest. Her insights contribute to a more general understanding of the ways sexual violence is employed in periods of conquest and war.

Sexual Violence in the Politics and Policies of Conquest: Amerindian Women and the Spanish Conquest of Alta California
ANTONIA I. CASTAÑEDA

In the morning, six or seven soldiers would set out together . . . and go
to the distant *rancherías* [villages] even many leagues away. When both
men and women at the sight of them would take off running . . . the
soldiers, adept as they are at lassoing cows and mules, would lasso Indian
women—who then became prey for their unbridled lust. Several Indian
men who tried to defend the women were shot to death.

Junipero Serra, 1773

From *Building with Our Hands: New Directions in Chicana Studies,* eds. Adela de la Torre and Beatríz M. Pesquera.

Junipero Serra, pictured here overseeing the establishment of a new mission, led the efforts of Spanish Catholics who founded nine missions in Alta, California from 1769–1782. Under Serra's leadership, Catholic missionaries offered California Indians food, clothing, and religious training, but also forced them to live and work at the missions.

In words reminiscent of sixteenth-century chroniclers Bernal Díaz del Castillo and Bartolomé de las Casas, the father president of the California missions, Junipero Serra, described the depredations of the soldiers against Indian women in his reports and letters to Viceroy Antonio María Bucareli and the father guardian of the College of San Fernando, Rafaél Verger. Sexual assaults against native women began shortly after the founding of the presidio and mission at Monterey in June 1770, wrote Serra, and continued throughout the length of California. The founding of each new mission and presidio brought new reports of sexual violence.

The despicable actions of the soldiers, Serra told Bucareli in 1773, were severely retarding the spiritual and material conquest of California. The native people were resisting missionization. Some were becoming warlike and hostile because of the soldiers' repeated outrages against the women. The assaults resulted in Amerindian attacks, which the soldiers countered with unauthorized reprisals, thereby further straining the capacity of the small military force to staff the presidios and guard the missions. Instead of pacification and order, the soldiers provoked greater conflict and thus jeopardized the position of the church in this region.

Serra was particularly alarmed about occurrences at Mission San Gabriel. "Since the district is the most promising of all the missions," he wrote to Father Verger, "this mission gives me the greatest cause for anxiety; the secular arm down there was guilty of the most heinous crimes, killing the men to take their wives." Father Serra related that on October 10, 1771, within a month of its having been founded, a large group of Indians suddenly attacked two soldiers who were on horseback and tried to kill the one who had outraged a woman. The soldiers retaliated. "A few days later," Serra continued, "as he went out to gather the herd of cattle . . . and [it] seems more likely to get himself a woman, a soldier, along with some others, killed the principal Chief of the gentiles; they cut off his head and brought it in triumph back to the mission."

The incident prompted the Amerindians of the coast and the sierra, mortal enemies until that time, to convene a council to make peace with each other and join forces to eliminate the Spaniards. The council planned to attack the mission on October 16 but changed the plan after a new contingent of troops arrived at the mission. Despite this narrowly averted disaster, the soldiers assigned to Mission San Gabriel continued their outrages.

The soldiers' behavior not only generated violence on the part of the native people as well as resistance to missionization, argued Serra; it also took its toll on the missionaries, some of whom refused to remain at their mission sites. In his 1773 memorial to Bucareli, Serra lamented the loss of one of the missionaries, who could not cope with the soldiers' disorders at San Gabriel. The priest was sick at heart, Serra stated: "He took to his bed, when he saw with his own eyes a soldier actually committing deeds of shame with an Indian who had come to the mission, and even the children who came to the mission were not safe from their baseness."

Conditions at other missions were no better. Missions San Luis Obispo also lost a priest because of the assaults on Indian women. After spending two years as the sole missionary at San Luis, Father Domingo Juncosa asked for and received permission to return to Mexico because he was "shocked at the scandalous conduct of the soldiers" and could not work under such abominable conditions. Even before San Luis Obispo was founded in the early fall of 1772, Tichos women had cause to fear. The most notorious molesters of non-Christian women were among the thirteen soldiers sent on a bear hunt to this area during the previous winter of starvation at Monterey.

The establishment of new missions subjected the women of each new area to sexual assaults. Referring to the founding of the mission at San Juan Capistrano, Serra wrote that "it seems all the sad experiences that we went through at the beginning have come to life again. The soldiers, without any restraint or shame, have behaved like brutes toward the Indian women." From this mission also, the priests reported to Serra that the soldier-guards went at night to the nearby villages to assault the women and that hiding the women did not restrain the brutes, who beat the men to force them to reveal where the women were hidden. Non-Christian Indians in the vicinity of the missions were simply not safe. They were at the mercy of soldiers with horses and guns.

In 1773, a case of rape was reported at San Luis Rey, one at San Diego, and two cases at Monterey the following year. Serra expressed his fears and concern to Governor Felipe de Neve, who was considering establishing a new presidio in the channel of Santa Barbara. Serra told Neve that he took it for granted that the insulting and scandalous conduct of the soldiers "would be the same as we had experienced in other places which were connected with presidios. Perhaps this one would be worse."

Native women and their communities were profoundly affected by the sexual attacks and attendant violence. California Amerindians were peaceable, non-aggressive people who highly valued harmonious relationships. Physical violence and the infliction of bodily harm on one another were virtually unknown. Women did not fear men. Rape rarely, if ever, occurred. If someone stole from another or caused another's death, societal norms required that the offending party make reparations to the individual and/or the family. Appropriate channels to rectify a wrong without resorting to violence existed.

Animosity, when it did surface, was often worked out ritualistically—for example, through verbal battles in the form of war songs, or song fights that lasted eight days, or encounters in which the adversaries threw stones across a river at each other with no intent actually to hit or physically injure the other party. Even among farming groups such as the Colorado River people, who practiced warfare and took women and children captive, female captives were never sexually molested. The Yumas believed that intimate contact with enemy women caused sickness.

Thus, neither the women nor their people were prepared for the onslaught of aggression and violence the soldiers unleashed against them. They were horrified and terrified. One source reported that women of the San Gabriel and other southern missions raped by the soldiers were considered contaminated and obliged to undergo an extensive purification, which included a long course of sweating, the drinking of herbs, and other forms of purging. This practice was consistent with the people's belief that sickness was caused by enemies. "But their disgust and abhorrence," states the same source, "never left them till many years after." Moreover, any child born as a result of these rapes, and apparently every child with white blood born among them for very long time, was strangled and buried.

Father Pedro Font, traveling overland from Tubac to Monterey with the Anza expedition between September 1775 and May 1776, recorded the impact of the violence on the native people he encountered. Font's diary verifies the terror in which native Californians, especially the women, now lived. Everybody scattered and fled at the sight of Spaniards. The women hid. They no longer moved about with freedom and ease. The people were suspicious and hostile. The priests were no longer welcome in the living quarters.

The Quabajay people of the Santa Barbara Channel, Font wrote, "appear to us to be gentle and friendly, not war-like. But it will not be easy to reduce [subordinate] them for they are displeased with the Spaniards for what they have done to them, now taking their fish and their food . . . now stealing their women and abusing them." Upon encountering several unarmed Indians on Friday, February 23, Font commented that "the women were very cautious and hardly one left their huts, because the soldiers of Monterey . . . had offended them with various excesses."

At one village, Font noted, he was unable to see the women close at hand because as soon as the Indians saw his party, "they all hastily hid in their huts, especially the girls, the men remaining outside blocking the door and taking care that nobody should go inside." Font attempted to become acquainted with the people of another village on the channel. He went to the door, but "they shut the inner door on me . . . this is the result of the extortions and outrages which the soldiers have perpetrated when in their journeys they have passed along the Channel, especially at the beginning." Font echoed Serra's concern that the sexual assaults and other outrages had severely retarded missionization in California.

Serra and his co-religionists had great cause for concern, because the missions were not meeting their principal objective of converting Amerindians into loyal Catholic subjects who would repel invading European forces from these shores. By the end of 1773, in the fifth year of the occupation of Alta California, fewer than five hundred baptisms and only sixty-two marriages had been performed in the five missions then existing. Since the marriages probably represented the total adult converts, that meant that the remaining four hundred converts were children. These dismal statistics fueled arguments for abandoning the California missions. While various reasons may be cited for the failure to attract adult converts, certainly the sexual attacks and the impact of that violence on women and their communities were primary among them.

Few historians have recognized that the sexual extortion and abuse of native women gravely affected the political, military, religious, and social developments on this frontier. In 1943, Sherburne F. Cook commented that "the entire problem of sexual relations between whites and the natives, although one which was regarded as very serious by the founders of the province, has apparently escaped detailed consideration by later historians." Cook tackled the issue in demographic terms and wrote about the catastrophic decline in the Indian population as a result of alien diseases, including venereal diseases, brought in by Europeans, as well as other maladies of the conquest.

Almost thirty years later, Edwin A. Beilharz wrote that "the major causes of friction between Spaniard and Indian were the abuse of Indian women and the forced labor of Indian men. . . . Of the two, the problem of restraining the soldiers from assaulting Indian women was the more serious." In his study of the administration of Governor Felipe de Neve, Beilharz notes that Neve recognized the seriousness of the problem and tried to curb the abuses.

Since the 1970s, the decade that saw both the reprinting of Cook's work and the publication of the Beilharz study, the development of gender as a category of analysis has enabled us to reexamine Spanish expansion to Alta California with new questions about sex and gender. Cook, Beilharz, and other scholars initiated but did not develop the discussion about the centrality of sex/gender issues to the politics and policies of conquest.

It is clear that the sexual exploitation of native women and related violence seriously threatened the political and military objectives of the colonial enterprise in California. Repeated attacks against women and summary reprisals against men who dared to interfere undermined the efforts of the priests to attract Amerindians to the missions and to Christianity. They also thwarted whatever attempts the military authorities might make to elicit political or military allegiance from the native peoples.

From the missionaries' point of view, the attacks had more immediate, deleterious consequences for the spiritual conquest of California, because such actions belied significant principles of the Catholic moral theology they were trying to inculcate. As the primary agents of Christianization/Hispanicization, the missionaries argued that they could not teach and Amerindians could not learn and obey the moral strictures against rape, abduction, fornication, adultery, and all forms of sexual impurity while the soldiers persisted in their licentiousness and immorality. Their actions repudiated the very morality the friars were to inculcate.

Early conflict between ecclesiastical and civil-military officials over deployment and discipline of the mission escort soon gave rise to constant bitter disputes centering on the question of authority and jurisdiction over the Indians in California. The conflict over control of the Indians revolved around the issue of their segregation from the non-Indian population. Rooted in the early conquest and consequent development of colonial Indian policy, the issue has been extensively discussed by other historians. The concern here is to examine it specifically from the point of view of sex/gender and to define a context for explaining why, despite strenuous efforts by church and state alike, there was little success in arresting the attacks on Indian women.

Serra, for his part, blamed the military commanders and, once appointed, the governor. They were, he said, lax in enforcing military discipline and unconcerned about the moral fiber of their troops. They failed to punish immoral soldiers who assaulted native women, were flagrantly incontinent, or took Amerindian women as concubines. In California, he stated, secular authorities not only condoned the soldiers' assaults on Indian women but interfered with the missionaries' efforts to counter the abuse, and thereby exceeded their authority with respect to Amerindians.

To argue his case against Lieutenant Pedro Fages, the military commander, and to muster political and economic support for the California establishments, Serra made the arduous trip to Mexico City for an audience with Viceroy Bucareli. He left California in September of 1772 and arrived in Mexico the following February. At the viceroy's request, Serra submitted a lengthy work entitled "Report on the General Conditions and Needs of the Missions and Thirty-Two Suggestions for Improving the Government of the Missions." Serra addressed sex/gender issues as part of several grievances against Fages's command. His recommendations for curtailing the sexual violence and general malfeasance of the soldiers were that Fages should be removed and that Spaniards who married Indian women should be rewarded.

Once the viceroy had removed the lieutenant, Serra continued, he should give strict orders to Fages's successor that, upon the request of any missionary, "he should remove the soldier or soldiers who give bad example, especially in the matter of incontinence . . . and send, in their place, another or others who are not known as immoral or scandalous."

Drawing on colonial tradition established much earlier in New Spain, wherein colonial officials encouraged intermarriage with Amerindian noblewomen in order to advance particular political, military, religious, or social interests, Serra suggested that men who married newly Christianized "daughters of the land" be rewarded. In the second to last of his thirty-two suggestions, Serra asked Bucareli to "allow a bounty for those, be they soldiers or not, who enter into the state of marriage with girls of that faraway country, new Christian converts."

Serra specified the three kinds of bounty to be given the individual: an animal for his own use immediately upon being married; two cows and a mule from the royal herd after he had worked the mission farms for a year or more; and, finally, allotment of a piece of land. Since soldiers were subject to being transferred from one mission or presidio to another, Serra further recommended that he who married a native woman should be allowed to remain permanently attached to his wife's mission.

With this recommendation, which he discussed in more detail in a subsequent letter to the viceroy, Serra hoped to solve several related problems. He sought to curb the sexual attacks on Indian women as well as to induce soldiers to remain and become permanent settlers in Alta California. Theoretically, soldiers would thereby remain on the frontier, and formal and permanent unions with Indian women would allay the natives' mistrust and help to forge a bond between them and the soldiers. These marriages would thus help to ease Indian-military tensions while also cementing Catholic family life in the region.

It was equally important to remove temptation and opportunity for licentious behavior. Thus, in a second memorial to the viceroy, written in April of 1773, a little over a month after his report, Serra forcefully argued against the proposal that the annual supply ships from San Blas be replaced with mule trains coming overland. In addition to the greater expense of an overland supply line, he reasoned, the presence of one hundred guards and muleteers crossing the country would add to "the plague of immorality" running rampant in California.

The document that resulted from the official review of Serra's memorial, the *Reglamento Provisional*—generally known as the *Echeveste Regulations*—was the first regulatory code drawn up for California. The *Echeveste Regulations* acted favorably on twenty-one of Serra's thirty-two original recommendations, including the removal of Fages as military commander.

Implementation of the new regulations, however, did not stop the abuse of women or the immorality of the soldiers. Serra continued to blame the civil-military authorities. He charged Captain Fernando de Rivera y Moncada, who replaced Fages, with currying the soldiers' favor; and he subsequently accused the newly appointed governor, Felipe de Neve, of antireligiosity and anticlericalism. Thus, in the summary of Franciscan complaints against Neve, which Francisco Panagua, guardian of the College of San Fernando, sent Viceroy Mayorga in 1781, Father Panagua wrote that "another consequence . . . of the aversion which the said Governor [Neve] has for the religious, is that the subordinates . . . live very libidinously in unrestrained and scandalous incontinence as they use at will Indian women of every class and strata." Serra further charged that Neve allowed fornication among the soldiers, "because, so I have heard him say, . . . it is winked at in Rome and tolerated in Madrid."

Serra's charges against Fages, Rivera, and Neve were not well founded. As head of the California establishments, each was fully congnizant that the soldiers' excesses not only undermined military discipline, and thus their own command, but also seriously jeopardized the survival of the missions and the presidios. Fundamentally, the assaults against women were unwarranted, unprovoked, hostile acts that established conditions of war on this frontier. Although the native peoples by and large did not practice warfare, they were neither docile nor passive in the face of repeated assaults. The people of the South were especially aggressive. The country between San Diego and San Gabriel remained under Indian control for a long time. It was in this region that the Indians marshaled their strongest forces and retaliated against the Spaniards. Some of the engagements, such as the one at San Gabriel in 1771, were minor skirmishes. Others were full-fledged attacks. In 1775 at Mission San Diego, for example, a force of eight hundred razed the mission, killed one priest and two artisans, and seriously wounded two soldiers. Women participated and sometimes even planned and/or led the attacks. In October 1785, Amerindians from eight *rancherías* united under the leadership of one woman and three men and launched an attack on Mission San Gabriel for the purpose of killing all the Spaniards. Toypurina, the twenty-four-year-old medicine woman of the Japchivit *ranchería*, used her considerable influence as a medicine woman to persuade six of the eight villages to join the rebellion. The attack was thwarted. Toypurina was captured and punished along with the other three leaders.

Throughout their terms, Fages, Rivera, and Neve were keenly aware that Amerindians greatly outnumbered Spain's military force in the fledgling settlement and that, ultimately, the soldiers could not have staved off a prolonged Indian attack. Neve's greatest fear, expressed in his request to Bucareli for more commissioned officers, was that "if an affair of this kind [disorders caused by soldiers] ever results in a defeat of our troops, it will be irreparable if they [the Indians] come to know their power. We must prevent this with vigor."

Therefore, during their respective administrations, the military authorities enforced Spain's legal codes, as well as imperial policy regarding segregation of Amerindians from non-Indians as a protective measure for the former. They prosecuted soldiers for major and minor crimes, and they issued their own edicts to curb the soldiers' abuse of Amerindians in general and women in particular. Their authority, however, was circumscribed by Spain's highly centralized form of government.

While the governor of the Californias was authorized to try major criminal cases such as those involving homicide and rape, judgment sentence were decided at the viceregal level in Mexico City. . . .

A 1773 case illustrates the complexity of legal procedures. This case—in which a corporal, Mateo de Soto, and two soldiers, Francisco Avila and Sebastian Alvitre, were accused of raping two young Amerindian girls and killing one of them near the mission of San Diego—dragged on for five years. Fages, Rivera, and Neve all dealt with the case, which occurred while Fages was military commander. Fages received the official complaint from Mariano Carrillo, sergeant at the San Diego presidio, who had interviewed the young survivor at that presidio in the presence of four soldiers acting as witnesses. The girl was accompanied to the presidio by two mission priests and an interpreter, who was also present at the interview.

Fages forwarded the documents to Viceroy Bucareli in Mexico City and, on Bucareli's order, subsequently sent a copy to Felipe Barri, then governor of the Californias, at Loreto. When Rivera replaced Fages, he complied with the viceroy's order to bind the men for trial and to send them to Loreto, the capital of the Californias, in Baja California. By 1775, when Rivera sent Avila and Alvitre to Loreto (Soto had deserted and was never apprehended), Neve had replaced Barris as governor of the Californias. It fell to Neve to hear testimony and conduct the trial, which he opened on October 19, 1775.

The trial, including testimony from six soldiers and comments from the accused after Carrillo's charges were read to them, produced voluminous documents. Neve concluded the trial on November 22 and sent a copy of the entire proceedings to the viceroy for final disposition, along with a statement noting certain discrepancies from proscribed judicial procedure. Upon receipt of the proceedings, Bucareli turned the file over to Teodoro de Croix, recently appointed commandant-general of the Interior Provinces, which included the Californias.

Almost three years elapsed before Croix called in the case. On August 26, 1778, his legal adviser, Pedro Galindo Navarro, submitted his opinion to Croix. In Navarro's opinion, the accusation of rape and homicide was not proven. The dead child's body, he argued, was not examined or even seen; the identification of the soldiers accused was unsatisfactory, since it appeared to have been prompted by the interpreter; the entire charge rested on the testimony of a child, "poorly explained by an interpreter." Finally, the accused denied the charge.

Navarro recommended that the penalty for Avila and Alvitre, who had been detained during the five years of the trial, be commuted to time served and that they should be sentenced to remain and become citizens of California. Croix accepted these recommendations. He issued the order, and the two discharged soldiers were enrolled in the list of settlers at the new pueblo of San José de Guadalupe.

Whether local officials would have convicted the soldiers of rape and homicide must remain a matter of conjecture. In any event, despite laws and prosecutions, the sexual exploitation of Indian women did not cease. The missionaries continuously reported that soldiers "go by night to nearby villages for the purpose of raping Indian women." And while some cases were recorded, many more must surely have gone unreported. Nevertheless, it is clear that the commandants and the governors did prosecute and take disciplinary action when charges were filed against individual soldiers. Contrary to Serra's charges of laxity and complicity, Fages, Rivera, and Neve did exert the full measure of their authority in this and other reported cases of sexual violence or abuse. Abundant evidence details the dual policy of prevention and punishment implemented by the three seasoned frontier administrators in their ongoing effort to check the soldiers' excesses.

Even concerned that Amerindians would discover the real weakness of the Spanish position in California, Neve sought to prevent the sexual attacks, and thereby to defuse the military and political conflicts they gave rise to, by forbidding all troops, including sergeants and corporals, from entering Indian villages. Only soldiers escorting the priests on sick calls were exempt from this order, and then the soldier was not to leave the missionary's side. Escort guards were strictly admonished against misconduct and were severely punished if they disobeyed.

In the same vein, he prohibited soldiers of the mission guard from spending the night away from the mission—even if the priests demanded it. Neve emphatically repeated this same order in the instructions he left to Pedro Fages, who succeeded him as governor in September of 1782. "It is advisable," Neve further instructed Fages, "that we muzzle ourselves and not exasperate the numerous heathendom which surround us, conducting ourselves with politeness and respect. . . . It is highly useful to the service of the King and the public welfare that the heathen of these establishments do not learn to kill soldiers."

Governor Fages was equally emphatic when he issued the following order in 1785: "Observing that the officers and men of these presidios are comporting and behaving themselves in the missions with a vicious license which is very prejudicial because of the scandalous disorders which they incite among the gentile and Christian women, I command you, in order to prevent the continuation of such abuses, that you circulate a prohibitory edict imposing severe penalties upon those who commit them."

A decade later, Viceroy Branciforte followed up Neve's earlier order with his own decree prohibiting troops from remaining overnight away from the presidios, because among other reasons this practice was "prejudicial to good discipline and Christian morals." Governor Diego de Borica, who succeeded Fages in 1794, issued a similar order the following year. These edicts had little effects.

Soldiers and civilian settlers alike disregarded the civil laws against rape as well as military orders against contact with Amerindian women outside of narrowly pro-scribed channels. The records verify that sexual attacks continued in areas adjacent to missions, presidios, and pueblos throughout the colonial period. Amerindian women were never free from the threat of rapacious assaults.

Why, despite strenuous efforts by officials of both church and state, did the sexual attacks persist unabated? Why, despite the obviously serious political and military conflicts the assaults ignited, did they continue? In view of extensive leg-islation, royal decrees, and moral prohibitions against sexual and other violence, what, in the experience of the men who came here, permitted them to objectify and dehumanize Indian women to the degree that chasing and lassoing them from mounted horses and then raping them reveals?

Until recently, scholars attributed sexual violence and other concurrent social disor-ders in early California to the race and culture of the mixed-blood soldier-settler popu-lation recruited or banished to this frontier. Institutional historians concluded . . . that the "original settlers, most of them half-breeds of the least energetic classes . . . , were of a worthless character." Institutional studies generally concurred with Serra's view that the soldiers were recruited from the scum of the society. Serra had repeatedly beseeched Bucareli to send "sturdy, industrious Spanish families" and asked him to advise the governor of the Californias "not to use exile to these missions as punishment for the soldier whom he may detest as insolent or perverse."

In the last two decades, the conditions that shaped institutional development on this frontier have been reexamined. In addition, studies of the social history of the people recruited to Alta California have been undertaken. As a result, the earlier interpretations have been rejected. Scholars now conclude that the slow develop-ment of colonial institutions in California was attributable to limited resources, lack of uniform military codes, and other structural problems—and not to the racial or social-class origins of the soldier-settler population.

Instead, the mixed-blood recruits—who themselves derived from other frontier settlements—were admirably able to survive the harsh privations and onerous condi-tions. In so doing, they established lasting foundations of Spanish civilization in California and the Southwest. Although the *cuera* (leather-jacket) soldiers were indeed unruly and undisciplined, their behavior reflected a particular informality and a "peculiar attitude of both officers and men." According to revisionist studies, the isola-tion and distance from the central government, a shared life of hardship and risk, and the fact that blood and marriage ties existed among officers and common soldiers—all contributed to this attitude of informality and independence. . . . [T]he racially mixed settlers responded to the often brutal conditions on the far northern and Pacific fron-tiers by creating a distinct frontier culture, characterized by self-reliance, individualism, regionalism, village orientation, resistance to outside control, innovativeness, family cohesiveness, and the preservation of Roman Catholicism as a unifying force.

But these revisionists do not address sex/gender issues. The informality of disci-plinary codes does not explain the origins or the continuation of sexual violence against native women. Moreover, as the documents for Alta California clearly reveal,

This map traces the establishment of Catholic missions and presidios (forts) by the Spanish in Alta California between 1760 and the early 1800s. The missions and forts sought both to convert and to conquer the various Indian nations in Alta California, from the Yuma and Cahulla in the South to the Costanoan and Miwok in the North.

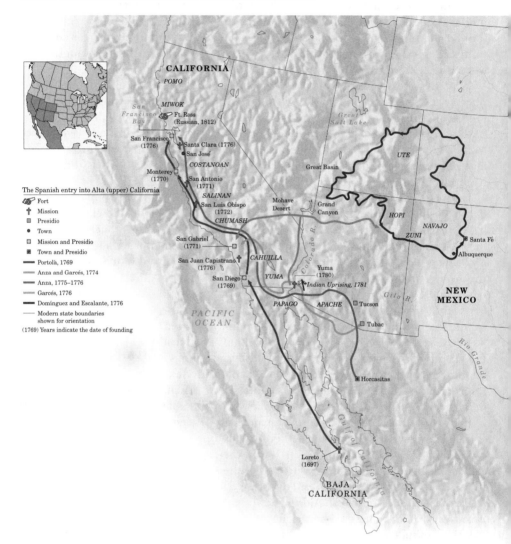

Spanish officials enforced colonial criminal statutes and punished sexual crimes to the extent of their authority. However, neither the highly regulatory Laws of the Indies (the extensive legislation enacted to protect the rights of Amerindians), which mandated nonexploitive relations with Amerindians, nor punishment for breaking the laws arrested the violence.

To begin to understand the soldier-settler violence toward native women, we must examine the stratified, patriarchal colonial society that conditioned relationships between the sexes and races in New Spain; the contemporary ideologies of sex/gender and race; and the relations and structures of conquest imposed on this frontier. While rape and other acts of sexual brutality did not represent official policy on this or any other Spanish frontier, these acts were nevertheless firmly fixed in the history and politics of expansion, war, and conquest. In the history of Western civilization writ large, rape is an act of domination, an act of power. As such, it is a violent political act committed through sexual aggression against women.

"The practice of raping the women of a conquered group," writes historian Gerda Lerner, "has remained a feature of war and conquest from the second millennium to the present." Under conditions of war or conquest, rape is a form of national terrorism, subjugation, and humiliation, wherein the sexual violation of women represents both the physical domination of women and the symbolic castration of the men of the conquered group. These concepts and symbolic meanings of rape . . . are rooted in patriarchal Western society—in the ideology that devalues women in relation to men while it privatizes and reifies women as the symbolic capital (property) of men. In this ideology, rape has historically been defined as a crime against property and thus against "territory." Therefore, in the context of war and conquest, rape has been considered a legitimate form of aggression against the opposing army—a legitimate expression of superiority that carries with it no civil penalty. In nonmilitary situations, punishment for rape and other crimes of sexual violence against women in Western civilization has, until very recently, generally been determined by the social condition or status of the women violated and by the status of the violator.

In eighteenth-century California, the status of Amerindian women—as members of non-Christian, indigenous groups under military conquest on Spain's northernmost outpost of empire—made them twice subject to assault with impunity: They were the spoils of conquest, and they were Indian. In the mentality of the age, these two conditions firmly established the inferiority of the Amerindian woman and became the basis for devaluing her person beyond the devaluation based on sex that accrued to all women irrespective of their sociopolitical (race, class) status. The ferocity and longevity of the sexual assaults against the Amerindian woman are rooted in the devaluation of her person conditioned by the weaving together of the strands of the same ideological thread that demeaned her on interrelated counts: her sociopolitical status, her sex, and her gender.

From their earliest contact with Amerindian peoples, Europeans established categories of opposition, or otherness, within which they defined themselves as superior and Amerindians as inferior. These categories were derived from the Aristotelian theory that some beings are inferior by nature, and therefore should be dominated by their superiors for their own welfare, and from the medieval Spanish concept of "purity of blood," which was based on religion and which informed the sense of national unity forged during the reconquest. These ideas—which were fundamentally political concepts that separated human beings into opposing, hierarchical subject-object categories—prevailed during the era of first contact with Amerindians and the early conquests of the Americas.

By the late eighteenth century, a different political concept—racial origin—defined place and social value in the stratified social order of colonial New Spain. Race was inextricably linked to social origin and had long been a symbol for significant cleavages in society; it was one primary basis for valuation—and devaluation—of human beings. In the contemporary ideology and society, Amerindian women were thus devalued on the basis of their social and racial origins, which placed them at the bottom of the social scale, and as members of a conquered group.

Two aspects of the devaluation of Amerindian women are especially noteworthy. First and foremost, it is a political devaluation. That is, it is rooted in and driven by political considerations and acts: by war, conquest, and the imposition of alien sociopolitical and economic structures of one group over another. Second, the devaluation rationalized by conquest cuts across sex. At this level, women and men of the conquered group are equally devalued and objectified by the conquering group. Amerindian women and men were both regarded as inferior social beings, whose inferiority justified the original conquest and continued to make them justifiably exploitable and expendable in the eyes of the conqueror. The obverse, of course, also holds in this equation: Women and men of the conquering group share the characterization and privileges of their group. In this instance, the primary opposition is defined by sociopolitical status, not sex.

Although the ideological symbols of sociopolitical devaluation changed over time—from religion to socioracial origins to social class—the changing symbols intersected with a sex/gender ideology that has remained remarkably constant from the fifteenth to the twentieth century. As the term implies, the sex/gender ideology defines two categories of opposition—sex and gender—within which women are characterized as superior or inferior in relation to others.

With respect to sex stratification, women are placed in opposition and in an inferior position to men, on the assumption that in the divine order of nature the male sex of the species is superior to the female. In this conception, the ascribed inferiority of females to males is biologically constructed.

The opposition centering on gender revolves around sexual morality and sexual conduct. This opposition creates a level of superior-inferior or good-bad stratification based on social and political value-centered concepts of women's sexuality. This dichotomization provides a very specific, socially constructed, "sexual morality" category for valuing or devaluing women.

Rooted in the corollary patriarchal concepts of woman as the possession of man and of woman's productive capacity as the most important source of her value, this ideology makes woman a pivotal element in the property structure and institutionalizes her importance to the society in the provisions of partible and bilateral inheritance. It also places woman's value, also termed her "honor," in her sexual accessibility—in her virginity while single and, once wed, in the fidelity of her sexual services to the husband to ensure a legitimate heir.

Within this construct, women are placed in opposition to one another at two extremes of a social and moral spectrum defined by sexuality and accessibility. The good woman embodies all the sexual virtues or attributes essential to the maintenance of the patriarchal social structure: sexual purity, virginity, chastity, and fidelity. Historically, the norms of sexual morality and sexual conduct that patriarchal society established for women of the ruling class have been the norms against which all other women have been judged. These norms are fundamentally rooted in questions of the acquisition and transference of economic and political power, and of women's relationship to that power base.

Since the linchpins of these ideological constructs are property, legitimacy, and inheritance, a woman excluded from this property/inheritance structure for sociopolitical reasons (religion, conquest, slavery, race, class), or for reasons based on sexual immorality (any form of sexual misconduct), is consequently excluded from the corresponding concepts and structures of social legitimacy. A woman so excluded cannot produce legitimate heirs because she is not a legitimate social or sexual being.

The woman who is defined out of social legitimacy because of the abrogation of her primary value to patriarchal society, that of producing heirs, is therefore without value, without honor. She becomes the other, the bad woman, the embodiment of a corrupted, inferior, unusable sex: immoral, without virtue, loose. She is common property, sexually available to any man that comes along.

A woman (women) thus devalued may not lay claim to the rights and protections the society affords to the woman who does have sociopolitical and sexual value. In colonial New Spain, as in most Western societies until the very recent period, the woman so demeaned, so objectified, could be raped, beaten, worked like a beast of burden, or otherwise abused with impunity.

The soldiers, priests, and settlers who effected the conquest and colonization of Alta California in the last third of the eighteenth century perceived and acted toward Amerindians in a manner consistent with the ideology and history of conquest—regarding them as inferior, devalued, disposable beings against whom violence was not only permissible but often necessary. For, despite the Laws of the Indies, the contradictions in the ideology and corresponding historical relations of conquest were great from the very beginning. These contradictions were generally exacerbated, rather than resolved, across time, space, and expansion to new frontiers.

From the very beginning, the papal bulls and scholarly (ideological) debates that affirmed the essential humanity of Amerindians and initiated the legislation to effect their conversion and protection sanctioned violence and exploitation under certain conditions. Loopholes in the royal statutes that were technically intended to protect Amerindians and guarantee their rights, but more specifically protected the crown's interest in Indian land and labor, had permitted virulent exploitation of Indians since the laws were first passed.

More contemporary military and civil laws, such as those enacted by Neve, Fages, and Borica, carried severe penalties for illegal contact with or maltreatment of Indians; but these laws were especially contradictory because they were intended to curb certain kinds of violence by soldiers who were trained to kill Indians and who were sent to California to effect the temporal (military) conquest of this region. Thus, violence against Amerindians was permissible when it advanced the particular interests of the Spanish Conquest, but punishable when it did not. Since the sexual violence that occurred in this region was but the most contemporary manifestation of a national history that included the violation of enemy women as a legitimate expression of aggression during conquest, it would seem that sexual violence became a punishable offense only when it was the source of military or political problems.

Finally, perhaps the greatest contradictions were those of the greatest champion of Amerindian rights—the Catholic church. On the one hand, Catholic clergy sought to remove Amerindians from contact with Spaniards, in order to protect them from the exploitation and violence of conquistadores, soldiers, and colonists; on the other hand, Jesuits, Franciscans, and other religious orders relied heavily on corporal punishment in their programs to Christianize and Hispanicize native people. While proclaiming the humanity of Amerindians, missionaries on the frontier daily acted upon a fundamental belief in the inferiority of the Indian. Their actions belied their words.

Accordingly, in his lengthy memorial of June 19, 1801, refuting the charges of excessive cruelty to Amerindians leveled against the Franciscans by one of their own, Father President Fermín Francisco de Lasuén disputed the use of extreme cruelty in the missions of the New California. Force was used only when absolutely necessary, stated Lasuén; and it was at times necessary because the native peoples of California were "untamed savages . . . people of vicious and ferocious habits who know no law but force, no superior but their own free will, and no reason but their own caprice." Of the use of force against neophyte women, Lasuén wrote that women in the mission were flogged, placed in the stocks, or shackled only because they deserved it. But, he quickly added, their right to privacy was always respected—they were flogged inside the women's dormitory, called the *monjero* (nunnery). Flogging the women in private, he further argued, was part of the civilizing process because it "instilled into them the modesty, delicacy, and virtue belonging to their sex."

A key element in the missionaries' program of conversion to Christianity included the restructuring of relations between the sexes to reflect gender stratification and the corollary values and structures of the partriarchal family: subservience of women to men, monogamy, marriage without divorce, and a severely repressive code of sexual norms.

In view of the fact that the ideologies, structures, and institutions of conquest imposed here were rooted in two and a half centuries of colonial rule, the sexual and other violence toward Amerindian women in California can best be understood as ideologically justified violence institutionalized in the structures and relations of conquest initiated in the fifteenth century. In California as elsewhere, sexual violence functioned as an institutionalized mechanism for ensuring subordination and compliance. It was one instrument of sociopolitical terrorism and control—first of women and then of the group under conquest.

Questions for Study and Review

1. How were the lives of Indian women and men transformed by the Spanish conquest of Alta California?

2. Analyze the differences and similarities in ideas about and treatment of Amerindian women by Spanish soldiers and Catholic missionaries.

3. What were the relationships between Spanish ideas about gender and race and their use of sexual violence against women to conquer Amerindians?

4. Compare the Spanish conquest of Indians in Alta California and the English conquest of the Powhatan Confederacy in Jamestown, Virginia.

Suggested Readings and Web Sites

Ramón A. Gutierrez, *When Jesus Came, the Corn Mothers Went Away: Marriage, Sexuality and Power in New Mexico,1500–1846* (1991)

Jane T. Merritt, *At the Crossroads: Indians & Empires on a Mid-Atlantic Frontier, 1700–1763* (2003)

Gwenn Miller, "'The Perfect Mistress of Russian Economy': Sighting the Intimate on a Colonial Alaskan Terrain, 1784–1821," in *Haunted by Empire: Geographies of Intimacy in North American History*, ed. Ann Laura Stoler (2006)

Paige Raibmon, "Naturalizing Power: Land and Sexual Violence along William Byrd's Dividing Line," in *Seeing Nature Through Gender*, ed. Virginia J. Scharff (2003)

Sylvia Van Kirk, *Many Tender Ties: Women in Fur Trade Society, 1670–1870* (1980)

Online Archive of California
   http://www.oac.cdlib.org/texts

First American West: The Ohio River Valley, 1750–1820
   http://memory.loc.gov/ammem/award99/icuhtml/fawhome.html

PART III

The Revolution and Early Republic

This 1782 engraving of a "Spinner" represents an important task for women that carried different political and economic meanings for female patriots, domestic servants, and early industrial workers.

T he process of revolution and nation building is most often understood in terms of military strategy and formal political development. In recent decades, increasing attention has been focused on the social and economic upheavals that preceded and followed the American War for Independence. The demonstrations and boycotts that fed revolutionary fervor in the 1760s and 1770s as well as the revolts against "hard money" and taxation that the Revolution fostered can be fully understood only by examining the experiences of common women and men in their local communities. Yet even these studies usually emphasize male-centered events—the Boston Tea Party, Paul Revere's ride, Shays' Rebellion, the Whisky Rebellion—or at least men's participation in such events.

The authors included in this section focus instead on women's experience of and involvement in the birth of the nation. Even in the mid-eighteenth century, women were in charge of buying most items for household consumption, including sugar, molasses, tea, and cloth. Thus, if boycotts against British goods were to succeed, women's support was essential. Such support required real devotion to the patriot cause since the loss of imported goods required housewives to replace British-made linen with homespun cloth and processed tea with home brews or coffee (the latter relatively unpopular in North America before the Revolution). These and other substitutions meant increased labor for women. A Massachusetts leader of the Daughters of Liberty, the organization that coordinated women's boycott efforts, assured her fellow colonists that added work or diminished comfort would not deter her patriot sisters: "I hope there are none of us but would sooner wrap ourselves in sheep and goatskin than buy English goods of a people who have insulted us in such a scandalous way."

Other women organized anti-tea leagues, sewing circles, and petition drives to support the patriot cause. In these ways, the economic necessity of women's work, which had been recognized for centuries, now took on political significance as well. A few saw in the politicization of women's domestic labor the first step toward women's participation in formal politics. Abigail Adams was only the most famous of those who asked their patriot brothers (or, in her case, husband) to "remember the ladies" in the nation's new code of laws and to "be more generous and favorable to them than your ancestors!" More astonishingly, perhaps, a group of fifty-one women from Edenton, North Carolina, wrote a proclamation in 1774 that insisted on their right and duty to participate in the political activities of the day.

Some women took a more direct approach. Deborah Sampson (alias Robert Shurtleff) disguised her sex in order to join the Continental army. So did several hundred other women. The women of Groton, Massachusetts, though not interested in full-time soldiering, dressed in men's clothing and defended the local bridge from British troops retreating from Lexington and Concord. They captured a courier carrying valuable information, along with a number of comrades, and turned them over to military authorities. Many more women sought simply to protect hearth and home and for their efforts frequently endured exploitation or abuse at the hands of enemy forces.

Not all colonists, however, supported the patriot cause or sympathized with the British. Perhaps a third of all colonists were unmoved by revolutionary and parliamentary proclamations, unless or until troops appeared at their doorsteps. These women and men were caught up in other struggles—to grow a good crop, to last out a bad winter, or to survive a difficult birth.

American Indians and African Americans had different choices to make than did European colonists. They rarely participated directly in the events leading to the Revolution, but they could not escape its impact on their lives. Indian nations calculated the benefits of siding with or opposing the patriots, but African Americans more often made choices as individuals or families. In Chapter Seven, Carol Berkin analyzes the opportunities that the war created for African American women and their families. She highlights the ways that British military strategy fueled proclamations of emancipation for enslaved women and men in the South while revolutionary rhetoric inspired some in the North to claim freedom for themselves. Yet enslaved blacks who sought freedom faced numerous hardships, including responsibility for family members, especially young children.

In the midst of the Revolution, as well as before and after, women continued to bear children. But even this most personal of events was reshaped by the battle for independence. Women whose husbands fought in the war bore greater burdens in having to manage family farms and businesses as well as their households. Yet their husbands' absence probably relieved them of other burdens by increasing the interval between births. At the same time, the number of premarital pregnancies increased in the late eighteenth century, perhaps because of fears that sweethearts and fiancés might never return from battle.

The number of children raised by mothers alone grew after Americans defeated Great Britain and gained their independence. Of course, many widows were left to care for sons and daughters. In addition, the birthrate among unmarried women also continued to rise. The upheavals of a protracted war made it even more difficult than earlier for families and communities to coerce men into marrying young women who discovered they were pregnant. And in many American towns and cities, where the population surged immediately following the war, family and community ties were limited. At least in one way, however, single mothers had an easier time after the war. Many affluent housewives were eager for servants in the late eighteenth century and more readily accepted the children who might accompany them. In Chapter Eight, Marla Miller traces the lives of several servant women, black and white, who worked in the household of Elizabeth Porter Phelps. These women either brought children with them into the Phelps home or gave birth while employed there. We thus get a rare glimpse into the family lives of women who lived on the margins of society in the new nation.

Well-to-do women like Elizabeth Porter Phelps must have worried about the example that unwed mothers in the household set for their own daughters and granddaughters. Fortunately for young women of means, independence created new opportunities that were far more enticing than an unplanned pregnancy. The desire for a national identity and the cultivation of virtue among "American" citizens encouraged the establishment of schools of all kinds, including seminaries for young women.

Believing that only educated mothers could properly train sons for citizenship in the new nation, many writers supported these expanded educational opportunities. Although the curriculum offered to the new generation of "Republican Mothers" tended to focus on domestic arts and traditional female skills, it still expanded horizons for women. In other ways, however, women's spheres continued to be restricted, even for affluent and middling white women.

Still, the concept of "republican motherhood" enhanced the opportunities for many women in the new nation. After many years of war, some women had come to enjoy and excel at managing households, farms, and businesses, duties that had initially seemed burdensome. Others, especially well-educated women, made direct connections between the language of natural rights proclaimed by patriots and their own position in society. At the same time, some ministers, politicians, and male educators advocated a more elevated role for women in their families and communities. Educated mothers could raise children nurtured in the ideals of republicanism, and virtuous wives and daughters could strengthen the moral fiber of the nation and provide charity to the needy.

In the new system of laws, neither John Adams nor his fellow patriots did "remember the ladies." Instead, by codifying situations previously left to custom, they more often narrowed than expanded women's political and property rights in the years immediately following the British surrender at Yorktown. Thus, while women's indirect influence on politics expanded and women's early connections with evil were replaced by paeans to female moral and spiritual superiority, the ideal woman was now confined even more tightly within the bounds of domesticity.

More than educational or political innovations, economic change most thoroughly transformed the opportunities available to women in the New Republic. Here, too, a concern with national autonomy affected the policies advocated by political leaders, which in turn shaped everyday life. In his famous *Report on Manufactures*, for instance, Secretary of the Treasury Alexander Hamilton argued that the new nation could free itself from economic dependency on Europe only by establishing its own industries. The development of manufacturing, however, would require a new division of labor between women and men. The farmer, Hamilton insisted, would be provided "a new source of profit and support from the increased industry of his wife and daughters, invited and stimulated by the demands of neighboring manufactories." Thomas Jefferson, the first U.S. Secretary of State and an opponent of Hamilton, placed greater faith in America's agrarian values and traditions. "I think our government will remain virtuous for many centuries," he wrote, "as long as they [the people] are chiefly agricultural." For Jefferson, wives and daughters were best employed as helpmates on the family farm.

When translated into everyday life, both Hamilton's and Jefferson's visions proved problematic. As Paul Johnson shows in Chapter Nine, too many children, too little land, and the "exhaustion" of what acres remained often left younger sons and daughters of all ages without an inheritance, at least one that allowed them to remain near their families and communities of origin. Such dispossessed individuals, male or female, had little opportunity to fulfill the Jeffersonian promise of agrarian peace and prosperity. Rather, these new citizens were both freed and forced from traditional entanglements of family and farm, released to fuel the industrial development planned by Hamilton. The families who supplied labor to industries, such as the family of Greenleaf and Abigail Patch, found themselves facing entirely new difficulties and dangers. In this new order, women and men often faced quite different obstacles and were offered different rewards. Thus did women and men, in families and communities up and down the Atlantic seaboard, begin to conceive of their choices in new ways as the nation itself struggled to life.

Suggested Readings and Web Sites

Catherine Allgor, *Parlor Politics: In Which the Ladies of Washington Help Build a City and a Government* (2000)

Linda Kerber, *Women of the Republic: Intellect and Ideology in Revolutionary America* (1980)

Benjamin Quarles, *The Negro in the American Revolution* (1961; reprint 1996.)

Laurel Thatcher Ulrich, *A Midwife's Tale: The Life of Martha Ballard Based on Her Diary, 1785–1812* (1990)

How Did the Ladies Association of Philadelphia Shape New Forms of Women's Activism during the American Revolution, 1780–1781?
http://womhist.binghamton.edu/index.html

Betsy Ross, Molly Pitcher, Deborah Sampson, Abigail Adams—all heroines of the Revolution—are exceptional only in the attention they have attracted from scholars and novelists. The domestic and public activities of these heroines were quite common among colonial women, whose labors were critical to sustaining families and communities as tensions between the colonies and Great Britain erupted into war. Beginning in the mid-seventeenth century, housewives began translating domestic skills, such as sewing and brewing, into marketable commodities. It was the disruption of trade with Britain, however, from the 1760s through the 1780s, that encouraged women to adapt household resources to political ends.

Historians have traced this politicization of the household in both rebel and Tory families to demonstrate how women's involvement in the Revolution—on either side—challenged traditional notions of virtue and citizenship. African American women, too, were roused to action by the outbreak of war. And as Carol Berkin shows, they had much to gain and much to lose from the battle between the colonies and Great Britain.

In their justifications for the American Revolution, patriot leaders pitted independence and virtue against tyranny and greed. Yet many of the most celebrated advocates of independence, including Thomas Jefferson and George Washington, were slaveholders. We know that some patriot slaveowners recognized the tensions between ideals of independence for white colonists and the enslavement of black women and men. Yet most of them learned to live with the contradictions. For many African Americans, however, demands for political freedom echoed their most heartfelt desires for personal emancipation. And the American Revolution did provide a chance for some enslaved women and men to escape their bondage. Still, the risks were high, and not all who escaped managed to maintain their independence.

Carol Berkin analyzes the choices made by African American women and their families as they confronted the Revolution throughout the colonies. In some places like Virginia, royal officials offered freedom to enslaved women and men who took up arms for the British. The danger, of course, was that should armed slaves be captured by patriot forces or the British defeated, these black loyalists would likely pay with their lives. In addition, how would African Americans who joined with British troops protect family members left behind on plantations? For enslaved women living in the North, the chances for freedom were more closely tied to the courts than to the armies. Here, too, blacks faced significant barriers to emancipation, but one enslaved woman, Mumbet, who sued for her freedom in Massachusetts, set a precedent that would aid others in her state.

The African Americans who escaped the brutality of slavery during the Revolution faced enormous challenges in the war's aftermath. Some fled to

Canada under protection of the British army, but conditions there were harsh and few provisions were made for establishing freed blacks in homes or jobs. Others were forced back into slavery. At the same time, however, the number of slaves manumitted, that is, freed, by their owners increased substantially in the decade following independence. The nation's first president, George Washington, left instructions in his will that slaves on his plantation should be freed upon the death of his wife, Martha. Martha Washington, fearing that slaves now had good reason to hasten her end, freed them sooner.

In the North, the Revolution inspired many states to end slavery, though most did so very gradually. Slavery did not officially end in New York, for example, until 1828. Moreover, once freed, black women and men faced prejudice and hostility as they tried to find homes, jobs, and education.

The struggle for national independence sparked demands for freedom among enslaved African Americans just as it inspired calls for more economic and political rights for women. In the war's aftermath, however, most women—patriot or loyalist, black, white, or Indian—found themselves struggling to survive and support their families.

Looking forward, Marla Miller's and Paul Johnson's articles suggest that women's contributions to the patriot effort were not fully rewarded in the New Republic. Perhaps fortunately for the success of the Revolution and the struggle for emancipation, women who sustained these efforts could not see into the future.

"The Day of Jubilee Is Come": African American Women and the American Revolution

CAROL BERKIN

Molly Brant [a Mohawk who supported the English] and Thomas Jefferson shared a desire for freedom and independence—and went to war with each other to ensure that these ideals became reality. The same dream of freedom motivated African American women and their families to wage their own war against those who enslaved them. In the struggle that Joseph Brant called a war between English "brothers," African American loyalties were to their own future, not to Congress or to king.

While leading patriots decried the king's efforts to enslave his American subjects, African American slavery was an accepted social institution in every American colony. Black slaves could be found working in shops in Boston, on the docks of New York

City, in the elegant homes of Philadelphia's merchant elite, in the tobacco fields of Virginia, and in the rice paddies of South Carolina. By 1770, there were more than 47,000 enslaved blacks in the northern colonies, almost 20,000 of them in New York. More than 320,000 slaves worked the tobacco and wheat fields of the Chesapeake colonies, making 37 percent of the population of the region African or African American. More than 187,000 of these slaves were Virginians. In the Lower South, more than 92,000 slaves could be found wading deep in the putrid waters of the rice paddies or laboring at trades in the cities of Charleston or Savannah. South Carolina alone had more than 75,000 slaves, and by 1770 planters there were importing 4,000 more Africans a year. More than a third of the thriving plantations of the Lower South boasted slave populations of fifty or more, so that in many counties the black population far outnumbered the white. Although free black women and men could also be found in every colony, the trend toward emancipation had slowed greatly by the middle of the eighteenth century. In New York, Pennsylvania, and New England, colonial governments had placed obstacles in the way of any master wishing to free his slaves.

No matter where they lived, slaves endured hard and demeaning lives. But labor in the southern colonies was most severe. Tobacco production, done by gang labor, was both tedious and demanding, but rice production was, as one observer declared, "I think the hardest work I have seen [slaves] engage in." On the whole, slaves were poorly fed and poorly clothed, and subject to both physical and psychological abuse. From humiliating names to humiliating punishments, slaves learned the meaning of freedom every day by its absence.

Whether slave or free, African American women struggled to establish and maintain a family. Free black women who worked as household servants were usually not allowed to set up an independent household with a husband or children. Enslaved black women working in northern household were often sold away when they became pregnant, separating them from their husbands and relatives. On the plantations of the Chesapeake, slave gangs were usually housed at a distance from other gangs, and frequently their members were segregated by age or sex. Husbands and wives who lived on different plantations had even greater difficulty keeping up their relationships. And as planters opened up new lands in the Piedmont regions and further west, families were split apart. In every southern colony, the death of a master or the marriage of a master's child could mean a black family divided, for widows rented out slaves and fathers gave slaves to their daughters as wedding gifts. Planters often put young slave boys up for sale, separating them from their parents, or sold family members as punishment for insolence or bad work habits.

Throughout the colonial period, enslaved people had made their bids for freedom, either in groups or as solitary runaways. On plantations that bordered Spanish, French, or Indian territory, or in areas where an escape to a busy port city was possible, runaways had some chance of finding refuge or melting into the crowds. Most runaways, however, were male. Pregnant women, mothers with infants and small children, and women who cared for elderly parents or friends, could not—and would not—abandon those who depended upon them.

The year 1775 brought new possibilities to slave and free women in every colony. The emerging conflict between mother country and colonies led loyalists, British officials, army commanders, and patriots to appeal to African Americans for support.

The near-constant presence of British armies in the Lower South, the American army's desperate need for soldiers and laborers, and recruitment by guerrilla loyalist and patriot bands in the southern backcountry all created opportunities for black women as well as men to escape slavery. The disruption of daily life, the chaos and confusion that marked the war in the South, the flight of masters and their families to safer ground—these realities, more than any broadening of the meaning of "free-dom" embraced by patriots, allowed tens of thousands of African Americans to enjoy small blessings of liberty at last.

The British were certainly the first to recognize the potential benefits of an alliance between the Crown and the enslaved. On November 7, 1775, with the colonies on the verge of revolution, the governor of Virginia, the Earl of Dunmore, issued a proclama-tion that terrified white plantation owners and brought hope to their slaves. As a "Body of . . . Traitors, and their Abettors" threatened to attack the king's troops in Virginia, Dunmore declared "all indented Servants, Negroes, or others . . . free that are able and willing to bear Arms, they joining his MAJESTY'S Troops as soon as may be. . . . " Dunmore assumed, rightly, that many black men would be willing to fight against their masters. He also hoped that the loss of slave labor would be an economic blow to the rebels. As the war progressed, both proved to be true: black soldiers would fight side by side with British regulars, in their own black regiments, and in Hessian regiments, and an estimated 80,000 to 100,000 African Americans, both male and female, would desert their masters before the war ended, damaging the tobacco economy of the Chesapeake and leaving the plantation economy of the Carolinas in ruins.

By December 1, some three hundred runaway male slaves had enlisted in what Dunmore called his Ethiopian Regiment. Across their chests, these men wore a ban-ner that read "Liberty to Slaves." With them came women and children, hoping that Dunmore's protection would extend to them as well. To counter the effect of Dunmore's proclamation, the Virginia Committee of Safety issued a warning to the colony's slaves: "To none is freedom promised but to such as are able to do Lord Dunmore's service: The aged, the infirm, the women and children, are still to remain the property of their masters." What would become of those left behind? The committee's answer was a chilling threat: "masters . . . will be provoked to severity, should part of their slaves desert them . . . should there be any amongst the Negroes weak enough to believe that Dunmore intends to do them a kindness, and wicked enough to provoke the fury of the Americans against their defenceless fathers and mothers, their wives, their women and children, let them only consider the difficulty of effecting their escape, and what they must expect to suffer if they fall into the hands of the Americans."

Dunmore's biracial army could not withstand the force of Virginia's rebels, how-ever. It was defeated outside Norfolk, and the governor fled to British ships waiting in the Chesapeake. He took the surviving members of the Ethiopian Regiment and other black refugees aboard with him. But worse was to follow. A smallpox epidemic broke out on board the ships, and Dunmore, hoping to contain it, ordered the African Americans to be isolated on an island in the bay. Later, when the Americans took the island, they found "many poor Negroes . . . dying of the putrid fever, others dead in the open fields; a child was found sucking at the breast of its dead mother." Before the disease ran its course, half the Ethiopian Regiment had died.

Virginia planters moved quickly to prevent any further loss of slaves to the British. Virginia's patriot leadership threatened death or resale to the West Indies to "all Negro or other Slaves, conspiring to rebel or make insurrection," and to make their point, they sold thirty-two of the Ethiopian Regiment soldiers they had captured in battle to planters in the Caribbean. Threats like these did not prevent the flight of some five thousand African Americans from Virginia and the surrounding Chesapeake region during the course of the war. But the British army would not be there to shelter them. The war moved out of Virginia before independence was declared, and did not return until General Cornwallis made his last stand at Yorktown in 1781.

The greatest push for self-emancipation came in the Lower South, the scene of brutal civil war and two major British military campaigns. Slave women, like slave men, took advantage of the violent confusion to seek safety behind British lines. Some British commanders were willing to arm able-bodied black men, but the majority of male and female refugees were set to work making musket cartridges, tending to the sick and wounded in hospitals, or performing the backbreaking labor of building fortifications and repairing roads. Not a few were assigned to work as personal servants for British officers.

Despite all the difficulties and dangers, wherever the British army went in the South, black men and women followed in its wake. The number of runaways increased dramatically after June 1779 when the British commander, Sir Henry Clinton, issued a second proclamation, known as the Philipsburg Proclamation. In it, General Clinton declared that "every NEGRO who shall desert the Rebel Standard" would be granted "full security to follow within these Lines, any Occupation which he shall think proper." Although Clinton intended the proclamation to encourage African Americans serving in the Continental Army to desert, thousands of civilian blacks read it as a general promise of emancipation. Men, women, and children poured into the British camps. Others, taking advantage of the confusion and chaos that the war in the South produced, made their escape to Maroon communities in Florida or on the borderlands of Carolina and Georgia.

When Cornwallis's army moved north from the Carolinas to Virginia in 1781, over four thousand black men and women trailed behind the baggage carts. Dianah and Hannah of the Linning plantation were perhaps typical of the women who chose to run away. Before the Revolution, escape would have been impossible for this elderly woman and her half-blind daughter. But when the British army crossed the Linning fields on their way to Charleston, Dianah and Hannah went with them. When the British surrendered Charleston to the American army, mother and daughter sailed with them to New York and from there, at last, to freedom in Canada aboard the British transport ship *Elijah.*

Although Dianah and Hannah made it safely to Canada when the loyalists were finally evacuated from New York, the majority of slaves who sought their freedom did not. Half of the women and men who answered the call issued in Clinton's Philipsburg Proclamation did not survive the war. And despite the proclamation's promise, many who survived were not allowed their freedom. Both loyalists and British regulars considered them, like the slaves captured on American plantations, to be prizes of war.

Even official documents of emancipation sometimes failed to protect African Americans. In Charleston, for example, a loyalist named Jesse Gray made a career of false claims of ownership and the resale of emancipated blacks. Mary Postill was one of his victims. Postill was the slave of a wealthy South Carolina planter who fled with her children to British-held Charleston. Here the military gave her a certificate of freedom. When the American army reclaimed Charleston in 1782, Mary, her husband, and her family went to St. Augustine, Florida, as the hired servants of Jesse Gray. But Gray had managed to take Postill's certificate and now declared that she and her family were legally his slaves. Soon after they arrived in St. Augustine, Jesse Gray sold Mary Postill to his brother Samuel. When the Gray brothers emigrated to Canada, they took Mary and her daughters with them. In Canada, Samuel Gray sold Mary Postill back to his brother. Fearful that Jesse Gray would sell her once again, this time separating her from her children, Mary took her daughters and fled the Gray household. Gray went to court to recover her. Although Postill swore in court that she was a free woman when she left Charleston, Gray won his suit. To punish Postill, he took her down the river and sold her to another loyalist for one hundred bushels of potatoes.

As the war in the South turned in the Americans' favor, retreating British troops left many blacks behind. Most of these were re-enslaved. Left behind, too, were the enslaved women and men who had chosen not to leave their plantation homes. Few records exist to tell us why the majority of African American slave women did not flee. Some may have feared for the safety of their children in the midst of battlefields and disease-ridden camps. Others may have feared reprisals if they were captured or returned to their masters. For many, the desire to be in familiar surroundings and among friends and family in a time of chaos and violence kept them at home.

Remaining home did not ensure a woman's safety or secure the well-being of her family, however. Ironically, the flight of so many others left them vulnerable. On South Carolina plantations, where desertions ran high, there were not enough field hands to plant or harvest crops. Food grew scarce, and it was "the poor Negroes" who remained behind who starved. Wartime decisions made by planters harmed them as well. Slave owners hoping to protect their human property from confiscation or theft chose to send their slaves to places of safety like Florida, Louisiana, or the West Indies, where they could be kept until peace returned. If plantation owners chose to flee themselves, they were rarely willing or able to take all members of a slave family with them. Black parents were thus separated from their children and wives from their husbands. Slaves who remained on rebel plantations also fared badly when British troops seized their masters's possessions, for the soldiers considered them to be spoils of war. In an effort to prevent individual soldiers from claiming these slaves as personal property, General Henry Clinton ordered that they be treated as British property. His efforts were not always effective, however, for soldiers learned to quickly sell the captured slaves before officers could intervene. This wartime trafficking in slaves, observed South Carolina patriot Henry Laurens, condemned African Americans to a "ten fold worse slavery in the West Indies."

Perhaps twenty thousand fugitive slaves left the Lower South when the British abandoned Savannah and Charleston at war's end. Along with other loyalists, most were taken to New York City, where the final evacuation of British forces and their supporters was to take place. Even here, however, freedom was not final. Loyalist masters rushed to reclaim former slaves from among the refugee groups and patriot masters demanded the return of runaways. As preparations got under way, a rumor spread that the British intended to turn over all former slaves to their owners. "This dreadful rumour," recalled a black man, "filled us all with inexpressible anguish and terror, especially when we saw our old masters coming from Virginia, North Carolina, and other parts, and seizing their slaves in the streets of New York, or even dragging them out of their beds." Among those who were reclaimed by their masters were a "man, his wife, and a kinswoman of theirs," who had served the Baroness Riedesel during the years her family spent as prisoners of war in America. "They had served us faithfully," wrote the baroness, while their former master had "treated them shockingly." She remembered vividly the "shrieks and lamentations of these poor people" as they were taken away.

Despite the successes of some slaveholders in reclaiming their human property, the worst fears of the refugees in New York proved unfounded. The British refused to turn blacks over to their former masters wholesale, although they did allow loyalists to bring their slaves with them as they boarded the ships for Canada. The British ultimately issued certificates of manumission to more than 1,300 men, 914 women, and 740 children as a reward for their wartime services. Their names, along with the names of slaves belonging to white loyalists, were recorded in a log known as *The Book of Negroes*, which contained a description of each person. To guard against ship captains putting free black loyalists in irons and carrying them to the West Indies for sale, *The Book of Negroes* also recorded the name of the ship they boarded, the name of the captain, and the official port of destination.

On evacuation day, November 25, 1783, British transport ships began their journeys to Nova Scotia, New Brunswick, and the Caribbean. Each passenger list contained a sliver of the histories of African American freedom and bondage: For example, the *Spring*, headed for Saint John's, carried Ann Black, a twenty-five-year-old woman, and Sukey, a five-year-old girl, both free. Twenty-year-old Rose Richards, described as a "healthy young woman," was aboard the *Aurora*, traveling to Canada as the property of a white Philadelphia loyalist. On the same ship was Barbarry Allen, a "healthy stout wench" of twenty-two, who was the property of a Virginian, and twenty-four-year-old Elizabeth Black, a free mulatto woman. The *Ariel* carried thirty-two-year-old Betsy Brothers, traveling with two children and a certificate of manumission; thirty-year-old Dinah Mitchell, a "stout healthy Negress" with a child in her arms who had been freed by her master; and twenty-year-old Clara, a "stout wench," once the property of a Colonel De Bois, but left behind by him. The *Spencer* carried several emancipated women, including twenty-one-year-old Sarah Fox, a "stout healthy wench" who had somehow managed to purchase her freedom; the "stout little woman" Phebe Lynch, forty-two, once owned by a Mr. Lynch of South Carolina but now holding a certificate declaring her free; and young Hagar Corie, with her small child, once slaves on Great Neck, Long Island. On the *Peggy*, bound for Port Roseway, were Major Coffin's slave, the twenty-one-year-old Phebe, listed like so many other black women as a "stout wench"; and twenty-six-year-old Lettie, whose certificate showed her to be a freeborn woman from Montserrat. The *Peggy* also carried a young woman named Mary, listed as the property of her husband Joe, who "owned himself."

In Canada, former slaves were indeed free, but prejudice and poverty replaced their earlier bondage. The free black loyalists taken to Canada were segregated into black settlements like Little Tracadie and Brindley Town. The largest of these towns, Birchtown, was named in honor of the British general who authorized the certificates of manumission. Here, some 2,500 refugees began their new lives as free women and men. But whatever their hopes, few were realized. A racial as well as a class hierarchy determined the rations provided in the first years of settlement, with white officers and gentlemen served first, white veterans and working people next, and African Americans last of all. Of 649 male heads of household in Birchtown in 1784, only 184 had received the land grants promised to them by the Crown. White settlers, unhappy with their allotments, soon discovered means to deprive Birchtown residents of what land they did receive. The Anglican Church took property to the east of the settlement, and white settlers snatched up farmland to the north, carving lots out of the more valuable property surrounding the harbor.

Conditions were little better in the smaller settlements. Sharecropping developed in some areas where whites had received large land grants they could not cultivate on their own. Many desperate blacks, giving up all hope of farmland, flocked to cities like Halifax, where low-paying jobs could be found. Even here, they found no peace. In 1784, poor white veterans in Shelburne rioted against blacks, whom they accused of forcing them out of the labor market. Black men and women were beaten, homes were destroyed, and many were forced to take refuge in nearby Birchtown. Landless and jobless women and men indentured themselves to white settlers or were sold as servants as punishment for vagrancy. Sometimes the motives for acts of violence were not economic but social. When a black Birchtown Baptist minister, David George, began to baptize white Christians, a mob destroyed his home.

By the 1790s, couples like Violet and Boston King, formerly of Massachusetts, were ready to emigrate once again. In 1791, their opportunity came in the form of the Sierra Leone Company, which offered refuge to "such Free Blacks as are able to produce to their Agents, Lieutenant Clarkson, of His Majesty's Navy, and Mr. Lawrence Hartshorne, of Halifax, or either of them, satisfactory Testimonials of their Characters, (more particularly as to Honesty, Sobriety, and Industry)." In February 1792 fifteen ships carrying 1,196 blacks from Nova Scotia and New Brunswick sailed from Halifax to the colony in West Africa. Legend has it that, as they disembarked, these women and men sang, "The day of jubilee is come, return ye ransomed sinners home."

And what of the African Americans who remained in the new United States? When the Revolution began, a small number of whites and blacks had voiced their hopes that the principles of liberty and freedom would bring an end to the institution of slavery. One of the most impressive voices was that of a young slave woman named Phillis Wheatley. Phillis was brought to America in 1761 at the age of seven, and sold to a prosperous Boston tailor named John Wheatley. John and his wife recognized and nurtured the talents of this young girl, allowing her to study Latin and Greek as well as to master English. Before the decade was over Phillis had created a sensation in Massachusetts with the publication of a poem honoring the evangelical preacher George Whitefield. In 1776, she published a collection of her poetry, which asserted that Africans, like Europeans, were children of God and thus deserved respect and sympathy. Phillis understood the racism that pervaded much of white society: "Some view our sable race with scornful eye / 'Their colour is a diabolic die,'" she wrote. But she continued:

> *Remember,* Christians, Negroes, *black as* Cain,
> *May be refin'd, and join th'angelic train.*

Phillis won her own freedom from her master, but other blacks were not so fortunate. Indeed, there were few avenues to emancipation during the war for those who supported the patriot cause. Service in the military, for example, did not guarantee black men their freedom. The Massachusetts state government did buy and emancipate slaves who were willing to serve in the military, but other states did not follow suit. Instead, slave owners in every region began a practice of sending able-bodied slaves as their substitutes when they were drafted. In several southern states, governments chose to offer a healthy black male slave as a bonus to any white recruit who signed up for the duration of the war.

The American army did not issue proclamations offering freedom to slaves who deserted their loyalist masters, nor was it American policy to encourage runaways. When loyalist plantations were captured, slave women and children were frequently taken and sold for the soldiers' profit. Slave women could be found in American army camps, where they were set to work building roads, constructing fortifications, and laundering uniforms, but they remained slaves rather than refugees. Masters usually hired these women out to the military, sometimes hiring out their children as well.

Slowly, the new northern states did take steps to eliminate slavery. Vermont's state constitution, drafted in 1777, specifically prohibited the institution. Three years later, in 1780, the Pennsylvania legislature enacted a gradual emancipation law that directly connected the ideals of the Revolution with the rights of African Americans to freedom. In its preamble, these legislators declared that "we conceive that it is our duty, and we rejoice that it is in our power, to extend a portion of that freedom to others, which hath been extended to us, and release them from the state of thralldom, to which we ourselves were tyrannically doomed, and from which we have now every prospect of being delivered." And, in a statement that echoed, unintentionally no doubt, Phillis Wheatley's insistence on universal humanity, they added: "It is not for us to inquire why, in the creation of mankind, the inhabitants of the several parts of the earth were distinguished by a difference in feature or complexion. It is sufficient to know that all are the work of the Almighty Hand." And, in Massachusetts, a judge ruled that slavery was unconstitutional because it was in conflict with the state's bill of rights, which declared "all men . . . free and equal."

The Massachusetts decision was the result of a lawsuit by a middle-aged slave woman known as Mumbet. Mumbet belonged to a prominent and respected Massachusetts lawyer and member of the state legislature, Colonel John Ashley. In 1781, Mumbet sued for her freedom in the Berkshire County Court of Common Pleas at Great Barrington, Massachusetts. Theodore Sedgwick, a rising young lawyer and political leader who would later become an abolitionist, agreed to take Mumbet's case. He successfully argued that slavery was incompatible with the guarantee of liberty in the 1780 state constitution. After the court ruled in her favor, Mumbet took the name Elizabeth Freeman. When asked what motivated her to demand her freedom, Mumbet is alleged to have said she learned about liberty by "keepin' still and mindin' things."

In the southern states, however, the legacy of the Revolution was a hardening of attitudes toward emancipation and harsher laws regulating African American life. The war had taken a brutal toll in this region; by the time peace came, the plantation-based

Susan Anne Sedgwick painted this portrait of Elizabeth Freeman, also known as Mum Bett (or Mumbet), in 1811. Such portraits of African Americans were rare, especially one that showed an African American woman so well attired and looking directly at the viewer.

economy of the Chesapeake was badly damaged and the economy of the Lower South was in ruins. White southerners, returning home from military service, recorded their shock at the devastation and destruction. In South Carolina, the labor force had all but vanished. In the months before the British evacuated Savannah, fewer than eighty slaves were for sale in the entire state of Georgia. The destruction of property and fields and the disappearance of a labor force meant agricultural production for the market was impossible in the years immediately following Yorktown. Any slaves remaining on the plantations had to be set to work producing basic necessities such as cloth or repairing roads and houses. Thus, after the Revolution it was not an end to slavery that rice planters wanted; it was a massive infusion of new slaves from Africa or the Caribbean.

The presence of black leaders, whose wartime experiences equipped them to organize resistance to slavery, acted to deepen white hostility to and fear of African Americans in these southern states. In the decade after the Revolution, assaults on whites increased across the South. More than 148 blacks were convicted of murdering whites between 1785 and 1794 in Virginia alone. From the swamps along the Savannah River, runaway slaves, both women and men, launched guerrilla attacks on plantations. In response, the new state governments tightened regulations on African Americans, forbidding slave literacy and enforcing rigid segregation laws.

Individual planters inflicted brutal reprisals against slaves suspected of plotting rebellions. A racial ideology that declared African Americans inherently and irrevocably inferior took hold. This ideology could be seen during the debate over the Virginia Declaration of Rights. When some members voiced concerns that the first article, stating that "all men are by nature equally free," might spur slaves to demand their rights, supporters of the article dismissed these concerns. They assured their fellow political leaders that "slaves not being constituent members of our society could never pretend to any benefit from such a maxim."

In the end, there would be no winning side for Hannah or Mary Postill, or for the many nameless African American women who died of starvation and enemy attack. Many African American women who won their freedom lost it again through violence and trickery and the venality of men entrusted with their care. Many more died in the attempt to gain it. Those who succeeded faced racial prejudice in exile that resulted in poverty and injustice. Those who remained behind in the South found the reins of slavery tighten around them. The American Revolution had brought no "day of jubilee" after all.

Questions for Study and Review

1. What opportunities did the American Revolution create for women and African Americans to improve their lives and their status in society?

2. How did African American women's chances for freedom differ in northern and southern colonies during the Revolution?

3. What were the greatest hardships faced by African American women who escaped slavery? By those whose husbands and sons escaped slavery?

4. What does this article suggest about the changes in enslaved women's lives between the emergence of slavery in North America during the seventeenth century and the Revolution?

Suggested Readings and Web Sites

Sylvia Frey, *Water from a Rock: Black Resistance in the Revolutionary Age* (1991)
Mary Beth Norton, *Founding Mothers and Fathers: Gendered Power and the Forming of American Society* (1996)
Sheila L. Skemp, *Judith Sargent Murray: A Brief Biography with Documents* (1998)
Alfred Young, *Masquerade: The Life and Times of Deborah Sampson, Continental Soldier* (2004)
Colonial Williamsburg
    http://www.history.org
American Revolution Digital Learning Project
    http://www.amrevonline.org/museum/
New Jersey History Partnership
    http://www.njhistorypartnership.org/contents

Chapter 8

ollowing the American Revolution, many more women than ever before had to find ways to support themselves and their families. For those with few resources or connections, domestic service remained one of the few options. From the earliest settlements, women and men had worked as servants in the households of others. But by the late eighteenth century, women far outnumbered men among domestic servants. The job itself had changed as well, especially in the North. In the colonial era, farm families often sent their daughters to work in one another's households, or orphans were put out to service by the town. In these relatively small and tight-knit communities, women who worked as domestic servants one year might get married the next and eventually employ servants in their own households. Some women preferred the word "help" to "servant," distinguishing between strangers who worked to pay off passage to North America and friends or relatives who assisted with childcare, cooking, sewing, or other chores.

By the late eighteenth century, however, more women were forced to seek jobs as domestic servants, many far from home. Growing numbers had children or parents to support as well, and fewer were able to escape from service until they were simply too old to find work. Household labor required great strength and perseverance in this period. Loads of heavy, wet wash had to be done each week by hand; clothes, diapers, blankets, and socks had to be made and mended; water and firewood had to be fetched and hauled on a daily basis; gardens had to be weeded and hoed; eggs gathered, cows fed, and milked, chickens plucked; meals prepared and cooked; and children had to be fed, clothed, and kept safe from the thousand dangers that lurked in houses, barns, fields, woods, and streams. For housewives with sufficient money, hiring domestic servants seemed the only way to manage the workload, since wealthier families had larger houses, extensive gardens, more clothes, and often more people to feed.

Yet as Marla Miller shows, many housewives found the need to hire and keep help burdensome. Domestic servants not only worked in the household, they also usually lived there. So servants had to be trustworthy as well as hardworking, and most women preferred them to be clean and respectful, too. From an employer's perspective, servants with children added one more complication to the mix. And as premarital pregnancy rates rose in the late eighteenth century, a growing number of those seeking jobs as servants were unwed mothers. The upheavals of war and the increasing mobility of the population meant that older familial and community controls over marriage were less effective, leaving more pregnant women to bear and raise children alone.

From the point of view of domestic servants, the employment risks were mostly on their side. They were forced to live in the employer's home, usually in a back, attic, or basement room, and depended on the employer as well for food, heat, and time off. Servants were also vulnerable to sexual exploitation by men in the household or the neighborhood. Moreover, if they had their own children to care for along with the employer's family, it was difficult to juggle all the demands on their time and energy. Yet how else, given the few occupations open to women, could they keep a roof over their heads and food on the table? African American women had even fewer options than their white counterparts.

Not surprisingly, few domestic servants left diaries or letters to tell us about their lives. Most received little if any education, and those who were literate had little time to record their thoughts. Thus, knowledge of their lives comes to us through court records, most often when the domestic servants were accused of a crime, or through the letters and diaries of their employers. Marla Miller analyzes the writings of Elizabeth Porter Phelps to illuminate the experiences of white and black domestic servants in Hadley, Massachusetts. All of these servants either had a child when first employed or bore a child while in the Phelpses' household. The sources used by Miller reveal as much about the hopes and frustrations of Mrs. Phelps as they do about those of the young women working in her employ. Yet it is precisely because Elizabeth Porter Phelps agonized over these women's circumstances that we gain a glimpse into lives that otherwise might have stayed hidden from history.

Eggs on the Sand: Domestic Servants and Their Children in Federal New England
MARLA R. MILLER

> Now I look back, I cannot help attributing the greater part of my misery,
> to the misfortune of having been thrown into the world without the great
> support of life—a mother's affection. I had no one to love me; or to
> make me respected, to enable me to acquire respect. I was an egg
> dropped on the sand; a pauper by nature, hunted from family to family,
> who belonged to nobody—and nobody cared for me.

When Mary Wollstonecraft penned these lines in her 1798 novel *The Wrongs of Woman*, she described the conditions of life experienced by Jemima, the bastard child born of a servant who had been seduced and abandoned by her lover, a fellow servant. Jemima, like many children born to unmarried domestic servants, had been thrust into an uncertain world. Her mother had died in childbirth, leaving her wholly without parental protection and advice, but other children born in similar

---

From *Women's Work in New England, 1620–1920,* ed. Peter Benes. Copyright © 2003 by Boston University for the Dublin Seminar for New England Folklife.

These pages from Elizabeth Porter Phelps' diary, housed at the Amherst College Archives and Special Collections, suggest the effort that went into her daily entries. While a large percentage of American women could read by 1800, far fewer could write. Though most often kept by well-to-do women, diaries such as this one offer rare direct evidence of women's own thoughts and experiences.

circumstances found that their mother's ability to care for them was compromised by her circumscribed social and economic options. "Eggs on the sand," the children Wollstonecraft observed and wrote about in her fiction, were born to mothers whose position as unmarried domestic servants shaped their ability to parent, to provide for their children's upbringing, and to direct their growth.

The papers of Hadley, Massachusetts, gentlewoman Elizabeth Porter Phelps allows us to compare fact with fiction and to observe the strategies employed by rural New England women who struggled to reconcile motherhood with other demands. As the eighteenth century gave way to the nineteenth, Phelps employed a number of women whose unexpected pregnancies—often, as with Jemima's parents, the result of unsanctioned relationships among servants employed by the household—created dilemmas for both the employer and the employee. Some women came to their workplace with a child in tow; Susanna Whipple Blodgett brought her daughter, Mitte West, to work with her when she secured a place at the Phelps farm, Forty Acres, and left her there when another pregnancy and subsequent marriage produced a new family. Others, like Persis Morse, became pregnant while in the Phelps family's employ, gave birth, and remained in the household, raising their children for a few months, or a few years, in their workplace. Finally, some single working mothers struggled to keep their family life out of their workplace; Polly Randall took a position as a domestic at Forty Acres while her young daughter remained in the care of Randall's aunt in Pelham, a situation that ultimately proved untenable.

Peg and Her Daughters Phillis and Roseanna

Raising one's family in one's workplace was, of course, nothing new in federal New England. African-American women had been doing it for generations, in the North as well as the South, and in much more trying conditions. Enslaved African-American women raised children even under the roof of Forty Acres. In 1754, Elizabeth's father Moses purchased Peg (ca. 1742–1792), who lived and worked in the Phelps family for some forty years. In the 1760s, when Peg was in her late teens and twenties, she had two daughters, Roseanna (1761–1781) and Phillis (1765–1775). She raised her little girls at Forty Acres until 1772, when she and Jon Warner's slave Pomp convinced their respective owners to sell them both to Stephen Fay of Bennington, Vermont, in order to facilitate their marriage. Pomp and Peg had been pressing for this arrangement for over a year, since at least May 1771, when town clerk Josiah Pierce recorded that "Jon Warner's Pomp desires to be published with Charles Phelps's Peg." Pomp told Pierce that "the masters are consenting," but when Pierce's son tried to confirm the matter, Warner "denies consent . . . and says he shall forbid, if published." Given the circumstances, Pierce refused to publish marriage banns for the two slaves. But after a year of what must have been persistent lobbying, the deal was eventually struck, and Peg left for Vermont, leaving her children behind.

For six years the family was separated. During those years, Roseanna became pregnant at fourteen, while Phillis became desperately ill. Charles and Elizabeth carried Phillis from doctor to doctor, but nothing, it seemed, could be done. In a twist of fate, in April 1775 Roseanna gave birth just as Phillis drew her final breaths. Roseanna named her daughter after her dead sister and raised the child at Forty Acres until her own death in 1781. In March 1778, the young mother gained the help of her own parent when Charles Phelps repurchased Peg, who rejoined the Hadley household. Perhaps Peg had been widowed by this point and desired to return home, but it seems likely too that Fay's decision to sell was prompted by the July 1777 Vermont constitution which declared slavery to be illegal in the fledgling state. Peg was there to nurse Roseanna during her fatal illness in 1781 and surely thereafter assumed care for her six-year-old granddaughter. But as Massachusetts followed Vermont's lead, entertaining a series of lawsuits in the early 1780s that would abolish slavery by 1783, Peg eagerly "went off free" in June 1782 (whether the Phelpses believed her to be emancipated or manumitted her themselves is at present unclear), although she did return the following year to nurse her ailing granddaughter, Phillis, in her own final illness. In the end, Peg outlived both her daughters and granddaughter, surviving until 1792.

Peg's ability to make choices involving her family were clearly circumscribed by her legal status and her race; she had to appeal to the good offices of her owners when seeking marriage and had little say over the care and disposition of her children. The circumstances of her life after emancipation are more difficult to track, but it seems likely that Peg, like other freedwomen in Hadley, continued to perform household labor for local families, often related to laundry. The Anglo-American women who worked for the Phelps household had more alternatives. Though their marginal economic status surely constrained their options, white women employed a variety of strategies when faced with the challenge of raising their children while earning an income. With few occupations open to them, unmarried women in rural New England often found themselves seeking positions as domestic servants, which required them to find ways to care for their children while working. Some women opted to keep their children with them in their places of employment, acting simultaneously as mothers and wage workers. Others left their children with relatives. Whatever choices they made, the balancing act was a difficult one.

Susanna Whipple Blodgett and Her Daughter, Submit West

On December 1791, Lucy Marshall, a hired woman from Leverett, left after some eight or nine years in the Phelpses' employ—an unusually long tenure in the world of domestic service. In her place, Elizabeth hired seventeen-year-old Susanna Whipple, who came with a six-week-old baby in tow, named Submit. The child was apparently the daughter of Daniel West, whose family lived on the south end of town. For whatever reason, Susanna could not compel a marriage and so found herself in need of shelter and employment, both of which were secured at Forty Acres. For the following fourteen months, she nursed her infant daughter in between chores for the Phelps household. Elizabeth Phelps's memorandum book for 1792 suggests a steady round of chores punctuated by visits to and from relatives.

Susanna would not remain a single mother for long; on 16 March 1793, Susanna married Samuel Blodgett, a hired man who was also living on the property. At the time of her marriage, she was once again pregnant—three months along by the time the Reverend Mr. Hopkins arrived to tie the knot. Two weeks later, the newly married Blodgetts moved out. In Susanna's place, Elizabeth engaged a "Mrs Hancock," who herself brought two children along with her. The Hancock family remained in the Phelps household for just over a year, until the fall of 1794, when they moved to Whately. By July, however, Susanna was having a difficult time managing both her pregnancy and little "Mitte," prompting her to ask whether she might return the child to the Phelpses. On 21 September, Susanna gave birth to twins, a boy and a girl. On 28 September Elizabeth Phelps recorded in the pages of her memorandum book, "*We* had *our* little girl Submit West christened," suggesting that already the little girl had made her way into the Phelps family circle (emphasis added).

Susanna Blodgett may have initially assumed that she and her new husband would eventually retrieve little Mitte, but for whatever reason, that was not to be. In the spring of the following year, the Blodgetts and their twins moved north, to Deerfield, but Mitte, now three-and-a half years old, did not join them. Instead, Mitte remained in the Phelps household, where she was raised as a ward of the family. She learned to knit, spin, help with the milking, and to perform other chores typically undertaken by children; at the same time, she became a treasured companion for Elizabeth Porter Phelps, whose own daughters were just themselves leaving the nest. In August 1794 Phelps reported to her daughter that she made Mitte "a little bed by ours every night and sometimes She will be in it at night others she will be up and down a number of times jest as she happens to feel—but on the whole she makes not much trouble in the night . . . indeed she is a great deal of company for me." The toddler was a steady source of amusement: "I love dearly to hear her talk. Yesterday it rained a little she was standing at the door looking out very serious then turning to me 'I is paid twil 'ain on Besse—un tamp un Porter'—I told her I thought there was more danger of its raining in on her—there she talks all day and is very diverting I can tell you." But even at the age of three, there were early signs that the young girl would not be easy to raise; Elizabeth assured her daughter Betsy that Mitte "is a much better girl than when you was here—no body to flee to now—but expects to do as I bid her."

Mitte's unruly behavior was a source of constant worry for Elizabeth Phelps and her daughter. From the time she was a toddler, it appears, Mitte was a handful. She was apparently uninterested in contributing to the work of the family, and had an insolent streak. Her conduct was a constant topic of conversation for Elizabeth, who regularly observed how "Mitte plods on, sometimes good and sometimes bad." When Betsy offered to take her into her home in Connecticut, Elizabeth called it a "relief." In the years to come, Mitte shuffled between the Hadley and Litchfield households until November 1804, when she left the Phelps household to live with her "grandmother West." Exhausted and disappointed, Elizabeth sighed, "O how pitiful I feel for her. I commit her Lord unto thee, do thou dispose of her as seemeth good in thy sight."

Persis and Dolly Morse

It was not just Mitte's conduct that Elizabeth Porter Phelps found difficult to control; Phelps constantly had a hard time enforcing among her hired help the same codes of behavior embraced by members of her family. Drunkenness was rampant among the hired men (at least as far as Elizabeth was concerned), and her kitchen was perpetually full of "talk and brawl." As the eighteenth century gave way to the nineteenth, Elizabeth found her household affairs regularly disrupted by the sexual behavior of the people in her employ. Although labor contracts from the latter half of the eighteenth century routinely forbade fornication, Elizabeth Porter Phelps had little luck controlling her servants' sexual activities. Among the first experiences with the unhappy consequences of unsanctioned intimacies concerned a hired woman named Judith who had joined the family sometime before February 1801. The family had been quite satisfied with her work, but when she became pregnant in the winter of 1802, her condition was an embarrassment, so much so that when Elizabeth was away visiting Betsy in Litchfield, she instructed her husband Charles, if company should come, "don't introduce Judith."

By mid March, it was becoming increasingly difficult for Judith to keep up with her duties: "Jude is quite feble. She has made out to dress a fowl for her Self, and a few other chores, she discharged her blood on Wednesday. Mrs Prince has been here to help her ever since. But I hope to get along if I can hire the washing." Though she was "not certain how it will be," whether Judith would indeed "venture off," she took the opportunity to inquire whether her daughter-in-law in Boston, Sarah Parsons Phelps, might be able to help secure Judith's replacement: "if you could find a good black girl down there I should be willing to give a good price, or a white girl, tho a black one would be best on some accounts for us." Phelps's predilection for women of color probably stemmed from longstanding cultural preferences among Connecticut Valley elites, but it seems possible, too, that she hoped that women of color would find fewer opportunities for romantic entanglements in Hadley than their Anglo-American counterparts.

Elizabeth seemed truly torn by her employee's difficult situation. She hoped that Judith appreciated "her own mercies" (perhaps a reference to the kindness she had heretofore received at Forty Acres) but felt too that her "long tarry has made her assume too much importance," suggesting that Judith had begun to take her position in the Phelps family for granted. In the end, Elizabeth Porter Phelps seemed to feel that "[Judith] has been here perhaps nearly long enough." For her part, Betsy Phelps Huntington recognized how few options were available to single mothers: "I pity poor Judith—should she be unable too work for her living, what would become of her?" Her father, she believed, would never turn her out, "destitute and distressed," but apparently Judith had no other means of support beyond her own labor. By May 1802, for whatever reason or by whatever means, Judith had left the household.

The experience left a lasting impression on Elizabeth Porter Phelps and her daughter Betsy, herself a young woman of twenty-three when Judith found herself with child. In January 1804, when discussing the care of Susanna Blodgett's daughter Mitte, Betsy suggested that she might come to live with her in Litchfield: "I feel as if she was not in so great danger here, as she was with your girls—from some things I understood from her, Persis [Morse—or Marsh, as she was also called] is a poor example for a girl of her years, [and] Meriam [Wire] was quite as bad." Well aware of the circumstances surrounding Mitte's own birth, Betsy was especially concerned that the young woman seemed a little too "sociable" in the kitchen with the hired boy Almond, a situation particularly troubling to her since twelve-year-old Mitte had already "had the sign" that Betsy and Elizabeth did not get until they were fourteen. Betsy's concern for the girl proved well founded: in a month's time Persis *was* pregnant by another of the hired boys, nineteen-year-old Reuban Bedell, who had lived at the farm since he was brought there in April 1791 at the age of five.

Persis Morse had joined the Phelps household in October of 1803. Reuban Bedell had lived at the farm nearly his whole life, having been brought there as a small child whose father was apparently dead, though he had other relatives in the area, and his mother visited him from time to time. The first hint of trouble for the two young servants came by early February 1805, when Elizabeth wrote to remind her daughter of "one thing I forgot to desire you to keep a profound secret, you recollect a Suspicion I mentioned of a person in our family—whether it be true, or false, keep it close." A month later, with Persis now nearly three months pregnant, Elizabeth reported to her daughter Betsy that Reuban had "took leg"; he told his employers that he was going to see his brother and sister in Vermont and proposed to return at the beginning of the next week, but when the whole week passed with no sign of the young man, the Phelpses concluded that Persis had been abandoned.

Persis herself seemed oddly unconcerned. She "ventured to say he would not be seen here again," and Elizabeth concurred, adding that "if lifting a finger would have kept him I'm sure mine would have try'd hard to have lain still." Still, Persis's calm puzzled her: "I should think it was of some consequence to her where he was—but as she appears to be well pleased." As to Charles and Elizabeth, they tried to keep out of it as much as was possible—"we say not much"—though Elizabeth remained concerned: "sometimes I almost tremble—& can tell you, I do now feel, as if I hardly dare go to bed." Within a few weeks the family heard that Reuban was back and was living with an uncle nearby, though he "has not been near here *that we know of*," conceding that the young couple may be in greater communication than she realizes. Though Elizabeth was genuinely fond of Persis, this situation presented a real dilemma. Betsy encouraged her mother to dismiss Persis, but Elizabeth was less certain.

> Pierces does not seem to have any inclination to quit here, says she can do as much work as last summer, says work does her no hurt, indeed she is as good as ever for ought I see. . . . yesterday [she] did all of the washing and all the work in that part of the house, cleard out that buttery, which you know is a great job, scoured it and replaced all the things, washed the floor done all and set down to knitting before four. I never expect to have another girl so kind, and willing to wait on me, and yet I know some things are very disagreeable. Your father and I talk, and talk, about it, and leave it just where we begun.

Persis's exemplary work in this period—washing the kitchen, scouring the buttery, getting everything back in order before 4 o'clock, and sitting down then to knit—appears to have been a calculated effort to convince Charles and Elizabeth that her pregnancy would not interfere with her responsibilities at work. And the campaign seems to have been working. In the summer Elizabeth described to her daughter a difficult week in which they had not only entertained important guests, "Col Chester and his Lady," but had also fed more than a dozen hired men. "I don't know how it is," she sighed, "but I do think Persis is really the best help I ever had, or ever shall have." Partly inclined to release Morse from her duties, Elizabeth was equally afraid that Persis herself would announce her departure, a prospect so disconcerting that Elizabeth was "almost in tremors every time I leave home."

This is apparently exactly the conclusion that Persis intended her employers to draw. While Charles and Elizabeth were stewing over what the outcome of this troubling situation might be, Persis herself was imagining her future at Forty Acres. In July she provided Elizabeth with some new information that she hoped would put her employer more at ease, and secure her place.

> P. is jest [ ] as ever . . . she says when she [ ] other one, she did not mind it, any more than a [ ] was round doing any thing in a few days—& [ ] was no trouble, quiet as a lamb, she went back [ ] time to the place where she liv'd before, & did all the work of a large tavern—the child liv'd about 2 years—& before it died, its work used to be to go round into all the rooms and chambers, & gather the candlesticks for P. to clean, that it was a very forward child. Thus stands the matter.

It is unclear whether this was the first time Elizabeth learned of Persis's other child, or whether Persis only just revealed this chapter in her life in order to persuade her employer to keep her on. In any event, apparently, Persis hoped to reassure Elizabeth that the last time she found herself pregnant, while employed at a "large tavern," her child proved to be no trouble at all and in fact helped Persis complete her regular duties. "She continues jest as alert as ever," Elizabeth concluded, adding that "perhaps she intends to go way—but she takes care not to tell of it."

Finally, on Wednesday, August 10, at about 11 o'clock p.m., Persis gave birth to a daughter, called Dolly. Interestingly, though she was living under the same roof, she did not call Elizabeth until after the child had arrived, and there is no mention of the midwife's arriving, as was usual, until the next day, when Charles brought Mrs. Montague to the house to see to the new mother and child. Elizabeth had to hire an African-American woman to come in and help with Monday's wash, but on the following Tuesday, true to her word, Persis came down to do some chores and "gained a little in the business every day" thereafter. By 28 August, Elizabeth reported that "she is now nearly as good as ever. The child is very quiet, & she pays every attention to it, that is necessary. I dare not let her do the washing this week, tho she said she could."

For almost two years, Persis and Dolly remained members of the Phelps household. No records survive to shed light on how well the two families coexisted under Forty Acres' roof, but Persis's departure late in 1807 seems to have come on awkward terms. A year earlier a letter from Elizabeth hinted that having Dolly in the house was starting to strain her nerves. Early one Saturday morning she wrote, "I feel just as unable to write now as last night—for my patience is so much try'd with this young one that it really disturbs my peace—I beg for more patience if I must have this thorn in the flesh or in the spirit I don't know which—we were quite dirty eno' I tho't before, but now it is much worse than ever." By spring Phelps was again asking Betsy to be on the lookout for new help: "if you could find a good Negro woman for us, I hope we should be thankful, as our present help is nearly worn out." Phelps recalled that her hired woman had been "very kind to me, & very good tempered the first part of the time," but "the trouble which is attached to her now, and the crosses which we have to bear, is rather troublesome, how long we shall have it I can't guess, unless she should be so kind as to say she will tarry no longer, which I am something suspicious will take place." The nature of the "trouble attached to her" remains unstated, but eight months later, in November 1807, Elizabeth sighed to her daughter-in-law Sarah, "I suppose [Persis] will leave us soon." As she did with Judith, she suggests that she would be grateful if Sarah could recommend anyone, noting that a "good black girl would suit very well."

Polly Randall and Child

Persis Morse actively promoted her ability to raise a child while keeping up with her household assignments, even suggesting that a child could contribute to the household labor; other women took a different tack, struggling to sustain families far distant from their places of employment. Polly Randall, like both Susanna Whipple and Persis Morse, had a small child in her care when she worked at Forty Acres. But unlike Susanna, she did not wish to bring the child with her to her new workplace. Instead, Polly left her young child at home with an aunt in Pelham, a hilltown roughly ten miles to the east.

Polly Randall came to work at Forty Acres in July 1809, and remained until November of the following year. The period of her employment was a difficult one, both for Polly and for her employers. Polly was trying to juggle the care of an elderly aunt and of her own young child with full-time work in the Phelps household. Elizabeth Porter Phelps keenly felt the inconveniences Polly's family obligations caused her own household. In writing to her daughter Betsy, she explained, "I was obliged to break off abruptly last Wednesday as Polly went away last Tuesday to

Pelham, & has not got home yet, she has a great deal to do, to take care of her old Aunt & her own child, I think it uncertain whether we shall be able to get along with her much longer." Polly was apparently trying to find new lodgings for her aunt, who had been sick for most of the winter. Nearly once every two weeks she had been borrowing a horse from the Phelpses and riding to Pelham to attend to matters there "without any charge made of it," leaving Elizabeth without reliable help: "Now I have had the work to do about three days & when she will come is altogether uncertain." As to Polly's dilemma, Elizabeth was unsympathetic: "Her folly, & sin, has been the occasion of a great deal of trouble to her & others."

Randall struggled on through the spring, summer, and fall, but by the end of the year, she had decided that enough was enough. In mid-November, Randall quit her position and returned to Pelham. Her wages were $1.00 per week, but she found that, burdened with the care of both her elderly aunt and young child, she could not make ends meet. Elizabeth Porter Phelps seemed a bit dismayed at Polly's decision, or at least at the circumstances surrounding it. "I am the only female in the house and have been about two weeks," she reported to her daughter in December 1810; "We gave Polly great wages, & she could not support a family at Pelham and half cloath herself, so she tho't best to try some other method, & braiding straw hats was the one proposed." Like growing numbers of girls in Pelham and Amherst, Polly Randall embraced a new source of income that would allow her to remain at home, converting locally grown rye into lengths of straw plaits, to be made into women's bonnets. At the end of her tenure, Charles' accounts show that Polly owed the family $25.98 for the purchase of gloves, wool, a shawl, shoes, and other miscellaneous items, as well as several visits to the doctor. She was also in debt for pork, cheese, butter, and sugar, which she supplied to her aunt in Pelham. Subtracting some $19 in unpaid wages, Polly Randall left Forty Acres with a balance due of $6.65.

What became of these women, and of their children, those "eggs on the sand"? As is too often the case, once their paths diverged from that of their well-heeled employer, few records survive to shed light on their lives. Susanna Whipple Blodgett and her husband Samuel remained in Deerfield. When Susanna had another child in January 1802, Elizabeth Phelps wrote her daughter Betsy that she may inform Mitte or not, as she pleases, suggesting that the mother and daughter had become at least somewhat estranged. Susanna's daughter, despite the continuing concern and efforts of the Phelps and Huntington families, remained unreconciled to social constraints; in 1810 Phelps recorded that "submit west had a child in Conway, said to be a negro, shocking affair." The child's father may well have been Prince, an African-American hired man in the neighborhood of Forty Acres and occasional employee of the farm there; when Sarah Parsons Phelps heard the news about Mitte she wrote "My heart sickens within me when I think of her or Prince, what will become of her I know not." Persis and Dolly Morse vanish from local records; whatever happened next for them, Elizabeth Porter Phelps never seems to have learned. Polly Randall and child, we know, returned to Pelham, though their subsequent fortunes remain a mystery.

Though the ultimate fates of Mitte West, the Morses, and Randalls are as yet unknown, the brief tenure of each family in the household at Forty Acres suggests some of the strategies employed by working mothers in federal New England. Each of these women chose different means by which to cope with the challenges of parenting while at the same time ensuring an income for herself and her child. Close examination of these women, their relationships with their employers, their strategies and choices in raising their own families, and the consequences of those decisions for their children sheds important light on the world of laboring women and children in early New England. The world of Forty Acres allows us to imagine the world of early America's working women as they struggled to balance their needs, desires, and values with the needs, desires, and values of their employers.

Questions for Study and Review

1. How did New Englanders define concepts like family and household in the early years of the new nation?

2. How did pregnancy and childrearing shape the lives of married and single women in late eighteenth- and early nineteenth-century New England?

3. How had daily life changed for families in North America between the early eighteenth and early nineteenth centuries?

4. Compare the difficulties of tracing the life of Pocahontas through the records of Englishmen and the lives of domestic servants through the letters of their employer.

Suggested Readings and Web Sites

Faye Dudden, *Serving Women: Household Service in Nineteenth-century America* (1983)
Linda Kerber, *No Constitutional Right to Be Ladies: Women and the Obligation of Citizenship* (1998)
Laurel Thatcher Ulrich, *The Age of Homespun: Objects and Stories in the Creation of an American Myth* (2001)
Betty Wood, *Gender, Race, and Rank in a Revolutionary Age* (2000)
Doing History: Martha Ballard's Diary Online
    http://DoHistory.org
Colonial House from PBS
    http://www.pbs.org/wnet/colonialhouse/history

Individuals, families, and communities reacted differently to the economic and social changes of the postrevolutionary era. Battles over hard currency and increased taxes led some to active resistance, as in Shays's Rebellion and the Whisky Rebellion. Most citizens, however, like Greenleaf and Abigail Patch, sought to adapt to new conditions, hoping for the break that would send them on their way to financial security and a better life.

Uprooted from family and community by the death of parents, a failure to inherit land, and an inability to succeed at his trade of shoemaking, Greenleaf Patch almost did find through marriage the stability that had earlier eluded him. Alternating between agrarian, artisan, and industrial pursuits, however, he never achieved the success that seemed within his grasp. Abigail, whose upbringing prepared her to labor alongside but not in place of her husband, was perhaps fortunate to live in an era when a woman and her daughters could find in factories the means of supporting themselves. Yet she was no feminist foremother, seeking liberation from family claims. Rather, only a deep religious faith seems to have carried her through the economic trials and personal tragedies of a life filled with anxiety and disappointment.

Through a detailed portrait of a couple considered unremarkable in their own day, Paul Johnson demonstrates the halting first steps in what would one day culminate in a full-blown "industrial revolution." The social and economic transformations that began the process are here described as a series of disjointed and often disruptive modifications in the opportunities and expectations available to those living on the margins of society. Limited in their choices and often unaware of the consequences resulting from them, husbands and wives, parents and children, sons and daughters might suddenly find their places in the family and community significantly altered, even reversed.

When Alexander Hamilton called for women to enter factories or Thomas Jefferson for men to stay on farms, both seemed to envision stable and prosperous families in which men were breadwinners and women helpmates. Johnson shows that such a life was not obtainable by those Americans for whom economic upheaval coincided with other disruptions wrought by war and its aftermath—indebtedness, transiency, premarital pregnancy, alcoholism. Though in the mid-nineteenth century, farmers' daughters did finally live out Hamilton's dream in factory towns like Lowell, Massachusetts, industrialization continued to subvert as often as it supported individual prosperity and familial stability.

The Modernization of Greenleaf and Abigail Patch: Land, Family, and Marginality in the New Republic

PAUL E. JOHNSON

This is the story of Mayo Greenleaf Patch and Abigail McIntire Patch, ordinary people who helped write a decisive chapter in American history: they were among the first New Englanders to abandon farming and take up factory labor. They did so because rural society had no room for them, and their history is a tale of progressive exclusion from an agrarian world governed by family, kinship, and inherited land. Mayo Greenleaf Patch was the youngest son of a man who owned a small farm. He inherited nothing, and in his early and middle years he improvised a living at the edges of the family economy. He grew up with an uncle and brother, combined farming and shoemaking with dependence on his wife's family in the 1790s, recruited a half-sister into schemes against his in-laws' property, then lived briefly off an inheritance from a distant relative. Finally, having used up his exploitable kin connections, he left the countryside and moved to a mill town in which his wife and children could support the family.

That is how Greenleaf and Abigail Patch made the journey from farm to factory. But they experienced their troubles most intimately as members of a family; their story can be comprehended only as family history. Greenleaf Patch was a failed patriarch. His marriage to Abigail McIntire began with an early pregnancy, was punctuated by indebtedness and frequent moves, and ended in alcoholism and a divorce. Along the way, a previously submissive Abigail began making decisions for the family, decisions that were shaped by an economic situation in which she but not her husband found work and by her midlife conversion into a Baptist church.

The outlines of the Patch family history are familiar, for recent scholarship on New England in the century following 1750 centers on its principal themes: the crisis of the rural social order in the eighteenth century, the beginnings of commercial and industrial society in the nineteenth, and transformations in personal and family life that occurred in transit between the two. The Patches shared even the particulars of their story—disinheritance, premarital pregnancy, alcoholism, transiency, indebtedness, divorce, female religious conversion—with many of their neighbors. In short, Abigail and Greenleaf Patch lived at the center of a decisive social transformation and experienced many of its defining events.

The story of the Patches throws light on the process whereby farmers in post-Revolutionary New England became "available" for work outside of agriculture. That light, however, is dim and oblique, and we must confront two qualifications

The New England Quarterly, v. 55, December 1982 for "The Modernization of Mayo Greenleaf Patch: Land, Family and Marginality in New England, 1766–1818" by Paul Johnson. Copyright held by *The New England Quarterly*. Reproduced by permission of the publisher and the author.

at the outset. First, the Patches were obscure people who left incomplete traces of their lives. Neither Greenleaf nor Abigail kept a diary or wrote an autobiography, their names never appeared in newspapers, and no one bothered to save their mail. Apart from one rambling and inaccurate family reminiscence, their story must be reconstructed from distant, impersonal and fragmentary sources: wills and deeds, church records, tax lists, censuses, the minutes of town governments, court records, and histories of the towns in which they lived and the shoe and textile industries in which they worked. The results are not perfect. The broad outlines of the story can be drawn with confidence, and a few episodes emerge in fine-grained detail. But some crucial points must rest on controlled inference, others on inferences that are a little less controlled, still others on outright guess-work. Scholars who demand certainty should stay away from people like Greenleaf and Abigail Patch. But historians of ordinary individuals must learn to work with the evidence that they left behind.

A second qualification concerns the problems of generalizing from a single case. It must be stated strongly that the Patches were not typical. No one really is. The Patches, moreover, can claim uniqueness, for they were the parents of Sam Patch, a millworker who earned national notoriety in the 1820s as a professional daredevil. The younger Patch's life was an elaborate exercise in self-destruction, and we might question the normality of the household in which he grew up. Indeed the history of the Patch family is shot through with brutality and eccentricity and with a consistent sadness that is all its own. The Patches were not typical but marginal, and that is the point: it was persons who were marginal to rural society who sought jobs outside of agriculture. The number of such persons grew rapidly in post-Revolutionary New England. This is the story of two of them.

● ● ●

New England men of Greenleaf Patch's generation grew up confronting two uncomfortable facts. The first was the immense value that their culture placed on ownership of land. Freehold tenure conferred not only economic security but personal and moral independence, the ability to support and govern a family, political rights, and the respect of one's neighbors and oneself. New Englanders trusted the man who owned land; they feared and despised the man who did not. The second fact was that in the late eighteenth century increasing numbers of men owned no land. Greenleaf Patch was among them.

Like nearly everyone else in Revolutionary Massachusetts, Patch was descended from yeoman stock. His family had come to Salem in 1636, and they operated a farm in nearby Wenham for more than a century. The Patches were church members and farm owners, and their men served regularly in the militia and in town offices. Greenleaf's father, grandfather, and great-grandfather all served terms as selectmen of Wenham; his great-grandfather was that community's representative to the Massachusetts General Court; his older brother was a militiaman who fought on the first day of the American Revolution.

The Patches commanded respect among their neighbors, but in the eighteenth century their future was uncertain. Like thousands of New England families, they owned small farms and had many children; by mid-century it was clear that young

Patch men would not inherit the material standards enjoyed by their fathers. The farm on which Greenleaf Patch was born was an artifact of that problem. His father, Timothy Patch, Jr., had inherited a house, an eighteen-acre farm, and eleven acres of outlying meadow and woodland upon his own father's death in 1751. Next door, Timothy's younger brother Samuel farmed the remaining nine acres of what had been their father's homestead. The father had known that neither Timothy nor Samuel could make a farm of what he had, and he required that they share resources. His will granted Timothy access to a shop and cider mill that lay on Samuel's land and drew the boundary between the two farms through the only barn on the property. It was the end of the line: further subdivision would make both farms unworkable.

Timothy Patch's situation was precarious, and he made it worse by overextending himself, both as a landholder and as a father. Timothy was forty-three years old when he inherited his farm, and he was busy buying pieces of woodland, upland, and meadow all over Wenham. Evidently he speculated in marginal land and/or shifted from farming to livestock raising. He financed his schemes on credit, and he bought on a fairly large scale. By the early 1760s Timothy Patch held title to 114 acres, nearly all of it in small plots of poor land.

Timothy Patch may have engaged in speculation in order to provide for an impossibly large number of heirs. Timothy was the father of ten children when he inherited his farm. In succeeding years he was widowed, remarried, and sired two more daughters and a son. In all, he fathered ten children who survived to adulthood. The youngest was a son born in 1766. Timothy named him Mayo Greenleaf.

Greenleaf Patch's life began badly: his father went bankrupt in the year of his birth. Timothy had transferred the house and farm to his two oldest sons in the early 1760s, possibly to keep the property out of the hands of creditors. Then, in 1766, the creditors began making trouble. In September Timothy relinquished twenty acres of his outlying land to satisfy a debt. By March 1767, having lost five court cases and sold all of his remaining land to pay debts and court costs, he was preparing to leave Wenham. Timothy's first two sons stayed on, but both left Wenham before their deaths, and none of the other children established households in the community. After a century as substantial farmers and local leaders, the Patch family abandoned their hometown.

Greenleaf Patch was taken from his home village as an infant, and his family's wanderings after that can be traced only through his father's appearances in court. By 1770 the family had moved a few miles north and west to Andover, where Timothy was sued by yet another creditor. Nine years later Timothy Patch was in Danvers, where he went to court seven times in three years. The court cases suggest that the family experienced drastic ups and downs. Some cases involved substantial amounts of money, but in the last, Timothy was accused of stealing firewood. He then left Danvers and moved to Nottingham West, New Hampshire. There Timothy seems to have recouped his fortunes once again, for in 1782 he was a gambler-investor in an American Revolutionary privateer.

That is all we know about the Patch family during the childhood of Mayo Greenleaf Patch. About the childhood itself we know nothing. Doubtless Greenleaf shared his parents' frequent moves and their bouts of good and bad luck, and from his subsequent behavior we might conclude that he inherited his father's penchant for economic adventurism. He may also have spent parts of his childhood and youth in other households. Since he later named his own children after relatives in Wenham, he probably lived there in the families of his brother and uncle. We know also that during his youth he learned how to make shoes, and since his first independent appearance in the record came when he was twenty-one, we might guess that he served a formal, live-in apprenticeship. Even these points, however, rest on speculation. Only this is certain: Greenleaf Patch was the tenth and youngest child of a family that broke and scattered in the year of his birth, and he entered adulthood alone and without visible resources.

In 1787 Mayo Greenleaf Patch appeared in the Second (North) Parish of Reading, Massachusetts—fifteen miles due north of Boston. He was twenty-one years old and unmarried, and he owned almost nothing. He had no relatives in Reading; indeed no one named Patch had ever lived in that town. In a world where property was inherited and where kinfolk were essential social and economic assets, young Greenleaf Patch inherited nothing and lived alone.

Greenleaf's prospects in 1787 were not promising. But he soon took steps to improve them. In July 1788 he married Abigail McIntire in Reading. He was twenty-two years old; she was seventeen and pregnant. This early marriage is most easily explained as an unfortunate accident. But from the viewpoint of Greenleaf Patch it was not unfortunate at all, for it put him into a family that possessed resources that his own family had lost. For the next twelve years, Patch's livelihood and ambitions would center on the McIntires and their land.

The McIntires were Scots, descendants of highlanders who had been exiled to Maine after the Battle of Dunbar [1650]. Some had walked south, and Philip McIntire was among those who pioneered the North Parish in the 1650s. By the 1780s McIntire households were scattered throughout the parish. Archelaus McIntire, Abigail's father, headed the most prosperous of those households. Archelaus had been the eldest son of a man who died without a will, and he inherited the family farm intact. He added to the farm and by 1791 owned ninety-seven acres in Reading and patches of meadowland in two neighboring townships, a flock of seventeen sheep as well as cattle and oxen and other animals, and personal property that indicates comfort and material decency if not wealth. Of 122 taxable estates in the North Parish in 1792, Archelaus McIntire's ranked twenty-third.

In 1788 Archelaus McIntire learned that his youngest daughter was pregnant and would marry Mayo Greenleaf Patch. No doubt he was angry, but he had seen such things before. One in three Massachusetts women of Abigail's generation was pregnant on her wedding day, a statistic to which the McIntires had contributed amply. Archelaus himself had been born three months after his parents' marriage in 1729. One of his older daughters had conceived a child at the age of fourteen, and his only son would marry a pregnant lover in 1795.

Faced with yet another early pregnancy, Archelaus McIntire determined to make the best of a bad situation. In the winter of 1789/90, he built a shoemaker's shop and a small house for Greenleaf Patch and granted him use of the land on which they sat. At a stroke, Patch was endowed with family connections and economic independence.

Greenleaf Patch took his place among the farmer-shoemakers of northeastern Massachusetts in 1790. The region had been exporting shoes since before the Revolution, for it possessed the prerequisites of cottage industry in abundance: it was poor and overcrowded and had access to markets through Boston and the port towns of Essex County. With the Revolution and the protection of footwear under the first national tariffs, with the expansion of the maritime economy of which the shoe trade was a part, and with the continuing growth of rural poverty, thousands of farm families turned to the making of shoes in the 1790s.

Their workshops were not entrepreneurial ventures. Neither, if we listen to the complaints of merchants and skilled artisans about "slop work" coming out of the countryside, were they likely sources of craft traditions or occupational pride. The trade was simply the means by which farmers on small plots of worn-out land maintained their independence.

The journal of Isaac Weston, a Reading shoemaker during the 1790s, suggests something of the cottage shoemaker's way of life. Weston was first and last a farmer. He spent his time worrying about the weather, working his farm, repairing his house and outbuildings, and trading farm labor with his neighbors and relatives. His tasks accomplished, he went hunting with his brothers-in-law, took frequent fishing trips to the coast at Lynn, and made an endless round of social calls in the neighborhood. The little shop at the back of Weston's house supplemented his earnings, and he spent extended periods of time in it only during the winter months. With his bags of finished shoes, he made regular trips to Boston, often in company with other Reading shoemakers. The larger merchants did not yet dominate the trade in country shoes, and Weston and his neighbors went from buyer to buyer bargaining as a group and came home with enough money to purchase leather, pay debts and taxes, and subsist for another year as farmers.

Isaac Weston's workshop enabled him to survive as an independent proprietor. At the same time, it fostered relations of neighborly cooperation with other men. He was the head of a self-supporting household and an equal participant in neighborhood affairs; in eighteenth-century Massachusetts, those criteria constituted the definition of manhood. Mayo Greenleaf Patch received that status as a wedding present.

Greenleaf and Abigail occupied the new house and shop early in 1790, and their tax listings over the next few years reveal a rise from poverty to self-sufficiency with perhaps a little extra. In 1790, for the first time, Greenleaf paid the tax on a small piece of land. Two years later he ranked fifty-sixth among the 122 taxpayers in the North Parish. Patch was not getting rich, but he enjoyed a secure place in the economy of his neighborhood. That alone was a remarkable achievement for a young stranger who had come to town with almost nothing.

With marriage and proprietorship came authority over a complex and growing household. Few rural shoemakers in the 1790s worked alone; they hired outside help and put their wives and children to work binding shoes. Isaac Weston brought in apprentices and journeymen, and Greenleaf Patch seems to have done the same. In 1790 the Patch family included Greenleaf and Abigail and their infant daughter, along with a boy under the age of sixteen and an unidentified adult male. In 1792 Patch paid the tax on two polls, suggesting that again the household included an adult male dependent. It seems clear that Greenleaf hired outsiders and (assuming Abigail helped) regularly headed a family work team that numbered at least four persons.

During the same years, Patch won the respect of the McIntires and their neighbors. When Archelaus McIntire died in 1791, his will named Patch executor of the estate. Greenleaf spent considerable effort, including two successful appearances in court, ordering his father-in-law's affairs. In 1794 he witnessed a land transaction involving his brother-in-law, again indicating that he was a trusted member of the McIntire family. That trust was shared by the neighbors. In 1793 the town built a schoolhouse near the Patch home, and in 1794 and 1795 the parish paid Greenleaf Patch for boarding the schoolmistress and for escorting her home at the end of the term. Those were duties that could only have gone to a trusted neighbor who ran an orderly house.

• • •

Greenleaf Patch's marriage to Abigail McIntire rescued him from the shiftless and uncertain life that had been dealt to him at birth. In 1787 he was a propertyless wanderer. By the early 1790s, he was the head of a growing family, a useful member of the McIntire clan, and a familiar and trusted neighbor. Greenleaf Patch had found a home. But his gains were precarious, for they rested on the use of land that belonged not to him but to his father-in-law. When Archelaus died, the title to the McIntire properties fell to his nineteen-year-old son, Archelaus, Jr. Young Archelaus was bound out to a guardian, and Patch, as executor of the estate, began to prey openly on the resources of Abigail's family. In succeeding years bad luck and moral failings would cost him everything that he had gained.

With Archelaus McIntire dead and his son living with a guardian, the household that the senior Archelaus had headed shrank to two women: his widow and his daughter Deborah. The widow described herself as an invalid, and there may have been something wrong with Deborah as well. In the will that he wrote in 1791, Archelaus ordered that his heir take care of Deborah. His son would repeat that order ten years later, when Deborah, still unmarried and still living at home, was thirty-five years old. Shortly after the death of Archelaus McIntire (and shortly before Patch was to inventory the estate), the widow complained to authorities that "considerable of my household goods & furniture have been given to my children" and begged that she be spared "whatever household furniture that may be left which is but a bare sufficiency to keep household." At that time two of her four daughters were dead, a third lived with her, and her only son was under the care of a guardian. The "children" could have been none other than Greenleaf and Abigail Patch, whose personal property taxes mysteriously doubled between 1791 and 1792. Greenleaf Patch had walked into a house occupied by helpless women and walked off with the funiture.

Patch followed this with a second and more treacherous assault on the McIntires and their resources. In November 1793 Archelaus McIntire, Jr. came of age and assumed control of the estate. Greenleaf's use of McIntire land no longer rested on his relationship with his father-in-law or his role as executor but on the whim of Archelaus, Jr. Patch took steps that would tie him closely to young Archelaus and his land. Those steps involved a woman named Nancy Barker, who moved into Reading sometime in 1795. Mrs. Barker had been widowed twice, the second time, apparently, by a Haverhill shoemaker who left her with his tools and scraps of leather, a few valueless sticks of furniture, and two small children. Nancy Barker, it turns out, was the half-sister of Mayo Greenleaf Patch.

In November 1795 Nancy Barker married Archelaus McIntire, Jr. She was thirty-one years old. He had turned twenty-three the previous day, and his marriage was not a matter of choice: Nancy was four months pregnant. Archelaus and Nancy were an unlikely couple, and we must ask how the match came about. Archelaus had grown up with three older sisters and no brothers; his attraction and/or vulnerability to a woman nearly nine years his senior is not altogether mysterious. Nancy, of course, had sensible reasons for being attracted to Archelaus. She was a destitute widow with two children, and he was young, unmarried, and the owner of substantial property. Finally, Greenleaf Patch, who was the only known link between the two, had a vital interest in creating ties between his family and his in-law's land. It would be plausible—indeed it seems inescapable—to conclude that Nancy Barker, in collusion with her half-brother, had seduced young Archelaus McIntire and forced a marriage.

Of course, that may be nothing more than perverse speculation. Nancy and Archelaus may simply have fallen in love, started a baby, and married. Whatever role Greenleaf Patch played in the affair may have added to his esteem among the McIntires and in the community. That line of reasoning, however, must confront an unhappy fact: in 1795 the neighbors and the McIntires began to dislike Mayo Greenleaf Patch.

The first sign of trouble came in the fall of 1795, when town officials stepped into a boundary dispute between Patch and Deacon John Swain. Massachusetts towns encouraged neighbors to settle arguments among themselves. In all three parishes of Reading in the 1790s, only three disagreements over boundaries came before the town government, and one of those was settled informally. Thus Greenleaf Patch was party to half of Reading's mediated boundary disputes in the 1790s. The list of conflicts grew: after 1795 the schoolmistress was moved out of the Patch household; in 1797 Patch complained that he had been overtaxed (another rare occurrence), demanded a reassessment, and was reimbursed. Then he started going to court. In 1798 Greenleaf Patch sued Thomas Tuttle for nonpayment of a debt and was awarded nearly $100 when Tuttle failed to appear. A few months earlier, Patch had been hauled into court by William Herrick, a carpenter who claimed that Patch owed him $480. Patch denied the charge and hired a lawyer; the court found in his favor, but Herrick appealed the case, and a higher court awarded him $100.52. Six years later, Patch's lawyer was still trying to collect his fee.

There is also a question about land. In the dispute with John Swain, the description of Patch's farm matches none of the properties described in McIntire deeds. We know that Patch no longer occupied McIntire land in 1798, and town records identified him as the "tenant" of his disputed farm in 1795. Perhaps as early as 1795, Patch had been evicted from McIntire land.

Finally, there is clear evidence that the authorities had stopped trusting Mayo Greenleaf Patch. Nancy Barker McIntire died in 1798 at the age of thirty-four. Archelaus remarried a year later, then died suddenly in 1801. His estate—two houses and the ninety-seven-acre farm, sixty acres of upland and meadow in Reading, and fifteen acres in the neighboring town of Lynnfield—was willed to his two children by Nancy Barker. Archelaus's second wife sold her right of dower and left town, and the property fell to girls who were four and five years of age. Their guardian would have use of the land for many years. By this time Greenleaf and Abigail Patch had moved away, but surely authorities knew their whereabouts and that they were the orphans' closest living relatives. Yet the officials passed them over and appointed a farmer from Reading as legal guardian. The court, doubtless with the advice of the neighbors, had decided against placing Greenleaf Patch in a position of trust. For Patch it was a costly decision. It finally cut him off from property that he had occupied and plotted against for many years.

Each of these facts and inferences says little by itself, but together they form an unmistakable pattern: from the date of his marriage through the mid-1790s, Greenleaf Patch accumulated resources and participated in the collective life of Abigail's family and neighborhood; from 1795 onward he entered the record only when he was fighting the neighbors or being shunned by the family. The promising family man of the 1790s was a contentious and morally bankrupt outcast by 1798.

Late in 1799 or early in 1800 Greenleaf and Abigail and their four children left Reading and resettled in Danvers, a community of farmer-shoemakers on the outskirts of Salem. We cannot know why they selected that town, but their best connection with the place came through Abigail. Danvers was her mother's birthplace, and she had an aunt and uncle, five first cousins, and innumerable distant relatives in the town. Indeed Abigail's father had owned land in Danvers. In 1785 Archelaus McIntire, Sr. had seized seven acres from John Felton, one of his in-laws, in payment of a debt. Archelaus, Jr. sold the land back to the Feltons in 1794 but did not record the transaction until 1799. Perhaps he made an arrangement whereby the Patches had use of the land. (Doubtless Archelaus was glad to be rid of Greenleaf Patch, but he may have felt some responsibility for his sister.)

Danvers was another shoemaking town, and the Patches probably rented a farm and made shoes. In 1800 the household included Greenleaf and Abigail, their children, and no one else, suggesting that they were no longer able to hire help. But this, like everything else about the family's career in Danvers, rests on inference. We know only that they were in Danvers and that they stayed three years.

Late in 1802 Greenleaf Patch received a final reprieve, again through family channels. His half-brother Job Davis (his mother's son by her first marriage) died in the fishing port of Marblehead and left Patch one-fifth of his estate. The full property included a butcher's shop at the edge of town, an unfinished new house, and what was described as a "mansion house" that needed repairs. The property, however, was mortgaged to the merchants William and Benjamin T. Reid. The survivors of Job Davis inherited the mortgage along with the estate.

Cartoons such as these were popular in the mid- and late-nineteenth century. They focused primarily on the effects of alcohol, gambling and other vices on the American family. As a result of giving in to some vice, the father forfeits his role as family patriarch, the wife is forced to take on paternal as well as maternal duties, and the children are both estranged from and frightened of the father.

The other heirs sold to the Reids without a struggle, but Greenleaf Patch, whether from demented ambition or lack of alternatives, moved his family to Marblehead early in 1803. He finished the new house and moved into it, reopened the butcher's shop, and ran up debts. Some of the debts were old. Patch owed Ebenezer Goodale of Danvers $54. He also owed Porter Sawyer of Reading $92 and paid a part of it by laboring at 75¢ a day. Then there were debts incurred in Marblehead: $70 to the widow Sarah Dolebar; a few dollars for building materials and furnishings bought from the Reids; $50 to a farmer named Benjamin Burnham; $33 to Zachariah King of Danvers; $35 to Joseph Holt of Reading; another $35 to Caleb Totman of Hampshire County. Finally, there was the original mortgage held by the Reids.

Patch's renewed dreams of independence collapsed under the weight of his debts. In March 1803 a creditor repossessed the property up to a value of $150, and a few weeks before Christmas of the same year the sheriff seized the new house. In the following spring, Patch missed a mortgage payment, and [the] Reids took him to court, seized the remaining property, and sold it at auction. Still, Patch retained the right to reclaim the property by paying his debts. The story ends early in 1805, when the Reids bought Greenleaf Patch's right of redemption for $60. Patch had struggled with the Marblehead property for two years, and all had come to nothing.

With this final failure, the Patches exhausted the family connections on which they had subsisted since their marriage. The long stay in Reading and the moves to Danvers and Marblehead were all determined by the availability of relatives and their resources. In 1807 the Patches resettled in Pawtucket, Rhode Island, the pioneer textile milling town in the United States. It was the climactic event in their history: it marked their passage out of the family economy and into the labor market.

When the family arrived in Pawtucket early in 1807, they found four textile mills surrounding the waterfall at the center of town. The mills were small and limited to the spinning of yarn, and much of the work was done by outworkers. Children picked and cleaned raw cotton in their homes, then sent it to the mills to be carded by other children. The cotton next went to the spinning rooms, where, with the help of water-driven machinery, a few skilled men, and still more children, it was turned into yarn. Millers put the yarn out to women, many of them widows with children, who wove it into cloth. There was thus plenty of work for Abigail and her older children, and it was they who supported the family in Pawtucket. Samuel, the second son, spent his childhood in the mills, and his sisters probably did the same. It is likely that Abigail worked as a weaver; certainly the wool produced on her father's farm suggests that she knew something about that trade.

That leaves only the father. Pawtucket was booming in 1807, and if Greenleaf Patch were willing and physically able, he could have found work. We know, however, that he did not work in that town. He drank, he stole the money earned by his wife and children, and he threatened them frequently with violence. Then, in 1812, he abandoned them. Abigail waited six years and divorced him in 1818. She recounted Greenleaf's drinking and his threats and his refusal to work, then revealed what for her was the determining blow: Greenleaf Patch had drifted back to Massachusetts and had been caught passing counterfeit money. In February 1817 he entered the Massachusetts State Prison at Charlestown. He was released the following August. Patch was fifity-two years old, and that is the last we hear of him.

• • •

In a society that located virtue and respectability in the yeoman freeholder, Mayo Greenleaf Patch never owned land. We have seen some public consequences of that fact: his lifelong inability to attain material independence, the troubled relations with in-laws, neighbors, creditors, and legal authorities that resulted when he tried, and the personal and moral disintegration that accompanied unending economic distress.

Now we turn to private troubles, and here the story centers on Abigail McIntire Patch. Recent studies of late eighteenth- and early nineteenth-century family life have documented a decline of patriarchal authority, the creation of a separate and female-dominated domestic sphere, an increase in female religiosity, and, bound up with all three, the elevation of women's status and power within the home. Most of these studies center on middle- and upper-class women, and we are left to wonder whether the conclusions can be extended to women further down the social scale. In the case of Abigail Patch, they can: her story begins with patriarchy and ends with female control. In grotesque miniature, the history of the Patches is a story of the feminization of family life.

Abigail grew up in a family that, judged from available evidence, was ruled by her father. Archelaus McIntire owned a respected family name and a farm that he had inherited from his father and that he would pass on to his son; he was the steward of the family's past and future as well as its present provider. As a McIntire, he conferred status on every member of his household. As a voter he spoke for the family in town affairs; as a father and church member he led the family in daily prayers; and as a proprietor he made decisions about the allocation of family resources, handled relations with outsiders, and performed much of the heavy work.

Archelaus McIntire's wife and daughters were subordinate members of his household. He had married Abigail Felton of Danvers and had brought her to a town where she lived apart from her own family but surrounded by his; her status in Reading derived from her husband's family and not from her own. On the farm, she and her daughters spent long days cooking and cleaning, gardening, tending and milking cows, making cloth and clothing, and caring for the younger children—work that took place in and near the house and not on the farm. That work was essential, but New England men assumed that it would be done and attached no special importance to it. The notion of a separate and cherished domestic sphere was slow to catch on in the countryside, and if we may judge from the spending patterns of the McIntires, it played no role in their house. Archelaus McIntire spent his money on implements of work and male sociability—horses, wagons, well-made cider barrels, a rifle—and not on the china, tea sets, and feather beds that were appearing in towns and among the rural well-to-do. The McIntires owned a solid table and a Bible and a few other books, and there was a clock and a set of glassware as well. But the most valuable item of furniture in the house was Archelaus's desk. Insofar as the McIntires found time for quiet evenings at home, they probably spent them listening to the father read his Bible (the mother was illiterate) or keeping quiet while he figured his accounts.

As the fourth and youngest of Archelaus McIntire's daughters, Abigail had doubtless traded work and quiet subordination for security, for the status that went with being a female McIntire, perhaps even for peace and affection in the home. As she set up housekeeping with Mayo Greenleaf Patch, she doubtless did not expect things to change. Years later Abigail recalled that in taking a husband she wanted not a partner but "a friend and protector." For her part, Abigail spoke of her "duties" and claimed to have been an "attentive and affectionate wife." It was the arrangement that she had learned as a child: husbands protected their wives and supported them, wives worked and were attentive to their husbands' needs and wishes. All available evidence suggests that those rules governed the Patch household during the years in Reading.

Abigail and Greenleaf Patch maintained neither the way of life nor the standard of living necessary for the creation of a private sphere in which Abigail could have exercised independent authority. The house was small and there was little money, and the household regularly included persons from outside the immediate family. Greenleaf's apprentices and journeymen were in and out of the house constantly. For two summers the Patches boarded the schoolmistress, and Nancy Barker may have stayed with Greenleaf and Abigail before her marriage. With these persons present in hit-and-miss records, we may assume that outsiders were normal members of the Patch household.

At work, rural shoemakers maintained a rigid division of labor based on sex and age, and Greenleaf's authority was pervasive. Abigail's kitchen, if indeed it was a separate room, was a busy place. There she bound shoes as a semiskilled and subordinate member of her husband's work team, cared for the children (she gave birth five times between 1789 and 1799), did the cooking, cleaning, and laundry for a large household, and stared across the table at apprentices and journeymen who symbolized her own drudgery and her husband's authority at the same time. As Abigail Patch endured her hectic and exhausting days, she may have dreamed of wallpapered parlors and privacy and quiet nights by the fire with her husband. But she must have known that such things were for others and not for her. They had played little role in her father's house, and they were totally absent from her own.

Greenleaf Patch seems to have taken his authority as head of the household seriously. Available evidence suggests that he consistently made family decisions—not just the economic choices that were indisputably his to make but decisions that shaped the texture and meaning of life within the family.

Take the naming of the children. Greenleaf Patch was separated from his own family and dependent on McIntire resources, so when children came along we would expect him and Abigail to have honored McIntire relatives. That is not what happened. The first Patch child was a daughter born in 1789. The baby was named Molly, after a daughter of Greenleaf's brother Isaac. A son came two years later, and the Patches named him Greenleaf. Another daughter, born in 1794, was given the name Nabby, after another of Isaac Patch's daughters. A second son, born in 1798, was named for Greenleaf's uncle Samuel. That child died, and a son born the following year (the daredevil Sam Patch) received the same name. The last child was born in 1803 and was named for Greenleaf's brother Isaac. None of the six children was named for Abigail or a member of her family. Instead, all of the names came from the little world in Wenham—uncle Samuel's nine-acre farm, the shared barn and outbuildings, and the eighteen acres operated by brother Isaac—in which Greenleaf Patch presumably spent much of his childhood.

Religion is a second and more important sphere in which Patch seems to have made choices for the family. Abigail McIntire had grown up in a religious household. Her father had joined the North Parish Congregational Church a few days after the birth of his first child in 1762. Her mother had followed two months later, and the couple baptized each of their five children. The children in their turn became churchgoers. Abigail's sisters Mary and Mehitable joined churches, and her brother Archelaus, Jr. expressed a strong interest in religion as well. Among Abigail's parents and siblings, only the questionable Deborah left no religious traces.

Religious traditions in the Patch family were not as strong. Greenleaf's father and his first wife joined the Congregational church at Wenham during the sixth year of their marriage in 1736, but the family's ties to religion weakened after that. Timothy Patch, Jr. did not baptize any of his thirteen children, either the ten presented him by his first wife or the three born to Thomasine Greenleaf Davis, the nonchurchgoing widow whom he married in 1759. None of Greenleaf's brothers or sisters became full members of the church, and only his oldest brother Andrew owned the covenant, thus placing his family under the government of the church.

Among the Wenham Patches, however, there remained pockets of religiosity, and they centered, perhaps significantly, in the homes of Greenleaf's brother Isaac and his uncle Samuel. Uncle Samuel was a communicant of the church, and although Isaac had no formal religious ties, he married a woman who owned the covenant. The churchgoing tradition that Greenleaf Patch carried into marriage was thus ambiguous, but it almost certainly was weaker than that carried by his wife. And from his actions as an adult, we may assume that Greenleaf was not a man who would have been drawn to the religious life.

As Greenleaf and Abigail married and had children, the question of religion could not have been overlooked. The family lived near the church in which Abigail had been baptized and in which her family and her old friends spent Sunday mornings. As the wife of Greenleaf Patch, Abigail had three options: she could lead her husband into church; she could, as many women did, join the church without her husband and take the children with her; finally, she could break with the church and spend Sundays with an irreligious husband. The first two choices would assert Abigail's authority and independent rights within the family. The third would be a capitulation, and it would have painful results. It would cut her off from the religious community in which she had been born, and it would remove her young family from religious influence.

The Patches lived in Reading for twelve years and had five children there. Neither Greenleaf nor Abigail joined the church, and none of the babies was baptized. We cannot retrieve the actions and feelings that produced these facts, but this much is certain: in the crucial area of religious practice, the Patch family bore the stamp of Greenleaf Patch and not of Abigail McIntire. When Greenleaf and Abigail named a baby or chose whether to join a church or baptize a child, the decisions extended his family's history and not hers.

Abigail Patch accepted her husband's dominance in family affairs throughout the years in Reading, years in which he played, however ineptly and dishonestly, his role as "friend and protector." With his final separation from the rural economy and his humiliating failure in Marblehead, he abdicated that role. In Marblehead Abigail began to impose her will upon domestic decisions. The result, within a few years, would be a full-scale female takeover of the family.

In 1803 the sixth—and, perhaps significantly, the last—Patch child was baptized at Second Congregational Church in Marblehead. And in 1807, shortly after the move to Rhode Island, Abigail and her oldest daughter joined the First Baptist Church in Pawtucket. At that date Abigail was thirty-seven years old, had been married nineteen years, and had five living children. Her daughter Molly was eighteen years old and unmarried. Neither followed the customs of the McIntire or Patch families, where women who joined churches did so within a few years after marriage. Abigail and Molly Patch presented themselves for baptism in 1807 not because they had reached predictable points in their life cycles but because they had experienced religion and had decided to join a church.

At the same time (here was feminization with a vengeance) Abigail's daughters dropped their given names and evolved new ones drawn from their mother's and not their father's side of the family. The oldest daughter joined the church not as Molly but as Polly Patch. Two years later the same woman married under the name Mary Patch. Abigail's oldest sister, who had died in the year that Abigail married Greenleaf, had been named Mary. The second Patch daughter, Nabby, joined the Baptist church in 1811. At that time she was calling herself Abby Patch. By 1829 she was known as Abigail. The daughters of Abigail Patch, it seems, were affiliating with their mother and severing symbolic ties with their father. It should be noted that the father remained in the house while they did so.

In Pawtucket Abigail built a new family life that centered on her church and her female relatives. That life constituted a rejection not only of male dominance but of men. For five years Abigail worked and took the children to church while her husband drank, stole her money, and issued sullen threats. He ran off in 1812, and by 1820 Abigail, now officially head of the household, had rented a house and was taking in boarders. Over the next few years the Patch sons left home: Samuel for New Jersey, Isaac for the Northwest, Greenleaf for parts unknown. Abigail's younger daughter married and moved to Pittsburgh. Among the Patch children only Mary (Molly, Polly) stayed in Pawtucket. In 1825 Mary was caught committing adultery. Her husband left town, and Mary began calling herself a widow. Abigail closed the boardinghouse and moved into a little house on Main Street with Mary and her children sometime before 1830. She and her daughter and granddaughters would live in that house for the next quarter-century.

The neighbors remembered Abigail Patch as a quiet, steady little woman who attended the Baptist church. She did so with all of the Patch women. Mary had joined with her in 1807, and each of Mary's daughters followed in their turn: Mary and Sarah Anne in 1829, Emily in 1841. First Baptist was a grim and overwhelmingly female Calvinist church, subsidized and governed by the owners of Pawtucket's mills. The Articles of Faith insisted that most of humankind was hopelessly damned, that God chose only a few for eternal life and had in fact chosen them before the beginning of time, "and that in the flesh dwelleth no good thing." It was not a cheerful message. But it struck home among the Patch women.

Apart from the church, the women spent their time in the house on Main Street. Abigail bought the house in 1842—the first land that the Patches owned—and her granddaughters Mary and Emily taught school in the front room for many years. The household was self-supporting, and its membership was made up of women whose relations with men were either troubled or nonexistent. Abigail never remarried. We cannot know what preceded and surrounded the instance of adultery and the breakup of Mary's marriage, but she too remained single for the rest of her life. Sarah Anne Jones, one of the granddaughters, was thirty-six years old and unmarried when called before a church committee in 1853. Although she married a man named Kelley during the investigation, she was excommunicated "because she has given this church reason to believe she is licentious." Sarah Anne's sisters, the schoolteachers Mary and Emily, were spinsters all their lives. The lives of Abigail Patch and her daughter Mary Jones had been blighted by bad relations with men; the women whom they raised either avoided men or got into trouble when they did not. Abigail Patch lived on Main Street with the other women until 1854, when she died at the age of eighty-four.

We know little of what went on in that house. The women lived quietly, and former pupils remembered Abigail's granddaughters with affection. But beyond the schoolroom, in rooms inhabited only by the Patch women, there was a cloistered world. Within that world, Abigail and her daughter Mary reconstructed not only themselves but the history of their family.

Pawtucket celebrated its Cotton Centennial in 1890, and a Providence newspaperman decided to write about the millworker-hero Sam Patch. He asked Emily Jones, one of Abigail's aged granddaughters, about the Patch family history. Emily had been born after 1810, and her knowledge of the family's past was limited to what she had picked up from her mother and grandmother. Her response to the reporter demonstrated the selective amnesia with which any family remembers its history, but in this case the fabrications were sadly revealing.

Miss Jones told the newspaperman that her oldest uncle, Greenleaf Patch, Jr., had gone off to Salem and become a lawyer. That is demonstrably untrue. No one named Greenleaf Patch has ever been licensed to practice law in Massachusetts. About her uncle Sam Patch, Emily said: in the 1820s he operated a spinning mill of his own north of Pawtucket, but failed when his partner ran off with the funds; it was only then that he moved to New Jersey and became a daredevil. That too is a fabrication. What we know about Sam Patch is that he was an alcoholic with powerful suicidal drives, and that he succeeded in killing himself at the age of thirty. Miss Jones remembered that her youngest uncle, Isaac, moved to Illinois and became a farmer. That was true: in 1850 Isaac Patch was farming and raising a family near Peoria. It seems that Abigail Patch and Mary Patch Jones idealized the first two Patch sons by giving them successes and/or ambitions that they did not have. The third son was born in 1803 and grew up in a household dominated by Abigail and not by her dissipated husband; he became a family man. By inventing a similar ordinariness for the older sons, Abigail may have erased some of the history created by Mayo Greenleaf Patch.

Emily's memory of her grandfather provokes similar suspicions. We know that Greenleaf Patch lived in Pawtucket until 1812. But Miss Jones remembered that her grandfather had been a farmer in Massachusetts, and that he died before Abigail brought her family to Rhode Island. Greenleaf Patch, it seems, was absent from Abigail's house in more ways than one.

Questions for Study and Review

1. Analyze Hamilton's and Jefferson's plans for national development in light of the Patch family's history.

2. In what ways did Abigail Patch gain and demonstrate authority in the household as a result of the family's changing economic fortunes? Did she regard these as gains?

3. How did the options available to the Patch sons and daughters differ, and which were the most attractive alternatives for them?

4. Compare the choices available to Abigail Patch and her daughters with those available to the domestic servants described by Marla Miller and the African Americans analyzed by Carol Berkin.

Suggested Readings and Web Sites

Christopher Clark, *The Roots of Rural Capitalism: Western Massachusetts, 1780–1860* (1990)

Thomas Dublin, *Women at Work: The Transformation of Work and Community in Lowell, Massachusetts, 1820–1860* (1979)

Paul E. Johnson, *Sam Patch: The Famous Jumper* (2003)

Christine Stansell, *City of Women: Sex and Class in New York City, 1789–1860* (1986)

Lowell Mill Girls
   http://faculty.uml.edu/sgallagher/Mill_girls.htm

Autobiography of a Mill Worker: Lucy Larcom
   http://digital.library.upenn.edu/webbin/gutbook/lookup?num=2293

PART IV

Expansion and Division

The gauze-draped woman in this lithograph offers inspiration to men. In real life, women played crucial roles in western migration and in the settlement of western lands.

Expansion was the watchword of nineteenth-century North Americans. With the purchase of the Louisiana Territory in 1803, the United States doubled in size. Over the next half-century, the population grew from fewer than seven million to almost thirty million, including an increase from less than one million to nearly four million slaves and an influx of several million new immigrants. Technological advances in agriculture, industry, transportation, and communication increased production of food, clothing, and hundreds of other goods and sped the movement of individuals and information across the nation. Americans traveled to both unexplored western territories and turbulent seaboard cities.

In 1810, New York became the first city to house 100,000 residents; after 1825, with the opening of the Erie Canal, it became the nation's unrivaled commercial as well as population center. Along the paths of canals, wagon trains, and railroads, boom towns sprang up, some to become thriving metropolises and others to fade away as the frontier passed. Chicago, a mere trading post in the early 1830s, had over 100,000 inhabitants by 1860.

Expansion fed the development of distinct regional economies in the North, South, and West and nurtured the accompanying social and political divisions. Expansion also reinforced divisions within each region—between long-settled American Indians and the newcomers who wanted their land, between African and African American slaves and their ever more vigilant masters, between workers and employers both bent on gaining their fair share of new wealth, and between women and men on southern plantations and western wagon trains and in Indian villages and northern urban neighborhoods. Sometimes division meant confrontation, other times resistance, resignation, accommodation, or peaceful co-existence.

Geographic expansion, economic growth, and the political debates that each engendered transformed the place of women in American society. On the one hand, the rise of factories and the growth of slavery pulled women into the world of work. On the other hand, the availability of cheap labor and of manufactured goods allowed more well-to-do women to withdraw from manual labor and adopt new notions of proper behavior.

The emergence and dissemination of a new ideal of womanhood depended greatly on improvements in printing that allowed newspapers, magazines, and that relatively new literary form, the novel, to reach mass audiences. A careful reading of these sources suggests that the "true woman" of the early nineteenth century was pious, pure, domestic, and submissive, enclosed within her separate sphere of family, home, and church. Such images were both reinforced and modified by the teachings of a new breed of evangelical ministers. The Reverend Charles Grandison Finney was the most famous of the revivalists who led the evangelical movement known as the Second Great Awakening. Tempering older messages about original sin and predestination, Finney and his followers stressed the individual's ability to participate in his or her own salvation and to pursue good works as a means of hastening the millennium. Often relying on women to carry the tidings to the unchurched, evangelical preachers reinforced claims for female moral and spiritual superiority. The new ideal was primarily directed at and embraced by the emerging middle class.

Women had long used the church as a vehicle for organizing voluntary efforts on behalf of the sick, orphaned, and destitute, and they expanded these benevolent activities throughout the early nineteenth century. In the 1830s, under the influence of evangelicalism, members of these organizations began to believe that such problems could be not only lessened but eliminate'd. The perfection of society would then open the door for Christ's Second Coming and a thousand years of joy, serenity, and justice. New associations emerged that were more fully infused with this millennial vision, encouraging women to step beyond home and church and into the public streets. These associations included temperance, peace, and moral reform societies, the last of which sought to rescue and rehabilitate prostitutes.

Some evangelicals also joined free blacks and small circles of radical whites to demand the abolition of slavery. It was male and female abolitionists who then formed the core of a new movement for women's rights. The first meeting devoted solely to the rights of women was held in Seneca Falls, New York, in July 1848. By that time women had entered the public sphere on behalf of a wide array of causes, and Americans hotly debated which activities were appropriate to women's sphere.

In Chapter Ten, Anne Boylan traces the development of women's organizations and activities in Boston and New York in the decades before the Seneca Falls Woman's Rights Convention of 1848. She reveals the ways that women justified their entrance into the public sphere and the effects this had on the responses to their public labors. In particular, she compares the efforts of "benevolent" ladies, who assisted those in need, and women "reformers," who mobilized to change society, law, and public policy.

One movement that bridged the divide between female benevolence and reform emerged in the 1820s and early 1830s. It was inspired by the U.S. government's effort to move thousands of Cherokee families to the Oklahoma Territory in order to open up the lands they occupied in Georgia and the Carolinas to white farmers. Although focused on changing federal policy, women who joined the movement claimed that they were motivated by the desire to save Christian Indians and their families from the greedy demands of planters. They thus sought to frame political demands in the language of religion and morality.

The expansion of European settlements had, from the beginning, forced changes in the lives of American Indians. By the early nineteenth century, those Indian nations on the eastern seaboard that had not been exterminated had adapted to new conditions. This involved changes in women's and men's roles. Iroquois and Cherokee women, for instance, wielded significant economic, political, and religious power prior to colonization. Such influential positions for females were at odds with European customs and expectations, encouraging Old World settlers to scorn Indians as uncivilized because they practiced a different sexual division of labor.

By the early nineteenth century, Americans of European descent were sufficiently dominant to force the reassignment of male and female tasks within many Indian societies. Among southeastern Indians, such as the Creek and Cherokee, Christian missionaries and govermment agents encouraged individuals to adopt "civilized" ways by introducing them to new technology—metal hoes for men and spinning wheels for women. Such interventions helped expand the influence of American Indian men in the family and the larger community, but did not provide them with the power to stop their tribes' removal to the West once white southerners' search for fertile cotton fields led to the Indians' land.

In Chapter Eleven, Theda Perdue chronicles women's efforts to maintain their power, especially over land, in the Cherokee Nation. She also examines what happens to the Cheroke when such efforts failed.

White southerners' search for land was fueled by the success of the cotton gin, invented in 1793 by Eli Whitney. This simple machine dramatically increased the speed with which slaves could separate seeds from short staple cotton. At a time when even some southerners were considering the advisability of freeing the slaves, the cotton gin's success ensured that slavery and the slave trade would continue. An increase in the numbers of slaves and their concentration on larger plantations unintentionally encouraged the elaboration of family and community life among those in bondage. Since slave children were considered the property of the mother's owner, African American females were central figures in the development of these more extensive kinship networks.

Slave women played critical roles in sustaining both communities and families, and all-female work groups as well as extended kinship networks bound slaves together across plantations and generations. Yet as Stephanie Camp demonstrates in Chapter Twelve, enslaved women did not simply accept their bondage in order to protect their families and friends. She analyzes truancy, that is, short-term absences from plantations, and argues that this comprised an important dimension of women's resistance to their enslavement. In addition, she shows how mothers, daughters, and wives supported male truants by providing them with food and other forms of support.

During the early to mid-nineteenth century, many plantation owners moved west to find more fertile land on which to grow cotton or raise sugar cane. Such moves shattered slave families and often inspired truancy and other acts of resistance. Yet westward migration could not be contained. North and South, people packed up their households and moved west: Small farmers and shopkeepers as well as planters, whites and free blacks as well as slaves, women and children as well as men all joined the procession.

The construction of canals and then railroads increased both the speed and the comfort of travel, as well as the profitability of shipping western agricultural goods eastward. Still, before the Civil War most migrants ventured beyond the Mississippi by wagon. The trip placed unusual demands on all those heading west—and in the 1840s and after, a significant proportion of these travelers were women and children. Physical demands included crowded wagons, constant motion, fear of Indians (despite the relatively few hostile incidents), hot and dry or cool and wet weather, and the continuous need to haul water and collect fuel. In addition, the migrants had to deal with the psychological demands of the journey. Sorrow at leaving loved ones behind, anxiety about an unknown future, tensions increased by daily contact among fellow travelers, or isolation faced by a family traveling alone contributed significant stress.

Women, sometimes burdened with young children, sought to maintain high domestic standards and Sabbath rest on the trail, and were often asked to jettison family heirlooms when the load had to be lightened. Even as their numbers increased, women were nearly always outnumbered by men on wagon trains, and some found themselves isolated from female companionship. Yet many also found a new freedom and a personal pride by persevering in these struggles. The end of the journey offered much the same scenario—hardship and isolation combined with new opportunities and a heightened sense of self-worth.

The most dramatic episode that spurred westward migration was the California Gold Rush. After gold was discovered in 1848, thousands and then tens of thousands of men rushed to California from the eastern United States, South America, and other parts of the world. In Chapter Thirteen Albert Hurtado explores the male-dominated society that developed in California in this period. He also examines the opportunities offered those rare women who settled in California in the midst of gold fever.

The mass migration westward that occurred in the early decades of the nineteenth century had different meanings for American Indians, African Americans, and Euro-Americans and held different promises and possibilities for women and men in each of these groups. Expansion and division on the national level were two of the most important developments in the history of the United States in the mid-nineteenth century. So, too, were these same processes critical in the many local communities in which ordinary women challenged the boundaries of their spheres and demanded the right to participate in the many debates inspired by rapid geographic, economic, and political change.

Suggested Readings and Web Sites

John Mack Faragher, *Men and Women on the Overland Trail* (1979)
Albert Hurtado, *Intimate Frontiers: Sex, Gender and Culture in Old California* (1999)
Mary P. Ryan, *Women in Public: Between Banners and Ballots* (1990)
Judith Wellman, *The Road to Seneca Falls: Elizabeth Cady Stanton and the First Woman's Rights Convention* (2004)
Deborah G. White, *Ar'n't I a Woman? Female Slaves in the Plantation South* (1985)
Women and Social Movements in the United States, 1600–2000
    http://womhist.binghamton.edu
Trails to Utah and the Pacific
    http://memory.loc.gov/ammem/award99/upbhtml/overhome.html
Slave Movement during the Eighteenth and Nineteenth Centuries
    http://dpls.dacc.wisc.edu/slavedata

Chapter 10

The Seneca Falls Woman's Rights Convention of 1848 is often used to mark women's entrance into the political sphere. One hundred of the participants (thirty-two men and sixty-eight women) signed a Declaration of Sentiments at the end of the two-day meeting that included a resolution demanding that women be granted the right to vote. In recent years, scholars have demonstrated that even before 1848 a few women had called for voting rights for women, and single property-owning women in New Jersey had actually cast votes in the late eighteenth and early nineteenth centuries. Even more importantly, historians have now unearthed women's participation in hundreds of organizations, campaigns, and social and political movements across the Northeast and Midwest in the early decades of the nineteenth century.

Both African American and white women participated in voluntary associations and reform movements as did working-class, middle-class, and upper-class women. Not surprisingly, however, women differed in the kinds of issues they advocated, in the strategies they employed, and in the goals they supported. Race and class certainly shaped competing networks of women's activism but so, too, did ideology, familial support, region, and religious affiliation. By mid-century American women could choose to join benevolent societies and hospital boards, work on behalf of orphans or prostitutes, campaign against alcohol or slavery, demand higher wages or higher education, protest racism and capital punishment, embrace vegetarianism and health reform, condemn tobacco or organized religion, establish asylums for the insane or for widows, advance literacy and prison reform, and support rights for Indians or for themselves. This vast panoply of issues and organizations was rooted in the history of women's associations that stretched back before the founding of the United States.

Anne Boylan traces the development of two paths to public activism among women from 1800 through the 1840s. She makes clear that women gained considerable support, from men as well as other women, for their "non-political" efforts on behalf of the poor, sick, orphaned, and widowed. It was only when women's activities were perceived as political that condemnations flowed from press and pulpit. In part, this may have been in response to increasingly popular notions about women's proper role. The cult of domesticity and the concept of true womanhood emerged at the same time that more women were leaving their private households to take on public responsibilities. Popular magazines like *Godey's Lady's Book* disseminated the idea that respectable ladies should demonstrate piety, purity, and submissiveness while devoting themselves to home and family. Yet in general such strictures only led to condemnations of women's public efforts when those efforts touched too closely on overtly political concerns like slavery.

In their language and choice of tactics, women in public dispelled or invited criticism. As Anne Boylan shows, benevolent ladies appealed to city fathers and ministers by framing their activities in the rhetoric of self-sacrifice and moral necessity. At the same time, their organizations often raised large sums of money, and many formed corporations in order to dispense funds that married women normally could not control. They also established informal partnerships with mayors, city councils, and other political and business leaders. At the other end of the spectrum, women abolitionists, black and white, signed petitions, held conventions, and spoke to "promiscuous," that is, mixed-sex, audiences. Some antislavery societies included both women and men and African Americans and whites as members. Even though abolitionist women wielded less money and rarely sought legal incorporation, they were considered far more radical, and political, than their benevolent sisters. By examining women's organizations in two cities in the early to mid-nineteenth century, Boylan helps us recognize both the range of female activism and the public's changing responses to it.

Women and Politics in the Era before Seneca Falls: Boston and New York City
ANNE M. BOYLAN

To most Americans of the early nineteenth century, "women" and "politics" were mutually exclusive categories. Politics was a public endeavor and as such belonged to the world of men. Women's world, or "sphere," to use the widely employed term, was to revolve around the private arena of home and family. "Home is [women's] appropriate sphere of action," wrote Mrs. A. J. Graves in 1841; and "whenever she neglects these duties, or goes out of this sphere of action to mingle in any of the great public movements of the day, she is deserting the station which God and nature have assigned to her." "If man's duties lie abroad," she reasoned, "woman's duties are within the quiet seclusion of the home." Such sentiments were part of the accepted wisdom of early nineteenth-century life.

Even as Graves wrote, the conventional wisdom was under challenge by abolitionists and moral reformers. Indeed, her critique of women who "mingle in any of the great public movements of the day" clearly referred to them. By speaking out on issues such as slavery, by mobilizing women to lobby for specific legislation, and by engaging in petition campaigns to Congress, activist women had already defied accepted conventions. They had also begun to reconceptualize women's relationship to politics and to question their exclusion from voting, which emerged in the 1840s as a key symbol of male political privilege. The debate at the Seneca Falls Convention (1848) over whether women should exercise "their sacred right to the elective franchise" culminated a decade of discussion concerning acceptable political activities for women.

From *Journal of the Early Republic,* Vol. 10, No. 3, 1990. Copyright © by The Society for Historians of the Early American Republic. Reprinted with Permission of University of Pennsylvania Press.

NO. 226.

FEMALE

INFLUENCE AND OBLIGATIONS

You are the very persons to collect the little wanderers—*Page 6.*

The American Tract Society published numerous pamphlets and lithographs like this one from 1842 that encouraged women to take responsibility for the moral and spiritual education of children. Although such benevolent ladies were not expected to wield power, they could use their influence to uplift the community through the establishment of Sunday schools and other charitable ventures.

It would be misleading, however, to assume that the provocative actions of abolitionists and moral reformers represented American women's first foray into politics. As Paula Baker has pointed out, since the 1760s "a tradition of women's involvement in government" had been evident in crowd actions, organized boycotts, and fund-raising efforts. In the early nineteenth century, through the formation of permanent organizations, women expanded and institutionalized this tradition by undertaking to provide social services—caring for widows and orphans, assisting the aged, providing health care to pregnant women—previously assumed by families and local governments. As they did so, women entered the political realm, lobbying for shares of public money, joining with local governments in delivering welfare assistance, seeking political influence or favors, and engaging in critiques of the public welfare system. Clearly, organized women were involved in politics and government well before 1848.

Yet such organizational activities were seldom perceived as political, nor were they accompanied by the storms of criticism that greeted abolitionist petitioning and lobbying in later years. Why not? An analysis of women's groups in two cities—Boston and New York—during the first four decades of the nineteenth century suggests that benevolent groups founded to aid the widow or orphan differed substantially in political style from reform-oriented societies such as female abolition groups. Both types of organizations were politically involved when needs dictated. Yet benevolent societies adhered to a deferential mode of politics that was essentially eighteenth-century in tone, whereas reformist organizations adopted a nineteenth-century style that sought to mobilize women in a mass, democratic fashion. If benevolent women utilized influence to achieve their goals, reformist women in effect created interest groups to pressure politicians. It was this difference in style, dictated by their very different goals, that enabled benevolent groups to enter politics in an era when "women" and "politics" theoretically did not mix.

From the very outset at the turn of the nineteenth century, women's organizations provided opportunities for members to be political actors and behave in ways ordinarily defined as male. Because every group—no matter how small or how modest—had a constitution and bylaws, held regular elections, and followed set agendas, members were able to vote, run for office, hammer out platforms, and make decisions that affected others directly. The stakes, to be sure, were usually small, and the women themselves did not explicitly connect their activity to the broader political world of their husbands, fathers, and brothers. Disavowing any conception of themselves as "legislators and governors" who "have to enact laws, and compel men to observe them," organized women nevertheless became, in a limited fashion, voters and "governors."

New legal rights came to some women through their organizations. Securing an act of incorporation . . . enabled groups of women to exercise collective rights that they did not possess individually, especially if they were married. Although only some women's groups incorporated, the laws permitted those that did to own substantial amounts of property (usually set at $20,000 to $50,000, but the limitation could be adjusted to fit an organization's changing circumstances), invest their financial resources in stocks and bonds, sue and be sued, construct and manage institutions such as orphanages, and indenture children. Virtually all of these were powers that individual married members lacked in their own lives. Until the passage of married women's property acts, beginning in the 1840s, wives generally could not hold property or control money separately from their husbands; moreover, early nineteenth-century family law conferred legal guardianship of children on their fathers, although in contests over custody, courts frequently awarded the care of very young children, especially girls, to their mothers.

The contrast between their individual powerlessness and their collective empowerment was not lost on organized women. Their acts of incorporation explicitly reminded them that married women had few legal rights by requiring (in the case of Boston) that an organization's treasurer be single, over 21 years of age, and post a substantial bond, or (in the case of New York) that members' husbands be free of any financial liability for their wives' work with the organization. Awareness of their vulnerability as individuals often made women careful to preserve the power and autonomy they possessed as a public corporation but lacked in private life. When the members of the Boston Female Asylum petitioned for incorporation in 1802, for example, several legislators tried to convince them to let a group of male trustees handle the society's funds. The ladies refused, arguing that "[we] could not have any legal control over these Trustees, nor prevent their transferring the property of the Society." Although most women's groups solicited the advice of knowledgeable men on subjects such as investments or real estate, and some established formal advisory "committees of gentlemen," the members nevertheless resisted efforts to curtail their group rights.

Armed with these collective rights, organized women entered the political arena, learned some of the political ropes, and sought to wield influence. Involvement in politics was dictated by their plans: many early women's societies were formed to provide social services to needy urban residents. Thus, the New York Society for the Relief of Poor Widows with Small Children came into being in 1797 as an effort to provide winter relief to the families of yellow fever victims. The Boston Female Asylum (1800) attempted to assist young orphaned girls, the Association for the Relief of

Respectable, Aged, Indigent Females (1814) in New York sought to assist women who fit that description, and the Boston Children's Friend Society (1833) provided refuge for neglected and abused children, as well as the children of working mothers. In these and other cases, women organizers saw their groups as taking responsibility for individuals and groups overlooked by existing programs—both public and private.

In delivering city services, benevolent women's groups often assumed a kind of partnership with elected officials. Pointing out that they had removed "a vast number" of children from the city almshouse, and kept them off the public relief rolls, the managers of New York's Orphan Asylum Society suggested in 1818 that they were entitled to a share of city funds. In a similar vein, the Association for the Relief of Respectable, Aged, Indigent Females asked the mayor and city council in 1815 for a donation, arguing that their work had saved the city money by keeping many elderly women out of the almshouse. Indeed, benevolent groups often approached every available public and quasi-public organization as potential partners in their work. Just as they requested city and state funds, the managers of the New York Society for the Relief of Poor Widows with Small Children asked Trinity Church for land, suggested to the Free School Society that it educate their clients' children, and approached the St. Patrick's Society for aid to an Irish client.

Politicians accepted benevolent women's claims, trickling tax monies into their treasuries and adopting the women's own descriptions of their public service. Recommending in 1814 that the newly formed House of Industry receive $500, a New York city council committee simply lifted words from the women's petition: quite apart from the "intrinsic merit" of its program, the House of Industry would "be a real saving to the City[;] it will greatly relieve the pressure on the public charity." A similar committee in 1818 repeated the women's claim that their "Institution has already kept from the Alms House a number of persons who . . . would . . . have become a public charge." A grant of $750 to the Society for the Relief of Poor Widows with Small Children was approved on the grounds that it had "rendered to the Community great and essential services" saving hundreds of widows and children from "the necessity of taking refuge in the Alms House." And an 1824 city council committee, though reluctant "to establish any more precedents for annual donations to charitable Institutions," nevertheless agreed that the Orphan Asylum Society deserved $500 because, without its work, the city "would have been compelled to support many of the Orphans who are thus taken care of by this Society." Such monetary grants placed women's charitable organizations on the same political (though not necessarily economic) footing as men's, and established the principle that private women's groups, like men's, could aid elected officials in relieving public burdens.

Official favors, both large and small, also resulted from this informal partnership between politicians and women. In 1803, for example, the New York state legislature authorized the holding of a lottery to raise $15,000 for the Society for the Relief of Poor Widows with Small Children; the New York city council supervised the actual lottery, appointing lottery managers, supplying them with an office, and permitting them to advance cash to the society. The Orphan Asylum Society received similar help in the form of a $5,000 lottery grant in 1808, and annual $500 grants beginning in 1811. Indeed, this society had a knack for acquiring public funds; it received annual appropriations from the city's Common School Fund (in 1828, the asylum's school, with 175 pupils—2.8 percent of the city's total—received over 3.5 percent of the fund) as well as special donations from the city council. Besides money, there were other favors. Some societies received land grants on which to build benevolent institutions; others had their tax assessments paid or rescinded. The New York city council on occasion bought supplies for private charities, and regularly saved them storage costs by permitting them to stack wood at the almshouse. One gift offered a particularly pungent symbol of public largesse: in 1808 New York's aldermen paid a carter $191.50 to collect and deliver manure to the Orphan Asylum Society's kitchen garden.

In seeking such favors, leaders of women's organizations employed the only tactics they considered appropriate: deferential, personal ones. Choosing well-connected women as officers and using powerful men as intermediaries were two sides of this tactical coin. For the Boston Female Asylum, it was very useful to have Sarah Bowdoin, daughter-in-law of a former governor and wife of a prominent state politician, serving as manager and "giving it her name and influence," as her grateful associates acknowledged, "thereby encouraging its friends and adding to its respectability." Isabella Graham was so closely associated with respectable benevolence in New York that her daughter, Joanna Bethune, felt it politic to place the ill and elderly Graham's name at the head of a petition to establish the House of Industry.

In a similar fashion, the patronage of powerful men helped oil the political gears when an organization needed something done. As the first women's society to incorporate in Massachusetts, the Boston Female Asylum could call on the services of two officers' husbands: James Bowdoin, Jr., and Samuel Parkman. Bowdoin drafted the act, while Parkman, a wealthy merchant and member of the state house of representatives, sponsored its passage. When the Widows' Society sought incorporation in 1828, its vice president ("second directress," to use her official title), Maria Theresa Appleton, offered her husband's assistance. Nathan Appleton, one of the Boston Associates, was wealthy, well known, and well connected. And New York's Orphan Asylum Society enjoyed the support of Mayor De Witt Clinton, who twice lent his name to legislative petitions.

Organized women often exhibited a good deal of savvy in their quest for favors. When the managers of New York's Asylum for Lying-In Women needed land to build a new asylum, they shrewdly dispatched a committee of ladies to consult informally with the mayor and aldermen before writing their petition for a land grant. After being advised by the mayor that they were unlikely to receive a city-owned lot, the asylum ladies instead requested a $3,000 donation. They received $1,500. Some groups issued special invitations to political leaders both to show off their programs and to get favorable patronage. The trustees of New York's House of Industry, whose work received regular support from the city council, found it useful occasionally to invite the aldermen to attend their meetings in order to "examine the proceedings" of the house, and "judge the beneficial effects" for themselves. Such visits invariably evoked a panegyric on the group's contributions to the city, and another public donation. Organized women often had a keen sense of how the political winds were blowing and tailored their applications to existing realities. When rejection of a petition signaled that the current aldermen were tightening the city's purse strings, women's societies stopped requesting funds for a while, and bided their time. The return of more sympathetic men to public office brought renewed applications for assistance.

During Roger Strong's tenure as a New York City alderman, the Female Assistance Society, of which his wife was a manager, received regular city donations.

The deferential and personal nature of these tactics obscured the reality that organized women were involved in politics, primarily through the exercise of their right to petition their rulers. Yet these women did not view petitioning as political because it involved private efforts to influence powerful men, not attempts to seek collective power for women. In the increasingly democratic political environment of the early nineteenth century, as virtually all white men acquired voting rights and politics came to mean mass mobilization of specific groups in pursuit of public power, benevolent women's adherence to personal tactics defined their actions as private, feminine, and non-political. Reflecting Catharine Beecher's view that women's power came through "influence," these tactics fit very well with the emerging ideology of women's proper place in a democratic society and cemented the connection between women's voluntary activity and women's "sphere."

Nevertheless, influence was available only to certain women. [I]t was heavily dependent upon social class: only women whose class position gave them personal access to politicians could seek favors for their organizations. Black women's groups, for example, had no entree into the political process. None applied for incorporation in either city during the early nineteenth century, and despite the prevalence of extreme poverty in urban free black communities, black women's groups received no monetary or other favors from public officials. No members with prominent names or influential husbands represented their cause. Instead, black women's organizations, such as New York's Abyssinian Benevolent Daughters of Esther and Boston's Colored Female Charitable Society, had to generate their meager resources from already hard-pressed members and friends, and occasionally from sympathetic whites.

For those with the requisite class standing, influence could operate in two ways. Not only could they use it to secure public aid if they chose (many groups did not), they could also mold it into a collective voice through which to discuss, criticize, and even attempt to shape public policy. In meetings and through their published reports, women's groups debated some key political issues of their day, especially the nature and causes of poverty, and the purposes of public and private charity. Often, their analyses sounded conventional and formulaic, and repeated the concepts that informed contemporary understanding of these issues. Yet some groups went beyond the conventional formulas of public discussions to criticize the conduct of public affairs, particularly the seemingly inhumane character of the public welfare system. As they did, they made a case for superiority of private women's benevolence at a time when cities like New York and Boston were attempting to define the extent and limits of public responsibility for the people's welfare.

Like their contemporaries, organized women usually distinguished between the "vicious" poor and the "respectable" poor and attempted to limit their assistance to the latter. Typically, Boston's Fragment Society reassured its supporters in 1822 that they "discriminate[d] between real and pretended want" and attempted "to soothe the miseries and mitigate the sufferings of indigent merit." Women's groups were quick at times to blame the poor for their own problems, suggesting, as did one member of New York's Society for the Relief of Poor Widows with Small Children, that "Misery, and Poverty . . . among the lower Classes in this City" arose "principally from the two following causes—viz. Intemperance among the Men and the love of dress among the Women." Only "the humble, the Virtuous, and the industrious poor" truly deserved charity.

In the same fashion, women's groups claimed that their work served "the interests of civil society" by improving the moral character of the poor and promoting social order. In petitioning for public money, for example, the members of the New York Orphan Asylum Society asked the city council to remember "how much the good order and happiness of the community depend on the early and virtuous instruction of its younger inhabitants," instruction which the asylum presumably offered in large amounts. Missionary, tract, and Sunday school organizations were especially prone to make such claims, perhaps because their activities were less visible than those of charitable relief societies. Thus, in 1818, the New York Female Union Society for the Promotion of Sabbath Schools suggested that their work effected "the reformation in our streets, [which] must be apparent to every one who walks out on the morning of the Lord's day."

But many groups were willing to criticize public relief programs in strong terms. They were not the only ones, at a time when expenditures were rising and the plight of the desperately poor seemed to be changing very little. But the comments of women's groups differed from those of other critics in their conviction that private, women's benevolence was invariably superior to the programs conducted by public officials. Benevolent women thus conceived of their work as something more complex than a mere partnership with local officials in the delivery of social services. They often saw their programs as mute testament to the failures of male leaders and to the superiority of women's methods.

The argument that their activities served individuals unreached by existing programs, for example, contained an implicit criticism of current policies. (It was also useful for generating donations.) When the Boston Female Society for Missionary Purposes hired two male missionaries in 1817 to minister to the city's poorest residents, their reports on urban conditions pointedly highlighted large gaps in civic and religious leadership. Not only had the churches abdicated their responsibilities by neglecting to build chapels or hold services in destitute areas, the group's secretary suggested, but neither ministers nor city leaders were fulfilling their obligations to assist the downtrodden. The women of New York's Female Missionary Society mounted similar, if veiled, criticisms against their own ministers and civic leaders. Over and over again, women organizers referred to their clients as "helpless," or as "neglected" and "forgotten" by existing programs. The use of such terms constituted a silent rebuke to male leaders who permitted the existence of huge gaps in social services.

Among "neglected" city-dwellers, however, there was one category of clients who received special sympathy in the reports of many benevolent groups. These were the "respectable" women who had "been reduced to penury" from "a state of ease or affluence" and who shrank from the prospect of receiving public assistance. The almshouse was the most visible symbol of public relief, representing the worst fears of indigent city-dwellers, fears that city fathers were quite willing to foster as a means of reducing the number of inmates. In the almshouse, "the virtuous and the vicious were indiscriminately treated," commented Mary W. Mason, explaining the need for New York's Asylum for Lying-In Women, a maternity hospital accepting only poor married women as clients. "[We] could not conscientiously advise a virtuous ~~woman~~ wife [*sic*],

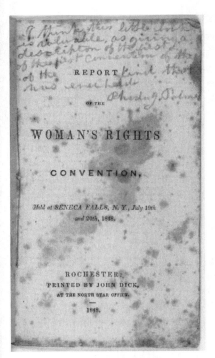

Those who attended the Seneca Falls Woman's Rights Convention in 1848, such as thirty-two year old Rhoda J. Palmer, remembered the event for the rest of their lives. In 1894, Palmer sent a copy of the published report of the convention to suffragist Anne Fitzhugh Miller, noting that it was "the first convention of the kind that was ever held." Palmer lived to cast a ballot in her hometown of Geneva, New York, in 1919 when she was 102 years old. Miller saved the rare first printing of the report in her suffrage scrapbook, now held at the Library of Congress, Washington, D.C.

to seek a home & companionship among *degraded, unmarried* mothers," she concluded. The clients of Boston's Widows' Society, reported one officer in 1819, "have a dread of our Alms-house; the apprehension seems to arise from the fear of being thrown into large rooms, with numbers and deprived of liberty."

For such clients, organization women believed, female benevolence was superior to public assistance because it protected their tattered dignity and permitted them to retain both privacy and a semblance of respectability. What was so horrifying about the almshouse was the prospect of being dumped into an undifferentiated mass of humans, promiscuously mixed together without regard for such standard distinctions of daily life as marital status or previous standing in the community. Whether their clients shared this revulsion toward public institutions is unclear; it is clear that comments about the horrors of the almshouse articulated benevolent women's own unspoken fears. Stories of once-respectable women impoverished by the death of a provider surely expressed the vulnerability shared by all women dependent upon a husband or father for economic support. Perhaps a collective shudder ran through the members of the Society for the Relief of Poor Widows with Small Children when they voted a ten-dollar gift to former donors, "reared in the bosom . . . of affluence" but now "reduced to the labor of their own hands for subsistence" by the death of the male breadwinner. Women who had once known the "elegancies" of life and were "unused to grappling with adversity" seemed to the members of this and other societies to "present to the heart a far more touching appeal than any other class of sufferers" because they would "feel more keenly the barbed points of poverty and want." With such comments benevolent women voiced their own fears while condemning the existing public welfare system.

Their critique of the almshouse underlined another reason why benevolent women saw their programs as superior: personal contact with clients. Such women believed that personal contact represented a particularly feminine approach to social problems. Unlike public welfare, women's organizations required clients to ask a manager personally for assistance, and often gave nothing until she visited the client's home. As an officer of the Society for the Relief of Poor Widows with Small Children put it in 1820, theirs was a "Charity which makes itself acquainted with the objects it relieves by entering into their Houses, informing itself not only of their wants but of their habits and dispositions." Such an approach, women's groups believed, benefited both the giver and the recipient. To the recipient, it brought uplifting contacts with her social betters, the opportunity to receive some useful advice, or in the case of the formerly affluent, charity without degradation. To the dispenser of aid, home visits helped detect "false and idle pretenders to poverty" but they also encouraged sympathy for the plight of the poor. As the ladies of Boston's Female Auxiliary Bible Society put it in 1823, home visits permitted them to converse "on terms of the most perfect familiarity" with poor women. The result was that "we more deeply feel, and perfectly understand their temporal necessities, and by becoming acquainted with their characters, are better able to afford them relief."

Both as critics of city fathers and as petitioners for their assistance, organized women exhibited a strong belief in the personal touch. Just as they sought funds for their organizations by attempting to influence individual politicians, they believed indigent city-dwellers were best assisted through personal involvement. Such an approach made them successful providers of social services, but it did not turn them into critics of existing social and economic arrangements. Benevolent women's complaints about the conduct of public welfare programs had little impact on those programs. Moreover, their concern for clients did not translate into a general analysis of women's position in the political economy. To be sure, there were occasions when members' acquaintance with poorer women led them to realize the enormous difficulties working women faced in attempting to support themselves. But even that realization usually led to an appeal for contributions, not a critique of the wage system that made it, in the words of one woman, "an impossibility for a widow, with the labour of her own hands, to support her infant family." The male advisory committee to one women's group, the Boston Society for Employing the Female Poor, commended the society for paying its needleworkers lower wages than were standard in private industry. Such a practice, the advisors believed, weeded out undeserving clients, encouraged thrift, and facilitated those "dependencies that so usefully and kindly subsist between the rich and the poor."

By the 1820s, it became increasingly clear that women's voices in these public debates were small indeed. Faced with spiraling costs and a new belief in the mutability of poverty, cities like New York and Boston turned increasingly to institutional approaches, building new and more work-oriented almshouses, and attempting to eliminate outdoor relief entirely. Moreover . . . , it was during this period that "the lines between public and private pursuits, between public and private leadership, and public and private generosity" which during the eighteenth century had been "indistinct," received much clearer definition. For many women's groups, this redefinition brought increased uncertainty about how politicians would view their work. In 1829, for example, the New York city council's committee on charities approved a grant to the Orphan Asylum Society but denied one to the Female Assistance Society, claiming that its work was not "of that *Public Character* that it ought to be supported" by municipal funds. Nine years later, the committee rejected personalist critiques of public welfare and urged reduction of the city's support for all charitable societies, arguing that they "promote[d] a lamentable dependency" on the part of the poor. Whereas earlier political leaders had viewed dependence between the rich and poor as laudable, by the Jacksonian era the idea that society was "characterized by mutuality, reciprocity, and familial relationships between high and low" was fast disappearing. In adopting different, more bureaucratic forms of charity, politicians redefined most women's charities as private, hence undeserving of public funds.

At the same time, women's moral reform and antislavery groups, whose members came from more varied social backgrounds than their benevolent counterparts, began to forge a new style of female politics. Unlike benevolent women who presented to local politicians deferential petitions from prominent individuals for specific favors, antislavery women circulated their petitions to mass audiences. Whereas benevolent women working with prostitutes prided themselves on the discreteness of their labor and the obscurity of their organizations, moral reformers in the 1830s shouted their cause from the housetops and invited controversy as a means of publicizing their work. Reform groups also intruded themselves into the political process by lobbying for the passage of specific laws (abolition of slavery in the District of Columbia, establishment of seduction as a crime, criminalization of prostitution), thereby suggesting that organized womanhood had the right to formulate its own political agenda. While no group proposed that women be permitted to vote, their use of mass petitioning and public lobbying signaled that women might use their organizations to move into politics in new ways, precisely at a time when politics itself was being fundamentally altered by the extension of suffrage to most white men.

Not surprisingly, reformist politics met a very different reaction from that accorded benevolent politics. Although initially the formation of public corporations by women had elicited some criticism (one commentator had objected to the incorporation of a Boston group in 1803, arguing that women "has a province of her own, and should not interfer[e] in the busy and active employment of men," particularly "the direction of property"), occasional reservations about women's participation in "organized associations" paled into insignificance in contrast to the revulsion expressed toward antislavery and moral reform groups. In the most famous criticism of women's reform work, a group of Congregationalist clergymen in Massachusetts attacked women abolitionists for speaking in public to mixed audiences, and rebuked moral reformers for "promiscuous conversation . . . with regard to things which ought not to be named" (namely, prostitution). Invoking "the appropriate duties and influence of woman," the clergymen suggested that "unobtrusive," "private," and "unostentatious" activities, such as forming Sunday schools, were acceptable, while assuming "the place and tone of man as a public reformer" was not.

Clearly, what these and other critics objected to was not the mixing of women with politics but the political goals these women espoused and the political style they adopted. Prominent clergymen had routinely sermonized on behalf of benevolent women's work, even when it involved forming public corporations and petitioning legislators for shares of tax monies. As long as women's political style remained deferential and "unostentatious," that is, as long as it had more in common with the politics of the eighteenth century than those of the nineteenth, it could be approved as private influence. When reformist women asserted their right to adopt the new democratic style of the 1830s in pursuit of sweeping social change, they challenged, not women's exclusion from politics, but the narrow, class-based nature of their access to it.

They also challenged their critics' view of the "public sphere." Because women's voluntary associations had always existed, in Mary Ryan's words, "along the sidelines of the public sphere," their members never envisioned their work as strictly private. The managers of the Society for the Relief of Poor Widows with Small Children had few qualms, for example, about assembling in public places (holding their annual meetings, first at the City Hotel, then at various churches), or about speaking to these annual assemblies. New Yorker Mary Morgan Mason cringed when she had to address eight hundred people at a school gathering in 1814, but she went ahead: "I was obliged to speak in public on various subjects." Whereas Bostonian Susan Huntington contrasted the "public duties" she performed for her organizations in 1815 with the "domestic cares" of family life, the novelist Catharine Maria Sedgwick, writing to a friend in 1833, found the "caballing and diplomatizing" involved in forming a church women's society faintly silly. "I do not think it is within a woman's prescribed destiny," she commented, "to do any public duty. We are, some of us, very ridiculous persons in full light." She nevertheless helped run a sewing school, referring to her efforts as a "ministry at large." Critics of abolition and moral reform ignored the ambiguities of past practice, preferring instead to redraw the public-private boundary and assume that women had always stayed on one side of it.

Defending themselves, reformist women pointed to the arbitrariness of public-private boundaries. "If our sphere of action is limited to private life exclusively," argued moral reformer Sarah Towne Smith, "then we have long since left our own province and entered that of the other sex." After all, she pointed out in 1837, for years women "have organized associations, held meetings and published reports, appointed solicitors, and resolved themselves into committees, without alarming the guardians of the public welfare or outraging public sentiment." What, she asked, made moral reform different from running a tract society or working to benefit sailors and their families? The answer, of course, was that moral reform, along with abolitionism and temperance, involved women in questioning basic economic and social institutions. By contrasting (often with stinging sarcasm) the approbation accorded benevolent groups with the condemnation afforded them, these activists highlighted the ways in which public-private distinctions or renderings of women's proper "sphere" were social constructions, functioning as much to prescribe proper behavior as to describe social reality. Even they, however, could not escape the pre-scriptive power of the ideology of spheres. Unlike Smith, the president of the Ladies New-York City Anti-Slavery Society denied that antislavery "call[ed women] . . . from their own firesides, or identif[ied] . . . them with the scenes of political strife." Such differences sparked the split within abolitionist circles in 1840.

To point to organized women's varied political activities and differing political styles is not to suggest that women had the same access to politics and the public sphere as most men. Some elite white women attempted to use influence to gain favors for their benevolent concerns, but such influence was dependent upon family or marital con-nections. Holding an annual meeting in a hotel or church did not give women entree to the public spaces—halls, clubs, taverns—where significant political discussions took place, or to the legislative chambers where decisions were made. Any influence they exerted was contingent and uncertain. Reformist women did enter legislative halls in order to lobby lawmakers directly or present women's collected signatures on petitions, but they had no guarantees of being heard. For some, the experience underlined the ways in which the rise of democratic politics had shut their sex out of the political community, and led them in the 1840s to endorse the goal of suffrage in order to eliminate gender as a mark of political exclusion (or political privilege).

The experiences of organized women in the early decades of the nineteenth century belied the commonplace claim that women had no place in politics. Whether as boycotters of British goods in the 1760s, petitioners for incorporation in the 1800s, or lobbyists for antiseduction laws in the 1830s, women were involved in government and politics. The contrasting political styles evident in each of these activities, however, suggests that not one, but several women's political traditions were at work in the era before Seneca Falls. The tradition of private influence, utilized so successfully by benevolent organizations, achieved widespread acceptance because it appeared non-political. The tradition of mobilized womanhood, which reform organizations adopted in the 1830s, elicited outraged condemnation because it involved women directly in politics in pursuit of unpopular causes. Throughout the nineteenth century, these and other traditions, expressed through crowd actions, labor strikes, and public commentary, provided voteless women with some access to politics and the public sphere.

Questions for Study and Review

1. Compare the work of city fathers, who led local political and economic ventures, with that of benevolent ladies, who sought to sustain and support local families and communities. Could benevolent ladies be considered city mothers, and how were their visions of family and community shaped by their religious affiliation and economic status?

2. What were the most important factors influencing the kinds of organizations and/or issues that women embraced when they decided to enter the public sphere?

3. What was the relationship between women's activism and the growing demands in cities to assist impoverished, sick, widowed, and otherwise needy residents?

4. Compare the benefits and limits of women's participation in benevolent and reform movements and discuss why certain activities were considered "political" and others were not.

Suggested Readings and Web Sites

Bruce Dorsey, *Reforming Men and Women: Gender in the Antebellum City* (2002)
Lori D. Ginzberg, *Women and Antebellum Reform* (2000)
Nancy A. Hewitt, *Women's Activism and Social Change: Rochester, New York, 1822–1872* (1984)
Julie Roy Jeffrey, *The Great Silent Army of Abolitionism: Ordinary Women in the Antislavery Movement* (1998)
Kathryn Kish Sklar, *Women's Rights Emerges within the Antislavery Movement, 1830–1870* (2000)
Roads from Seneca Falls
    http://roadsfromsenecafalls.org
Godey's Lady's Book
    http://www.history.rochester.edu/godeys/

Chapter 11

Among the eighteenth-century Cherokee and other southeastern tribes, women played prominent economic, political, and religious roles, supported by strong bonds among extended networks of female relatives. Yet by the 1830s, when the Cherokee were forcibly removed from Georgia, Alabama, North Carolina, and Tennessee to new lands in Oklahoma, the economic, political, and familial authority of the tribe's women had been severely undercut. Andrew Jackson, Martin Van Buren, and a long series of southern judges, politicians, and planters were responsible for the removal of the Cherokee. Government agents and Christian missionaries, including women, were responsible for the reorganization of sex roles among the Cherokee that diminished women's ability to resist removal.

The ideals of true womanhood and the evangelical preachings that inspired Anglo-American women to initiate charitable and reform efforts proved problematic when applied to Cherokee society. Among the aboriginal Cherokee, women farmed and men hunted. Women thus remained closer to home and labored on the land, which was inherited through the female line. Indeed, when he married, a husband went to live with his wife's family so that she could continue to work on the female-centered family farm. Women also held important positions in religion and politics and practiced a sexual openness considered at best immodest by European standards.

The arrival of missionaries and government agents brought dramatic transformation to the Cherokee community. Men were encouraged to farm and women to spin. Male authority and control over trade, war, and property were reinforced. Eventually large numbers of Cherokees adopted Christianity, constitutional law, the English alphabet, even slavery. This embrace of Anglo-American lifeways weakened not only women's power but the power of the Cherokee as a whole.

As Theda Perdue explains, southern planters began coveting Indian lands, and once they had the support of leading politicians, no amount of civilization, not even a favorable ruling by the U.S. Supreme Court, could save the Indian nation. The resistance of some tribal members to further Anglo-American intrusions was considered an additional rationale for the tribe's removal.

In either case—the adoption of Anglo-American culture or its rejection—Cherokees and especially Cherokee women lost economic and political independence and power as King Cotton moved west. As Stephanie Camp shows in the next article, slave women and men also had to contend with challenges from planters and politicians that disrupted their families and communities. Yet as African and African American presence in the South rapidly increased, that of American Indians declined. They left behind lessons about the dangers of "civilization," especially for women, and a trail of tears.

Cherokee Women and the Trail of Tears

THEDA PERDUE

While President [Andrew] Jackson promoted the policy of removing eastern Indians to the west, he did not originate the idea. Thomas Jefferson first suggested that removal beyond the evils of "civilization" would benefit the Indians and provide a justification for his purchase of Louisiana. In 1808-10 and again in 1817–19, members of the Cherokee Nation migrated to the west as the Cherokee land base shrank. But the major impetus for total removal came in 1830 when Congress, at the urging of President Jackson, passed the Indian Removal Act which authorized the President to negotiate cessions of Indian land in the east and transportation of native peoples west of the Mississippi. Although other Indian Nations such as the Choctaws signed removal treaties right away, the Cherokees refused. The Nations's leaders retained legal counsel and took its case against repressive state legislation to the United States Supreme Court (*Cherokee Nation v. Georgia*). The Cherokee Nation won, however, on the grounds that the Cherokees constituted a "domestic dependent" nation—not a foreign state under the U.S. Constitution. The state's failure to respond to the decision and the federal government's refusal to enforce it prompted an unauthorized Cherokee faction to negotiate removal. In December 1835, these disaffected men signed the Treaty of New Echota by which they exchanged the Cherokee Nation's territory in the southeast for land in the west. The United States Senate ratified the treaty, and in the summer of 1838, soldiers began to round up Cherokees for deportation. Ultimately, the Cherokees were permitted to delay until fall and to manage their own removal, but this leniency did little to ameliorate the experience the Cherokees called the "trail of tears." The weather was unusually harsh that winter; cold, disease, hunger, and exhaustion claimed the lives of at least 4,000 of the 15,000 people who travelled the thousand miles to the west.

The details of Cherokee removal have been recounted many times by scholars and popular writers. The focus of these accounts has tended to be political: they have dealt primarily with the United States' removal policy, the negotiation of removal treaties, and the political factionalism which the removal issue created within Cherokee society. In other words, the role of men in this event has dominated historical analysis. Yet women also were involved. It seems appropriate to reexamine the "trail of tears" using gender as a category of analysis. In particular, what role did women play in removal? How did they regard the policy? Did their views differ from those of men? How did the removal affect women? What were their experiences along the "trail of tears"? How did they go about reestablishing their lives in their new homes in the West? How does this kind of analysis amplify or alter our understanding of the event?

The Treaty of New Echota by which the Cherokee Nation relinquished its territory in the Southeast was signed by men. Women were present at the rump council that negotiated the treaty, but they did not participate in the proceedings. They may have met in their own council—precedents for women's councils exist—but if they did, no record remains. Instead, they probably cooked meals and cared for children while their husbands discussed treaty terms with the United States commissioner.

Perdue, Theda. Cherokee Women and the Trail of Tears. *Journal of Women's History* 1:1 (1989), 14–30.

This drawing by Charles O. Walker depicts the homestead of a Cherokee man, Lying Fish, and his family in the early 1830s. Lying Fish had cleared nineteen acres of land, planted peach trees and apple trees, and built two log houses, a corn crib and a stable. He and his family would lose it all when forced to move to Oklahoma Territory with other members of the Cherokee Nation.

The failure of women to join in the negotiation and signing of the Treaty of New Echota does not necessarily mean that women were not interested in the disposition of tribal land, but it does indicate that the role of women had changed dramatically in the preceding century.

Traditionally, women had a voice in Cherokee government. They spoke freely in council, and the War Woman (or Beloved Woman) decided the fate of captives. As late as 1787, a Cherokee woman wrote Benjamin Franklin that she had delivered an address to her people urging them to maintain peace with the new American nation. She had filled the peace pipe for the warriors, and she enclosed some of the same tobacco for the United States Congress in order to unite symbolically her people and his in peace. She continued:

> I am in hopes that if you Rightly consider that woman is the mother of All—and the Woman does not pull Children out of Trees or Stumps nor out of old Logs, but out of their Bodies, so that they ought to mind what a woman says.

The political influence of women, therefore, rested at least in part on their maternal biological role in procreation and their maternal role in Cherokee society, which assumed particular importance in the Cherokee's matrilineal kinship system. In this way of reckoning kin, children belonged to the clan of their mother and their only relatives were those who could be traced through her.

The Cherokees were not only matrilineal, they also were matrilocal. That is, a man lived with his wife in a house which belonged to her, or perhaps more accurately, to her family. According to the naturalist William Bartram, "Marriage gives no right to the husband over the property of his wife; and when they part she keeps the children and property belonging to them." The "property" that women kept included agricultural produce—corn, squash, beans, sunflowers, and pumpkins— stored in the household's crib. Produce belonged to women because they were the principal farmers. This economic role was ritualized at the Green Corn Ceremony every summer when an old woman presented the new corn crop. Furthermore, eighteenth-century travelers and traders normally purchased corn from women instead of men, and in the 1750s the garrison at Fort Loudoun, in present-day eastern Tennessee, actually employed a female purchasing agent to procure corn. Similarly, the fields belonged to the women who tended them, or rather to the women's lineages. Bartram observed that "their fields are divided by proper marks and their harvest is gathered separately." While the Cherokees technically held land in common and anyone could use unoccupied land, improved fields belonged to specific matrilineal households.

Perhaps this explains why women signed early deeds conveying land titles to the Proprietors of Carolina. Agents who made these transactions offered little explanation for the signatures of women on these documents. In the early twentieth century, a historian speculated that they represented a "renunciation of dower," but it may have been that the women were simply parting with what was recognized as theirs, or they may have been representing their lineages in the negotiations.

As late as 1785, women still played some role in the negotiation of land transactions. Nancy Ward, the Beloved Woman of Chota, spoke to the treaty conference held at Hopewell, South Carolina to clarify and extend land cessions stemming from Cherokee support of the British in the American Revolution. She addressed the assembly as the "mother of warriors" and promoted a peaceful resolution to land disputes between the Cherokees and United States. Under the terms of the Treaty of Hopewell, the Cherokees ceded large tracts of land south of the Cumberland River in Tennessee and Kentucky and west of the Blue Ridge Mountains in North Carolina. Nancy Ward and the other Cherokee delegates to the conference agreed to the cession not because they believed it to be just but because the United States dictated the terms of the treaty.

The conference at Hopewell was the last treaty negotiation in which women played an official role, and Nancy Ward's participation in that conference was somewhat anachronistic. In the eighteenth century, the English as well as other Europeans had dealt politically and commercially with men since men were the hunters and warriors in Cherokee society and Europeans were interested primarily in military alliances and deerskins. As relations with the English grew increasingly important to tribal welfare, women became less singificant in the Cherokee economy and government. Conditions in the Cherokee Nation following the American Revolution accelerated the trend. In their defeat, the Cherokees had to cope with the destruction of villages, fields, corn cribs, and orchards which had occurred during the war and the cession of hunting grounds which accompanied the peace. In desperation, they turned to the United States government, which proposed to convert the Cherokees into replicas of white pioneer farmers in the anticipation that they would then cede additional territory (presumably hunting grounds they no longer needed). While the government's so-called "civilization" program brought some economic relief, it also helped produce a transformation of gender roles and social organization. The society envisioned for the Cherokees, one which government agents and Protestant missionaries zealously tried to implement, was one in which a man farmed and headed a household composed only of his wife and children. The men who gained power in eighteenth-century Cherokee society—hunters, warriors, and descendants of traders—took immediate advantage of this program in order to maintain their status in the face of a declining deerskin trade and pacification, and then diverted their energy, ambition, and aggression into economic channels. As agriculture became more commerically viable, these men began to farm or to acquire African slaves to cultivate their fields for them. They also began to dominate Cherokee society, and by example and legislation, they altered fundamental relationships.

In 1808, a Council of headmen (there is no evidence of women participating) from Cherokee towns established a national police force to safeguard a person's holdings during life and "to give protection to children as heirs to their father's property, and to the widow's share," thereby changing inheritance patterns and officially recognizing the patriarchal family as the norm. Two year later, a council representing all seven matrilineal clans, but once again apparently including no women, abolished the practice of blood vengeance. This action ended one of the major functions of clans and shifted the responsibility for punishing wrongdoers to the national police force and tribal courts. Matrilineal kinship clearly did not have a place in the new Cherokee order.

We have no record of women objecting to such legislation. In fact, we know very little about most Cherokee women because written documents reflect the attitudes and concerns of a male Indian elite or of government agents and missionaries. The only women about whom we know very much are those who conformed to expectations. Nancy Ward, the Beloved Woman who favored peace with the United States, appears in the historical records while other less cooperative Beloved Women are merely unnamed, shadowy figures. Women such as Catherine Brown, a model of Christian virtue, gained the admiration of missionaries, and we have a memoir of Brown's life; other women who removed their children from mission schools incurred the missionaries' wrath, and they merit only brief mention in mission diaries. The comments of government agents usually focused on those native women who demonstrated considerable industry by raising cotton and producing cloth (in this case, Indian men suffered by comparison), not those who grew corn in the matrilineage's fields. In addition to being biased and reflecting only one segment of the female population, the information from these sources is second-hand; rarely did Indian women, particularly traditionalists, speak for themselves.

The one subject on which women did speak on two occasions was land. In 1817 the United States sought a large cession of Cherokee territory and removal of those who lived on the land in question. A group of Indian women met in their own council, and thirteen of them signed a message which was delivered to the National Council. They advised the Council:

> The Cherokee ladys now being present at the meeting of the Chiefs and warriors in council have thought it their duties as mothers to address their beloved Chiefs and warriors now assembled.

Our beloved children and head men of the Cherokee nation we address you warriors in council. [W]e have raised all of you on the land which we now have, which God gave us to inhabit and raise provisions. [W]e know that our country has once been extensive but by repeated sales has become circumscribed to a small tract and never have thought it our duty to interfere in the disposition of it till now, if a father or mother was to sell all their lands which they had to depend on[,] which their children had to raise their living on[,] which would be bad indeed and to be removed to another country. [W]e do not wish to go to an unknown country which we have understood some of our children wish to go over the Mississippi but this act of our children would be like destroying your mothers. Your mother and sisters ask and beg of you not to part with any more of our lands.

The next year, the National Council met again to discuss the possibility of allotting Cherokee land to individuals, an action the United States government encouraged as a preliminary step to removal. Once again, Cherokee women reacted:

We have heard with painful feelings that the bounds of the land we now possess are to be drawn into very narrow limits. The land was given to us by the Great Spirit above as our common right, to raise our children upon, & to make support for our rising generations. We therefore humbly petition our beloved children, the head men and warriors, to hold out to the last in support of our common rights, as the Cherokee nation have been the first settlers of this land; we therefore claim the right of the soil. . . . We therefore unanimously join in our meeting to hold our country in common as hitherto.

Common ownership of land meant in theory that the United States government had to obtain cessions from recognized, elected Cherokee officials who represented the wishes of the people. Many whites favored allotment because private citizens then could obtain individually owned tracts of land through purchase, fraud, or seizure. Most Cherokees recognized this danger and objected to allotment for that reason. The women, however, had an additional incentive for opposing allotment. Under the laws of the states in which the Cherokees lived and of which they would become citizens if land were allotted, married women had few property rights. A married woman's property, even property she held prior to her marriage, belonged legally to her husband. Cherokee women and matrilineal households would have ceased to be property owners.

The implications for women became apparent in the 1830s, when Georgia claimed its law was in effect in the Cherokee country. Conflicts over property arose because of uncertainty over which legal system prevailed. For example, a white man, James Vaught, married the Cherokee, Catherine Gunter. She inherited several slaves from her father, and Vaught sold two of them to General Isaac Wellborn. His wife had not consented to the sale and so she reclaimed her property and took them with her when the family moved west. General Wellborn tried to seize the slaves just as they were about to embark, but a soldier, apparently recognizing her claim under Cherokee law, prevented him from doing so. After removal, the General appealed to Principal Chief John Ross for aid in recovering the slaves, but Ross refused. He informed Wellborn: "By the laws of the Cherokee Nation, the property of husband and wife remain separate and apart and neither of these can sell or dispose of the property of the other." Had the Cherokees accepted allotment and come under Georgia law, Wellborn would have won.

The effects of the women's protests in 1817 and 1818 are difficult to determine. In 1817 the Cherokees ceded tracts of land in Georgia, Alabama, and Tennessee, and in 1819 they made an even larger cession. Nevertheless, they rejected individual allotments and strengthened restrictions on alienation of improvements. Furthermore, the Cherokee Nation gave notice that they would negotiate no additional cessions—a resolution so strongly supported that the United States ultimately had to turn to a small unauthorized faction in order to obtain the minority treaty of 1835.

The political organization which existed in the Cherokee Nation in 1817–18 had made it possible for women to voice their opinion. Traditionally, Cherokee towns were politically independent of one another, and each town governed itself through a council in which all adults could speak. In the eighteenth century, however, the Cherokees began centralizing their government in order to restrain bellicose warriors whose raids jeopardized the entire nation and to negotiate as a single unit with whites. Nevertheless, town councils remained important, and representatives of traditional towns formed the early National Council. This National Council resembled the town councils in that anyone could address the body. Although legislation passed in 1817 created an Executive Committee, power still rested with the Council which reviewed all Committee acts.

The protests of the women to the National Council in 1817 and 1818 were, however, the last time women presented a collective position to the Cherokee governing body. Structural changes in Cherokee government more narrowly defined participation in the National Council. In 1820 the Council provided that representatives be chosen from eight districts rather than from traditional towns, and in 1823 the Committee acquired a right of review over acts of the Council. The more formalized political organization made it less likely that a group could make its views known to the national government.

As the Cherokee government became more centralized, political and economic power rested increasingly in the hands of a few elite men who adopted the planter lifestyle of the white antebellum South. A significant part of the ideological basis for this lifestyle was the cult of domesticity in which the ideal woman confined herself to home and hearth while men contended with the corrupt world of government and business. The elite adopted the tenets of the cult of domesticity, particularly after 1817 when the number of Protestant missionaries, major proponents of this feminine ideal, increased significantly and their influence on Cherokee society broadened.

The extent to which a man's wife and daughters conformed to the idea quickly came to be one measure of his status. In 1818 Charles Hicks, who later served as Principal Chief, described the most prominent men in the Nation as "those who have for the last 10 or 20 years been pursuing agriculture & kept their women & children at home & in comfortable circumstances." Eight years later, John Ridge, one of the first generation of Cherokees to have been educated from childhood in mission schools, discussed a Cherokee law which protected the property rights of a married woman and observed that "in many respects she has exclusive & distinct control over her own, particularly among the less civilized." The more "civilized" presumably left such matters to men. Then Ridge described suitable activities for women: "They sew, they weave, they spin, they cook our meals and act well the duties assigned them by Nature as mothers." Proper women did not enter business or politics.

Despite the attitudes of men such as Hicks and Ridge, women did in fact continue as heads of households and as businesswomen. In 1828 the *Cherokee Phoenix* published the obituary of Oo-dah-less who had accumulated a sizeable estate through agriculture and commerce. She was "the support of a large family," and she bequeathed her property "to an only daughter and three grandchildren." Oo-dah-less was not unique. At least one-third of the heads of household listed on the removal roll of 1835 were women. Most of these were not as prosperous as Oo-dah-less, but some were even more successful economically. Nineteen owned slaves (190 men were slaveholders), and two held over twenty slaves and operated substantial farms.

Nevertheless, these women had ceased to have a direct voice in Cherokee government. In 1826 the Council called a constitutional convention to draw up a governing document for the Nation. According to legislation which provided for election of delegates to the convention, "No person but a free male citizen who is full grown shall be entitled to vote." The convention met and drafted a constitution patterned after that of the United States. Not surprisingly, the constitution which male Cherokees ratified in 1827 restricted the franchise to "free male citizens" and stipulated that "no person shall be eligible to a seat in the General Council, but a free Cherokee male, who shall have attained the age of twenty-five." Unlike the United States Constitution, the Cherokee document clearly excluded women, perhaps as a precaution against women who might assert their traditional right to participate in politics instead of remaining in the domestic sphere.

The exclusion of women from politics certainly did not produce the removal crisis, but it did mean that a group traditionally opposed to land cession could no longer be heard on the issue. How women would have voted is also unclear. Certainly by 1835, many Cherokee women, particularly those educated in mission schools, believed that men were better suited to deal with political issues than women, and a number of women voluntarily enrolled their households to go west before the forcible removal of 1838–39. Even if women had united in active opposition to removal, it is unlikely that the United States and aggressive state governments would have paid any more attention to them than they did to the elected officials of the nation who opposed removal or the 15,000 Cherokees, including women (and perhaps children), who petitioned the United States Senate to reject the Treaty of New Echota. While Cherokee legislation may have made women powerless, federal authority rendered the whole Nation impotent.

In 1828 Georgia had extended state law over the Cherokee Nation, and white intruders who invaded its territory. Georgia law prohibited Indians, both men and women, from testifying in court against white assailants, and so they simply had to endure attacks on person and property. Delegates from the Nation complained to Secretary of War John H. Eaton about the lawless behavior of white intruders:

> Too many there are who think it an act of trifling consequence to oust an Indian family from the quiet enjoyment of all the comforts of their own firesides, and to drive off before their faces the stock that gave nourishment to the children and support to the aged, and appropriate it to the satisfaction to avarice.

Elias Boudinot, editor of the bilingual *Cherokee Phoenix,* even accused the government of encouraging the intruders in order to force the Indians off their lands, and he published the following account:

> A few days since two of these white men came to a Cherokee house, for the purpose, they pretended, of buying provisions. There was no person about the house but one old woman of whom they inquired for some corn, beans & c. The woman told them she had nothing to sell. They then went off in the direction of the field belonging to this Cherokee family. They had not gone but a few minutes when the woman of the house saw a heavy smoke rising from that direction. She immediately hastened to the field and found the villains had set the woods on fire but a few rods from the fences, which she found already in a full blaze. There being a very heavy wind that day, the fire spread so fast, that her efforts to extinguish it proved utterly useless. The entire fence was therefore consumed in a short time. It is said that during her efforts to save the fence the men who had done the mischief were within sight, and were laughing heartily at her!

The Georgia Guard, established by the state to enforce its law in the Cherokee country, offered no protection and, in fact, contributed to the lawlessness. The *Phoenix* printed the following notice under the title "Cherokee Women, Beware.":

> It is said that the Georgia Guard have received orders, from the Governor we suppose, to inflict corporeal punishment on such females as shall hereafter be guilty of insulting them. We presume they are to be the judges of what constitutes *insult.*

Despite harassment from intruders and the Guard, most Cherokees had no intention of going west, and in the spring of 1838 they began to plant their crops as usual. Then United States soldiers arrived, began to round up the Cherokees, and imprisoned them in stockades in preparation for deportation. In 1932 Rebecca Neugin, who was nearly one hundred years old, shared her childhood memory and family tradition about removal with historian Grant Foreman:

> When the soldier came to our house my father wanted to fight, but my mother told him that the soldiers would kill him if he did and we surrendered without a fight. They drove us out of our house to join other prisoners in a stockade. After they took us away, my mother begged them to let her go back and get some bedding. So they let her go back and she brought what bedding and a few cooking utensils she could carry and had to leave behind all of our other household possessions.

Rebecca Neugin's family was relatively fortunate. In the process of capture, families were sometimes separated and sufficient food and clothing were often left behind. Over fifty years after removal, John G. Burnett, a soldier who served as an interpreter, reminisced:

> Men working in the fields were arrested and driven to stockades. Women were dragged from their homes by soldiers whose language they could not understand. Children were often separated from their parents and driven into the stockades with the sky for a blanket and the earth for a pillow.

Burnett recalled how one family was forced to leave the body of a child who had just died and how a distraught mother collapsed of heart failure as soldiers evicted her and her three children from their homes. After their capture, many Cherokees had to march miles over rugged mountain terrain to the stockades. Captain L. B. Webster wrote his wife about moving eight hundred Cherokees from North Carolina to the central depot in Tennessee: "We were eight days in making the journey (80 miles), and it was pitiful to behold the women & children, who suffered exceedingly—as they were all obliged to walk, with the exception of the sick."

Originally the government planned to deport all the Cherokees in the summer of 1838, but the mortality rate of the three parties that departed that summer led the commanding officer, General Winfield Scott, to agree to delay the major removal until fall. In the interval, the Cherokees remained in the stockades where conditions were abysmal. Women in particular often became individual victims of their captors. The missionary Daniel Butrick recorded the following episode in his journal:

> The poor Cherokees are not only exposed to temporal evils, but also to every species of moral desolation. The other day a gentleman informed me that he saw six soldiers about two Cherokee women. The women stood by a tree, and the soldiers with a bottle of liquor were endeavoring to entice them to drink, though the women, as yet were resisting them. He made this known to the commanding officer but we presume no notice was taken of it, as it was reported that those soldiers had those women with them the whole night afterwards. A young married woman, a member of the Methodist society was at the camp with her friends, though her husband was not there at the time. The soldiers, it is said, caught her, dragged her about, and at length, either through fear, or otherwise, induced her to drink; and then seduced her away, so that she is now an outcast even among her own relatives. How many of the poor captive women are thus debauched, through terror and seduction, that eye which never sleeps, alone can determine.

When removal finally got underway in October, the Cherokees were in a debilitated and demoralized state. A white minister who saw them as they prepared to embark noted: "The women did not appear to as good advantage as did the men. All, young and old, wore blankets which almost hid them from view." The Cherokees had received permission to manage their own removal, and they divided the people into thirteen detachments of approximately one thousand each. While some had wagons, most walked. Neugin rode in a wagon with other children and some elderly women, but her older brother, mother, and father "walked all the way." One observer reported that "even aged females, apparently nearly ready to drop in the grave, were traveling with heavy burdens attached to the back." Proper conveyance did not spare well-to-do Cherokees the agony of removal, the same observer noted:

> One lady passed on in her hack in company with her husband, apparently with as much refinement and equipage as any of the mothers of New England; and she was a mother too and her youngest child, about three years old, was sick in her arms, and all she could do was to make it comfortable as circumstances would permit. . . . She could only carry her dying child in her arms a few miles farther, and then she must stop in a stranger-land and consign her much loved babe to the cold ground, and that without pomp and ceremony, and pass on with the multitude.

This woman was not alone. Journals of the removal are largely a litany of the burial of children, some born "untimely."

Many women gave birth alongside the trail: at least sixty-nine newborns arrived in the West. The Cherokees' military escort was often less than sympathetic. Daniel

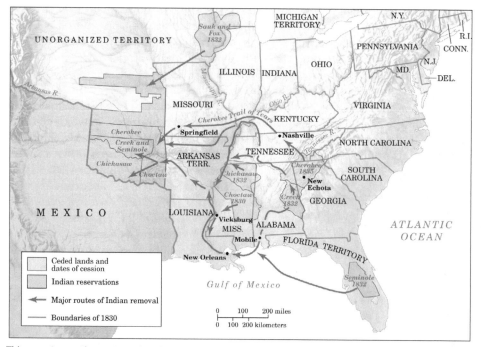

This map traces the routes taken by members of the Seminole, Choctaw, Creek, Chickasaw, and Cherokee Nations who were forced to move from their homelands in the southeastern United States to territories set aside for them in Oklahoma. The Trail of Tears, located furthest north, led the Cherokee through bitterly cold terrain and created enormous suffering for those forced to move west.

Butrick wrote in his journal that troops frequently forced women in labor to continue until they collapsed and delivered "in the midst of the company of soldiers." One man even stabbed an expectant mother with a bayonet. Obviously, many pregnant women did not survive such treatment. The oral tradition of a family from southern Illinois, through which the Cherokees passed, for example, includes an account of an adopted Cherokee infant whose mother died in childbirth near the family's pioneer cabin. While this story may be apocryphal, the circumstances of Cherokee removal make such traditions believable.

The stress and tension produced by the removal crisis probably accounts for a post-removal increase in domestic violence of which women usually were the victims. Missionaries reported that men, helpless to prevent seizure of their property and assaults on themselves and their families, vented their frustrations by beating wives and children. Some women were treated so badly by their husbands that they left them, and this dislocation contributed to the chaos in the Cherokee Nation in the late 1830s.

Removal divided the Cherokee Nation in a fundamental way, and the Civil War magnified that division. Because most signers of the removal treaty were highly acculturated, many traditionalists resisted more strongly the white man's way of life and distrusted more openly those Cherokees who imitated whites. This split between "conservatives," those who sought to preserve the old ways, and "progressives," those committed to change, extended to women. We know far more, of course, about "progressive" Cherokee women who left letters and diaries which in some ways are quite similar to those of upper-class women in the antebellum South. In letters, they recounted local news such as "they had Elick Cockrel up for steeling horses" and "they have Charles Reese in chains about burning Harnages house" and discussed economic concerns: "I find I cannot get any corn in this neighborhood, so of course I shall be greatly pressed in providing provision for my family." Nevertheless, family life was the focus of most letters: "Major is well and tryes hard to stand alone he will walk soon. I would write more but the baby is crying."

Occasionally we even catch a glimpse of conservative women who seem to have retained at least some of their original authority over domestic matters. Red Bird Smith, who led a revitalization movement at the end of the nineteenth century, had considerable difficulty with his first mother-in-law. She "influenced" her adopted daughter to marry Smith through witchcraft and, as head of the household, meddled rather seriously in the couple's lives. Interestingly, however, the Kee-Too-Wah society which Red Bird Smith headed had little room for women. Although the society had political objectives, women enjoyed no greater participation in this "conservative" organization than they did in the "progressive" republican government of the Cherokee Nation.

Following removal, the emphasis of legislation involving women was on protection rather than participation. In some ways, this legislation did offer women greater opportunities than the law codes of the states. In 1845 the editor of the *Cherokee Advocate* expressed pride that "in this respect the Cherokees have been considerably in advance of many of their white brethren, the rights of their women having been amply secured almost ever since they had written laws." The Nation also established the Cherokee Female Seminary to provide higher education for women, but like the education women received before removal, students studied only those subjects considered to be appropriate for their sex.

Removal, therefore, changed little in terms of the status of Cherokee women. They had lost political power before the crisis of the 1830s, and events which followed relocation merely confirmed new roles and divisions. Cherokee women originally had been subsistence-level farmers and mothers and the importance of these roles in traditional society had made it possible for them to exercise political power. Women, however, lacked the economic resources and military might on which political power in the Anglo-American system rested. When the Cherokees adopted the Anglo-American concept of power in the eighteenth and nineteenth centuries, men became dominant. But in the 1830s the chickens came home to roost. Men, who had welcomed the Anglo-American basis for power, now found themselves without power. Nevertheless, they did not question the changes they had fostered. Therefore, the tragedy of the trail of tears lies not only in the suffering and death which the Cherokees experienced but also in the failure of many Cherokees to look critically at the political system which they had adopted—a political system dominated by wealthy, highly acculturated men and supported by an ideology that made women (as well as others defined as "weak" or "inferior") subordinate. In the removal crisis of the 1830s, men learned an important lesson about power; it was a lesson women had learned well before the "trail of tears."

Questions for Study and Review

1. Why was the transition from matrilineal to patrilineal descent important when it came to Cherokee women's roles in the debates over Indian removal?

2. What were the perceived benefits of Anglo-American gender roles and social customs that encouraged many Cherokee to adopt the programs put forth by missionaries and government agents?

3. Compare the roles of traditional Cherokee women with those of the West African women discussed by Jennifer Morgan.

4. What were the similarities and differences in the ways that the Spanish treated California Indians and the United States treated the Cherokee?

Suggested Readings and Web Sites

Mary Hershberger, "Mobilizing Women, Anticipating Abolition: The Struggle Against Indian Removal in the 1830s," *Journal of American History* (1999)

Albert Hurtado, *Indian Survival on the California Frontier* (1987)

Theda Perdue, *Cherokee Women: Gender and Culture Change, 1700–1835* (1998)

Claudio Saunt, *A New Order of Things: Property, Power, and the Transformation of the Creek Indians, 1733–1816* (1999)

The Cherokee Indians
   http://ngeorgia.com/history/cherokee.html

Chapter 12

Historians of American slavery began in the 1980s to explore the particular roles and experiences of women. The first studies, by Deborah Gray White, emphasized the importance of enslaved women as laborers, healers, cooks, and mothers. She argued that slavery necessitated—and the slave community recognized—female strength, expertise, and authority. Thus, even though slavery was brutal for both sexes, that brutality did not negate differences in the roles and experiences of enslaved women and men. Indeed, because slave status was carried through the mother's line, mothers were more likely to live with their children than were fathers, and enslaved families carried on ideas about the centrality of motherhood from West African cultures, in which adult women were central to the formation and sustenance of enslaved families and communities.

More recently, scholars have begun to explore enslaved women's experience in more detail, focusing on their roles in reproduction and the maintenance of extended families and households, in medical care within white families and slave quarters, and in their communities' resistance to bondage. Still, it has been assumed until recently that men dominated the two most celebrated forms of resistance, running away and rebellion. While the issue of women's roles in slave rebellions has yet to be fully explored, Stephanie Camp offers us a new perspective on running as a challenge to planters' control. She argues that truancy, which involved slaves leaving plantations temporarily and then returning, was a standard means by which women and men responded to beatings, threats of sale, and other oppressive conditions. Rather than simply letting off steam, truancy provided a means to disrupt plantation routines, cut into planters' profits, and gain much-needed respite from hard labor. In some cases, truancy even provided slaves with leverage to negotiate changes in their situation.

Not only did women practice truancy in significant numbers, but they also facilitated the truancy of other women and men. Those who fled plantations for even brief periods required food, shelter, and often clothing. If they were traveling to another plantation to see family members or loved ones, they might also need assistance in sneaking into the slave quarters at night or being hidden during the daytime. Women were central in efforts to support truants and facilitate their communication with other enslaved women and men.

One of the reasons that scholars have given for the low number of women who ran north to freedom is the important role they played in their families, and particularly their responsibilities to their children. Running away with children in tow was difficult; but leaving them behind often seemed impossible. Truancy, however, provided mothers with a means of resisting their exploitation without abandoning their children to a planter's wrath. Here, too, female truants depended on other women, in this case to care for children in their absence.

It took the resources of both women and men to survive slavery. Similarly, the development of African American families and cultures cannot be understood without recognizing women's central role in their preservation. At the same time, the centrality of women to survival, to families, and to culture and customs should not blind us to their importance in resisting black bondage. Stephanie Camp reminds us that there were many ways to challenge the power of planters, and women chose those that fit best with their roles and responsibilities.

"I Could Not Stay There": Enslaved Women, Truancy and the Geography of Everyday Forms of Resistance in the Antebellum Plantation South

Stephanie M. H. Camp

Like many other antebellum planters, Sallie Smith's Louisiana owner hoped to control his labour force and to affirm his position as head of the plantation household by limiting the movement of enslaved people around and, especially, off his property. Accordingly, he forbade his bondpeople from leaving his plantation without a pass. When his enslaved people broke the rules that determined where they ought to be—in the field, in the yard, in their quarters—and when they ought to be there, Smith's owner punished them violently, as was his prerogative. After running away temporarily, Smith was tortured inside of "a big barrel he kept to roll us in, with nails drove all through it." But Sallie Smith continued to run away: "I did not stay more than a month before I ran away again. I tell you, I could not stay there."

Unwilling or unable to "stay there," Sallie Smith was like many other bondwomen who, for short periods of time, ran away from overwork and abuse on antebellum plantations. Smith was not a typical bondwoman in that most did not run away nearly so frequently as she. But many other enslaved women and men did run away on occasion throughout their lives. Called "runaways" by antebellum Southern blacks and whites, and termed "truants" and "absentees" by historians, they did not intend to make a break for freedom in the North, but sought short-term escapes from work, from planter and overseer control and from the prying eyes of family and friends. Their movement challenged the regulations dictating bondpeople's location, regulations that were designed to affirm slave holders' dominion over the movement of the enslaved and, thereby, to maximize the exploitation of bondpeople's labour.

This engraving shows Margaret Garner, who fled her Kentucky master with her four children in the early 1850s, being captured in Ohio. Faced with returning to the South, Garner killed two of her children before she was captured and drowned herself in the Ohio River on the trip back to Kentucky. Her story inspired an acclaimed nineteenth-century painting by Thomas S. Noble, on which this engraving was based, and Toni Morrison's twentieth-century novel, *Beloved*.

Winthrop Jordan found that it was confinement "more than any other single quality" that differentiated slavery from servitude in the early years of American slavery's formation: "enslavement was captivity." By the antebellum period, slave-holding elites had created a "geography of containment" that aimed to control slave mobility in space and in time. Bondpeople everywhere were forbidden by law and common practice to leave their owners' property without passes, and slave patrols attempted to ensure obedience to the law. With the rise of paternalism among the slave-holding elite in the early national years came great attention to black bodily minutiae: nutrition, dress, hygiene and pleasure all became the targets of planter meddling, as did black movement in space and in time. Advice manuals proliferated to help planters establish orderly plantations in large measure by dominating and controlling the bodies of the people they owned. Laws, customs and ideals came together into a systematic constriction of slave movement as one of the most important bases of mastery.

Mississippian William Ethelbert Ervin personified the paternalist paradigm of his class and historical moment. In December 1846, Ervin sat down to write out his ideal of slave behaviour. First, he indicated that plantation borders not only marked the edges of his estate, but also hemmed in his bondpeople: no one was to "leave the place without leaf of absence." Secondly, within those spatial borders, he added temporal limits that bound enslaved people's movement even more: "at nine o'clock every night the Horne must be blown Which is the signal for each to retire to his or her house and there to remain until morning." Ervin directed his overseers to check up on people in the quarters, and if anyone was found "out of their places," they would be "delt with . . . according to discretion."

While planters dreamt and schemed about the creation of orderly plantations in which the location of enslaved people was neatly determined by curfews, rules and the demands of crops, enslaved people engaged in truancy with a persistence that disturbed and alarmed most slave holders. Though common, truancy never became an acceptable part of plantation life in slave holders' minds. Rather, truancy was the source of a fundamental conflict of interest between owner and owned. When bondpeople engaged in absenteeism, they withdrew their labour and they challenged the authority of their owners. Most of all, they created alternative ways of knowing and using plantation space that were inconsistent with planters' requirements. Their distinct mapping of the plantation might best be called a "rival geography." Enslaved people's rival geography was not a fixed spatial formation for it included quarters, outbuildings, woods, swamps and neighbouring farms as opportunity granted them. Absentees' movement to and between these places wove them together into an alternative mapping of plantation space. Where planters' mapping of the plantation was defined by fixed places for its residents, the rival geography was characterized by motion: the movement of bodies within and around plantation space. Truancy, a practice that facilitated independent activity (thereby denying planters' desire for control of bondpeople's movement and their labour) was the foundation of this rival geography. As such, absenteeism was an endemic problem of labour and social discipline in the antebellum plantation South.

Much of the existent literature on the topic considers truancy to have been a "safety valve" in plantation life; that is, an individual expression of dissatisfaction that released anger and frustration but posed no danger to the system. This interpretation, however, misses the broader operation of politics in the Old South. Places, boundaries and movement were central to how slavery was organized, and to how it was resisted. Truancy threatened planters' sense of mastery and their security in the moneymaking purpose of their farms. At least as importantly, through absenteeism enslaved people established a form of spatial knowledge that granted them room and time for themselves, and that they would put to emancipatory uses during the Civil War.

Gender difference informed the practice of truancy. Compared with their numbers among permanent fugitives, women were much more highly represented among absentees, and while men and women both engaged in it, truancy served somewhat varying purposes for and imposed distinct responsibilities on each. In different time periods and in various parts of the South, women consistently made up a minority of those who ran away to permanent freedom in the North. In a recent study, John Hope Franklin and Loren Schweninger found that, between 1838 and 1860, Virginia's bondwomen were a mere nine per cent of fugitives, while women in South Carolina made up 19 per cent of the group. Fourteen per cent of North Carolina's and 12 per cent of Tennessee's runaways were women. Louisiana had the largest percentage of female runaways, still less than a third (29 percent) of all fugitives.

The factors that held women within plantation space more firmly than men were many. Paramount among them were women's family responsibilities and bondpeople's gender ideals. Women, as a group, were enmeshed in networks of extended family and friends where they played central roles in the black family. "Abroad" marriages, the disproportionate sale of men into the slave-trade supplying labour to the new cotton lands in the deep South and the Old Southwest, and African cultural legacies resulted in many female-headed families throughout the antebellum South. Such "matrifocal" families depended on women for their survival. Many women understood themselves as persons in terms deeply connected to community; and they identified as women in part through their activities on behalf of their families. Thus enmeshed in dense social relations, women appear to have considered permanent escape to be even more difficult than did many men.

Such day-to-day realities reinforced gender ideals among enslaved people. Community sanctions against women abandoning their children normalized female dedication to the family, and were another pressure that limited the number of women who could escape to the North. Invoking a standard of respectable womanhood, Molly Horniblow chastised her granddaughter for even thinking of running away: "Nobody respects a mother who forsakes her children." Taught community ideals, children held their mothers to them. Expressing a feeling of betrayal uncharacteristic among former bondpeople remembering their fathers' escapes from bondage, Patience M. Avery was heartbroken by her mother's escape: "No, chile, I can never fergit dat. You see my mother gimme dem pennies to mek me hush crying. Yes, yes, I can 'member dis as good as ef 'twas yestidy; how my mother stole out and lef' me." Avery murmured to her interviewer the plaintive refrain of ultimate loss: "I was a po' motherless chile." Women, like Avery's mother, who did dare to escape left behind children whose grief would be a lesson to other women who considered running away.

The point must not be overstated: enslaved fathers were important to their families, as their families were to them. Most enslaved men did not attempt to run away at all, partly because of their own roots in their communities. And some women did leave lovers and families to head north. But different roles within the family nonetheless created diverse responsibilities and conceptions of acceptable behaviour for women and men. These duties and gender norms helped to shape fugitive behaviour by diminishing women's rates of flight.

A final factor preventing women from running away in the same numbers as men was their relative lack of knowledge of geography beyond the plantation. Men in the skilled trades, men who performed transportation or communication work, and men with wives and lovers in other places had occasions to leave the farm on which they lived. For all of these reasons, men sometimes received passes and the opportunity to learn the lie of the land, roads and waterways, an opportunity implicitly denied to women. In addition to generally being unfamiliar with local geography, women were especially noticeable to passers-by. While it was dangerous for both men and women to be seen while escaping, it was more so for women. Men could have a plausible excuse for traversing roads and estuaries; enslaved men transporting letters, messages, goods and materials and men visiting their girlfriends and families were an ordinary part of the landscape—as was the mandatory presentation of the pass that legitimated their travel. Women, on the other hand, did not generally perform such work and thus rarely became familiar with neighbourhood geography or with watercraft. As fugitives, if they needed to abandon the byways for a main road, they were sure to draw attention—and suspicion. Their conspicuousness would only have been highlighted by their awkwardness on unfamiliar terrain and by the possible presence of children, who would have further complicated matters: they needed to be fed, carried, hurried along and kept quiet.

All in all, the social and the logistical difficulties were nearly insurmountable for the majority of women who even bothered to contemplate flight to the North. Most bond-women apparently concluded that permanent escape was impossible or undesirable, and they were thus bound more narrowly than men. Yet, enslaved women did not sub-mit to planters' schemes for spatial and temporal order by remaining obediently in their assigned places. Instead, like men, they chose truancy, a temporary escape from the plantation. Absenteeism, generally to the nearest woods or swamps and occasion-ally to nearby towns, allowed bondwomen to remain in immediate proximity to their families, yet offered escape from slave holders' demands and control. Truancy was par-ticularly important in the lives of enslaved women, but not because it was a "female from" of resistance. It was not: men made up the majority of truants most of the time. Rather, truancy is an important part of the story of women's lives in and resistance to slavery because women engaged in it more frequently than they ran away as fugitives, and because they played a critical role supporting other truants even when they them-selves did not run away.

Women's participation in truancy on three plantations with exceptional docu-mentation of the practice shows quite a contrast with their fugitive rates. All three plantation records come from the lower South: South Carolina and Mississippi. In general, planters from the lower South appear to have complained about truancy more than slave holders in the upper South. Or, at least they were driven to record their frustrations in their journals more commonly, a phenomenon that itself sug-gests that enslaved people in the lower South may have engaged in truancy more fre-quently and consistently than those in the upper South. Perhaps their great distance from freedom in the North, and the near-hopelessness of running away to the North made flight in other, more local, directions for shorter periods of time a more urgently needed, and therefore more commonly practised, method for escaping bondage. Much planter documentation also survives from the upper South, though. Moreover, black testimony comes from both sections; consequently, conclusions about distinctions between the upper and lower South must remain speculative.

In Adams County, Mississippi, John Nevitt presided over Clermont plantation, located on fertile land along the Mississippi River's southwestern border of the state. Nevitt's bondpeople worked Clermont's land, producing cotton, tobacco and rice which Nevitt easily traded in nearby Natchez whence it was quickly transported along the river. But the production of these goods was not smooth; rather, multiple incidents of truancy per month marred Nevitt's ideal of orderly production and sale. Nevitt kept an extraordinarily methodical log of truants' escapes, mutual assis-tance, returns and punishment, providing an important source for the history of truancy. The frequency of absenteeism at Clermont may indicate that enslaved people there engaged in truancy more intensely than those in other places. Yet herein lies the diary's strength. While Nevitt's diary cannot (as no single source can) tell us about truancy everywhere, the heightened activity it documents allows us an unusual glimpse into patterns of gender difference.

Compared with their numbers among fugitives, women's rates of truancy are striking. When women on Nevitt's estate ran away, they generally represented signif-icant proportions of the total numbers of incidents of absenteeism and of the num-ber of truants: with two years excepted, women constituted from 19 to 41 per cent of truants. The differing behaviours of men and women at Clermont plantation are similar to those in other, relatively more opaque but still instructive, plantation records. In the summer of 1828 the sole year documenting incidents of truancy at the Rockingham plantation in the Beaufort District of South Carolina, 55 per cent of the truants were women. And during the peak of recorded truancy at James Henry Hammond's Silver Bluff plantation in South Carolina, the time between his assumption of ownership in December 1831 and the end of his first full and highly tumultuous year, 32 per cent of the truants were women. Clearly, at least on these three plantations with detailed records of truancy, women made up a greater proportion of truants than they did of runaways.

Much of bondpeople's autonomous and semi-autonomous social activity depended upon truancy, as Christian worshippers and secular party-goers alike produced rare moments of leisure by absenting themselves to congregate in the woods, swamps or in outbuildings. But absenteeism was often a solitary affair, frequently a spontaneous response to violence, which enslaved people saw as a physical violation and as offensive to their sense of human dignity. North Carolina slave holder George D. Lewis was disdainful of the behaviour of his "negro girl," but he probably accurately detected her outrage when she "took umbrage at a little flagellation and left." Sometimes dey beat 'em so bad," William Brooks said of planters' treatment of women, "dey run away an' hide in de woods." Women also ran away to evade sexual violence, of which they were the disproportionate targets.

Absentees ran away to assert some control over their labour. "Sometimes," Lorenzo L. Ivy recalled, "slaves jes' run' 'way to de woods fo' a week or two to git a res' fum de fiel', an' den dey come on back." Chronic truant Sallie Smith went to the woods not only to escape her master's violence, but also to take a break from the demanding regimen of the plantation on which she lived. "Sometimes," she said, remembering the distance she could obtain from the sounds of morning and the beginning of another workday, "I'd go so far off from the plantation I could not hear the cows low or the roosters crow."

On Nevitt's farm, truants ran away more often at the beginning and end of the cotton-picking season's intensive labour. The number of incidents of truancy (for all years together) remained relatively steady between March and October, but rose in November, just as labour intensified around cotton picking. The number dropped again in December, perhaps in response to the holiday that Nevitt gave his enslaved labourers for Christmas. By January first, bondpeople at Clermont were back at work finishing picking the cotton crop, as well as clearing the fields, making fence posts and shingles, and repairing local roads, fences and the quarters. At the same time, the number of incidents of truancy once again rose, often at the very beginning of the month, suggesting that absentees may have been extending their holidays as well as evading the rush to complete the cotton harvest.

Truants who left during November and January must have been in search of rest and amusement, but they may have also been escaping increased violence. Nevitt's demands for increased labour during harvest would certainly have been underscored by the lash, no doubt spurring some to run away. Furthermore, the consumption of alcohol was a part of harvest and holiday celebrations among both black and white men, and may have led to an escalation in violence by planters and overseers against bondpeople, and by bondmen against bondwomen. In addition, drinking might have incited more incidents of sexual abuse of women. The merciless work schedule may have combined with a rise in violence to impel more people to run away during this time of year.

The plantation's "push" factors (exhaustion, desperation, terror, anger) were only some of the reasons people ran away. Marginal spaces offered opportunities that drew runaways to them. Bondmen ran away to visit their wives and girlfriends, for instance, hiding in their cabins or meeting them in the woods near the women's homes. Ellen Campbell knew a woman whose abroad husband once ran away to the woods near her home farm when he was denied permission to visit her. While he hid out, she went to the woods to meet him and to give him dinner, until he was caught one night and summarily shot dead.

The separation of family members through sale and abroad marriages was one of slavery's greatest atrocities. But historians have shown that while separation was devastating to individuals, the slave family as an institution adapted to, and was not annihilated by, personal loss. When the distance was not too far, family separation was also remedied by secret visits in the night-time. Frederick Douglass's classic 1845 autobiography opened with his faint memories of his mother who lived some 12 miles from him in Maryland. "I never saw my mother, to know her as such," Douglass recounted, "more than four or five time in my life; and each of these times was very short in duration, and at night." Douglass wrote with open admiration for his mother, who ran away from her hirer as often as she could, which was not very often, to visit him "in the night, traveling the whole distance on foot after the performance of her day's work." Douglass's account of his relationship with his mother is a mixture of bitterness about what slave holders did to the enslaved, sorrow that he did not have more time with his mother (his father was her owner), and tenderness for what his mother struggled to provide him. "I do not recollect of ever seeing my mother by the light of day," he wrote. "She was with me in the night. She would lie down with me, and get me to sleep, but long before I waked she was gone." Douglass walked a delicate line, stressing the brutalities of the system, the lingering emotional trauma of early orphanage and the agency of his truant mother.

In woods or swamps, runaways faced extremely difficult living conditions. They ate berries in the woods and, as one absentee put it, "any thing we came upon." They also were commonly blamed by their slaveholding neighbours for the disappearance of chickens and hogs. But not everyone was skilled at hunting, foraging or reappropriating; in any case, fruits and the occasional chicken made for skimpy fare. At times Smith experienced hunger so severe she "could not sleep," and weather so cold she "did not know what to do." Often afraid to build a fire lest it call attention to their location, absentees had a difficult time staying warm in cold seasons. They collected branches, twigs, moss and leaves to make the "brush harbors" in which they slept; and serendipity or detailed knowledge of the woods led some to tree hollows for shelter from the rain. Needless to say, such structures proved adequate only in mild weather; in the cold, wind, or rain, runaways could only endure. And all the while, they had to look out for patrols, whites in general and opportunistic bondmen, any of whom might turn them in. Absentees withstood these hardships for anywhere from a few days to two weeks; and sojourns of even several months were hardly unknown.

The tenacity of female and male runaways was due in part to community efforts to assist them. Truants needed the collaboration of the larger community, and often they got it. Women, in particular, supported runaways by extending the meals they prepared for their families to truants. In so doing, they turned their reproductive labour, which partially functioned to maintain the labour supply and partially to sustain the people they loved or to whom they felt a sense of duty, into a source of resistance. Thus, even women who did not run away themselves were active in the alternative uses of plantation space. Men and women both created the rival geography, but women performed most of the reproductive work that enabled truants to occupy it for longer periods of time than would otherwise have been possible. When Lorenzo L. Ivy's grandmother ran away to the woods, as she did regularly to protest and prevent ill treatment, she would "stay in hidin' in de day time an' come out onlies' at night. My mama say she used to always put out food fo' her an' she would slip up nights an' git it."

Among women, field and household workers alike secretly helped outlaws. Even favoured women, such as "aunt Fanny" of Virginia, had lives hidden from their owners. When someone "had the presumption to break in our meat house" the elite Aylett family initiated an investigation. Some suspected a new neighbour, and others believed that the longtime-runaway Jim was "at the bottom of it all." The Aylett family matriarch had always "thought well of" Fanny, one of the "house servants," and placed her above suspicion. But when "Brother Henry had the servants houses searched on Friday," the source was found. In Fanny's house Henry found a reserve of food ("a basket of corn"), as well as "a piece of bridling." It would appear that Fanny was outfitting Jim for an escape on horseback, perhaps to the North. And that was not all; Jim, it turned out, had been "staying [in] her house for the last 12 months."

Unlike Jim, most truants tended to move back and forth between relatively remote hiding places and the quarters, sometimes on paths with which only enslaved people were acquainted. Hammond's runaways Nancy and Abram made a habit of going back and forth between the swamp and the quarters, where they would visit and be fed, but not only after dark. "Day and night," Hammond fumed, they came in from the swamp where they were "encamped" and passed their time "about the lot." Women absentees ran to and fro not only to receive sustenance, but also to return at night and feed their families. Camilla Jackson's mother "would run away ter the woods" when her mistress hit her, "but at night she would sneak back to nurse her babies." Movement back and forth might have been easier and more common in black-majority counties, such as those of the Black Belt and coastal South Carolina and Georgia, than in other parts of the South where greater surveillance may have forced truants to be relatively more cautious and self-reliant.

The flow of movement between hiding places and the quarters both helped and hurt absentees. On the one hand, truants needed the assistance of willing fellow bondpeople, and this support enabled them to survive and to stay out longer than if they had been left on their own. As a Virginia planter informed the traveller Frederick Law Olmsted, the runaways were "often hunted after, but it was very difficult to find them, and, if caught, they would run away again, and the other negroes would hide and assist them." On the other hand, much of slaves' rival geography—the quarters, outbuildings—was space to which planters had access and over which they had a large measure of control. When runaways ventured in from woods and swamps to these places, they at once helped themselves by gaining access to material support and increased their risk of capture. Louisiana planter Bennet Barrow, for instance, was able to capture runaways when they returned to the quarters. "Caught a runaway yesterday," Barrow once wrote in his journal. "Came to the hands." Olmsted, too, commented on the risk of detection raised by absentees' return to the quarters. He noted first of all that "runaways . . . almost always kept in the neighbourhood, because they did not like to go where they could not sometimes get back to see their families." As a result, "the overseer would soon get wind of where they had been; they would come round their quarters to see their families and to get food, and as soon as he knew it, he would find their tracks and put the dogs out again."

In an effort to get around the problem of capture in the quarters, some absentees and their helpers arranged meeting places in the woods. Cornelia Carney's mother "used to send John, my oldes' brother, out to de woods wid food" for her father when he hid from his abusive owner. Runaways and their supporters sometimes exploited their intimate knowledge of plantation geography, as did two enslaved women, Lorendo Goodwin and Hattie, who lived on a Louisiana sugar plantation. The two women coordinated the rhythm of Goodwin's fieldwork to Hattie's location in the woods bordering the cane fields. One morning Hattie waited at the edge of the woods where she hid for Goodwin who unknowingly worked her way toward Hattie. When Goodwin was "getting toward the end of my row of cane I heard somebody over the fence in the woods calling me." Goodwin spotted Hattie, who "asked me to give her something to eat; and I did give her all I had in my bucket." In like manner, when Sallie Smith got hungry she would, "find out where the hands on the place were working, and if the overseer was away I'd get something from them." She could even count on them to bring their food to her in the woods, once they knew she was there. She would go to the "edge of the woods every day, and when they would come to hunt for me they called out in a low piercing voice, 'Sallie! Sallie!' I'd come running and sometimes I was nearly perished."

Women's work supporting truancy complicates the distinction between individual and collective resistance, and between the personal and the political. Absenteeism was very often a sudden, solitary reaction to a particular grievance. At the same time, individual truants partially depended upon others for assistance. Many bondwomen helped runaways because they understood runaways to be protesting their conditions of labour and life. Moreover, some bondpeople assisted truants because the distinction between wrongs committed against an individual and those committed against a group were less important within communities of extended family, friends, and occasionally even strangers. The distinction between individual and collective resistance, then, offers only an aphoristic description of truancy in practice. The reasons bondpeople ran away—violence, exhaustion, humiliation—resonated with wrongs others had suffered, or could, at any moment, be made to suffer.

Just as the difference between individual and collective resistance is misleading, so is the separation of political principal and personal sentiment. Many women helped truants—husbands, lovers, family members and friends—because they loved them or because they felt loyal to them. Perhaps otherwise disinclined to support opposition, some women were motivated by intimate feelings to help support the actions of people who defied their owners' authority, withheld their labour and who broke the law. Many people in enslaved communities recognized absenteeism for what it was: social protest in which many bondpeople participated collectively for political and personal reasons.

But cooperation coexisted with ambivalence, fear and self-interest and many bondpeople refused to get deeply involved in punishable activities. When the weather turned too cold for the "mossbed" Sallie Smith made for herself to sleep in at night, she sometimes stayed with different enslaved families. After being caught by the overseer in one home, Smith found it impossible to get shelter in the quarters. Just as absentees' movement back and forth between hiding places and quarters connected these places in a common rival geography, so the cooperation of truants and their supporters blurred the difference between resistant and compliant bondperson. It was an elision that slave holders upheld, punishing those who helped runaways and exploiting truancy's collective nature to force absentees to return, and successfully undermining feelings of solidarity with the runaways that might have emerged in the quarters. Both James Henry Hammond and John Blount Miller, a South Carolina planter, cut off the meat allowance "of all," as Miller put it, "until return". The apparent success of this tactic indicates that there were limits to what residents would sacrifice for truants.

Truants knew the secret mapping of the plantation expertly, could locate other absentees and were thus in a perfect position to win favour with or payment from their owners by turning in other runaways. Men appear to have been especially able to do so; at Clermont plantation, every single one of the truants who turned in another was a bondman, probably because women lacked the physical presence and the social authority to compel an absentee to return against his or her will. These men, mainly Rubin and Jerry, were unlikely intermediaries: they were themselves regular absentees. Rubin frequently visited his wife without a pass for days and even weeks at a time, and Jerry was once shot at while being chased from the neighbouring farm where his own wife lived. Yet again and again, these two men "brought home" other truants for the benefits they gained: pardons for their own absences and sometimes pay. Once, when Rubin returned from a one-day absence, Nevitt turned him right around and "sent him out for Maria," who had been gone for a few days. By evening Rubin had returned with her. As a reward, Nevitt "forgave Rubin his fault an gave Maria a severe whiping," Rubin and Jerry were hardly unique: neighbouring bondmen also returned truants to Nevitt, as they did on other plantations. Cooperation between truants and their neighbours presented benefits as well as dangers.

Far from understanding truancy as a routine part of plantation life and taking it in stride, slave holders viewed it as an egregious violation of labour and social discipline. One reason that planters objected so strenuously to truancy was that truants withheld their labour from their owners for the period of time they were absent: crops were neglected, livestock untended, maintenance chores undone. Contemporaries noticed the economic cost that absentees caused. Olmsted met one Virginia farmer who compared the economic sabotage caused by bondpeople who feigned illness and by absentees, concluding that a "more serious loss frequently arises, when the slave, thinking he is worked too hard, or being angered by punishment or unkind treatment, 'getting the sulks,' takes to 'the swamp,' and comes back when he has a mind to." Household bondwomen's absences were disruptive, as well; someone had to do their work. At times, fellow bondwomen took up the slack; on other occasions a slaveholding woman was forced to make up the difference. When Clarissa, a household bondwoman "took it into her head to run away," a miserable Mahala P. Eggleston Roach found herself "obliged to work some." Clarissa returned two days later and

$100 REWARD

WILL be given for the apprehension and delivery of my Servant Girl HAR-RIET. She is a light mulatto, 21 years of age, about 5 feet 4 inches high, of a thick and corpulent habit, having on her head a thick covering of black hair that curls naturally, but which can be easily combed straight. She speaks easily and fluently, and has an agreeable carriage and address. Being a good seamstress, she has been accustomed to dress well, has a variety of very fine clothes, made in the prevailing fashion, and will probably appear, if abroad, tricked out in gay and fashionable finery. As this girl absconded from the plantation of my son without any known cause or provocation, it is probable she designs to transport herself to the North.

The above reward, with all reasonable charges, will be given for apprehending her, or securing her in any prison or jail within the U. States.

All persons are hereby forewarned against harboring or entertaining her, or being in any way instrumental in her escape, under the most rigorous penalties of the law.

JAMES NORCOM.

Edenton, N. C. June 30

Ads for runaway slaves, such as this one, were published and posted throughout the South and in northern cities as well, especially after passage of the Fugitive Slave Law in 1851. Most slave owners could not easily distinguish between those slaves who ran seeking permanent freedom and the "truants" described by Stephanie Camp.

Roach delivered what may have been the kindest punishment an enslaved person ever received: Roach "would not speak to her."

The most basic requirement of slavery as a system was the presence of labouring slaves; by creating absences, truants initiated an ongoing struggle with slave holders. Slave patrols were charged with the task of capturing runaways of any sort and bringing them back to work. But planters were not above personally venturing out to search for absentees, to "hunt" them as they often put it. Alone, in teams and sometimes with dogs, planters pursued truants ruthlessly. When one of the "negro dogs" that Bennett Barrow and his neighbours regularly used to chase truants once caught a man, they stood by as the animal "nearly et his legs off—near killing him." Generally, such "hunts" failed to locate their prey, and absentees were driven back by hunger and cold, encountering grave punishments on their return.

In the inchoate language of violence, planters registered strong objections to truancy. A great many truants were flogged, often along with other abuses—a combination that was neither rare nor a trifle, even in the very violent Old South. Absentees were also forced "to work harder den ever," put on bread-and-water diets "for long time," caned, put in stocks, shackled with a ball-and-chain at their feet, chained from the leg to the neck, confined alone in outbuildings, and jailed. One man had an iron cage with bells on it locked over his head for three months; another received a "decent smoking" in the smoke house; one was made to "ware womens cloths," more than a few were even shot at or shot. Some truants were sold, as were many captured fugitives; John Nevitt and John Blount Miller both sold their greatest recidivists. Repeat offenders were not the only ones cast into the slave market: enslaved North Carolinian Hasty made for the woods after her mistress slapped her. Upon her return, Hasty learned that she had been sold. Bennet Barrow, who shot at, shot, chained, whipped, clubbed and ducked his truants in water—and whose treatment of runaways did not stand out among his neighbours—explained why he punished absenteeism so severely: "I had rather a negro do any thing Else than runaway."

Women's sex did not protect them from the full force of their owners' indignation; they were whipped, chained, put in stocks and sold for their transgressions, just as men were. In many instances female gender seems to have served as a license for planters' full expression of violent rage, exposing women to cruel punishment more consistently than men. On John Nevitt's plantation there were disparities in the distribution of punishment along gender lines. In the diary entries that record a punishment, women were slightly more consistently punished—by flogging, shackles, ball-and-chain, or jail—than men. Whereas three-quarters of male truants were reported to have been punished, 83 per cent of women were; and while Nevitt "forgave" a quarter of male runaways, only 16 per cent of women were absolved. In part the skewed distribution of punishment was due to Nevitt absolving Rubin and Jerry for running away when they turned in other truants. But other men were acquitted, so other reasons were at play as well.

According to the customary norms of the rural South, there were potentially legitimate reasons for enslaved men to leave plantations, while there were almost none for women. Planter's expectations regarding women's locations, then, may have varied from those they had for men; what counted as truancy in women may have been somewhat more acceptable in men, who had families to visit, as many of Nevitt's men did. Women's alternative movement, then, may have been more easily perceived as a trespass, and more quickly punished. Another issue may have been that Nevitt viewed women as easier to punish and to use as examples. Overall, it is clear that Nevitt's bondwomen were subjected to disparate treatment based on their gender.

In his travels, Olmsted came to a similar conclusion. The "severest corporeal punishment of a negro" that he ever "witnessed at the South" was visited upon Sall, a woman truant. Sall had "slipped out of the gang when they were going to work," her overseer explained to Olmsted. "She's been dodging about all day," he complained. Furious that "she meant to cheat me out of a day's work, and she has done it, too," the overseer stripped the woman from head to foot and laid into her. The sadistic act became a lewd spectacle before Olmsted's eyes, as he watched the overseer give Sall "thirty or forty blows across the shoulders" with a rawhide, and another set of the same number on "her naked loins and thighs."

Truancy impacted the two major forms of labour organization in the Old South differently, but introduced similar conflicts of interest to the spatial and temporal logic of each. For the majority of enslaved people who worked in the gang system, absenteeism punctuated their gruelling, "sunup to sundown" labour, especially during harvest seasons, granting them escapes from otherwise almost unrelenting work and the violence required to make it possible. For those who worked in the task system, truancy extended the late afternoon and evening "off-times" that shaped the core of slave life and culture in the South Carolina low country into days and weeks for oneself. In both cases, absenteeism muddied the vision of spatial and temporal order toward which slave holders strove, occasionally provoking questions about their mastery. Ada Bacot spoke out loud the anxiety planters sometimes felt when bondpeople ran away, on the day she discovered that "some of my young negroes have been disobeying my orders[.] they were found away from home without a pass." Though Bacot had "never had any trouble with them until now," their autonomous movement caused her to worry. "I hope that I may be able to make them understand," she fretted, "that I am mistress and will be obeyed."

But more was at stake than money; more, indeed, was at stake than even mastery. Truants' greatest accomplishment was in furthering bondpeople's long-term freedom struggle. During the Civil War, enslaved people ran to advancing Union lines, seeking freedom under the aegis of the federal army. The fugitives, who quickly came to be called "refugees," received diverse treatment from the Yankees, but their growing numbers placed tremendous pressure on the Union army to make a uniform policy. A reluctant Abraham Lincoln followed the example of many of his officers in the field and decided to admit blacks into the army, but first he had to emancipate them. Lincoln announced the Emancipation Proclamation in September of 1862, effective January 1863, manumitting bondpeople in the Confederate states, and allowing the federals to arm these refugees and muster them into the army, along with free blacks in the North. Military expediency demanded the use of "the power which slaves put into the hands of the South," as W.E.B. DuBois put it. DuBois detailed the effect of the exodus—which he termed a "general strike"—on the morality of the war: "with perplexed and laggard steps, the United States Government followed the footsteps of the black slave." Enslaved people's massive movement out of slavery to what they believed would be freedom with the Union army forced emancipation onto the federal war agenda.

Wartime migration did not erupt suddenly and without precedent. Rather, it was the product of a history begun in slavery and in the tradition fostered in truancy of moving beyond the bounds of the plantations's legitimated spaces. During their bondage, enslaved people had established alternative ways of knowing and using Southern space that violated the laws and customs constricting black mobility. In so doing, they created a mapping of Southern space that would play an important role in the exodus from slavery during the Civil War. Truant bondpeople—not fugitives who left the South—gained and transmitted to others the infrastructure of geographical knowledge that was a considerable and crucial part of the foundation of wartime activity. The role that enslaved people played in their own emancipation had been long in the making. During their enslavement women and men—in rage, indignation and desperation—fled the worst aspects of their bondage, paving as they did so the routes that would become in wartime literal roads to freedom.

Questions for Study and Review

1. What are the most useful definitions of resistance if we consider the lives of enslaved women as well as the lives of enslaved men?

2. How does enslaved women's knowledge of the plantation's geography affect the forms of their resistance, and how might this differ for enslaved men?

3. What experiences were most likely to drive women to employ truancy?

4. Given earlier discussions of African women's roles—in slavery and the slave trade before and during the American Revolution—do you see more continuity or discontinuity in black women's lives from the seventeenth to the mid-nineteenth century? What are the major similarities and differences?

Suggested Readings and Web Sites

Catherine Clinton, *The Plantation Mistress: Women's World in the Old South* (1982)
Sharla M. Fett, *Working Cures: Healing, Health and Power on Southern Slave Plantations* (2002)
Sally G. McMillen, *Southern Women Black and White in the Old South* (1992)
Brenda E. Stevenson, *Life in Black and White: Family and Community in the Slave South* (1996)
Marlie F. Weiner, *Mistresses and Slaves: Plantation Women in South Carolina, 1830–1860* (1998)
Slave Narratives from the 1930s
    http://lcweb2.loc.gov/ammem/snhtml
The Atlantic Slave Trade and Slave Life in the Americas
    http://hitchcock.itc.virginia.edu/slavery/index.php

Chapter 13

J ames K. Polk won the presidency of the United States in 1844 with the promise to annex Texas and expand the nation's boundaries. Editor John L. O'Sullivan assured his fellow Americans that annexation was "the fulfillment of our manifest destiny to overspread the continent allotted by providence for the free development of our yearly multiplying millions." In the 1830s, 1840s, and 1850s, thousands of young men—mostly northern, native-born, and white—committed themselves to forwarding that destiny. After the defeat of Black Hawk's forces in 1832 removed the fear of hostile Indians, the Midwest became the haven for those seeking to escape overused agricultural areas and over-crowded cities of the East.

Pioneer wives were often less enthusiastic than their husbands at the prospect of moving west, but before and after the Gold Rush, most wagon trains included a significant number of families. The trip itself expanded women's work as they continued to clean, cook, and care for children while taking on new tasks—such as collecting buffalo chips for fuel or substituting for men as drivers and scouts when emergencies demanded they do so. Although women's contributions to the move and to the new settlement were rarely rewarded with increased status or authority, western communities did recognize women's importance in other ways.

The Gold Rush to California provides examples of both western men's denigration and appreciation of women. The territory of California had been acquired from Mexico by the Treaty of Guadalupe-Hidalgo, which ended the Mexican-American War in March 1848. Two months earlier, James Marshall had discovered gold in a millrace in central California. By year's end, news of the discovery had traveled around the United States and to many areas of the world. Tens of thousands of Americans from the East and Midwest headed to California in 1849 alone. Nearly all of them were men, either single men who sought to make their fortunes or married men who hoped to strike it rich before sending for their families to join them.

The scarcity of women in California, and especially in the gold mining areas, had dramatic consequences. As we know from Antonia Castañeda's article, many Indian communities were decimated in the late eighteenth century by the Spanish conquest. And Spain itself sent few women into its California colony. During the Mexican-American War, more Americans moved to the area, but most of them were soldiers and thus predominantly men. Yet traditional histories of the Gold Rush have rarely focused on the gender dynamics of this event, although most have assumed that the lawlessness and disorder that plagued the region resulted, in large part, from the absence of women. When historians of the Gold Rush did attend to women, it was most often to note the sudden surge in prostitution the Gold Rush inspired.

Only recently have scholars begun to look closely at the way that a society with few women fulfilled the tasks normally performed by them. Susan Johnson offers one intriguing analysis. She argues that Chinese, Mexican, and Indian men were assigned feminine roles and responsibilities. Some of these men embraced such roles. Chinese men, for instance, were used to cooking and doing laundry. Regularly run off of their mining claims, they were more likely to survive and prosper by using their "domestic" skills to make a living. Others, like Mexican men long resident in California, more often rejected the efforts of Anglo-American newcomers to force them into subordinate roles. Still, as tavern keepers and farmers, they knew they might well benefit from the increased demand for food and drink among mining men.

Albert Hurtado focuses on a different aspect of California's gender dynamics during the Gold Rush: the opportunities available to and the stir created by the presence of those few women who moved to California in these years. Capturing the excitement and danger that women faced in California in the mid-nineteenth century, he details the ways that white men in particular treated white women, Indian women, and Mexican women. In the process, he demonstrates how race continued to play a critical role in social relations even when men were desperate for women as wives and helpmeets. Moreover, he suggests that even white women, if poor, were vulnerable to abuse in the frontier atmosphere created by gold-smitten men.

Sex, Gender, Culture, and a Great Event: The California Gold Rush

ALBERT L. HURTADO

I suspect that there are many historians who believe that sex and gender are trivial subjects. Sex and gender are merely manifestations of biology that are common to all humans. What have they to do with the big things in history? How does knowledge of sex and gender help us discover some of the truth about the past?

This essay addresses those questions. Surely the California gold rush qualifies as one of the "Big Things" in history. The discovery of gold in 1848 set off a human migration that was truly global in scope. Hundreds of thousands of people from every continent set off for California. As a national event, the gold rush provided a muscular punctuation to the Mexican-American War as Anglo Americans swept westward and around the Horn to the gold fields. They were the human "facts on the ground" who validated the provisions of the Mexican cession and the Treaty of

Albert L. Hurtado, "Sex, Gender, Culture and a Great Event: The California Gold Rush," *Pacific Historical Review*, Vol. 68, No. 1:1–19. © 1999, The Pacific Coast Branch, American Historical Association. Used by permission. All rights reserved.

Guadalupe Hidalgo. Regionally, the gold rush set a pattern of mineral rushes, industrial mining, and environmental despoliation that marked the West from the mid-nineteenth century to the present day. The gold rush earthquake set off political, social, and demographic tremors that continue to shake the American West and the wider world as well.

So how do sex and gender fit into the Big Event? First, a few basic definitions are in order. I agree with many other scholars who theorize that gender is a social construction. In other words, each society construes gender—that is, what it means to be a "man" or a "woman"—and defines what kind of behavior is acceptable and desirable. Gender signifies far more than sexual difference; it is a status that determines power relationships in society. Likewise, sexuality is a social construction that varies among cultures. Thus, gender and sexuality are fluid circumstances of human life, and their manifestations—such as heterosexual monogamy—are not "natural" biological conditions but constructions that manipulate the range of biological and social possibilities and that change over time.

California—at any time, and especially during the gold rush—is a particularly complicated place to look at gender and sexuality. It has always been a multicultural frontier and is likely to remain so. Multiculturalism implies that several cultures with assorted notions of sexuality and gender met and mingled. Mixing, however, did not lead to amalgamation, at least not on a large scale. The trend toward separation and domination in the face of diversity is one of the themes of this essay.

The gold rush is about swift demographic change. In 1848, before the discovery of gold, perhaps 165,000 people lived in California. The vast majority of them—approximately 150,000—were Indians, most of whom lived autonomously in what came to be known as the mother lode and other isolated regions away from Mexican settlements. Approximately 7,500 Californios and 6,500 other people of American and European extraction accounted for the rest of the population. Then John Marshall discovered gold, word leaked out, and the rush to California was on. It is impossible to give more than rough estimates for the number of hopeful people who poured into California from 1848 to the early 1850s. No one made an official count until the 1850 federal census, and that enumeration was seriously flawed. The state of California made another stab at census-taking in 1852, but that effort was also incomplete. Federal officials finally made a reasonably accurate count for the 1860 census after the gold rush was over. Flawed as they are, these documents consistently describe a population with far more men than women (see Table 1). In 1850 there were 12.2 men for each woman in California. The ratio declined to 7.2 men per woman in 1852 and 2.4 men per woman in 1860. The ratio of men to women was even higher in the mining districts than for the state as a whole, and it held true for every racial and ethnic category in the censuses—including Indians. While the 1860 ratio was significantly lower than it had been in previous census years, details for age cohorts show that the older the population, the higher the ratio of men to women (see Table 2). These statistics indicate that women came later to California and in smaller numbers than men. Men rushed to California; women ambled. Changes in the sex ratio to 1860 were due to the immigration of families, births in California, and a modestly growing immigration of single females. In 1860 men

TABLE 1 SEX RATIOS, CALIFORNIA WHITE POPULATION

YEAR	MALES PER FEMALE
1850	12.2
1852	7.2
1860	2.4

Derived from "Table No. 3—Population Cities, Towns, &c.," Joseph G. C. Kennedy, comp., *Population of the United States in 1860* (Washington, D.C., 1864), 30.

who were over thirty had only a slim chance of marrying a woman from their own age cohort. Patterns of age and gender imbalance that dated from the gold rush era remained embedded in the censuses until the twentieth century.

Historians and contemporary observers have naturalized the maleness of the gold rush population—even celebrated the masculine social world that emerged as a result. In 1855 Frank Soulé, John Gihon, and James Nisbet published their first-hand observations of the brief, tumultuous history of California's first city in *Annals of San Francisco.* They summarized the dynamics of gold and society:

> [Gold] Dust was plentier than pleasure, pleasure more enticing than virtue. Fortune was the horse, youth in the saddle, dissipation the track, and desire the spur. Let none wonder that the time was the best ever made.

These three men, at least, greeted the wide-open, vice-ridden advent of the Barbary Coast with unalloyed enthusiasm. And who should be surprised at a population of young men who responded positively to the voluptuous opportunities that gold dust provided? In "the States" drinking, gambling, and open prostitution were condemned, even if they were not completely expunged from society. Large cities—especially ports—had vice districts, and the incipient temperance movement had just begun its long effort to reform Americans' drinking habits. Still, San Francisco and the gold rush towns seemed designed to satisfy precisely those appetites that reformers damned as un-Christian and immoral.

To be sure, the large male population demanded feminized service industries—laundresses, cooks, housekeepers, seamstresses, and prostitutes. The abundance of gold enabled men to pay handsomely for such services. This incarnation of Adam Smith's principle of supply and demand has inspired some historians to argue that gold rush demography raised the value of women's labor and enabled them to gain

TABLE 2 SEX RATIOS FOR WHITE AGE COHORTS IN 1860

AGE	MALES PER FEMALE
15–19	1.2
20–29	3.1
30–39	4.3

Derived from "Table No. 3—Population Cities, Towns, &c.," Kennedy, comp., *Population of the United States in 1860*, 30.

riches in the gold fields just as male miners and entrepreneurs made their fortunes. Certainly some women made a good living, bought property, and achieved a degree of independence that exceeded the nineteenth-century norm. Some women spoke eloquently about their achievements in California businesses.

Women's independence came at a cost to men who paid dearly for all kinds of women's labor. Men also set a high value on women as brides—wives who customarily provided unwaged labor for domestic duties including child rearing, cooking, cleaning, and sexual service. I do not mean to imply that men married merely to obtain a source of cheap labor and free sex, but rather to emphasize that women's household work had real economic value to their spouses and to society. Unpaid wives who cooked, sewed, and cleaned contributed to the general economy as well as to the hygiene and contentment of their men. In an industrial economy, even one as primitive as California's, someone would have to provide these services if men were to contribute their labor fully and exclusively to the industry at hand. Even child rearing has an economic value because it replaces the labor force. This was a lesson in household economy and subsistence reproduction, as it is called, that California men quickly learned.

Gold rush letters and diaries are full of evidence that men were incompetent at the basic domestic skills, but the value of women's work in the California economy was driven by more than their superior ability to darn socks, wash long johns, nurse babies, and change diapers. Henry Sheldon, a Methodist missionary who did not make much money from his preaching, soon gained an appreciation of woman's worth after sending for his Ohio sweetheart to marry. His wife, Priscilla, became something of a cultural cottage industry in Shasta. In 1854 Brother Sheldon reported that his wife put on a splendid Sunday school exhibition and collected $66. She also started a select school, for which she got $120 per month. The reverend thought her tuition was too cheap, but he did not want to start trouble by charging more in the little town. They were also boarding a little boy and three girls at $30 per month each (exclusive of washing), a business that a bachelor surely would not have undertaken. In her spare time, limited as it was, Priscilla gave piano lessons to two pupils and guitar lessons to two others. Evidently she borrowed a piano for the lessons (perhaps in a local saloon). The reverend intended to get a piano for Priscilla so she could take more students. Priscilla took in more than $300 in June from these pursuits, while her preaching husband found offerings in his collection plate that varied from $12 to $15 per week. Brother Sheldon may have made additional money laboring in the mines or in some other way, but he never commented on such things. Surely Priscilla's value as a teacher was enhanced in California because of the scarcity of women in the mining districts. Perhaps because of Priscilla's gender, Shastans were willing to pay far more for cultural edification than for religious uplift. It would be too much to say that Brother Sheldon got his living by selling sex, but gender seems to have been a marketable commodity.

The rarity of females in the mines led men to do extraordinarily foolish things when women appeared. William M. Stewart, a California miner who later became U.S. senator from Nevada, left a particularly colorful description of such an encounter. One morning in 1850 near Nevada City Stewart noticed a wagon with a woman's dress on a nearby clothesline. "When I saw the feminine raiment I raised the usual alarm, 'Oh Joe!'" Stewart recalled, "and this called the attention of the miners on Buckeye Hill, where I was, to the clothesline which had attracted my notice. They gathered around on the hill, nearly surrounding the covered wagon and its contents," Soon there were two or three thousand young men surrounding the wagon and clothesline. A young husband came out to ascertain what had attracted the mob, but his terrified wife remained in the wagon. Stewart, who showed leadership potential even then, took up a collection to entice the frightened woman from the wagon. Soon miners were pulling nuggets from their pokes, and Stewart held out a tidy pile for the woman if she would show herself. (Stewart does not say whether or not she was clothed for this exercise.) Finally she came out, and Stewart held the prize just beyond her reach while the woman chased after it like a carrot on a stick, "so the boys could have a good view of her," he said. "I suppose half an hour was occupied with her running back and forth while the boys looked on in admiration, when I finally gave her the bag with all the good wishes of the camp. She grabbed it and ran into the tent like a rabbit."

The rarity of white women was matched by the scarcity of white children. Many observers commented on the sentimentality of miners when they saw a child who reminded them of home, hearth, and domesticity. But there were ribald jokes, too. In the same year that William Stewart discovered a woman near Nevada City, John Paul Dart heard about "a man on the other side of the hill [who] had found a specimen on the Stanislaus that weighed 18 pounds." Thinking that it was a chunk of gold, he went to the place and asked the owner to show it to him. "'Certainly,' says he and went in the tent and brought out a boy baby about two months old. 'That is it,' says, he, but he didn't have the laugh all on his side. I told him I thought if he would continue to dig in the same old claim, he would probably find another. Somebody else asked him if he had reached the edge [of his claim] yet. The mother was a regular Californian," Dart said, "and enjoyed the joke."

Dart also remarked on a newspaper report concerning "the arrival of two ships, from France, with over 300 women aboard. Gads, what a rich cargo." He reckoned that the women would be "worth their weight in gold." "The imports of California are richer than the exports," he added. Dart's observation about the "worth" of the French women implies that he thought of them as commodities—prostitutes—an assumption that may have been rooted purely in his ethnocentric beliefs about the supposed immorality of French women. Still, the gold rush attracted prostitutes from around the world. Miners funneled much of their hard-earned gold dust through San Francisco, which quickly became a center of wealth that attracted prostitutes. Henry B. Sheldon, the Methodist missionary with a keen eye for wrong-doers, reported to his family that in San Francisco prostitutes numbered "nearly *one thousand* and there are no villages of any size in the country where they are not to be found—They are the *aristocracy*." Courtesans rode in "the most splendid *carriages*, and on the most showy studs."

As these examples show, the scarcity of women tended to raise their economic value, whether as prostitutes, cooks, seamstresses, or laundresses. Likewise, historians and contemporary observers contend, the scarcity of women raised their social value in California. At the very least, scarcity made men appreciate women more. Everywhere Californians remarked on the extreme deference that men paid to women. However, women had to "conduct themselves with the strictest propriety or be cast from the pale of good society," Sheldon reported, because of the presence of so many prostitutes.

Men certainly deferred to *some* women during the gold rush, but what if we introduce race and class into the equation? In the early years of the gold rush—say, until

A LIVE WOMAN IN THE MINES.—See page 16.

This sketch of "A Live Woman in the Mines" by Alonzo Delano suggests the boisterous enthusiasm caused by the appearance of a white woman in a California mining camp. Despite the rugged camp life, the woman is well dressed and demurely casts her eyes downward as she stands next to the cooking fire.

1851 or 1852—there were many Indian women in the state, although their numbers were declining rapidly. No one will be surprised to hear that white men extended few courtesies to Indian women. Blinded by racial prejudices and decades of frontier warfare, Anglo Californians seldom had a kind word for native women. Even Dame Shirley, that paragon of gold rush observers, could muster little sympathy for Indian women. "They are very filthy in their appearance," she wrote. "If one of them should venture out into the rain, grass would grow on her neck and arms." On another occasion she compared them with "Macbethian witches" for their "haggardness of expression and ugliness of feature."

Most white men were at least as critical of Indian beauty as Dame Shirley, although a few of them took Indian wives. Such alliances of convenience were seldom solemnized by church ritual or state license. These were the sort of custom marriages that were prominent among mountain men and fur traders in the nineteenth century. John A. Sutter, founder of New Helvetia where Sacramento now stands, is a prime example of this pattern. Sutter, who left his lawful spouse and children in Switzerland, pioneered in the Sacramento Valley in the 1840s. As lord of New Helvetia, Sutter kept Hawaiian and Indian mistresses. Some observers claimed that Sutter fathered several children by these women. Sutter's ways began to change when his oldest son unexpectedly arrived in California in 1848. The following year Sutter's son—evidently with his father's assent—financed passage for the rest of the family to California. The Sutter family reunion, however reluctant the patriarch may have been, put an end to his philandering with women of color. Other white men also abandoned their Indian consorts as soon as white spouses became available and when the development of frontier society made Indian marriages an embarrassing reminder of past conditions. Men who persisted in living with native women earned the racist sobriquet "squaw men," and their children were known as "half-breeds"—slurs that condemned racial mixing.

It is impossible to know the number of custom marriages in California, nor is it possible to quantify the incidence of rape. In the latter case, however, we know that the newspapers and agents of the Office of Indian Affairs and U.S. Army officers routinely complained about assaults on Indian women. Some observers went so far as to say that rapes were one of the principal causes of warfare in California—a strong accusation in a frontier country where conflict with Indians was more or less constant. Clearly, some men cared little for the niceties of gender relations when it came to women of color. What were the root causes of sexual violence? Most students of rape argue that assaults on women are attempts to assert power over the victims. Rapists often believe that their prey is especially blameworthy. In gold rush California, so lately conquered in the Mexican-American War, women of color were obvious targets for racist assailants, rapists and murderers alike. One gold rush hunter reported that he bagged "two grizzlys, one Antelope, and a digger squaw este noche," an ambiguous statement that may have had sexual as well as violent meaning.

Victorian notions about frail womanhood did not prevent some men from systematically murdering Indian women. One of the worst, but by no means the only, of these gendered mass killings occurred at Humboldt Bay in 1860. Bret Harte, a young newspaper reporter who subsequently became famous as the author of sentimental short stories about the gold rush, reported that several bands of white men mercilessly slaughtered about 150 Indians who lived peaceably around Humboldt Bay. One contingent attacked a sleeping Indian community on a small island in front of Eureka, killing three men and fifty-seven women and children. Tribesmen brought some of their murdered kin to Union where Harte saw them. "Old women, wrinkled and decrepit, lay weltering in blood, their brains dashed out and dabbled with their long gray hair," he wrote in the *Northern Calofornian*. He saw "infants scarcely a span long, with their faces cloven with hatchets and their bodies ghastly with wounds." As these vulnerable people "huddled together for protection like sheep, they were struck down with hatchets."

Nor were Indians the only women of color who were subject to violence. The lynching of the Mexican woman Juanita (also known as Josefa) is a well-known gold rush incident, for she was the only woman to die at the hands of a lynch mob. On the Fourth of July 1851 she was living in Downieville with a Mexican gambler. While celebrating the national holiday, Joe Cannon, a popular young Englishman, evidently knocked in the Mexican couple's door. The next morning he went to the shack to apologize. Juanita, who understood little English, perhaps thought Cannon was going to attack her lover; according to some accounts, she reacted to Cannon calling her a prostitute. In any case, she killed Cannon with a Bowie knife. A mob gathered, assembled a kangaroo court, and condemned Juanita to hang. All accounts agree that she ascended the makeshift scaffold without assistance, adjusted the noose so that it did not tangle her hair, and went to her death with uncommon courage. On the gallows she said that she would do the same thing again if her honor was similarly affronted. Then the mob hanged her.

Some believed that the hanging of Juanita was justified, but most Californians condemned it. Newspaper editors were appalled that Downieville men had hanged a woman, regardless of the provocation. Likewise, some eyewitnesses condemned the lynching of a woman on principles of gender as well as due process. The nineteenth-century philosopher-historian, Josiah Royce, was horrified that the mob had killed a woman, and modern historians—with justification—have argued that Juanita would not have been hanged if she had been an Anglo American woman.

Such incidents take us a long way from the sentimental forty-niner who doffed his hat and bowed to every woman he was lucky enough to meet. Singular as it was, it was not mere chance that made the Mexican Juanita the only woman to be lynched in California. When white pillagers burned Indian communities, raped Indian women, and then murdered them with axes, their corpses were not inadvertent collateral damage. Race trumped gender in California.

Class trumped gender, too, even among whites. The haunting story of Amelia Kuschinsky shows how dangerous sex and gender could be for a poor working girl. I use the term "girl" for two reasons. First, her contemporaries called her a girl, and she probably applied the term to herself. Second, "girl" is emblematic of the power relationship that doomed her. In the late 1850s, at age fourteen or perhaps even younger, Amelia was a servant in the home of a Shasta merchant named August Stiller, his wife, and three children. The Stillers were from Prussia and Wurtemburg, and Amelia was probably from Europe as well. Someone, probably Stiller, got Amelia pregnant when she was fifteen. After trying to abort her pregnancy using folk remedies, the Stillers called in a local physician, another German who was sympathetic to the Stillers' desire to keep the matter private. The doctor, or perhaps someone else, evidently used instruments to abort the fetus, but something went wrong. He perforated her uterus, an infection took root, and peritonitis killed her after a terrible, painful illness. After an autopsy a furious mob threatened to lynch the physician and Stiller, but the sheriff arrested them and held them for trial. Abortion was illegal in California, and some thought the two should be tried for murder. Evidence at trial proved inconclusive, and the men went free.

Amelia's short life and death tell us that even white women—especially poor white women—were subject to sexual abuse during the gold rush. Her youth, servant status, and possibly her foreign birth made her vulnerable to molestation. Arguably, the demographic conditions that were supposed to benefit women also put them at risk. Imagine being one woman among a hundred sexually alert young men. Imagine living in a community where most other women were prostitutes, circumstances that several women commented on. Would you feel somehow empowered in this situation? How would you regard the men who patronized the whores? Would you want to reinforce the boundaries in a stratified society that placed you above some women? Demography gave an advantage to women of the right race (whites, especially Anglophones) and class—the middling sort and above. Poor women took their chances. Women of color were among the ranks of the despised who were subject to the whims of individuals and the mob.

Still, it must be admitted that white women who wished to marry found California a very fertile field for investment. Conversely, the majority of men could not marry in California. They either remained single, returned east, or sent for brides. In short, there was a crisis in the marriage market. The crisis was evident in the lives of the Bullard family. Benjamin and Eleanor Bullard emigrated from Michigan to California with their three sons and five daughters in 1853. The family settled in Sacramento where they operated boarding houses. The oldest son, William, worked in the mines in Timbuctoo, Yuba County, while the daughters remained with their parents. "Girls are bound to get married in this country," brother William said, and were in "no danger of living to be old mades [*sic*] here." Mary, one of his sisters, explained that "California is a fast country and a girl gets to be a young lady at twelve." Another sister, Caroline, who was evidently in her early teens, soon had to beat the boys off with a stick. "Caroline has got to be a regular heart smasher," Mary revealed. "If you could only see the beaux that she has, and their hearts are ready to break on her account. Oh you would pity them." Caroline married a prosperous man when she was sixteen, and her other sisters also married well and quickly, except for Mary who died of tuberculosis.

Poor brother William, a successful miner, waited for years to find a mate, but it was not for want of effort. He corresponded with a young cousin in Michigan and thought he had a chance to lure her to California, but she disappointed him. Still, perhaps she could help. In his town of Timbuctoo there was "one Girle . . . & I should judge thare was about two hundred young men from the age of 20 to 30 years." The rest of the mining towns had similar conditions. "Now . . . you see that the chances are slim for me to get a wife in California (for Squaw time is about over . . .) so I think I shall have to go back to Michigan to get a Wife. " If she knew of a young woman who wanted a husband, "just tell her that I am the *chap*." In the case of Indian women, William would not allow his desire for a wife to override his racial preferences, but he had other prejudices, too. When he announced that there would be a Fourth of July ball a few miles from his mine, he declared that "as I don't like the kind I shant go. (The *kind* are Irish)," he added. William was not so picky as long as the woman met his racial, ethnic and probably religious preferences. "If one of your Sisters would like to hitch teams with your California Cousin just tell her to say so," he pleaded. None of them did, but the "honest miner," as he called himself, finally hit pay dirt in 1868, fifteen years after he had arrived in California. He married Mary Farrell, a native of Ireland. To marry in California, William had to relax at least one of his prejudices.

Not only was it difficult for men to marry in California, it was comparatively hard for men to keep their wives. "The devil gets in the women here, or perhaps it comes out of them. I suspect the latter," John Dart wrote. "Eight women in ten that comes leaves their husbands." "It is rather a dangerous thing to marry a woman here for fear that some hombre will prosecute you or her for bigamy," Dart claimed. He exaggerated but identified another effect of the crisis in the gold rush marriage market. Women could leave their old husbands for new ones who were richer or who otherwise suited them better.

If the devil motivated women to leave their husbands, California's divorce law permitted them to do so with relative ease. Women and men could sue for divorce on grounds of natural impotency, adultery, extreme cruelty, willful desertion, neglect, fraud, and conviction of a felony. The state legislature and courts progressively liberalized divorce law throughout the nineteenth century. Aggrieved wives and husbands alike took advantage of this law, but more women than men sued for divorce. Californians divorced at a much greater rate than other Americans, a difference that increased during the nineteenth century. By 1880 the ratio of married to divorced couples in California (239 to 1) was about half that of the United States as a whole (481 to 1).

Not all Californians were satisfied with the California divorce law. When the legislature considered the 1851 divorce bill, editors of the *Alla* (a San Francisco newspaper) categorically denounced it and all divorce laws:

> They are all reprehensible, all opposed to good morals, all at variance with the principle of marriage, all tending to encourage immorality, dissatisfaction and alienation of feeling, all incompatible with the great source whence the civilized world draws its ideas of the sanctity of an oath and the sacredness of the marriage contract, all an insult to the Bible and the principles of Christianity.

Unhappy California spouses could always discard their mates and obtain more suitable replacements, and, the editors fumed, women fished "for partners with as much unconcern as ever Isaac Walton flung a fly upon the surface of a brook." "California is becoming notorious for the rapid, steam-engine manner in which the family tie is severed," said the *Alta*, "and it has almost come to be considered that there is an alienating quality in our very air."

Alienating qualities were not located in the air but in the demographic imbalances of California's population. There were too many men competing for too few women. This basic fact was plain in the operation of the marriage market where women had many opportunities to marry and men had few. The same forces that impelled the marriage market drove the divorce mill. Relatively lax divorce proceedings in the Golden State certainly presented new opportunities and options to women, but dissolutions of marriage are best understood in economic rather than feminist terms. Whatever the legal and moral arguments for divorce may have been, divorce added women to the marriage market—if only briefly—where men could select them. The general effect of liberalized divorce was to redistribute scarce resources—women—in the competitive and inflated gold rush economy. Of course, the marriage market did not operate according to strict laws of supply and demand, nor did buyers and sellers follow only their own best material interests. Emotional, social, religious, and other factors were also at work. Still, it is noteworthy that, without prompting from women, a government of men enacted a law that made it easier for women to dissolve their marriages. This statue benefited some of California's horde of single men as well as the dissatisfied wives whom it briefly liberated.

Divorce was not intended to free women or to provide them with new opportunities outside of marriage. The conjugal couple, their offspring, and the nuclear family were considered the ideal social condition for Californians, just as they were for other Anglo Americans. Courtship, marriage, and even divorce (insofar as it led to remarriage) reinforced familiar social, racial, and gender patterns that prevailed in the states. Was the gold rush era "the best ever made," as *The Annals of San Francisco* put it? Perhaps it was for some young men who were emancipated for the first time from the restraints of home and family. But most men seemed to value the common domestic arrangements they had once known, mourned their absence, and hoped for their replication in the Golden State. Some white women who were willing to play the marriage market may well have thought of the gold rush as the best of times. But for others the blessings were mixed according to their race, class, and gender.

So, what did sex and gender have to do with the Big Event? Ideas about gender influenced the basic makeup of California society. Anglo Americans had no doubts about the superiority of their way of life compared to Mexican, Indian, and other Californians, and their ideas about gender were no exception. For Anglo Americans, the centripetal forces of homegeneity, cultural conformity, and continuity mastered the weaker centrifugal forces of diversity and cultural change. The gold rush distributed the benefits and liabilities of sex unequally according to gender, race, and class. Only the most attractive men—however attraction may be defined—operated advantageously in the marriage market. Some white women transcended their class by marrying men who had profited in the gold fields; some did not. In most cases nonwhite women were considered suitable only for sexual gratification as prostitutes or temporary helpmeets until more fitting potential spouses arrived. Worse, some white men easily put aside Victorian ideas about the "gentler sex" so that they could rape and murder Indian women. All women who used their bodies to attract men, whether as prostitutes or prospective spouses, ran significant risks—pregnancy, botched abortions, venereal diseases, and death. In the end, ideas about sex and gender influenced hundreds of thousands of individual decisions about marriage, family, and community relations. In turn, those decisions shaped the future population of California. Gender and sexuality were not trivial particularities that revealed only the incidental "natural" events of individuals' lives; they were fundamental threads woven into the fabric of culture and historical experience—the rudiments of life and death.

Questions for Study and Review

1. How did the scarcity of women in California during the Gold Rush affect the lives of women in different economic and racial groups?

2. Compare the ways that a scarcity of women affected their roles and status in the colonial Chesapeake and frontier California.

3. How representative is Gold Rush California of women's experiences in the West more generally?

4. What issues might the women activists discussed by Anne Boylan highlight if they lived in California during the 1840s and 1850s?

Suggested Readings and Web Sites

Deena Gonzalez, *Refusing the Favor: The Spanish-Mexican Women of Sante Fe, 1820–1880* (1999)
Elizabeth Jameson and Susan Armitage, eds., *Writing the Range: Race, Class and Culture in the Women's West* (1997)
Susan Johnson, *Roaring Camp: The Social World of the California Gold Rush* (2000)
Lillian Schlissel, ed., *Women's Diaries of the Western Journey* (1992)
The California Gold Rush
   http://www.museumca.org/goldrush/

PART V

The Civil War
and Its Aftermath

This 1864 photograph of nurses and officers of the U.S. Sanitary Commission in Fredericksburg, Virginia, shows Union women working alongside men in battlefield hospitals.

Civil War and Reconstruction—two events upon which both much blood and much ink have been spilled. As the nation was ripped in two and then partially repaired, families and communities North and South were transformed. High death and injury rates, inadequate transportation and communication, demands for more soldiers and more workers assured that mothers and sons, wives and husbands, sisters and brothers—whatever their race, region, or class—would be changed by the war.

In some cases, the war expanded opportunities for women—as nurses, as civil servants, and even as soldiers; as volunteer or paid workers in the thousands of local aid societies in the North and South; or as female slaves momentarily freed by the absence of owners and overseers from constant surveillance. Individual women engaged in an amazing array of activities. Rose O'Neal Greenhow, a Washington, DC, hostess, served as a Confederate informant and was honored by Jefferson Davis as the "hero" of Bull Run. Harriet Tubman was an even more valuable spy for the Union cause. An ex-slave who had made numerous journeys into the South to rescue runaways, she provided detailed reports on the southern terrain, worked as a nurse and courier, and guided several Union forays into Confederate territory.

Women performed medical as well as military miracles. Kate Cummings of Alabama and Hannah Ropes of Massachusetts were two of the tens of thousands of Civil War nurses, only 3,200 of whom were formally paid for services on either side. Catholic nuns, such as the Sisters of Charity, also served as nurses during the war. Many of these nuns were immigrants, and their service to the Union cause helped to soften anti-immigrant and anti-Catholic sentiments among northerners who observed their selfless efforts to care for the wounded. Dr. Maggie Walker, honored for her medical services to Union soldiers (some of which were performed after she was placed in a prisoner-of-war camp by Confederate troops), was the first woman to receive the Congressional Medal of Honor. Phebe Yates Pember, a South Carolina widow who served as superintendent in Richmond's largest hospital, gained a reputation as a brilliant administrator. Loretta Janeta Velasquez outfitted an entire cavalry unit after her planter husband's death in rebel ranks. Black women, North and South, were more likely to join the war effort as camp followers or to be pressed into service as cooks, laundresses, and nurses. Susie King Taylor, for example, served with an African American regiment in the South and recorded her experiences in *Reminiscences of My Life in Camp with the 33rd United States Colored Troops*. Ex-slave Harriet Jacobs and Quaker schoolteacher Julia Wilbur labored as agents of northern women's antislavery societies, assisting black women and men who found their way into "contraband" camps behind Union lines.

Thousands of women also served in the U.S. Sanitary Commission or in its local branches. These women produced and shipped tons of clothing, socks, bandages, medicine, books, and other items to Union soldiers. They also dramatically improved the medical care available to northern troops in the final years of the war. Their efforts reflected hardship as well as hope, frustration as well as innovation. War brought loneliness and poverty, widowhood and grief to many. It also brought separation from family and friends; it increased the number of poorly paid jobs for women who were suddenly forced to support themselves and their children; it lengthened the hours spent in fields for women left behind to manage farms; and it introduced the disruptions of migration for camp followers or those caught in the path of battle.

Black and white, northern and southern, rich and poor, women labored on behalf of Union and Confederate causes. Few gained fortune, some gained fame, most simply got along as best they could. Many recorded their thoughts in letters and diaries, perhaps fearing they would not survive the cataclysm or hoping to pass on a memento of these convulsive times to children and grandchildren. One such chronicler recorded the ambivalence of women toward war as deaths and prices mounted. Commenting on a series of inflation-induced bread riots in Richmond, Virginia, in 1863, she wrote:

> I am for a tidal wave of peace—and I am not alone. . . . Here, in Richmond, if we can afford to give $11 for a pound of bacon, $10 for a small dish of green corn, and $10 for a watermelon, we can have a dinner of three courses for four persons. . . . Somebody, somewhere, is mightily to blame for all this business, but it isn't you nor I nor yet the women who . . . were only hungry.

Irish women involved in the New York City draft riots of the same year, American Indian women whose husbands and sons fought for a nation that spurned them, frontier women struggling to keep the farm and family intact, textile operatives turning out both uniforms and burial shrouds, wives of the South's small farmers who battled to save a slave system from which they did not profit, and widows and orphans on all sides must have shared these thoughts, at least now and then.

Based on the letters between a Texas soldier and the wife he left behind, Drew Gilpin Faust examines in Chapter Fourteen the hardships women faced as they tried to manage farms and slaves in the absence of their husbands. In 1860, Will and Lizzie Neblett owned a six-thousand-acre farm, although only ninety-two acres were under cultivation, and eleven slaves. Will added to the money made in farming by practicing law and editing a local newspaper. But in 1863, Will joined the Confederate Army and left Lizzie to tend to the farm. They exchanged a series of letters over the next two years that provides a window into the challenges faced by wives forced to take on the management of the family business and the enslaved women and men who produced its profits. Although Lizzie Neblett survived the experience, she was certainly happy to see the war end, even with the Confederacy defeated.

When the "tidal wave of peace" came, it did not wash away the hardships and doubts, nor did it crush the spirit and pride of those who survived the war. Once again, the experiences of women and men differed by race, region, and class as well as by sex. Southern blacks had freedom but not the resources to enjoy it. Northern whites and blacks had victory, but the price in dead, wounded, maimed, imprisoned, and missing was high. Most southern whites had neither resources nor victory and harbored wounds that medicine and time did little to heal.

Americans shared the enormous consequences of the war—the loss of a generation of young men, more rapid industrialization and the intensified commercialization of agriculture, an increasingly powerful and centralized national government, the encouragement of further western migration, and the tensions of incorporating blacks, at least black men, into the country's ranks of voters. These changes and the national policies that spawned them comprised the formal history of Reconstruction, but it was their impact on and implementation in local communities that shaped the lives of most women and men.

Of the million men who served in the Confederate Army, more than one-fourth died. Another 360,000 perished in Union ranks. The South lost $2 billion in property, raising immense economic and social barriers for defeated whites and freed black women and men trying to build new lives. Though northern missionaries and teachers, many of them women, traveled south to educate freed blacks, and though the Freedmen's Bureau sent agents to assist needy families of both races, most Americans reconstructed their lives without outside help. Nonetheless, they were not untouched by state and federal programs. In Chapter Fifteen Jean Fagan Yellin traces efforts among northern and southern blacks to reconstitute families and give meaning to freedom. She offers a moving portrait of the limits and opportunities of freedom and the ways they were shaped by black initiative, federal and local barriers, and conflicts among former abolitionists over which rights freed blacks deserved.

One of the most fundamental transformations resulting from Reconstruction was the incorporation of African Americans into the political system. Former slaves were emancipated by the Thirteenth Amendment and granted citizenship by the Fourteenth. Black men were given voting rights by the Fifteenth, or, more precisely, could not be denied the vote "on account of race, color, or previous condition of servitude." For southern blacks of both sexes, attempts to claim these "rights" often led to retribution, including physical violence.

For some northern women who had fought for abolition and woman's rights, the ratification of the Reconstruction amendments spelled the end of their hopes for admission to full citizenship. The inclusion of the words "male inhabitants" to define voters in the Fourteenth Amendment dealt women of all races and regions a setback on the road to equality. As a result, many white women formerly sympathetic to the slave's plight became less enamored of racial equality as they pursued more ardently the advancement of women's interests. Jean Fagan Yellin traces these developments as well.

By the 1870s, many Americans were exhausted by the tumult of war and Reconstruction. An economic depression in 1873 discouraged many from pursuing efforts to ensure African American rights. Indeed, many northern whites grew tired of sectional battles and hoped that reconciliation with southern whites would speed economic recovery and development. Members of the old abolitionist coalition, who had once pushed for racial advancement, were now aging and at odds.

Yet women did not entirely abandon hope of reforming the South. As Leslie K. Dunlap demonstrates in Chapter Sixteen, the Woman's Christian Temperance Union began organizing in southern states during the 1880s. Their main goal, however, was not political rights or economic advancement for African Americans, but sexual protection for young women. Still, their efforts to raise the age of sexual consent in the South raised fears among white male legislators that they would no longer be able to abuse black women and girls with impunity. Thus even after managing to disenfranchise African American men and reclaim power for the planter class, white elites were forced to recognize that the intertwined dynamics of race and sex still dominated the southern political landscape.

Suggested Readings and Web Sites

Ira Berlin, et al., eds., *Freedom: A Documentary History of Emancipation, 1861–1867,* Ser. II: *The Black Military Experience* (1982)

Drew Faust, *Mothers of Invention: Women of the Slaveholding South in the American Civil War* (1996)

Nina Silber, *The Romance of Reunion: Northerners and Southerners, 1865–1900* (1993)

Jean Fagan Yellin, *Harriet Jacobs, A Life* (2004)

Civil War Women
http://scriptorium.lib.duke.edu/collections/civil-war-women.html

Lest We Forget: The Triumph Over Slavery
http://digital.nypl.org/lwf/flash.html

The conflicts that eventually erupted in the Civil War were fueled by western expansion. As the United States expanded into territories west of the Mississippi River, southern and northern residents hailed the opening of the West. But women and men in each region hoped to harness the opportunities thus created for their own benefit. Most importantly, northerners—white and black, immigrant and native-born, women and men—hoped the West would solve the crises that immigration and urbanization created by offering cheap land and more jobs for those who had a hard time surviving on worn-out farms and low-wage jobs back East. White southerners, on the other hand, imagined the West as providing space for the expansion of slavery and plantation agriculture. They felt that this, too, might help small farmers as well as larger planters by making fertile fields available at low prices.

One of the earliest conflicts over westward expansion occurred when white southerners began settling in Texas in the 1820s, when the region was still governed by Mexico. U.S. citizens, with the tacit backing of the federal government, led a revolt in Texas and established an independent republic. The Republic of Texas soon sought admission into the Union, but northern Congressmen were opposed to expanding slave territory. By 1845, however, Texas gained admission and the United States gained another slave state.

In the late 1830s, the fathers of both Will and Lizzie Neblett had migrated to the independent Republic of Texas and established themselves as professionals and planters. They raised their families in an area north of Houston and probably celebrated when Texas became part of the United States in the 1840s. When Will and Lizzie married in 1852, they settled near where they had grown up, and Lizzie's father gave them a gift of land and slaves. The Nebletts were comfortable, but they were not part of the planter elite. Still, Lizzie was saved from arduous labor by the presence of enslaved women and men, and she apparently knew little about the farm's management when Will joined the Confederate Army in 1863.

Faust traces Lizzie Neblett's experience with managing the family, the farm, and the slave labor force through letters she exchanged with Will, who was stationed along the Texas coast. Ironically, Will largely avoided the violence of the war because his health was too poor for him to be sent into combat, while Lizzie was forced to confront, or at least consider, the use of violence on a regular basis. Left to discipline the slaves laboring on her behalf, she wavered between leaving control in the hands of a brutal overseer or attempting to regulate the workers by alternately cajoling and threatening them. Her frustrations and failures in finding a way to manage the farm and its workers without resorting to violence endangered not only her slaves but her children.

Although Texas was spared the kind of devastation suffered by battle-ravaged areas in Virginia, Mississippi, Georgia, and other states, women like Lizzie Neblett nonetheless struggled mightily in their husbands' absences. The black men and women who worked the Neblett farm suffered mightily as well, although for them the war at least brought hopes of liberation. Indeed, it was such hopes that lessened their willingness to accept the commands of their owner or bend to her will, even when she employed violence.

Mistresses of larger plantations with staffs to oversee the slaves, or those able to take refuge in southern cities or with family members in the North, were spared some of the challenges faced by Lizzie Neblett. And Lizzie Neblett may have been more outspoken in both her anger and her analysis of physical violence as a means of control than most slave-owning women. But nearly all must have seen, if they took the time to notice, that look of defiance in the eyes of enslaved women and men as they heard the death knell of the Confederacy chime in the distance.

"Trying to Do a Man's Business": Slavery, Violence and Gender in the American Civil War
Drew Gilpin Faust

Between 1861 and 1865, three fourths of white southern men of military age entered the army of the Confederacy, removing from communities across the American South those very individuals whose unceasing exercise of power and vigilance had maintained order in the region's slave society. With their departure, the social relations of the Old South were necessarily and abruptly transformed. The threat—and often the reality—of physical force, together with the almost equally coercive manipulations of planter paternalism, had served as fundamental instruments of oppression and thus of race control. The white South had justified its "peculiar institution" as a beneficent system of reciprocal obligations between master and slave, defining slave labor as a legitimate return for masters' protection and support. But in the very notion of mutual duties, the ideology of paternalism conceded the essential humanity of the bondspeople, who turned paternalism to their own uses, manipulating it as an empowering doctrine of rights.

Desiring to see themselves as decent Christian men, most southern slaveholders of the antebellum years preferred the negotiated power of reciprocity to the almost unchecked exercise of force that was in fact permitted them by law. In the paternalistic

From *Gender and History,* Vol. 4, No. 2, 1992. Copyright © by Blackwell Publishers Ltd.

ideal, whipping was regarded as a last, not a first resort, as a breakdown in a control that was most properly exerted over minds, rather than bodies. Yet violence was implicit in the system, and both planters' records and slaves' reminiscences demonstrate how often it was explicit as well. The ideal of racial reciprocity, of hegemonic paternalistic domination was just that: an ideal articulated more often in proslavery tracts, plantation manuals or agricultural journals than in the day-to-day experience of plantation life. Violence was in fact never far from the minds of either blacks or whites, for overseers carried whips, slaves bore scars of past punishment, and almost everyone had personally witnessed masters' physical coercion of slaves.

In the antebellum years, white men had assumed the overwhelming responsibility for slavery's daily management and perpetuation. Just as paternalism was founded in a belief in the dominance of men within the family and household, so violence was similarly gendered as male within the ideology of the Old South. When the Civil War removed thousands of white men from households across the region, it became unclear how the slave system would be maintained. Called to fight for slavery on the battlefield, Confederate masters could not simultaneously defend it on the homefront.

In many ways, the daily struggle over coercion and control taking place on hundreds of farms and plantations was just as crucial as any military contest to defense of the southern way of life. Slavery was, as Confederate Vice President Alexander Stephens explained, the "cornerstone" of the region's social, economic and political order. Yet slavery's survival depended less on sweeping dictates of public policy than on tens of thousands of individual acts of personal domination exercised by particular masters over particular slaves. The nineteenth century southerner's designation of slavery as the "domestic institution" thus becomes in retrospect curious and even ironic, for such a term might be seen to imply a contrast with the public or the political. But the very domesticity of slavery in the Old South, its imbeddedness in the social relations of the plantation or yeoman household, made those households central to the most public, most political aspects of regional life. The direct exercise of control over slaves was the most fundamental and essential political act in the Old South. With the departure of white men, this transcendent public responsibility fell to Confederate women.

Although white southerners—both male and female—might insist that politics was not, even in the changed circumstances of wartime, an appropriate part of woman's sphere, the female slave manager necessarily served as a foundation of the South's political order. White women's actions as slave mistresses were critical to Confederate destinies, for the viability of the southern agricultural economy, the stability of the social order, as well as the continuing loyalty of the civilian population all depended upon successful slave control. On a microcosmic level, the daily interactions of particular women slaveholders with specific slaves yield a striking vision of the master-slave relationship in a new wartime guise, of war-born redefinitions of social power and social roles, and of a society in turmoil.

This essay will examine the experience of one woman in order to explore how the dynamics of war, slavery, gender and mastery played themselves out within a single richly documented context. Lizzie Scott Neblett lived in Texas, far from any direct threat of Union troops. Hers was a situation in which the forces and the internal logic of southern society operated in comparative freedom from the most direct intrusions of war. As a recent historian of Texas slavery has written, "The Peculiar Institution remained less disturbed in Texas than in any other Confederate state." Yet even without a Union military presence, the absence of white men would itself change the system profoundly, and transform the white women and black slaves who like Lizzie Neblett and her human property became caught up in slavery's wartime disintegration.

Slave management was not an opportunity white southern women eagerly sought. As one Georgia plantation mistress put it, a woman was simply not a "fit and proper person" to govern slaves. But like men conscripted into battle, Confederate women of the slave-owning classes often found they had little choice. When Will Neblett enlisted in the 20th Texas Infantry in March of 1863, his wife Lizzie explained that her impending service as agricultural and slave manager was "a coercive one." But, she vowed, she would be "faithful and conscientious in its discharge."

Already 37 years old, Will Neblett was in poor health—"Rheumatism, Neuralgia and Bronchial Affections, as well as General physical delicacy of organization," his service record described it. Designated as "unable to perform active field service," Neblett was assigned to the Quartermaster Corps and spent most of the two years remaining in the war stationed in Galveston on the Texas coast. Because the likelihood of losing her husband to Yankee fire was considerably less than that confronting many Confederate wives, the concerns Lizzie expressed about the difficulties of her own situation may have been proportionately increased. At age 30, she found herself in circumstances very unlike those she had envisioned as an idealistic girl, publishing romantic out-pourings in local Texas publications, dreaming of literary reputation, and maintaining an intense and intellectual correspondence with a circle of former schoolmates.

Marriage and motherhood had compelled a change in her aspirations. Ambition, she explained to her diary soon after her wedding in 1852, now must focus on her husband. "I am ambitious for *him*. . . . I can never gain worldly honors. Fame can never be mine." Even her hopes of teaching proved impossible, as Lizzie became caught up in a cycle of pregnancies, childhood diseases and family demands. When Will left home in the spring of 1863, Lizzie was awaiting her unwelcome fifth confinement. She was already mother of a ten year old daughter and three sons, ages eight, six and four. The much resented baby Bettie would arrive in May.

Born in Mississippi, Will and Lizzie were both children of slaveowning families who had migrated to the rich cotton lands of Grimes County, some fifty miles northwest of Houston, during the late 1830s. Will's father was a physician, and Lizzie's had been a circuit judge, as well as the master of more than 75 slaves, a holding large enough to place him in the top one percent of Texas slaveholders. When the war broke out, Will had been practicing law for well over a decade, and had just resigned after a year of service as editor of the *Navarro Express,* a staunchly secessionist Democratic paper. In addition, the Nebletts owned eleven slaves, who in 1860 had cultivated the 92 improved acres of a nearly 6000 acre farm to produce $15\frac{1}{4}$ bales of ginned cotton and 500 bushels of corn. With this force, which they had received from Lizzie's father Judge Scott, the young couple ranked among the top quarter of Texas slaveholders in 1860, but well below the upper three percent of the population who possessed more than 20 slaves and thus qualified as plantation owners. Nevertheless, with real estate valued at $12,500 and personal property worth $14,500 in 1860, the Nebletts stood well above the state mean, even among the 27% of Texas families who held slaves and averaged $7000 in real and $12,500 in personal property. Lizzie clearly had little right to her complaint that the neighbors were unjust in accusing her of being rich.

Lizzie set about the task before her in the spring of 1863 committed to "doing my best," but apprehensive both about her ignorance of agriculture and the behavior she might anticipate from the slaves. Their initial response to her direction, however, seemed promising. "The negros," she wrote Will in late April "seem to be mightily stirred up now, about making a good crop." Before his departure, Will had arranged to swap slave work with a neighbor in exchange for his assumption of a general supervisory eye over Lizzie and her slaves. Mr. Rivers seemed to Lizzie, however, to be taking advantage of the situation from the outset, using her slaves chiefly to his own profit. And, in her advanced state of pregnancy, dealing with outsiders was more trying than dealing with her own laborers. "I look so unsightly & feel that I do so sensibly that a man is a horror to me." Above all else, however, Lizzie was disgusted by Rivers' lack of shame in acknowledging his own slave children, and she was convinced that if the war did not end she must make different management arrangements after the current crop year.

Anxious about her confinement and then overwhelmed by a difficult and demanding infant, "cursed like her mother with the female sex," Lizzie wrote little of her agricultural dilemmas until the harvest season had nearly arrived. And by this time her initial optimism about the blacks' behavior had disappeared. A matching of Lizzie's scattered letter and diary references with the 1860 census count makes possible a rough recreation of the Neblett slaves and their family ties. But because Lizzie often borrowed slaves from other members of her family, it is difficult to achieve an exact congruence between those individuals regularly mentioned as part of her household and those officially listed as belonging to the Nebletts in the public record.

Although the 1860 census enumerator noted that the eleven Neblett slaves occupied two houses, they did not comprise two distinct family groups. Thornton and Nance, who had married in the mid 1850s, were in their late twenties or early thirties and parents of Lee, born in 1857, Henry, born in 1860, and Harrison, an infant when Will departed in 1863. Sarah, who worked chiefly in the house, was in her mid forties, and Lizzie's records make no mention of her family ties. Sam, the oldest male on the place, was of a similar age, and, like many slaves on such small holdings, had a wife belonging to another owner. Joe, probably in his thirties, also had an "abroad" wife and children, and Will's inability to meet Joe's request that he purchase them was in all likelihood the source of Joe's "propensity for running about at night and on Sundays." Tom, Randall, Bill and Kate were all in their mid teens, as was Polly, a house servant on loan from Lizzie's brother in the army. Anticipating the impressment of Randall for hospital detail in Brenham, about 50 miles away, Lizzie reckoned she would have five laborers to cultivate and harvest the corn and cotton crops.

But persuading them actually to work was another matter. "The negros are doing nothing," Lizzie wrote Will at the height of first picking in mid August. "But ours are not doing that job alone nearly all the negroes around here are at it, some of them are getting so high in anticipation of their glorious freedom by the Yankees I suppose, that they resist a whipping." Many slave-owners, she noted, had become "actually affraid to whip the negros." Lizzie harbored few doubts about the longterm loyalty of her own black family. "I don't think we have one who will stay with us."

Under these difficult conditions, Lizzie reported a cotton crop of eight bales, an achievement well below the 1860 average of 2.5 bales per slave for Texas farms of her size and only a bit more than half of what the Nebletts themselves had realized three years before. In the same letter in which she informed Will of these troubling realities, Lizzie announced her new arrangements for slave and crop management. She had, as she described it, "insisted" that another neighbor come to her aid. For $400 of Confederate money—the equivalent, she estimated, of $80 of "good money"—Mr. Meyers would spend a half day with her slaves three times a week. "He will be right tight on the negroes I think, but they need it, they never feared Rivers one single bit." And, she implied, they did not fear her either. "Meyers," she continued, "will lay down the law and enforce it." But Lizzie emphasized that she would not permit cruelty or abuse. She was sure he would not "have to whip but one or two before the others will take the hint."

But controlling Meyers would prove in some ways more difficult than controlling the slaves. His second day on the plantation Meyers whipped all three teenage boys for idleness, and on his next visit, as Lizzie put it, "he undertook old Sam." Gossip had spread among slaves in the neighborhood—and from them to their masters—that Sam intended to take a whipping from no man. Will Neblett had, in fact, not been a harsh disciplinarian, tending more to threatening and grumbling than whipping. Lizzie anticipated, however, that Sam might well prove a problem for Meyers, and her ten year old daughter, Mary, passed this concern along to Sam himself. Sam assured Mary and her eight year old brother Bob that he would run away rather than submit to Meyers' lash: "he shant whip me."

For Meyers, this very challenge was quite "enough." On his next visit to the farm, Meyers called Sam down from atop a wagon of fence stakes. Sam refused to come, saying he had done nothing to deserve a whipping. When Sam began edging away from Meyers, the white man ordered him to stop, then began shooting at him. Sam ran, but was soon cornered. At first he threatened to kill anyone who laid a hand on him, but when Meyers countered by waving his gun, Sam surrendered. Enraged, Meyers beat Sam so severely that Lizzie feared he might die. She anxiously called the doctor, who assured her Sam had no internal injuries and that he had seen many slaves beaten far worse.

Lizzie was torn about how to respond—to Meyers or to Sam. "Tho I pity the poor wretch," she confided to Will, "I don't want him to know it." To the other slaves she insisted that "Meyers would not have whipped him if he had not deserved it," and to Will she defensively maintained, "somebody must take them in hand they grow worse all the time I could not begin to write you . . . how little they mind me." She saw Meyers' actions as part of a plan to establish control at the outset: "he lets them know what he is, when he first starts, & then has no more trouble." But Lizzie's very insistence and defensiveness suggest that this was not, even in her mind, slave management in its ideal form, and the criticisms from her rejected neighbor Rivers—"a damed shame the way Sam was whipped"—stung all the worse when she was told of them indirectly by her own slaves, eager to report this fissure in white solidarity.

Over the next few days, Lizzie's doubts about Meyers and his course of action grew. Instead of eliminating trouble at the outset, as he had intended, the incident seemed to have created an uproar. Sarah, a cook and house slave, reported to Lizzie that Sam suspected the whipping had been his mistress's idea, and that when well enough, he would run away till Will came home. Perhaps this meant, Lizzie worried, that Sam was planning some act of vengeance against her.

To resolve the volatile situation and to salvage her reputation as slave mistress, Lizzie now enlisted another man, Coleman, to talk reasonably with Sam. Coleman had been her father's overseer and continued to manage her mother's property. In the absence of Will and of Lizzie's brothers, he was an obvious family deputy, and he had undoubtedly known Sam since the slave's days as the property of Judge Scott. Coleman readily agreed to "try to show Sam the error he had been guilty of." At last Sam spoke the words Coleman sought, admitting he had done wrong, promising "he would let Meyers whip him, one more time," as long as it was not so severe. But Coleman suggested an even more desirable survival strategy, promising him that "if only he would be humble & submissive . . . Meyers would never whip him so again."

Two weeks after the incident, Lizzie and Sam finally had a direct, and, in Lizzie's view at least, comforting exchange. Meyers had ordered Sam back to work, but Lizzie interceded in response to Sam's complaints of persisting weakness. Taking his cue from Lizzie's conciliatory gesture and acting as well in accordance with Coleman's advice, Sam apologized for disappointing Lizzie's expectations, acknowledging that as the oldest slave he had special responsibilities in Will's absence. Henceforth, he promised Lizzie, he was "going to do his work faithfully & be of as much service to me as he could. I could not help," Lizzie confessed to Will, "feeling sorry for the old fellow . . . he talked so humbly & seemed to hurt that I should have had him whipped so."

Sam's adroit transformation from rebel into Sambo helped resolve Lizzie's uncertainties about the appropriate course of slave management. Abandoning her defense of Meyers' severity, even interceding on Sam's behalf against her own manager, Lizzie assured Sam she had not been responsible for his punishment, had indeed been "astonished" by it. Meyers, she reported to Will with newfound assurance, "did wrong" and "knows nothing" about the management of slaves. He "don't" she noted revealingly, "treat them as moral beings but manages by brute force." Henceforth, Lizzie concluded, she would not feel impelled by her sense of helplessness to countenance extreme severity. Instead, she promised Sam, if he remained "humble and submissive," she would ensure "he would not get another lick."

The incident of Sam's whipping served as the occasion for an extended negotiation between Lizzie and her slaves about the terms of her power. In calling upon Meyers and Coleman, she demonstrated that despite appearances, she was not in fact a woman alone, dependent entirely on her own resources. Although the ultimate responsibility might be hers, slave management was a community concern. Pushed toward sanctioning Meyers' cruelty by a fear of her own impotence, Lizzie then stepped back from the extreme position in which Meyers had placed her. But at the same time that she dissociated herself from Meyers' action, she also reaped its benefit: Sam's abandonment of a posture of overt defiance for one of apparent submission. Sam and Lizzie were ultimately able to join forces in an agreement that Meyers must be at once deplored and tolerated as a necessary evil whom both mistress and slave would strive ceaselessly to manipulate. Abandoning their brief tryouts as Simon Legree and Nat Turner, Lizzie and Sam returned to the more accustomed and comfortable roles of concerned paternalist and loyal slave. And each recognized at last that his or her own performance depended in large measure upon a complementary performance by the other.

The lines of communication in this negotiating process are likewise revealing of the wider social structure of farm and neighborhood. Lizzie and Sam communicated

This picture of Will and Lizzie Neblett, taken after the Civil War, is typical of photographic portraits of the period. Here Will and Lizzie sit next to each other, with their arms linked, suggesting their shared roles in marriage and in rebuilding their life following the Confederate defeat and the abolition of slavery.

repeatedly through intermediaries: first her young children, whom Sam perhaps regarded as a means of blunting the impact of the defiance towards which he felt himself propelled; then through Sarah, a black woman to serve as translator between a white woman and a black man; then Coleman, a white man experienced in the language and manipulations of paternalism, who reminded Sam of his appropriate and, in this situation, most wisely calculated role. Slave management here involved not just master or mistress and slave, but, in the phraseology of the Old South, all the family white and black, as well as much of the surrounding neighborhood.

Meyers' actions, explicitly cited by Sam's physician as entirely within the law, were nevertheless quietly or overtly criticized by those for whom the paternalistic scenario of slavery remained, even in wartime exigency, far preferable to the harsh realities of physical domination. Rivers was gloating perhaps when he decried Sam's treatment as a "damed shame," but he also provided an opportunity for Lizzie's slaves to pressure their mistress to rebuke Meyers and offer Sam an opening for compromise. Eager for her to hear River's disapproval directly, the slaves took the initiative to inform Lizzie that Rivers wished to speak with her, thus demonstrating the part slaves played as communicators and negotiators not just within individual farms or plantations, but across neighborhoods. Yet Rivers, father of his own slave children, could hardly play the virtuous and upstanding paternalist. That role remained to Coleman, who as Scott family retainer and as Sam's former overseer stood midway between Lizzie and her defiant slave. Symbolizing both Sam's and his own longstanding ties with the Scott family, Coleman invoked the class language of paternalism to remind Sam of his place within these traditions of social order and obligation.

Lizzie's behavior throughout the crisis demonstrated as well the essential part gender identities and assumptions played in master-slave relationships. As a female slave manager, Lizzie exploited her apparently close ties to the woman house slave Sarah to secure information about the remainder of her force. "Sarah is worth a team of negro's with her tongue," Lizzie reported to Will. Yet Lizzie's gender more often represented a constraint than an opportunity. Just before the confrontation between Meyers and Sam, Lizzie had written revealingly to Will about the physical coercion of slaves. Acknowledging Will's reluctance to whip, she confessed to feeling the aversion even more forcefully than he. "It has got to be such a disagreeable matter with me to whip, that I haven't even dressed Kate but once since you left, & then only a few cuts—I am too troubled in mind to get stirred up enough to whip. I made Thornton whip Tom once."

Accustomed to occasional strikes against female slaves, Lizzie called upon a male slave to whip the adolescent Tom, then, later, a white male neighbor to dominate the venerable Sam. Yet even this structured hierarchy of violence was becoming increasingly "disagreeable" to her as she acted out her new wartime role as "chief of affairs." Lizzie knew she was objectively physically weaker than both black and white men around her, and she feared that wartime disruptions of established patterns of white male authority might encourage slaves to resist physical punishments—especially if inflicted by their new—and weaker—female managers. But she confessed as well to a "troubled . . . mind," to uncertainties about her appropriate relationship to the ultimate exertion of force upon which slavery rested. As wartime pressures weakened the foundations for the "moral" management that Lizzie preferred, what she referred to as "brute force" became simultaneously more necessary and more impossible as an instrument of coercion.

The resolution of the crisis concerning Sam hardly brought permanent peace to the Neblett farm. Even as she struggled with the aftermath of conflict, Lizzie found herself faced with unceasing demands from other slaves. When Thornton was gored in the hand by a wild pig, it was to Lizzie that he came for help. He seemed almost scared to death, but Lizzie remained calm, even though she saw his finger was almost severed. Calling upon her experience in domestic needlework, she took "two stitches through the flesh and tied it, to bring the cut together," then covered the wound with sugar and turpentine. It was, she reported, the "hardest sewing I ever done."

Lizzie's medical skills would be taxed more thoroughly, however, by the extended illness of six year old Lee, who in December of 1863 was seized by a flux. Lizzie sat with him for days and nights on end, and administered a veritable pharmacopeia of remedies: mustard plasters, rhubarb, soda, peppermint leaves, cinnamon bark. Removing him from his parents, Nance and Thornton, who Lizzie complained, "don't take care of their children," Lizzie installed the boy in a room in her own house. Although she took "every precaution," she assured Will, to prevent spread of the disease and tried to keep her own children out of Lee's room, she still worried that she herself, who had "spared neither hands nor nose," would contract the disease. Confident in her own course of therapeutics, Lizzie did not send for a doctor for almost two weeks, and then was gratified to have him entirely approve her course of treatment.

Yet at the same time Lizzie recognized and performed all the duties expected of the benevolent slave mistress, she reported to Will the half-heartedness she felt in executing her role. "I have nursed him closely," she assured her husband, "& done as much for him as if he was my own child, but have not of course felt the anxiety about him, that I would one of my own." "If it was not for the humanity of the thing I had much rather let him lay in his mothers house & died than to run the risk of myself & all the children taking it. . . . I have had a great deal of trouble with him, more than he is worth." But the "humanity of the thing," especially in the case of a child, still had a firm if grudging hold on Lizzie Neblett.

It was much harder to feel that benevolence towards Joe. In the fall of 1863, Lizzie's difficulties in managing Joe combined with fears that he would be seized by Confederate soldiers for military labor prompted the Nebletts to send Joe to Will in Galveston. But Will found his camp services of little use, and hired him out in Houston. Slave hiring was widespread in Texas, and seems to have become even more common during the Civil War when many families found they preferred reaping profit from their unfree property without bearing the responsibility for their direct supervision. And as Lizzie became increasingly exasperated with slave management, she would ever more strongly urge such a course on Will.

Joe's contract, however, was brief and at Christmas, he was to be returned to Lizzie in Grimes County. But the New Year of 1864 arrived with no sign of Joe, and Lizzie was not at all sure what had become of him. Perhaps, she feared, he had run away or had been seized for government service. By the middle of January, however, Joe appeared with a lengthy and, Lizzie thought, "plausible tale" to account for his delay: flooding en route, fear of impressment officers, an injury from being kicked by a horse. A letter from Will, who had spoken with Joe's boss, told another story—of Joe's eagerness to be rehired for another year, of his reluctance to return to Grimes, of his improvidence and his delay in departing. Lizzie should, Will urged, make Joe pay her in cash for the work days he had missed. Lizzie mocked Will's suggestion. "You seem to think I can do more with Joe than you can. You know I cant get money or work out of him."

Joe perfectly embodied the independence that southern critics of the hiring system feared as its inevitable outcome. Not only did Joe possess a keen sense of independence from the Nebletts' power, he had also acquired property and skills in transacting business that had made him into an energetic entrepreneur. Lizzie, far less experienced in such matters than he, found herself at a complete loss to control him. When Joe returned to Grimes County, he brought with him a mule, which he used to visit his wife and family. He began feeding the animal with Lizzie's corn, and soon took the girth and stirrup leathers from Will's saddle to put his own "in riding order." "I expect him to take all hands soon," Lizzie wryly remarked, "& build himself a stable." When Lizzie wanted to use the girth for her own animals, she found Nance had locked it up in one of the slave houses. Meanwhile Joe had begun negotiations to acquire a better mount from another slave in the neighborhood. By May, he had gained possession of a horse. He "is now too proud to ride his old mule," Lizzie reported.

Lizzie acknowledged to Will that the situation must seem on the face of it unthinkable. But, she explained resignedly, "necessity compels me to do many things I rebel at, when they first present themselves." She considered killing Joe's steed, but recognized that would just make the slave run away or cease work altogether. And yet Joe's influence threatened to transform the rest of her slave force into small businessmen. Tom had sold her hens to an "old negro" in the neighborhood, and was discovered cutting down trees to market to the neighbors as firewood.

Meyers sought to enforce control over both Tom and Joe exactly as he had Sam months before. He gave Tom an unprovoked whipping and succeeded in beating his back raw before Lizzie discovered that the young black had in response run away. When Meyers threatened Joe, however, the slave escaped through the woods and appeared in front of Lizzie before Meyers could lay a hand on him. Lizzie interceded. "I told him not to whip Joe, as long as he done his work well & that he must not shoot at him, that he might run away & we might never get him & if he never done me any good he might my children." Slavery in the present had become unworkable. Lizzie could only hope for its future. The balance of power between mistress and bondsmen seemed to have been reversed. "Joe, is doing very bad—it is his day now certainly, but whether my day will ever arrive or not is . . . exceedingly doubtful." Freedom had not yet officially come to Texas, but in Lizzie's despairing eyes, the bottom rail seemed already firmly situated on top.

Forbidden the physical severity that served as the fundamental prop of his system of slave management, Meyers requested to be released from his contract with Lizzie at the end of the crop year. Early on, Meyers had told Lizzie that he could "conquer" her slaves, "but may have to kill some one of them." It remained with Lizzie he explained, to make the decision. In her moments of greatest exasperation, Lizzie was ready to consent to such extreme measures. "I say do it." But with calm reflection, tempered by Will's measured advice, considerations of humanity inevitably reasserted their claim. Repeatedly she interceded between Meyers and the slaves—protecting them from whippings or condemning Meyers when he disobeyed her orders and punished them severely. Yet despite her difficulties in managing Meyers himself, and despite her belief that he was "deficient in judgment," Lizzie recognized her dependence upon him and upon the threat of physical coercion that he represented. She was determined to "hold him on as long as I can." If he quit and the slaves found that no one was coming to replace him, she wrote revealingly, "the jig will be up." The game, the trick, the sham of her slave management would be over. Without a man—or part of a man for three half days a week—without the possibility of recourse to violence that Meyers embodied, slavery was impossible. The velvet glove of paternalism required its iron hand.

The dependence of slavery upon violence and the Old South's gendering of physical force as male made women regard themselves as ineffective managers. "I am so sick," Lizzie wrote Will, "of trying to do a man's business when I am nothing but, a poor contemptible piece of multiplying human flesh tied to the house by a crying young one, look upon as belonging to a race of inferior beings." Her angry frustration seemed pointless, and only provoked the slaves to "meriment," so Lizzie resorted to private tears as a consolation for her "entire inability to help myself." Never had her dependence seemed greater than in this wartime situation of apparent independence and responsibility.

Central to Lizzie's dilemma were her ambivalence and confusion about the role of physical coercion in social relations. In the Old South, violence was anything but the monopoly of the state. Instead, recourse to physical violence in support of male honor and white supremacy was regarded as the right, even the responsibility, of each white man—within his household, on his plantaion, in his community. The outbreak of Civil War, the South's resort to the organized, region-wide violence of military conflict, simply underscored the legitimacy of force in social relations. In battle, white southerners embraced violence as a desirable, heroic means of resolving issues of power. But like the Old South's code of honor, military violence was to be fundamentally male; women were in the words of one female Confederate, "barred from the tented field."

Yet, as men moved in increasing numbers from the South's households to its battlefields, women of the region's plantation owning elite would be left as the custodians of social order and would find themselves confronting the dependence of their slave society upon the implicit threat, if not explicit use, of force. Throughout the history of the peculiar institution, slave mistresses had hit, slapped, even brutally whipped slaves—particularly slave women. But their relationship to this exercise of physical power was significantly different from that of their men. No gendered code of honor celebrated their physical power or dominance. A contrasting, yet parallel ideology extolled their female sensitivity, weakness and docility. In the prewar years, exercise of the violence that was fundamental to slavery was overwhelmingly the responsibility and prerogative of white men. A white woman disciplined and punished as the master's subordinate and surrogate. Rationalized, systematic, autonomous, instrumental use of violence belonged to men.

As a wartime slave manager, Lizzie soon discovered that she could live neither with violence nor without it. The manipulations of paternalism's velvet glove were growing progressively less effective as means of control, yet unrestrained terror, however appealing at times, was, Lizzie recognized, inhumane. Perhaps it had even become dangerous, threatening to provoke restive slaves themselves to act upon southern society's lessons about the primacy of force. Lizzie in fact worried about violence from her slaves—and especially feared retaliation for Meyer's cruelties. And she wondered too about the origins of mysterious fires that burned her mother's house, her father-in-law's gin and the Nebletts' own property now rented out in Navarro County, for she knew arson to be widely acknowledged as a characteristic slave "crime."

Violence seemed to permeate the white family as well. Lizzie's ill-behaved children were nearly as exasperating as her slaves and perhaps even more out of control. Bob mistreated the horses; Walter used a cowhide to beat the cat; all the children's faces bore the permanent scars of Billy's fingernails, and infant Bettie cried ceaselessly. Here Lizzie felt empowered to act in a way she dared not with her slaves. Here, with her own young children, a woman need not fear the use of physical force—even if considerations of humanity prompted doubt. Lizzie threatened she would whip Billy every day if necessary "& I do it well when I begin." "I can't get him to do anything unless I get the cowhide in hand." And Bob, she complained, just "don't mind me as well as he once did." By the time Bettie had reached 10 months, Lizzie confessed to Will "I have whipped her several times." Reporting her aunt's stern disapproval of beating such a small child, Lizzie admitted she was surprised when Will did not scold her as well. As she restrained herself from abusing her slaves, Lizzie turned to abusing her children.

Frustrated by feelings of powerlessness and incompetence as both slave manager and parent, Lizzie turned to brute force. Will's regime of "grumbling and threatening" slave management was replaced by the counterpoint of Meyers' cruelty and Lizzie's paternalism; Lizzie and Will's socialization of their children devolved into Lizzie's threats and punishments and the children's own resort to violence with their inferiors—siblings and animals.

Historians and social scientists exploring "family violence" have concentrated upon its appearances in urban settings, particularly in the industrial North. But the phenomenon, with its invaluable perspective on fundamental issues of social power, deserves historical attention in the South as well. Within slaveholding society, domestic violence took on a distinctive shape and meaning, one that suggests it would most usefully be examined not just in terms of biological family, but within the context of the wider household—the "family white and black" in which expressions of physical force were structured and influenced by intimate relationships of race as well as age and gender.

The South's social hierarchies created a spectrum of legitimate access to violence, so that social empowerment was inextricably bound up with the right to use physical force. Violence was all but required of white men of all classes and forbidden to black slaves, except within their own communities, where the dominant society regarded it as essentially invisible. White women stood upon an ill-defined middle ground, where behavior and ideology often diverged. The Civil War exacerbated this very tension, disrupting the broader structures of social order by removing a sizeable portion of the white men and thus compelling women in slaveowning households to become the reluctant agents of a power they could not embrace as rightfully their own. The centrality of violence in the Old South had reflected and reinforced white women's inferior status in that society. Within the Confederacy, it threatened to make women like Lizzie feel growing contempt for their identity as females trying, unsuccessfully, to "do a man's business." In their eyes, a man's business it would—and should—remain.

Violence was the ultimate foundation of power in the slave South, but gender prescriptions carefully barred white women—especially those elite women most likely to find themselves responsible for controlling slaves—from purposeful exercise of such authority. Even when circumstances had shifted to make female authority socially desirable, it remained for many plantation mistresses personally impossible. Lizzie's struggle with her attraction to violence and simultaneous abhorrence of it embodied the contradictions that the necessary wartime paradox of female slave management imposed on her individual life. Ultimately and tragically, she embraced violence by exercising power over the most helpless being of all. Lizzie turned in frustration and, I would suggest, self-loathing, to the beating of an infant child—a child who happened to be not just speechless and helpless, but, named for Lizzie herself and "cursed like her mother with the female sex."

The role of female slave manager was within the gender assumptions of the Old South a contradiction in terms that left Lizzie longing only for excape: she wished repeatedly to die; to be a man; or to give up the slaves altogether—except, tellingly, for one to wait on her in the house. White women had reaped slavery's benefits throughout its existence in the colonial and antebellum South. But they could not be its managers without ceasing to be what they understood as women. In the absence of men, a society based in the violence of slavery could not stand.

• • •

If he would not hire out his slaves and free her from their management, Lizzie begged Will in the spring of 1864, "give your negros away and, I'll . . . work with my hands, as hard as I can, but my mind will rest." A year later Lizzie would have to trouble her mind about slave management no longer. With war's end, Will returned safely from the coast and took up farming once again. By the time of the 1870 census, he was annually paying out $100 in wages to farm workers and raising 4 bales of cotton, as well as 200 bushels of corn. The value of his real estate had fallen sixty percent during the decade, and his personal property, with the freeing of his slaves, to just five and a half percent of its former value. Lizzie later described "seven years of struggle together after the war closed," for in the spring of 1871, Will died of pneumonia, leaving his wife five months pregnant with a third daughter.

A widow at thirty-eight, Lizzie had lived less than half her life. She would survive until 1917, returning to her early literary ambitions as a temperance columnist in the 1880s, and emerging by the end of the century as matriarch of a growing clan of descendants. Ironically, she would pass the last decades of her life in the Austin household of her second daughter, the unwelcome war-baby Bettie. Lizzie Neblett's scattered postbellum letters and papers cannot provide the vivid portrait of a woman's experience that emerges from her Civil War writings. We can never know whether the end of war and its responsibilities had indeed brought her sad and tormented mind to "rest."

Questions for Study and Review

1. How did the Civil War reshape race and gender relations on southern plantations, particularly regarding the use and meaning of violence?

2. In what ways was Lizzie Neblett's experience typical of southern slave-owning women and in what ways distinctive?

3. Does the practice of truancy among enslaved women and men described by Stephanie Camp illuminate the attitudes of blacks on the Neblett farm?

4. Compare the role played by Will Neblett in the midst of the Civil War with the ideals of domestic patriarchy outlined by Allan Kulikoff in the eighteenth-century Chesapeake.

Suggested Readings and Web Sites

Jean Attie, *Patriotic Toil: Northern Women and the American Civil War* (1998)

Laura Edwards, *Scarlett Doesn't Live Here Anymore: Southern Women in the Civil War Era* (2000)

Judith Ann Geisberg, *Civil War Sisterhood: The U.S. Sanitary Commission and Women's Politics in Transition* (2000)

Elizabeth Leonard, *All the Daring of the Soldier: Women of the Civil War Armies* (1999)

Susie King Taylor, *A Black Woman's Civil War Memoirs: Reminiscences of My Life in Camp with the 33rd U.S. Colored Troops, Late 1st South Carolina Volunteers*, ed. Patricia Romero (1902; reprint 1988)

The Valley of the Shadow: Two Communities in the American Civil War
   http://valley.vcdh.virginia.edu

Civil War Letters
   http://etext.virginia.edu/civilwar/nettleton/
   http://etext.virginia.edu/civilwar/brand/

Chapter 15

Harriet Jacobs suffered physical and sexual abuse as an enslaved woman
in North Carolina until she fled her master's house in 1835. She then spent seven
years hiding in a tiny attic in her grandmother's house before making her way to
freedom in the North. Forced to find work as a caregiver in a wealthy white family, she worked constantly to rescue her son and daughter from slavery and
locate her brother, who was also a fugitive. Befriended by abolitionists, including
Amy Post and Lydia Maria Child, Jacobs decided to write the story of her life,
which she published under the pseudonym Linda Brent in 1861. *Incidents in the
Life of a Slave Girl* did not achieve the fame that the narratives of Frederick
Douglass and Sojourner Truth gained for their authors, in part because the Civil
War broke out just as the book was published, but it provides a compelling
account of a southern black woman's life in slavery and freedom.

During the war, Jacobs returned south to assist black fugitives who
escaped behind Union lines. These contrabands, as they were called by the
government, were in dire straits, having left behind homes and families and
headed to freedom with the few possessions they could carry. Jacobs wrote
letters and articles for northern papers describing the needs of the fugitives
she met in Alexandria, Virginia, and urging abolitionists and Union supporters
to send clothing, medicine, food, and funds. She received assistance from antislavery societies in New York City, Rochester, New York, and elsewhere and
also from members of the National Women's Loyal League. The League was
formed at the beginning of the war by Elizabeth Cady Stanton and Susan B.
Anthony to demonstrate northern women's support for the Union cause and
to gain hundreds of thousands of women's signatures on petitions advocating
the abolition of slavery. They wanted to ensure that a victory in the war would
end slavery, and they also hoped to demonstrate the importance of women
to the war effort and thereby increase the chances for women's rights legislation in the war's aftermath.

When the war ended, Jacobs continued her work in the company of her
daughter, Louisa. They joined thousands of black and white teachers from the
North, many sent by missionary societies, and newly freed blacks in the South. All
of these women and men worked to give meaning to the freedom so recently
granted to former slaves. Southern blacks needed land, jobs, clothing, shelter,
and education; and for a brief moment it seemed that their needs might be
answered through a combination of federal intervention and the voluntary labor
of African Americans and their white allies. Congress established the Freedmen's
Bureau immediately after the war to assist former slaves in their efforts to find
jobs, legalize marriages, purchase land, and learn to read and write. Soon, however, white planters managed to regain control of their lands, demanding that the
federal government protect their rights to the property they owned prior to the

war. At the same time, it became clear that some of the whites who volunteered their services in the South believed that African Americans were racially inferior and were not ready for economic, political, or social equality with whites.

As conditions deteriorated in Savannah, Harriet and Louisa Jacobs decided to return North and work for the cause of freedpeople there. They arrived just as the American Equal Rights Association was formed to carry on the work of abolitionists and women's rights advocates in the postwar period. Within a year, however, the association was riven with conflicts over proposed amendments to the U.S. Constitution, which some members saw as crucial to maintaining the rights of African Americans and others viewed as privileging black men over black and white women. Unable to sustain the alliances that had supported her work as an abolitionist and an advocate for fugitives and then freedpeople, Jacobs retired from public life, a symbol of both the hopes and the bitter disappointments that African Americans faced in the postwar world.

Marching Without a Lance: Giving Meaning to Freedom

JEAN FAGAN YELLIN

> Be not discouraged. Deeds of mercy moveth even the heart of a man who may hate his Brother. We must march on though with but a broken lance, though we have no lance at all.
> —Harriet Jacobs, Alexandria, July 2, 1865

In November 1865, Harriet and Louisa Jacobs stepped off the gang plank onto the dock in Savannah and walked straight into the center of the epic national struggle for black autonomy. Georgia's superintendent of education had pleaded with the New England Freedmen's Aid Society to send teachers, and the Jacobs women had come as the Society's representatives. Their voyage had begun badly. They had booked staterooms, but when they boarded, the captain told them they would have to travel in steerage. They protested, and after prolonged negotiations, were offered a compromise. They could keep their quarters if they agreed to eat there alone, and not with the other travelers. The old sense of enclosure stifling her, Jacobs refused. "I don't care about the meals, but I cannot be shut up in the stateroom." Finally the captain backed down, warning, "Southerners never would stand it to be put on an equality with colored people."

Despite his warning, the voyage passed without incident, but when their ship docked in Savannah harbor, the superintendent came aboard to tell them that they were not

Harriet and Louisa Jacobs taught at this school for freedpeople in Alexandria, Virginia. The photo, taken in 1864, shows the wide range of men, women and children who benefited from the school's programs. Photographs like this one both documented the activities of Jacobs and her coworkers and encouraged organizations like the New York Society of Friends to continue to support such educational efforts.

needed. Jacobs and her daughter sensed something amiss and instead of complying, went ashore anyway. The city rose above them on a plateau forty feet higher than the river, its steep embankment bolstered by rocks. Its terraces were white, bleached with water-stained cotton worked by pickers—women paid twenty-five cents a day, men ten dollars a week. After picking the good cotton loose and spreading it out on large canvases, the workers threw aside the damaged fibers to be swept into windrows. "There you see our blood," an old woman said. "Three hundred weight when the sun went down or three hundred lashes, sure!" Beyond the wharves and embankments, in the city's parks, cows and goats grazed freely, shaded by willow-leaf live oaks and evergreens. Savannah's Forsyth Park, on the outskirts, boasted a fountain decorated with dolphins and a crane. But it was not the shady parks that most impressed Savannah's northern visitors that November. It was the softness of the air, sweet with the scent of jasmine and flowering plum, and the bird sounds everywhere welcoming them.

Although Jacobs told the superintendent she was staying on because her sponsors wanted her to report on the condition of Savannah's freedmen, she may also have been curious about the city. Famous for its live oaks and notorious as the port of the *Wanderer*—in 1859 thought to be the last slave ship to enter an American port—Savannah was the city that General William Tecumseh Sherman had famously presented to President Lincoln as a Christmas gift in 1864. Only weeks afterward, Sherman and Secretary of War Stanton had held an historic meeting with a delegation of local black leaders. When questioned, their spokesman, Reverend Garrison Frazier, said, "The freedom, as I understand it, promised by the proclamation, is taking us from under the yoke of bondage and placing us where we can reap the fruit of our own labor, and take care of ourselves and assist the Government in maintaining our freedom." Four days later, Sherman followed the ministers' lead by issuing his famous Special Field Order Number 15, setting aside for the freedmen "Sherman's Reservation"—the rice fields and the islands off the Georgia–South Carolina coast that the planters had abandoned.

Among activists, Savannah was known for its black-led Savannah Education Association. The city's African American community had met Sherman's victorious troops with praise and thanksgiving—and with an agenda. In January, the people were organizing schools and arranging for the establishment of a freedmen's hospital. In February, the thousand black men and women gathered at the Second African Baptist Church listened, rapt, as General Rufus Saxton, speaking in the name of the federal government, pronounced them all free and promised them forty acres and a mule. Led by their ministers, the community immediately began organizing the Savannah Educational Association to establish free schools for themselves and their children. At one meeting, an observer watched, amazed: "Men and women came to the table with a grand rush—much like the charge of Union Soldiers on a rebel battery! Fast as their names could be written, by a swift penman, the Greenbacks were laid upon the table in sums from one to ten dollars, until the pile footed up the round sum of *seven hundred* and *thirty dollars*." Within weeks, African American teachers were instructing black children in the Bryan and Oglethorpe schools.

White American Missionary Association representatives who traveled to Savannah to organize their own schools reported with surprise that "a goodly number" of the children already knew how to read and spell, and "others evinced considerable knowledge of arithmetic, geography and writing." They did not know that black schools had been operating in Savannah for decades, despite an 1817 city council ordinance that outlawed teaching slaves and free African Americans, and despite passage of a similar state law a dozen years later. Civil War nurse Susie King Taylor, now returned to the city, recalled that she had learned to read and write in the 1850s at the school on Bay Lane taught by Mrs. Mary Woodhouse and her daughter Mary Jane, free black women; later, her books wrapped in paper to mask them from the whites, she walked to Mrs. Mary Beasley's to continue her studies. Some of the secret schools operated for as long as thirty years. Officials seem to have known—and to have overlooked—the fact that James Porter was using his music classes to teach reading and writing. Among the underground teachers, only James M. Simms had been punished. Although publicly whipped, Simms had continued his work until he was fined $100; then he had gone to Boston.

Now Porter had become secretary of the Savannah Educational Association and principal of the Bryan Free School, housed in the old Bryan slave market at the corner of St. Julian and Bernard. Simms, too, was back. Recently ordained, he was serving as a missionary and as a Freedmen's Bureau superintendent of rice plantations on the river. While supporters of black autonomy cheered their work, Reverend S. W. Magill, sent to Savannah to organize the American Missionary Association schools, did not. "It will not do, of course, to leave these people to themselves," he counseled his northern brethren. "However good men they may be, they know nothing about educating . . . I fear they will be jealous & sullen, if I attempt to place t management in t hands of our white teachers. But this must be done, in order to make t schs effective for good."

Commenting on the tensions between the northern white-led group and the local black-led organization, a representative of the New England Freedmen's Aid Society noted "a rather peculiar feeling among the colored citizens here, in regard to the management of the schools. Among them are men of real ability and intelligence; and they have a natural and praiseworthy pride in keeping their educational institutions in their own hands. There is a jealousy of the superintendence of the white man in this matter. What they desire is assistance without control." Freedmen's Bureau Inspector of Schools John W. Alvord concurred: "Their management and teaching may not equal that of our northern instructors, but the people are ambitious to make their effort *themselves*—are proud of it—pay for it cheerfully according to their means." As the months passed, however, it was becoming increasingly obvious that Savannah's black-led schools were having funding and administrative problems, and the New England Freedmen's Aid Society, attempting to provide "assistance without control," began paying the salaries of Simms's "native teachers."

In the Georgia low country, the freedmen were planting the fields they believed their own. Up the rivers on the rice plantations (which for decades the masters had annually left to their overseers during the malarial season), the homogeneous and stable slave population shared a strong sense of community and a clear sense of autonomy. On the sea islands (abandoned by the planters during the war) black families from Beaufort, Hilton Head, and Savannah came and built settlements under the leadership of Freedmen's Bureau Agent Tunis Campbell, a black activist from the North. But the planters intended to have their land back and to restore plantation production. Although General Saxton reiterated that "the lands which have been taken possession of by this bureau have been solemnly pledged to the freedmen," President Andrew Johnson forced General Oliver O. Howard to issue Circular Number Fifteen, functionally restoring the plantations to the planters. Fearing that the Army would enforce compliance, Howard reluctantly began permitting the dispossession of black farmers who had claimed land under Sherman's order. After a military court restored St. Catherine's Island to Jacob Waldburg—in 1860 the largest landowner in Liberty County and, with 255 slaves, the second largest slaveholder—black settlers on the islands became deeply alarmed. Four days before Jacobs docked in Savannah, eighty freedmen, hearing that St. Catherine's and Ossebaw Islands had been returned to the planters, came to the city seeking refuge.

When Harriet and Louisa Jacobs arrived in Savannah in late November, both control of the schools and control of the land were at stake. This was, W.E.B. DuBois would write, the central struggle of Reconstruction, the issue that Reverend Frazier had addressed when he spoke to General Sherman of "placing us where we can reap the fruit of our labor, and take care of ourselves." Almost immediately, Harriet and Louisa began reporting to supporters in the North and in England. Their early letters seem to suggest that they might decide to settle in Savannah. Within a week, Louisa opened a school in the city poor-house, now a hospital for freedmen and refugees under the direction of their friend Major Augusta, with whom they had worked in Alexandria [Virginia]. They quickly became acquainted with the Savannah Education Association, reporting that it was operating "six schools in the city. Mr. Bradley is fitting up one of the slave auction rooms to open a seventh."

While Louisa was establishing her school, Jacobs, who had brought bundles of clothing with her, began distributing it to the hospital patients and organizing the convalescents to help. "If you could send me a barrel of hospital stores," she wrote the

New York Quakers, "it would be very acceptable. I have nothing on hand." With Christmas coming, Louisa repeated the strategy successfully used for the Alexandria fair, and "went among the colored people," collecting $25 so that she and mother could cook a holiday dinner for the hospital patients. The meal was simple, Jacobs wrote, "everything is very high." But "every one that could crawl out of bed was at the table, both black and white." In occupied Savannah, a dinner where blacks and whites sat down together was certainly not the norm. Generally the city's white citizens, Jacobs comments, "don't seem to think colored people have any rights or wants."

But change was in the air. Work was beginning on "the erection of an Orphan Asylum and Old Folks' Home," and Jacobs informed her northern sponsors, "my daughter has applied for the situation of matron in the Asylum. I expect to take the Home." The plans made the local papers. The *Savannah National Republican*, headlining "A Great Improvement—Proposed Erection of a Freedmen's Refuge," reported "a number of substantial wooden buildings are shortly to be erected . . . on the vacant land situated in a Southeasterly direction from Forsyth Park." Although approving the new hospital, however, the paper attacked the freedmen it would serve, opining that "hundreds of [them] seem unable to comprehend such a thing as the future. Come day, go day, God send Sunday, is their motto, and they care little to provide for the wants of tomorrow." Within this hostile public climate, work on the refuge quickly became stymied, and Jacobs's Savannah letters express the heightening tensions in the city. Increasingly, they suggest the growing violence. "We shall be badly off when the military protection is withdrawn."

The occupying Union Army was certainly functioning as protection, but it could also be used by Savannah's powerful to attack black efforts at independence, both in the city and out on the plantations. Military rule had ended in Savannah shortly before Jacob's arrival. The mayor and city fathers had just regained control when Aaron Bradley—like Jacobs, a fugitive slave who had worked with northern abolitionists—appeared and began speaking out for black autonomy. At meetings at the Second African Baptist Church, he advocated local black control of the schools and urged the people on the plantations to resist dispossession and to refuse to sign bad labor contracts with the planters. The American Missionary Association's representative complained: "We were getting along very pleasantly until this Bradley came and if he had stayed away and Mr. Alvord had not paid off the expenses of the Association and determined they should be sustained in this present shape I could have brought every thing under our control and made what is now working badly, more efficient." Bradley was promptly arrested, accused of voicing "seditious and treasonable language," quickly tried before a military commission, found guilty of using "insurrectionary language in public assemblages, inciting lawlessness and disturbance of public peace and good order," and sentenced to one year at hard labor at Fort Pulaski.

Jacobs's letters do not comment on Bradley's speeches or on his trial and sentence. Nor do they discuss the January convention of the Georgia Equal Rights and Education Association, organized to secure full citizenship rights for the freed people. They do, however, consistently address the land question. Visiting rice plantations on both sides of the river, Jacobs praises the work of the local black leader James Simms, reporting that she even has arranged "to teach an industrial department in connexion with some of his schools." She expresses concern, however, about the future of the freedmen's settlements where the schools are located: "Many of them will be turned over to their old masters the first of January."

Jacobs was eager to visit the people on the plantations, but violence ran unchecked in the countryside and, she explains to her northern supporters, "you have no protection. Things have come to such a pass, that you are not sure of it, even from our officers. The place Mr. Eberheart [state superintendent of schools] wished me to go, he refused to send a white teacher to, saying it was not a fit place for her." She could not even visit the smallpox patients, as she had in Alexandria. Here, "they are carried five miles in the country, put in tents, without stores, scarce any bedding. More have died from exposure and starvation than from the disease. I have made soup and sent it, but you are not always sure they get it."

Six weeks after arriving in Savannah, Jacobs tallied up the numbers to give her sponsors some idea of the scope of the refugee effort. The city's African American population numbered 10,500, with thousands more on the plantations on both sides of the river. James Simms was supervising 4,020 freedmen, and this group, she fears, are endangered. Although promised land, "now these people are found fault with for believing the government would help them. All the men that planted rice have done well," she reports, but "I am afraid they will not be allowed to plant again."

Two weeks later she wrote again, reporting the expulsion of the people from the plantations. Many, she explains, are refugees from Florida or South Carolina, where their masters had taken them early in the war to keep them from the Union armies. Now they are again being displaced. "It is a pitiful sight to go down to the Bluff where the poor creatures are landed. You will see crowds of them huddled around a few burning sticks, so ragged and filthy they scarce look like human beings."

At year's end, the *Savannah Daily Herald* announced that by Special Order of Brigadier General Tillson, all freedmen who refused or failed to sign contracts for their labor by January 10, 1866, "shall be hired under contract by the Authorized Agent of said Bureau." Jacobs explained to her northern audience what this meant: the planters were attempting to use the contracts to reestablish their authority over their former slaves. Many of these agreements, she writes, "are very unjust. They are not allowed to have a boat or musket. They are not allowed to own a horse, cow, or pig. Many of them already own them, but must sell them if they remain on the plantations." One master who owned 300 acres of rice land "wants to employ thirty hand; make the contract for the year, at ten dollars per month; gives them rations and four dollars a month out of their wages. When the crop is laid by, the master has two-thirds, the laborer has one-third, *deducting the pay for the rations.* Many of the freed people," she reports, "are leaving this place."

Ten days later, Jacobs reported, "In every direction the colored people are being turned from the plantations when unwilling to comply with the hard proposals of the planters. . . . The Bureau," she charged, "only assists them in making contracts," and these "are sometimes very severe and unjust." The people are not permitted to rent land or work on shares, but "must work under their former overseers. . . . They cannot leave the plantation without permission. If a friend calls to see them a fine is imposed of one dollar, and a second offence breaks the contract. They work for ten dollars and rations." On the river plantations, "the people are expecting the return of their old masters. Poor things! Some are excited; others so dispirited that they cannot work. They say, 'I can't eat, I can't sleep, for tinking of de hard time coming on me again; my heart 'pears to be all de time quiverin'; I knows 'tis trouble.' . . . On the rice plantations that I have visited, the people are badly off, God pity them. I lose sight of their rags when I see how degraded and hard-hearted slavery has made them."

Two weeks later, she wrote again. "I must tell you about my island poor; they have increased in numbers, mostly women and children. They are not allowed to plant, and are expecting every day to be driven off. These are the poor creatures from the interior of South Carolina; they did not know they were free until last month." Louisa, joining her mother's efforts to awaken their northern audience to the unfair conditions being forced on the people, indignantly detailed the contract demanded by one harsh master. "A boat, a mule, pigs and chickens, are prohibited; produce of any kind not allowed to be raised; permission must be asked to go off of the place; a visit from a friend punished with a fine of $1.00, and the second offence breaks the contract. Is this freedom, or encouragement to labor? Those who have had a taste of freedom will not make contracts with such men."

The people who resisted signing these contracts were being expelled by the Army. In mid-February, a *Savannah Daily Herald* report beginning, "There was nothing of any interest to our readers in this [Freedmen's] Court today," announced that a military squad had been sent to one plantation "to bring down some two hundred and fifty refractory negroes who refuse to make contracts."

Early in March, both Harriet and Louisa sent long letters north. Jacobs's was to L[ydia] Maria Child, who arranged to have it published in *The Independent*. For this newspaper's large northern audience, Jacobs again described the predicament of the thousands of freedmen who had landpasses allowing them to farm the land on the "Sherman reservation." "I visited some of the plantations, and I was rejoiced to see such a field of profitable labor opened for these poor people. If they could have worked these lands for two years, they would have needed no help from any one." Under Presidential Reconstruction, however, "Johnson has pardoned their old masters, and the poor loyal freedmen are driven off the soil, that it may be given back to traitors." She again condemns as unfair the contracts they are offered: "One of these laborers told me that, after working hard all the season to raise the master's crop, the share he received was only one dollar and fifty cents." Still, she tries to sound positive: "I am in hopes that something will yet be done for them by Congress; and therefore, I have earnestly exhorted them to remain on the plantations till ordered off by the authorities of the United States. But one by one the plantations have been given back to the rebels, till there are not five left." Then, dropping her public voice, she allowed herself a personal lament: "Oh, it is so discouraging!"

Louisa wrote to *The Freedmen's Record* to give her readers a sense of Savannah, where the old and new were colliding. "The old spirit of the system, 'I am the master and you are the slave,'" she explained, "is not dead in Georgia." She described a confrontation between their next door neighbors (who, though poor, had owned slaves), and their newly hired servant. The mistress struck the maid, a woman with "the look and air of one not easily crushed by circumstances." Louisa reports, "as I looked at the black woman's firey eye, her quivering form, and heard her dare her assailant to strike again, I was proud of her metal." When the mistress's husband appeared ready to hit her again, the maid "drew back, telling him that she was no man's slave; that she was as free as he, and would take the law upon his wife for striking her. He blustered, but there he stood deprived of his old power to kill her if it had so pleased him. . . . She went to the Bureau, and very soon had things made right."

Savannah's freedwomen were no longer complying with the ritualized subordination they had endured in slavery. Before the Union occupation, black people were not allowed to walk on the west side of Bull Street. Now, Louisa writes, when her friend was pushed off by a white man, "she gave him to understand that Sherman's march had made Bull Street as much hers as his." Not only access to the sidewalk, but fashion, too, was being revolutionized. Before the occupation, women of color had been forbidden to wear veils. Now they created a new style. "After the army came in, they went out with two on,—one over the face, the other on the back of the bonnet."

Life in the city was in transition, but all the changes were not necessarily empowering Savannah's black population. At the beginning of 1866, the superintendent of schools had privately proposed to reorganize the educational system and make the black school board "auxiliary only." By February, the American Missionary Association's Cooley could assert, "Now we have nearly all the schools in the Western part of the city and only the single school of Miss Jenness and that of Miss Jacobs in the Eastern part [are out of our control] if I may except a few private schools." Early in spring, he reports the total defeat of the black-led schools: "The teachers of the Savannah Educational Association have all withdrawn from that organization and are seeking employment elsewhere." He is, he writes, prepared "to place the whole management under our northern teachers and use any colored assistants in that position only." "The field is," he declared, "now virtually our own."

Louisa's Lincoln School, black-led and black-taught, survived. She had located it in the eastern section of the city where, upon first coming to Savannah, she had seen "hundreds of children . . . running in the streets that ought to be in school." When the new freedmen's hospital was built, she moved her classroom there. She and her mother also moved into Dr. Augusta's home, close to their work—and away from the supervision of whites. In Savannah, as in Alexandria, Louisa found "much to encourage me in my labors." A committed teacher, she delighted in the "bright faces" of her students. Acknowledging that her schoolroom (half of a hospital ward, with the old men on the other side of the partition) is "rough," she describes it as "large and airy." More important, "the freedmen," she assures her northern patrons, "are interested in the education of their children." She finds it odd that "the Southerners take no interest in the education of the freed people. It seems strange, when we consider how their interest must be linked in the future." A Pennsylvanian visiting at examination week wrote that he was impressed by her school, and other Northerners agreed. "I have children who could not spell when I organized the school in November, now reading well and studying Arithmetic and Geography," Louisa wrote in May. "This does not," she points out to her New England readers, "show inferiority of race." Still, "it will be a long time before things can be righted for the colored man South."

That spring, while Congress and the President warred over the shape of Reconstruction, Jacobs was appealing to her northern sponsors for seeds so the freedmen could plant. In response, the New York Quakers collected a large quantity, and L. Maria Child wrote, after hearing Jacob's plea, "I hastened to do up, label, and send through the mail fifty four different kinds of seeds; a job which took a day." In Georgia, Jacobs was giving them out, along with information on improved methods of agriculture, to freedmen who had rented plots of land.

But the seeds of violence were sprouting like weeds throughout the former Confederacy. The *Loyal Georgian* reported that in South Carolina "five white men, disguised with masks," entered a black family's house, raped the woman, then went to a shop nearby and robbed the black owner. In Memphis, a traffic accident involving two horse-drawn hacks, one driven by a black man and the other by a white, escalated into three days of racial violence. When it was over, forty-eight were dead—forty-six of them black—five black women had been raped, and hundreds of black homes, schools, and churches were ruined or burned. The Georgia Education Association commented that "in many counties, the intelligent colored men who attempted to organize educational Associations were driven by their employers from the plantation where they were employed. Many planters would not allow the children of those in their employ to attend the schools after they were established." In Jacobs's Savannah, the *Daily News and Herald* reported in July that near the canal on Fahn Street, a dispute between black and white cartmen resulted in one black man being severely beaten and another being shot to death. As the paper describes the incident, after a shouting match, the black man called the white "a rebel son of a b———." The white man started beating him with a stick and then tried to drive away, but found himself "surrounded with an excited and angry crowd of negroes threatening him. We are informed," the story continues, "that Samuel Whitfield pulled out a revolver and threatened to shoot, some of the crowd at the time urging him to do so. The white man then rose in the wagon, and leveling his gun at the crowd fired, the load, consisting of buckshot, taking effect on the body of Whitfield."

The *Boston Freedmen's Journal* presents a different picture. From Savannah, James Simms wrote that Whitfield "and some other Colored Persons Seeig A White Man A Citty Cartman Beating another Colored Man Cartman . . . Supposing the Colored Man Beated was Dead . . . Followed the two White Men up in the Citty that they May not Make their escape. . . . They Stoped the Cart and Commanded them to Halt and Not Follow them as they Would Shoot them, yet the party with Mr Whitfield continued to follow them . . . Whereupon the Man Allen that had a gun in the Cart fired into the Party following them, and the Load Taking effect in the Breast of Mr Whitfield Killed him Almost Amediately." Amazingly, Simms continues, the beaten man is recovering and the man who beat him is being held. But, he explains to his New England audience, "the State Court . . . Will Surely Justify Any White Man in Beating or Killing a Colored Man on a Trivial offence Such is the State of Law and Justice here."

Harriet and Louisa Jacobs—like both James Simms and the murdered Samuel Whitfield—were connected with the New England Freedmen's Aid Society. The day after Whitfield's murder, Harriet and Louisa Jacobs tried to leave Savannah. Whether they had planned their departure long before, or decided to leave when they heard of the shooting, is not known. As usual, Louisa bought their first-class tickets for New York, but when they tried to board the steamship *Leo*, they were told they would have to travel in steerage, and this time, their protests were useless. In Boston, *The Freedmen's Record,* recording the incident, writes that the mother and daughter "were both put off the boat in a very rough manner, and compelled to remain," and comments, "We hope the matter will be followed up, and the rights of citizens in public conveyances will be secured." In contrast, the report in Savannah's *Daily News and Herald* ends—not with the hope that Jim Crow will be stopped—but by dismissing Jacobs and her daughter as troublemaking outsiders: "The women, we understand, are from the North. They had been employed in some of the colored schools of this city and were about to return North for the summer." . . .

[In 1866,] when the issue of the freed people's citizenship was still unresolved, Harriet's and Louisa's co-workers in Georgia had formed an Equal Rights Association. Now in the North, Jacobs's colleagues in the Women's National Loyal League were again organizing, and at their first annual meeting since the war, the Eleventh National Woman's Rights Convention reconstituted itself as the American Equal Rights Association. Aware that New York State was facing its periodic constitutional revision, the delegates resolved to mount a campaign urging that the state constitution be changed to grant equal rights to all "without distinctions of color, sex or race."

Among the speakers was the black activist-poet Frances Ellen Watkins Harper. Harper's presentation alerted her New York audience to precisely the violence and racism that Jacobs and Louisa faced in Savannah: "You white women speak here of rights. I speak of wrongs. I, as a colored woman, have had in this country an education which has made me feel as I were in the situation of Ishmael, my hand against every man, and every man's hand against me." Then, she reversed the dominant notion that black women were backward and needed to change: "While there exists this brutal element in society which tramples upon the feeble and treads down the weak, I tell you that if there is any class of people who need to be lifted out of their airy nothings and selfishness, it is the white women of America." Now Louisa—in her middle thirties and without students to teach, a school to run, or an invalid to nurse—made a surprising decision. She would follow Harper onto the platform and speak for equal rights. She would fulfil her mother's old dream of becoming a public lecturer.

The *Standard* ran the announcement early in February: Louisa Jacobs had arrived in upstate New York and was lecturing in Herkimer County for the American Equal Rights Association. She was billed with Charles Lenox Remond, for thirty years committed to the movement—"the first black abolitionist lecturer and the most eloquent until the appearance of Frederick Douglass." . . . Now he was back on the lecture circuit, working for the Equal Rights Association. Although never an easy man and in his late fifties suffering from poor health, Remond reported positively on the "conventions" he and Louisa were holding.

At Johnstown, where Elizabeth Cady Stanton had made their arrangements, they held a "capital" meeting with a friendly audience. But as the days passed, the weather turned against them. Severe snowstorms and bad roads were hindering their progress, and worse, they were feeling cut off from everyone and everything. "Both Miss Jacobs and myself suffer exceedingly for want of the current news," Remond writes. "I have lost for three weeks all run of the proceedings of Congress, and wonder sometimes if New York city is still extant!" Despite this sense of isolation, however, "the movement is, so far, I think, a success. . . . the word *fail* finds no place in our vocabulary." They were working their way through the Mohawk Valley, and a week later Remond reports encountering some hostility—people "harsh and malignant towards our race and their rights." Nonetheless, he and Louisa were making headway. "They can curse and call us by all manner of names on the sidewalks, upon the corner of the streets, and in the bar-rooms; but in the meeting we pay them off with both principle and compound interest."

After years as a reviled "nigger teacher" in Alexandria and Savannah, Louisa was not unaccustomed to insults. Still, it was hard to be cursed in public, and having Remond with her on those hostile sidewalks was reassuring. When, a decade earlier, her mother had dreamed that she might "do something" for the cause by lecturing in England, she had never imagined that one day her [Louisa] would be touring upstate New York for the movement, doing the same public work as her elders Frances Harper and Maria Stewart. (Celebrated as the first American-born woman to mount the public platform, Stewart, like Louisa, had spent the war years teaching black refugees.) . . .

Louisa and Remond depended on the hospitality of their supporters. More than a decade earlier when William C. Nell had spoken in Herkimer County, he had enjoyed a warm welcome from Zenas Brockett's family, with whom Louisa was then staying. Now it was she who was the traveling lecturer. Louisa took the time to walk the grounds of her old school building in Clinton, although Kellogg's Domestic Seminary had long since closed. She also took advantage of her itinerary to renew old friendships with the family at Brockett's Bridge and to bask in their pride in her work. Then—like Nell before her—she collected their donation to the cause.

At Cohoes, famous for its cotton and knitting mills, Louisa and Remond were joined by John S.'s old fellow-lecturer Parker Pillsbury, Universalist minister Olympia Brown, and young Bessie Bisbee of Boston who, like Louisa, was new to the platform. Here the "factory girls" crowded the hall to hear Susan B. Anthony argue that women needed the vote. With it, they could put an end to their twelve-hour shifts and demand a ten-hour day—"to say nothing of the 8.—and also equal place & pay—the moment they should hold the ballot in their hands." Writing to Amy Post, Anthony enthused about these "capital" meetings and about her co-workers: "Louisa Jacobs—who was with us—promises first best.—She is everything proper & right in matter and manner—private and public—It is good to have two new helpers and *young* too—yes and good looking." The local press, which evidently did not recognize Louisa as African American, described her only as "a fair speaker . . . tall and quite dignified in appearance, a brunette, probably not thirty years of age."

At Syracuse, Stanton joined them and, with the Jacobses' old friend Samuel J. May in the chair, the audience formed its own Equal Rights Association. But as winter wore into spring, the speakers' heavy schedule—they were often addressing two meetings a day—wore them down. Pillsbury took to his bed, and Stanton's voice began to fail. At Orleans, the papers report, "in consequence of a severe cold, Mrs. Stanton was so hoarse that she was able to speak but a few minutes."

They needed better support. Privately, Anthony was complaining about their meager funds and about the half-hearted backing offered by the *Standard*—which, she protested, "does not officially plead the whole question of Suffrage as an inherent right of Woman as the Negro man." . . .

Short of money or not, the Equal Rights Association speakers arguing the need to extend the franchise consistently addressed the situation of the freedwoman. In New York City, Olympia Brown asserted: "If there be any person who needs the ballot, it is the negro woman. Some say the woman is protected by father and husband, and therefore needs not the ballot. But it may be in the case of the negro woman the father may perchance be the very white man who drove her to her daily toil, and the only man whom she had known as husband has been of the white cast, who made her only the object of his lust."

Linking the freedwoman's need for the vote with her historic sexual exploitation in slavery resonated for Jacobs and Louisa. But Equal Rights speakers were also arguing that the freedwoman needed the vote not to protect her from the abuses of her white former master, but to protect her from legal marriage to her freed husband. The papers quote Anthony as saying, "Remember that in slavery the black woman has known nothing of the servitude of the marriage laws of the Northern States. She has lived so far in freedom. . . . But under the new dispensation, with legal marriage established among the black race as among the white race, it subjects the black woman to all the servitude and dependence which the white woman has hitherto suffered in the North." Making this argument, Anthony was attacking the freedman's character: "What kind of master do you give her? Not one educated to the sense of woman's equality that we have here, but one whose only idea of having any right of control over another person is that which has been taught to him by his master, which is the tyranny of the lash. Those men, suddenly raised to power, in all their ignorance, will become, as husbands, the greatest tyrants the world has yet seen." Stanton, too, was making black men a target, along with immigrants, in her stock speech "Reconstruction." "In view of the fact that the freedmen of the south and the millions of foreigners now crowding our western shores are all in the progress of events to be enfranchised, the best interests of the nation demand that we outweigh this incoming poverty ignorance & degradation, with the wealth education & refinement of the women of the republic."

Equal Rights audiences were being given mixed messages. At Utica, Remond, condemning the widespread sexual abuse of slave women by their masters, asserted that "whites have so diluted color that few can tell where the white man commences and the African leaves off." But in Rochester, the press reports that Stanton claimed the oppression of women in slavery was not as terrible as the oppression of women in marriage. "She said that the black women of the South under slavery were more free than they would be under the restraint of church marriages, liberated from chattel slavery and made slaves to their husbands. . . . even the poor slave woman understood, how much worse was the slavery of woman to man than that which they endured as chattels."

At Troy, Anthony went even further. Reversing the roles of master and slave, she identified the white master as the black slave woman's rescuer and the male black slave as her tyrant: "She has not the master to appeal to against her husband as when they were slaves. Where, then, unless the ballot is placed in her hands, is she likely to secure her privileges?"

Louisa spoke on the second day. Uncomfortable, she nervously read her remarks, asserting that the events of the war years "have a tendency to melt the American people into one great family" and stating that woman's presence at the ballot-box would not "increase public dissentions." On the contrary, she argued, "woman needs the ballot to enable her to work out her mission in life, to ensure her support and keep her from temptation." But regaining her seat, Louisa found her situation increasingly difficult.

The problem was not only that she knew she was not a public speaker. The problem was also that she knew the freedwomen's condition. She had spent years working with refugees in Alexandria and Savannah—with women who had done everything they could to protect themselves, their children, and their men from their former masters. She well remembered these women coming asking to be married in church so that they could gain the security they believed free white women enjoyed. How could she share the platform with speakers who—in the name of asserting the rights of freedwomen— were attacking the freedmen? How could she face her audiences? Actually, how could she face any audiences? Perhaps the idea that she could fulfil her mother's dream of becoming a platform speaker was wrong-headed. If she were a public figure it might please her mother, but how could she live that life? Certainly she shared her mother's social conscience and her politics, but a life on the platform was not for her.

In the spring, the American Equal Rights Association held its annual meeting at the Church of the Pilgrims in New York City. Their effort to incorporate voting rights for women and African Americans into the new New York State constitution had been a failure. Nevertheless, Anthony announced hopeful signs of progress: nine U.S. senators voted in favor of suffrage for women as well as for black men in the District of Columbia, and the legislatures of Kansas and Wisconsin had struck the words "white male" from their constitutions.

Throughout this meeting, the attacks on the freedman continued, despite the presence of black leaders like Remond, Robert and Harriet Purvis, and George T. Downing. When Downing pointedly asked "whether he had rightly understood that Mrs. Stanton and Mrs. Mott were opposed to the enfranchisement of the colored man, unless the ballot should also be accorded to women at the same time," Stanton side-stepped and renewed her assault on the freedman. "I would not trust him with all my rights; degraded, oppressed himself, he would be more despotic with the governing power than even our Saxon rulers are. I desire that we go into the kindom together." Another white feminist, Frances D. Gage, exclaiming, "I shall speak for the slave woman at the South," recalled her refugee work. Gage asserted that "the men came to me and wanted to be married, because they said if they were married in the church, they could manage the women, and take care of their money. . . . But the women came to me and said, 'we don't want to be married in the church, because if we are our husbands will whip the children and whip us if they want to; they are no better than our old master.'" Sojourner Truth, the black evangelist and reformer, agreed: "if colored men get their rights, and not colored women theirs, you see the colored men will be masters over the women, and it will be just as bad as it was before. . . . Now colored men have the right to vote [in the District of Columbia]; and what I want is to have colored women have the right to vote."

But long-time white abolitionist Abby Kelley Foster protested that the condition of women and of former slaves were not analogous. In the South the freedman was "without wages, without family rights, whipped and beaten by thousands, given up to the most horrible outrages, without that protection which his value as property formerly gave him." Echoing Jacobs's letters from Savannah, with prescience she warned, "he is liable without farther guarantees, to be plunged into peonage." Is it not unjust, she asked, "to wish to postpone his security against present woes and future enslavement till woman shall obtain political rights?" As the meeting prepared to adjourn, Remond

SECOND READER.   35

LESSON XV.

cock	wash	pig	too
crows	dawn	dig	two
food	bound	hoe	scrub
wake	clean	plow	bake
home	know	noise	eyes
cheer	knives	kneel	school

What letter is silent in hoe? in clean? Say just, not *jist* catch, not *cotch;* sit, not *set;* father, not *fader.*

THE FREEDMAN'S HOME.

SEE this home! How neat, how warm, how full of cheer, it looks! It seems as if the sun shone in there all the day long. But it takes more than the light of the sun to make a home bright all the time. Do you know what it is? It is love.

The American Tract Society published *The Freedman's Second Reader* in 1865, which was used to educate former slaves throughout the South. Freedpeople eagerly sought education in the post-Civil War period, demanding to learn reading and writing skills that were denied them under slavery. Their lessons, like Lesson XV shown here, often combined practical education with moral guidance rooted in northern middle-class family ideals.

tried to retrieve at least minimal support for the extension of suffrage to black men. "Since this platform is the only place in this country where the whole question of human rights may now be considered, it seemed to me fitting that the right of the colored man to a vote, should have a place at the close of the meeting."

The discussion continued when the Equal Rights Association met the following year. The question was now tightly focused on the wording of the proposed Fourteenth Amendment—which, while naming the former slaves citizens, for the first time would insert the word "male" into the United States Constitution. Again Stanton and Anthony voiced their opposition to "the enfranchisement of another class of ignorant men to be lifted above their heads, to be their law-makers and Governors; to prescribe the moral code and political status of their daughters."

The debate climaxed in the spring of 1869. With full citizenship granted to blacks by the ratification of the Fourteenth Amendment, the Equal Rights Association met to discuss the proposed Fifteenth Amendment—which would award the suffrage to male freedmen—and to suggest a Sixteenth Amendment granting the vote to women. At this meeting, Stanton famously opposed extending the vote to black men and male immigrants while denying it to women: "Think of Patrick and Sambo and

Hans and Yung Tung, who do not know the difference between a monarchy and a republic, who can not read the Declaration of Independence or Webster's spelling-book, making laws for Lucretia Mott, Ernestine L. Rose, and Anna E. Dickinson." And from the floor, Douglass famously responded: "When women, because they are women, are hunted down through the cities of New York and New Orleans; when they are dragged from their houses and hung upon lamp-posts; when their children are torn from their arms, and their brains dashed out upon the pavement; when they are objects of insult and outrage at every turn; when they are in danger of having their homes burnt down over their heads; when their children are not allowed to enter schools; then they will have an urgency to obtain the ballot equal to our own."

Frances Harper, one of the few black women present, joined the debate in the evening. Stanton notes that "when it was a question of race, she let the lesser question of sex go. But the white women all go for sex, letting race occupy a minor position. . . . If the nation could only handle one question, she would not have the black women put a single straw in the way, if only the men of the race could obtain what they wanted."

Harper would continue to try to work with the white feminists, but Louisa Jacobs's 1867 speaking tour for equal rights marked the last time either mother or daughter would play a public role on behalf of social change in the United States. On the murderous streets of Savannah, they had learned that the struggle for land was lost. On the angry lecture platforms in the North, they discovered that the effort to mount a struggle for equal rights was also finished—at least for the present.

Questions for Study and Review

1. Describe the different roles played by northern and southern blacks, northern whites, the federal government, and the military in advancing the interests of newly freed African Americans in the aftermath of the Civil War.

2. In what ways did African American women and men express their newfound freedom?

3. What were the greatest hopes and the greatest disappointments of Harriet and Louisa Jacobs in the years following the Civil War? How did their relations to women's organizations and political power compare to that of the benevolent ladies and women reformers discussed by Anne Boylan?

4. How did debates over the Fourteenth and Fifteenth Amendments tear apart the prewar antislavery coalition?

Suggested Readings and Web Sites

Carol Faulkner, *Women's Radical Reconstruction: The Freedmen's Aid Movement* (2004)
Noralee Frankel, *Freedom's Women: Black Women and Families in Civil War Era Mississippi* (1999)
Jacqueline Jones, *Soldiers of Light and Love: Northern Teachers and Georgia Blacks, 1865–1873* (1980)
Nell Painter, *Sojourner Truth: A Life, A Symbol* (1996)
Leslie Schwalm, *A Hard Fight for We: Women's Transition from Slavery to Freedom in South Carolina* (1997)
Harriet Jacobs Paper Project
    http://harrietjacobspapers.org/
Women's Suffrage
    http://www.winningthevote.org/

Chapter 16

In the aftermath of the Civil War, most southern white women retreated from the public sphere. Chastened by defeat and anxious about the organized efforts of African American women and men to claim their rights as free people, those white women who were able returned eagerly to the domestic sphere. Of course, given the death and destruction suffered by the South during the war, many white women were forced to fend for themselves, find employment, or beg for assistance at government offices. Still, few engaged in organized efforts to rebuild their communities or reform their society. All this changed when white men, including former Confederates, reclaimed control of state governments across the South. It then seemed safe for their wives and daughters to claim a public role, at least in assisting the needy, raising funds for hospitals and other benevolent institutions, supporting women's education, and memorializing the Confederate cause.

One of the few national organizations that actively recruited southern members in the late nineteenth century was the Woman's Christian Temperance Union (WCTU). The WCTU managed to blend conservative and progressive impulses. In the Midwest, where it was founded in 1874, and in many northern cities, it allied itself with labor unions and with the Populist Party, which sought to advance the rights of farmers. Longtime WCTU president Frances Willard even identified herself as a socialist. At the same time, the WCTU accepted racial segregation as a necessary condition of organizing in the South, and Willard enraged some African American women by suggesting that black men who were lynched in the South might have deserved their fate. Ida B. Wells, a leading anti-lynching crusader, denounced Willard's position, arguing that white men used false accusations of rape against black men to justify their brutality. And indeed, Willard's willingness to accept the views of former slave owners reinforced the belief among reform-minded women and men in the North that lynching was a necessary evil.

Although Willard and the WCTU were unwilling to challenge directly the South's racial politics, they did confront southern politicians on matters involving the protection of young women and girls. In the 1880s, the WCTU launched a campaign across the country to raise the legal age of consent for sexual activity. They were concerned that the age of consent for girls was often defined as ten or twelve years old. In advocating for a higher age, preferably fourteen or sixteen, women reformers claimed that girls needed protection from older men—whether family members, neighbors, or employers—who sought to exploit them.

As Leslie Dunlap shows, when the WCTU campaigned in southern states to raise the age of consent, the members immediately confronted the prejudices and fears of white legislators who viewed any protections for women as endangering their "right" of sexual access to African Americans. African American women, too, sought to raise the age of consent, but they framed their demands differently than did the white women of the WCTU. The question, then, was whether and how far white women would compromise their demands in order to gain the support of white legislators in the South. Moreover, by the early twentieth century, some white southerners were revising their views of young white women, seeing them as less innocent than the plantation belles of the prewar era. Single wage-earning women, many of them clustered in the South's growing cities, were especially vulnerable to criticism. Like African American women, they were often portrayed as vixens, seducing unsuspecting men rather than being seduced by them. The age-of-consent campaign, then, touched sensitive nerves in the South and tested the commitments of WCTU leaders to campaign for protection of all women, white and black, rich and poor.

The Reform of Rape Law and the Problem of White Men: Age-of-Consent Campaigns in the Turn-of-the-Century South
Leslie K. Dunlap

> We have looked at the "Negro problem" long enough. Now the time has come for us to right-about-face and study the problem of the white man.
> —Lillian Smith (1945)

In September 1886 the *Atlanta Constitution* publicized a matter its editors preferred to keep silent. In response to a national campaign to reform rape laws led by the Woman's Christian Temperance Union, the *Constitution* excoriated reformers for raising "forbidden subjects."

> It is nothing more nor less than a public indecency for a lot of women to be moving about, discussing such a matter, getting up petitions and signatures, and bringing the subject into such prominence as to make it common talk. There are some evils unfit for public discussion, and this is one of them . . . Some reforms are not to be spoken of in mixed company or mentioned in print.

Women in the WCTU offered a trenchant retort. That very same issue of the newspaper, they pointed out, contained three explicit reports of alleged rape by black men, "dished up with startling headlines and needlessly disgusting particulars." Why, editors of the national WCTU paper asked, were these crimes fit for public discussion, while the legal reform that they proposed was deemed off-limits for public consideration?

Leslie Dunlap, "The Reform of Rape Law and the Problem of White Men," from *Sex, Love, Race*, Martha Hodes, ed. Copyright © by New York University Press. Used by permission of the publisher.

The forbidden subject was the sexual behavior of white men. White newspapers in the post-Reconstruction South featured lurid descriptions of alleged crimes committed by black men against women, especially white women. In contrast, white dailies rarely mentioned white men's crimes against women, black or white. African Americans had long criticized white men's sexual behavior. But the WCTU's campaign to reform rape law, which peaked in the South in the early 1890s, marked the first time that organized southern white women drew public attention to white men's sexual conduct.

Most historians have agreed . . . that late nineteenth-century sex reformers focused their anger on groups of men "other than their own husbands and fathers." Yet this was certainly not the case for black women activists, who regularly and sometimes angrily called upon black men to reform their sexual conduct in the service of "respectability" and "racial uplift." Nor, for a period of time, did white sex reformers displace their criticism of male abuse of sexual power onto men outside their kin networks and social circles. In the WCTU's age-of-consent campaigns, white sex reformers in the South did not invoke charged stereotypes about black rapists or immigrant brothel keepers. In fact, especially in the early years of the campaign, for the most part they avoided descriptions of women facing danger at the hands of black and foreign-born men or roving strangers. This is surprising, considering that these campaigns coincided with an explosion of inflammatory racialized rape rhetoric by white supremacists, escalating violence against African Americans, and the WCTU's own well-known apologies for lynching. Rather, this legal campaign revolved around the sexual behavior of those white men and boys who were assumed to be "respectable." Native-born white men—that is, reformers' "own" husbands, fathers, and sons—became the focus of debate. . . .

This essay examines how white reformers' changing racial ideology shaped their sexual ideology and their practical plans for sex reform in the South. Reform politics of the period brought labor and African American activists into tenuous coalition with WCTU reformers. These practical political alliances shaped sex reform in ways that distinguished them from later antiprostitution campaigns of the 1910s. Once disfranchisement [of African American men] quashed the reform movements that energized early age-of-consent campaigns, white women activists abandoned the African American and labor allies whose political activity had enabled them to challenge powerful white men. The solidification of segregation and white supremacy tempered white sex reformers' challenge; by 1910 reformers took pains to emphasize that white women were the primary focus of their reform efforts and that prostitution, not rape, constituted a threat to southern social order.

Southern white sex reformers, who had a distinctive stake in maintaining racial hierarchy, held white men accountable for both intraracial tension and interracial conflict. At the most immediate level, the sexual actions of many individual white men posed daily practical problems for black and white women, as well as black men. But for all these actors, elite white men's sexual power also indicated their systemic power over southern legal, political, and economic institutions. Challenging white men's sexual prerogatives, then, entailed confronting white men's political hegemony. Activists and scholars since Frederick Douglass and Ida B. Wells have argued that white southerners fashioned images of black male sexuality in response to African Americans' political agency. So, too, were images of white male sexuality tied to the political power of white men. Reformers' struggles to control the sexual conduct of white men were part and parcel of broader challenges to white men's political and economic control.

The efforts of African American activists and legislators set the precedent for white women's sex reform initiatives. In the 1890s black women criticized white men's sexual behavior; unlike white women, they focused consistently on white men's aggression against all women. At the height of the age-of-consent debates, Ida B. Wells directed the public spotlight at white men's sexual crimes, publicizing the names of those who had raped black women and girls. White men, she argued, were "not so desirous of punishing rapists as they pretend." In 1905 the Baptist activist Nannie H. Burroughs offered an incisive assessment of public silence surrounding white men and rape:

> Why is it that we do not "hear" of the white men of the United States committing out-
> rages upon white or black women? . . . White men in the United States were the first to
> begin the business of outraging women. They have outraged more women of both
> races than Negroes will ever outrage. . . . To publish such crimes perpetrated by them
> upon their own women would deprive their women of that protection of which the
> Anglo-Saxon delights to boast and which he wants his women to feel secure. . . . Let
> the thousands of white women whose mouths are shut by pride speak out.

Burroughs and other black reformers further challenged white women's refusal to confront sexual abuse of African American women by white men. Frances Ellen Watkins Harper, a national superintendent of the WCTU who lectured to black audiences nationwide under its auspices, devoted a number of poems to the sexual and racial double standard that held black women accountable for white men's advances. Popular opinion held that white men's "crimes were only foibles, and these were gently told," she observed. She warned white women to reform them-selves, calling their "hate of vice a sham." But she also urged white women to reform "their" men. In "A Double Standard," a poem written from the perspective of a "fallen woman," she concluded with a barbed suggestion:

> Yes, blame me for my downward course,
> But oh! remember well,
> Within your homes you press the hand
> That led me down to hell.

Harper not only indicated that white women associated intimately with immoral men, she also suggested that the sexual abuse of black women occurred under white women's noses—in their own homes. For example, she urged white reform-ers at an 1896 sex reform convention to include domestic servants in their social purity projects. Pronounced Harper, "no mistress of a home should be morally indifferent to the safety of any inmate beneath her roof." For Harper and other reformers, white women, especially in their capacity as employers of domestic ser-vants, were uniquely situated to protect black women but were not fulfilling these responsibilities. White women, they suggested, were complicit in white men's sexual offenses. As participants at a 1904 Atlanta University conference protested, domestic workers went "peculiarly unprotected" in white homes, since "the attitude of white women is not a protection, for many of them are indifferent to their husbands' or brothers' relations with Negroes." These activists pushed white women, then, to assume responsibility for protecting black women against white men.

Black activists sought not only publicity but legal change as well. Throughout the 1890s, African American politicians in the South sought sex legislation that would apply to African American women. Some, such as Texas representative Nathan Haller or Georgia legislator S.A. McIver, tried to ensure that bills for the "protection" or "reformation" of white girls explicitly included black girls as well. Others took on white men directly, pursuing legislation that would penalize them for sex with African American women. At the same session where South Carolina lawmakers debated age of consent, for instance, Robert Smalls objected to a law that criminalized interracial marriage but left informal sexual activity unregulated, thereby enabling white men to define the terms of interracial sex and leaving black women unprotected. In a gesture rich with mockery, he proposed barring white men who cohabited with black women from holding office. White officeholders rejected his proposals by a large majority. Like Smalls, other African Americans implied that the white men who framed the law might have a vested interest in stripping political rights from African Americans on the one hand, and leaving black women legally unprotected on the other. As a black newspaper wryly observed, "The very men who are abridging our rights are the ones who are ruining our daughters."

The African American WCTU activist Frances Joseph-Gaudet bemoaned the effects of laws that criminalized interracial marriage but not interracial sex. Observing that "the law is not respected by some of the men of the race who have helped to make it," she challenged white women to take action. Abuse of black women would continue, she argued, "until the white woman rises in her might and demands a higher standard of morals from the men of her race."

White women in the WCTU saw themselves as engaged in that very project, but they acted out of different motives. Age-of-consent campaigns in the South were part of a sweeping, nationwide sex reform program inaugurated in 1885 by the national WCTU. Through the legal branch of the work, activists sought, in Frances Willard's words, "the passage of such laws as would punish the outrage of defenseless girls and women by making the repetition of such outrage an impossibility." Specifically, the WCTU mobilized to amend rape statutes by raising the legal "age of consent." According to existing rape laws, most of which set the age at ten, a man who had sexual intercourse with a girl under that age would be punished as in the case of rape, whether or not she had consented and whether or not he had used force. Through revised consent laws, reformers intended to render questions about a woman's sexual character moot in court, in order to nullify the popular defense strategy of claiming that a woman did not resist. Most activists in this period took pains to distinguish between rape laws and laws regarding prostitution, although some confusion existed.

For the most part white southern women used the same organizing tactics and language as their northern counterparts. Southern WCTU chapters immediately and eagerly pursued sex reform projects; by 1886, within one year after the national organization launched its sex reform program, every state WCTU in the South, with one exception, had organized a department of "social purity." Yet the specific character of southern women's reform networks, race relations, and partisan politics in the South also influenced the timing and fate of age-of-consent legislation in the region.

White southern women were undoubtedly aware of black women's criticisms of the sexual conduct of white men, especially since their reform networks during this period brought them into interaction with African American educators, students, and activists. In the WCTU, which, although segregated, was the first biracial, inter-denominational venture in women's politics in the South, there was considerable overlap between sex reform networks and interracial coalitions. Those white women prone to participate in race reform initiatives were also likely to be active in sex reform. In Georgia, for example, numerous white WCTU superintendents of social purity projects worked with black women in African American institutions, drawing upon "neo-abolitionist" networks forged in the crucible of Reconstruction. White reformers promoted "White Shield" societies for African American women in Atlanta, where they aimed to "teach" students, mainly through moral exhortation, how to protect themselves from men's sexual advances. Black organizers who led the state WCTU for African American women assuredly brought the problem of white men to white women's attention. White women sex reformers followed black women's lead by suggesting that the best solution to the "race problem" lay in reforming white men's sexual practices.

White and black southern women faced a new set of problems from white men in the post-Reconstruction period. While it is not clear that white men's sexual behavior changed, responses to white men's actions by women, police, judges, and juries did change. According to the historian Laura F. Edwards, during Reconstruction poor black and white women brought a steady flow of sexual violence cases before the courts, attesting to their increased political power. "Redemption," the period in which elite white men beat back political challenges and reasserted control, reversed this trend. . . .

The impact of focusing on black men's alleged crimes, it seems, was to detract attention from those of white men. As the African American author Charles Chesnutt observed of the white popular fixation on the alleged rape of white women by black men, "from the hysterical utterances on the subject one would almost be inclined to believe that rape committed by a white man upon a white woman was scarcely any offense at all in comparison." Indeed, white supremacist propaganda culminated in such bald declarations as "The lust of the white man makes no menace . . . toward the women of the South. The negro has a monopoly on rape." Arrest statistics in at least one city—Savannah, Georgia—bear out the suggestion that white men's crimes against both black and white women went unnoticed by law enforcement officials: from 1899 to 1905 Savannah police arrested twenty black men for rape and three for seduction, but no white men whatsoever. Since white men so consistently avoided punishment for rape, the WCTU's rape reform campaign can be viewed as a response to this neglect. White men increasingly unrestrained by law posed new threats to all southern women.

New political conditions also laid the groundwork for age-of-consent campaigns, and help to explain the timing and fate of this legislation in the South. During the 1890s women successfully introduced age-of-consent bills in every state; by 1910 fifteen of eighteen southern legislative bodies had modified their rape laws to some degree in response to organized popular pressure. Georgia, the most notorious exception, did not pass a law raising the age from ten to fourteen years until 1918, despite the fact that women began petitioning the legislature to do so in 1887.

The sex reformers' success—be it simply introducing bills, pushing them through to a vote, or actually passing them—was tied to labor and African American political organization and independent party movement. Nationwide, Knights of Labor locals circulated thousands of petitions to raise the age of consent; in the South as well, WCTU members sought support from Knights in this campaign. Such legislation tapped into shared anxieties about exploitative bosses and sexual danger for women in the workplace. As WCTU literature explained, age-of-consent laws targeted the employer who "makes the price of [a working girl's] virtue the condition of her continued wages." Alliance with working people pushed WCTU reformers to emphasize the economic aspects of women's sexual vulnerability. Memphis women, for example, tied their age-of-consent agitation to a broader economic program, combining labor and sex reform slogans in their call for "Equal Purity, Equal Pay for Equal Work, and Self-Possession of Womanhood."

Sex legislation was among those political issues that could animate and unite organized white women, workers, and farmers. In Texas, age-of-consent reforms grew directly out of Populist politics. Mary Clardy, a Farmers' Alliance lecturer, Populist organizer, and laundress, began agitating for rape reform legislation in 1891. Ellen Lawson-Dabbs promoted age-of-consent legislation in 1894 under the banner of the Texas Farmers' Alliance, People's Party, Knights of Labor, and WCTU. In 1895 age-of-consent legislation was introduced by a Populist representative, and all the Populist legislators voted to raise the age. An opponent charged that the movement originated with "God forsaken Populistic Kansas . . . whose women are here now, the chief lobbyists for this amendment."

Developments in North Carolina also suggest the connections between sex reform and other political challenges to conservative Democrats. WCTU activists in the state began appealing for new rape laws in 1887. Not until 1895, after black and white Populists and Republicans combined to seize a majority in the state legislature from Democrats, did they finally receive a hearing. Notably, the most vigorous and vocal opponents of revising the rape law were also among the most staunch opponents of Populist and Republican reforms and were infamous for their obstructionist strategies. The WCTU's opponents surely exaggerated the threat that WCTU reforms posed to the racial and economic status quo. Yet conservative allegations that the WCTU promoted labor radicalism and "social equality" testify to the challenge posed by such coalitions.

Further evidence of rape reform's connections to the political challengers of the 1890s can be found in the political fate that befell those lawmakers who introduced age-of-consent bills in contrast to those who led the opposition. Age proponents mostly disappeared. In other words, those legislators who supported rape law reform were not among those who maintained power in the South well into the twentieth century. Conversely, contrary to the predictions of optimistic WCTU activists who maintained that opponents of rape reform "would be forever retired from public position," many of their antagonists went on to successful, and in some cases extremely long, political careers. In Tennessee the notorious and belligerent opponent John A. Tipton was voted Speaker of the House the year after he declared that legal rape reform was unneccessary, since "the shotgun remedy was the best that had ever been invented for the protection of virtue." . . .

Georgia representative Joe Hill Hall of Macon best illustrates the staying power of statesmen who opposed sex reform. A strong opponent of raising the age of consent above ten years when a bill was first proposed in 1900, he remained an intransigent foe of sex reform (and woman suffrage) to the last. In 1917 he still held a seat in the state legislature, where he continued to ridicule proposals to revise the age-of-consent law, insisting that girls of ten must be held responsible for their sexual conduct. Those men likely to introduce consent bills, then, generally did not demonstrate the political longevity of their opponents. Supporters' high turnover rate ensured that women reformers waged a constant battle to find new sponsors for their bills, while the opposition remained constant.

Opponents of age-of-consent reform benefited from keeping the issue quiet. The first step for white southern women who organized campaigns to raise the age of consent, then, was to claim a space for themselves in public discourse about sex, in order to change the law. Like the *Atlanta Constitution*, some newspapers did not deem this matter a fit subject for women to discuss publicly. As one editor patly put it, "THE LEAST TALKED ABOUT THE BETTER." Reformers did not "break the silence" in frank terms. Faced with the resistance of such editors as well as their own standards of "respectable" womanhood, these women adopted verbal strategies of indirection in order to hold serious public debate about what they themselves referred to as "the unmentionable." In fascinating comparison to what Darlene Clark Hine describes as middle-class black women's "culture of dissemblance," in which black women avoided public discussion of their private sexual practices even as they organized resistance to sexual exploitation, white women tiptoed around the subject of race and sex in the midst of a mass publicity campaign around the issue.

Women first publicized the issue by canvasing communities and gathering signatures on petitions. Activists in every southern state exerted sustained pressure on state lawmakers by submitting such petitions virtually every year until the legislation passed. In Texas, one of the most well-organized states, almost fifty thousand citizens signed petitions requesting the 1891 state legislature to raise the age of consent from ten to eighteen years. Ten years later, the pressure was still on: reformers in Florida submitted over fifteen thousand signatures in support of this reform. But the club meetings, sidewalks, and stores where reformers gathered signatures were not the only public spaces where this battle raged. Women brought their campaign into legislative halls.

Law was properly a matter for public discussion, women reformers maintained, not to be determined by men conversing alone behind closed doors. Out of the belief that "men will say in secret session things they would not say if they knew women to be present," women insisted that lawmakers publicly explain their reasons for not changing age-of-consent laws. Reformers attended legislative hearings in blocs to make their claims in person, punctuating the proceedings with commentary, even hissing at times. Legislators employed a variety of strategies to divert public attention from the matter, including inaction, evasion, and ridicule. Once age-of-consent bills were introduced, judiciary committees often simply rejected the proposed legislation, and the

TABLE 1 LEGAL AGES OF CONSENT IN SELECTED STATES, 1885 AND 1920

This table illustrates the problem faced by women reformers in the South. But it also makes clear that the age of consent battle had to be fought throughout the nation. Western and northern state laws were not significantly different from those in the South in defining the age of sexual consent. Still the debates over raising the age of consent do reveal concerns and fears specific to each state and region.

STATE	1885	1920
Alabama	10	16*
California	10	18
Delaware	7	16*
District of Columbia	12	16
Florida	10	18*
Georgia	10	14*
Kentucky	12	16*
Louisiana	12	18*
Maryland	10	16
Massachusetts	10	16
Mississippi	10	18*
New York	10	18
North Carolina	10	16*
South Carolina	10	16*
Tennessee	10	18*
Virginia	12	16
West Virginia	12	16

*The law in these states made sexual intercourse with underage females a criminal offense under a statute that typically referred to "carnal knowledge of female child"; the rape statute was a separate law.

Information for table from Mary E. Odem, *Delinquent Daughters: Protecting and Policing Adolescent Female Sexuality in the United States, 1885–1920* (1995), pp. 14–15.

bills never came to a vote. When a bill made it to the floor, opponents used every stalling tactic available to them. One legislator even invented a new filibustering technique: making a show of bolting from the house when a vote was called. As a last resort, legislators barred women from the galleries while they discussed age-of-consent bills. This move echoed the trend in this period to bar women from courtrooms. New laws enabling judges to clear the courtroom were in part a response to local WCTU chapters' practice of attending rape trials in a body.

Despite this resistance, reformers achieved some success, though not always on the terms that they had set. Southern lawmakers framed laws not necessarily in the ways women reformers intended. The opponents of rape reform shaped these laws just as much as reformers did. Legislators in most states made a distinction between rape and intercourse with an underage female. Referred to as the "age of protection," these laws set a higher age than the age of consent where sex with a woman would constitute a crime, but established milder penalties than for rape. Often no minimum penalty was established, and juries could recommend punishment by imprisonment or fines. No convictions would occur if the woman did not have a witness. Furthermore, when legislators named these bills, they shifted emphasis from men's behavior to the conduct of girls. They framed acts not to define the criminal action of men and prescribe penalties, but "to protect females of immature age and judgment from licentiousness," or "for the protection of girls and for the promotion of chastity," or "to establish the age of moral responsibility in girls." This marked a departure from the WCTU's intent, which was to place responsibility for sexual encounters largely upon men.

Reformers had a difficult time explaining the source and substance of this resistance. Although opposition in part stemmed from partisan allegiances, legislators did not represent a clear-cut body of interests. A legislator's occupation apparently had little bearing on his position: lawyers, farmers, and merchants were arrayed on both sides of the issue. Although lawmakers debated child labor throughout this period, no substantial correlation existed between support for raising the age of consent and support for child labor laws. Nor can geography help explain patterns of support or opposition: legislators from upcountry regions and plantation belts could be found in both camps. What unified opponents was a commitment to a particular conception of manhood, one based on opposition to women participating in politics or using the law to protect themselves. Opponents claimed that age-of-consent legislation deprived white southern men of their time-honored "right" to protect white women through individual acts of vengeance. But legislators also based their opposition on the perceived sexual interests of particular white men.

Ironically, opponents described white men not only as protectors of women, but also as potential victims of them. They described certain women as unusually powerful, and boys—not girls—as in need of special protection. "Is there nothing to be done for our boys?" objected one editorialist. "Do we mean that an amarous [*sic*] Venus of 17 years shall entice, if she chooses, a stripling Adonis of 16?" A Tennessee representative and self-proclaimed "father of boys as well as girls" protested that "he would not in the fear of God throw down the gate of blackmail against his sons." Another insisted that "he would not vote for a bill that would allow a designing prostitute to induce his boy into her house and make him a felon." That a substantial number of opponents had teenage sons or were single themselves helps explain the prevalence of this particular line of argument. They understood that their sons were at risk of being constrained by age-of-consent laws.

They also apprehended that adult men, including themselves, would be subject to these laws as well. A group of North Carolina legislators protested in 1895 that changing the age of consent would "prove a snare to some unfortunate and unwary man . . . [and provide] an instrument of oppression in the hands of some scheming female." Opponents expressed special alarm at the prospect of working women charging their employers with sexual abuse. As Texas senator William Bailey argued, raising the age above fourteen "gave rise to an opportunity for the typewriter girls and other females so disposed to blackmail their employers." A Texas newspaper insinuated that opponents feared that domestic workers would use this legislation to their advantage, but consoled anxious lawmakers that "defamation" could not touch the truly virtuous employer.

Opponents hinted that African American women, in particular, posed a threat to white men. One Tennesseean warned,

> All grades of society and all classes of population must be considered in such matters. To raise the age of consent . . . would enable loose young women, both white and black, to wreak a fearful vengeance on unsuspecting young men. . . . Who of us that has a boy 16 years old would be willing to see him sent to the penitentiary on the accusation of a servant girl?

The Kentucky legislator A. C. Tompkins expressed an unrestrained, and probably representative, opinion: "We see at once what a terrible weapon for evil the elevating of the age of consent would be when placed in the hands of a lecherous, sensual negro woman!" Yet overall, the white southern press was evasive when reporting on this feature of lawmakers' objections: newspapers reported on arguments of this type with innuendo. According to a Texas daily, Senator Walter Tips refused to support raising the age of consent "because legislation of this kind affects all classes." The South Carolina firebrand Ben Tillman, in uncharacteristic understatement, reportedly argued that opponents refused to raise the age of consent for white girls "because others were here."

Legislators fully understood that black girls and women could potentially use the law to protect themselves from white men. Tennessee senator Ernest Bullock objected that the law would extend to "both white and colored." In Mississippi an opponent explicitly argued "that this would enable negro girls to sue white men." A. C. Tompkins based his opposition precisely on the lack of distinction the age of consent law made among women. According to Tompkins, "The laws of the United States place the negro female on the same plane with the white female, declaring them identical in every particular."

With this lack of distinction in mind, lawmakers proceeded to make distinctions that would prevent black and working-class white women from effectively using these laws. Legislatures made provisions that the age-of-consent laws would include only women of "previously chaste character." In the words of one lawmaker, "The law is only beneficial inasmuch as it protects the innocent girls of the state." This shifted the burden of proof back onto a woman, who would not only have to prove in court that she was in fact "chaste," but further that she had a "reputation" for chastity. Legislators and reformers understood that this "reputation" requirement would be particularly difficult for African American women to meet, considering long-standing white stereotypes about their sexuality. Much like laws that prevented people whose grandfathers had not voted from voting themselves, this distinction was a way of writing racial distinctions into the law without using racial terminology.

Reformers objected strenuously to these clauses, arguing that the law had "teeth" only when women did not have to defend their character. They condemned legislators for drawing legal distinctions between the "innocent" and the sexually experienced. As one reformer exclaimed after North Carolina legislators enacted a prior chastity clause, "Fancy stopping to discuss whether a child ten and one-half years old is a virgin or has outlawed herself by having once before met a male brute! Is this 'Southern chivalry'?" An editorial in the African American journal the *Crisis* averred that through these clauses, southern lawmakers had "invented a [sure] method of damning the poor and helpless by making a distinction between 'chaste' and 'unchaste' children, the latter being given the least protection."

Lawmakers' opposition to strict rape laws extended only to those that might affect white men. Apparently, opponents did not see a contradiction in their advocacy of castration for rapists in one instance, and their vigorous defense of "men's rights" in the age-of-consent debates. Across the South at this time, legislators considered bills that would enable juries to recommend castration for men convicted of rape or attempted rape. These measures were clearly aimed at black men. Many of the same newspapers that played down age-of-consent campaigns gave these other draconian proposals a considerable amount of publicity and warm support. Thus, a Georgia paper observed that a proposed castration law was "peculiarly adopted to Southern conditions." In terrorist language, a Texas daily urged lawmakers to enact castration legislation for the protection of the "noble women of Texas" against black men.

Notably, in a number of cases it was the opponents of WCTU efforts who introduced these castration bills in the heart of debate over age of consent. Furthermore, a number of opponents proposed making penalties for attempted rape more broad—eliminating maximum limits to penalties and thereby giving juries greater power to determine punishments. In the South, where "attempt to rape" might include even a passing comment by an African American man to a white woman, and where juries were composed exclusively of white men, indeterminate sentences increased white southerners' ability to mete out harsher sentences to black men than to white men convicted of the same crime.

In the words of one African American editor who opposed leaving punishment, especially death, to jurors' discretion, "It is needless to say that the discretion is never thrown against white men, however heinous their offenses." The problem white southerners faced in framing criminal law, he observed, was "a hard one—how to [make] the law and yet save the white man from its provisions." In contrast to sex reformers, then, who wanted strict rape laws that would be universally and uniformly applied, their opponents wanted rape laws that could be selectively applied. . . .

White women activists endeavored to close up the very loopholes that their opponents labored to maintain. They intended rape laws to extend comprehensive protection to women and to cover all men. Though they shared a commitment to white supremacy with their opponents, their means of solidifying white control differed: they meant to compel white men to uphold its principles. Quite simply, white women hoped to prevent white men from having sex with black women, and saw the age-of-consent laws as a means to stop them from doing so. Texas WCTU president Helen Stoddard made this clear in an address before a state senate committee:

> I have heard a whisper—it was hardly meant for my ears—that this bill would protect the colored girl. As I pass along the streets of our cities and see the mulatto children, I think the colored girl needs protection, and more than that, the Anglo-Saxon man needs the restraints of this law to help him realize the dignity and sacred heritage he possesses by being born into the dominant race of the world.

Stoddard and her colleagues objected to any revisions in the proposed bill that "would withhold protection from the negro or colored girl against white men." In a circular letter, Georgia WCTU organizers referred to "the fact that certain legislators had openly objected to the protection [that an age-of-consent] bill would afford colored girls." This, the WCTU commented, stood as "an added reason for the bill's passage."

But reformers had rarely addressed the subject of sex between white men and black women in terms this direct. When they did, in marked contrast to their refusal to point fingers at African American men, many activists were ready to charge black women with immorality. In 1893 one activist editorialized, "I do not believe that negro men, *taking into consideration the low standard of morals among the women of the race*, are one whit more immoral than white men." While the white women activists emphasized the victimization of young white women, they studiously avoided naming African American women as victims.

Age-of-consent reformers presented themselves as protectors of "working girls" without ever alluding to what this meant in the South, where African American women constituted a large part of the labor force and the vast majority of domestic workers, and where many of these same white women unquestionably employed workers in their own households. When one white proponent tentatively broached the question of domestic service and African American women's sexuality, she put the onus on black women, urging employers to "require" virtue on the part of the women who would work in their homes. Not until the advent of southern interracial women's councils during World War I would organized white women frankly announce, "We acknowledge our responsibility for the protection of the Negro women and girls in our homes and on the streets."

White women in the WCTU expressed a range of racial perspectives in their sex reform work, and these attitudes changed in relation to shifting political conditions. Three examples illustrate the complex sources of white women's criticisms of white men, and the impact of the rising tide of white supremacy on their sexual ideology. Martha Schofield, a transplanted Quaker who ran a school for African Americans in South Carolina, made an intriguing suggestion at an 1896 purity conference. Women in the WCTU, she declared, "are sharing a weariness of so much talk and preaching about keeping *race* purity. They know what enemy is in the household and through them it must be cast out." Schofield reproached white men for their sexual advances toward black women, directing her criticism at "sons of respectable parents," men who "moved in the best society," public officials, and ministers "who led colored school girls from the path of virtue." "There are no young lives in America that have as much to contend with as the young *colored women*," maintained Schofield. "One cannot conceive the feelings of . . . colored women who know they are never safe from the insults of white men." For Schofield, the problem and the solution lay with white men; she exhorted women to "life men . . . to respect *all* women."

A decade later, even as white supremacy campaigns and politically manufactured "black brute" rape rhetoric reached a violent climax in the 1906 Atlanta riot, some white reformers still trained their critical sights on white men. Two editorials by WCTU activists in response to a barrage of sensationalist newspaper accounts of a "Reign of Terror for Southern Women" indicate different approaches to the white man problem. Mary Latimer McLendon made public her doubt over white men's will or ability to "protect" white women, especially in view of their refusal to raise the age of consent in Georgia. Although she did not dispute white stereotypes about "negro brutes," McLendon argued that certain white public officials, such as corrupt policemen, posed "as great danger" to all women, "white, black, red and yellow," as black rapists purportedly did. McLendon, who advised men to "stop all this foolish talk about disfranchising the negro," suggested that women needed political power in order to protect themselves. In effect, McLendon argued that white men's political conduct, not black men's sexual behavior, posed a threat to women.

Her fellow WCTU organizer Vara A. Majette—who later organized WCTU chapters among black women in Georgia in the 1920s and became a county juvenile court probation officer—also seized the opportunity to criticize white men. Majette's newspaper editorial appeared under the bold headline "The White Man to Blame." Unlike McLendon, who challenged white men's abuse of political and legal power, Majette focused her outrage on white men's betrayal of white supremacy. "Look at the hordes of mulatto children swarming in the cities, the towns and even the country," she protested, "and say how far is the white man responsible for conditions." Majette's white supremacist fury led her to lump black and white men together, even while she made a critical distinction about the nature of their crimes: "Accomplished by willing intercourse on the white man's part—brute force by the negro—the result is the same, outraged nature and degradation of our Southern blood!". . . .

As McLendon's editorial suggests, many white women in age-of-consent campaigns combined their consideration of white men's sexual behavior with a challenge to white men's political dominance. In the strong words of the Missouri WCTU activist Clara Hoffman, some reformers concluded that "Sex gives bias to law. Men legislate favorable for men." All of these white activists were less willing to conclude that race gives bias to law, much less to address how racial ideology shaped their own understanding of sexual relationships and their definition of sexual crime. . . .

By 1945, when Lillian Smith sought to break what she saw as white southern liberals' perpetual silence about the "white man problem," the earlier challenge to white men's sexual behavior had largely vanished from public memory. Age-of-consent campaigns indicate, however, that the subject of white men's sexuality garnered a significant amount of critical commentary in the period from 1885 to 1910. White men's sexual behavior, and the laws regulating it, were the subject of widespread public comment within black communities as well as among white women, and occasionally became points of discussion between white and black reformers as well. But disfranchisement and the solidification of racial segregation had effectively ensured that white women were even less likely to listen to African American women's insights on the problem of white men. This made it easier for white men to pursue their most effective strategy of sexual power: silence.

Questions for Study and Review

1. What motivated the Woman's Christian Temperance Union to campaign to raise the age of sexual consent in southern states in the late nineteenth and early twentieth centuries?

2. How did post–Civil War race relations shape the debate over the protection of young girls from sexual exploitation?

3. What were the similarities and differences between black and white women who advocated the reform of legislation concerning sexual abuse in southern states?

4. Compare the language and tactics of the benevolent ladies and female reformers studied by Anne Boylan in the pre–Civil War period and the women who worked with freedpeople discussed by Jean Fagan Yellin with those described by Leslie Dunlap.

Suggested Readings and Web Sites

Martha M. Hodes, *White Women, Black Men: Illicit Sex in the Nineteenth-century South* (1997)

Mary Odem, *Delinquent Daughters: Protecting and Policing Adolescent Female Sexuality in the United States, 1885–1920* (1995)

Peggy Pascoe, *Relations of Rescue: The Search for Moral Authority in the American West, 1874–1939* (1990)

Ronald G. Walters, ed., *Primers for Prudery: Sexual Advice to Victorian America* (1974)

Women and Social Movements in the United States, 1600–2000: Age of Consent Campaign
http://womhist.binghamton.edu

A Statistical Portrait

RUTH MILKMAN

To recapture the historical experience of women, scholars have pursued a host of new methods and turned to a variety of sources. Some famous or elite women left letters, diaries, and family papers, which historians have used to re-create these women's relations with their fathers and husbands as well as with female kin and friends. These documents also provide information about women's activities in churches, schools, and voluntary organizations as well as intimations of their attitudes toward children. A smaller number of poor, working-class, and minority women also wrote about their lives or had their spoken testimony transcribed by others. Yet uncovering and understanding the daily lives and thoughts of these nonelite and less well-known women, and their male kin and neighbors, requires investigation of more than the conventional literary sources. Examinations of physical artifacts such as housing or dress, the use of visual and aural documents in the form of photographs or recordings, the gathering of oral histories, and the analysis of quantitative data all provide important means of illuminating the past. The use of statistical information is especially important for reconstructing the objective boundaries of people's lives. Such data might include the relative numbers of women and men in a community, the average number of children borne by an adult women, the likelihood of a woman working for wages, the types of jobs she might hold and her average earnings, the life expectancy of women and men, and how each of these varied by region, race, class, and ethnic background as well as over time.

For most women, the size and makeup of their household, the amount and type of domestic labor they performed, and their access to paid employment set the framework of their lives. These factors shaped their relationships with relatives, neighbors, and the larger community and powerfully affected the opportunities open to them for education, recreation, and participation in public activities or institutions. For most of our nation's history, women of all regions, races, classes, and ethnic backgrounds shared certain experiences. More than 90 percent of all women did housework, were married or lived in marriage-like relations, and bore children at some point in their lives. Yet more often it was not these broad similarities but rather the differences among women that were important in shaping the contours of individual, family, and community history. Thus, it is critical to locate women in place as well as in time and to chart change over time both for women as women and in relation to men.

In the colonial period, for instance, men often outnumbered women by large margins, limiting opportunities for creating stable family lives. Life expectancy was relatively short by modern standards, a factor that also shortened the length of marriages and reduced the number of children that might be born to any given couple. Still, fertility rates were high as these early Americans sought to increase the new nation's population. One benefit of a larger population was a larger labor force, yet at least into the nineteenth century, Americans relied on immigration and enslavement, along with the natural increase supplied by births, to provide factory and field hands. Native-born white, African American, and immigrant women differed in their life expectancy, the size of their families, and the likelihood that they would work for someone other than their own family. Yet overall, from the first colonial settlements to the end of Reconstruction, fertility rates declined and women's participation in the labor force increased, setting the stage for more dramatic changes in the next century.

In the tables, figures, and graphs that follow, Ruth Milkman provides quantitative portraits of women from a range of families and communities and across the expanse of American history. Though limited by the amount, types, and quality of data collected in past centuries, these statistical snapshots allow us to view our ancestors with a new clarity and to compare their experiences—their life expectancy, the size of their families, the racial and sexual balance in their communities, their opportunities for paid work, and their participation in various occupations—with our own.

The articles in this volume describe women in specific times and places and engaged in a variety of activities—childbirth and childrearing, slave labor, factory or farm work, wartime service, or political or religious pursuits. Consulting the graphs and tables provided here as you read the articles will help you place the women you read about within the larger context of the American experience. For example, the figures indicate that in the early 1800s fewer than 10 percent of all women in the United States over the age of ten were gainfully employed. Thus, you can obtain some sense of both the excitement and the fear felt by the thousands of farm daughters who entered the textile mills at that time. Similarly, the statistical information here will help you grasp better the different relationships among slave, free black, and immigrant women and men in mid-nineteenth-century families. You will see, for example, that in the first group, there were roughly equal numbers of women and men; in the second, there were substantially more women than men; while among immigrants, there were far more men than women. Examining the high rates of fertility among nineteenth-century women will help you appreciate the importance of domestic servants in middle-class and upper-class households. When we examine these fertility rates and the limited employment opportunities for women, we can also begin to understand the difficulties faced by single mothers and widows who were trying to support their families through work in the textile mills or as domestic servants. At the same time, you can imagine what dramatic changes in individual and family life occurred as the average woman bore fewer and fewer children over the course of the century, with a woman of the Reconstruction era bearing perhaps only half the number of children borne by her Revolutionary-era grandmother.

These statistical portraits throw into sharp relief the outlines of women's lives across the first two and one-half centuries of our nation's history. Tracing the common as well as the quite different experiences of women of various ethnic backgrounds, classes, and races across both time and place, the charts, graphs, and tables included here set the contours of our own lives in a larger context and help us understand the conditions and the constraints under which earlier Americans carved out their individual, familial, communal, and national identities.

Suggested Readings and Web Sites

W. Elliott Brownlee and Mary M. Brownlee, *Women in the American Economy* (1976)
Sandra Opdyck, *The Routledge Historical Atlas of Women in America* (2000)
U.S. Bureau of the Census, *Historical Statistics of the United States, Colonial Times to 1970* (1976)
U.S. Bureau of the Census, *Negro Population, 1790–1915* (1918)
Lynn Weiner, *From Working Girl to Working Mother: The Female Labor Force in the United States, 1820–1980* (1985)
United States Historical Census Data Browser
    http://fisher.lib.virginia.edu/collections/stats/histcensus
Slave Movement during the Eighteenth and Nineteenth Centuries
    http://dpls.dacc.wisc.edu/slavedata
Women Working, 1800–1930
    http://ocp.hul.harvard.edu/ww/

In the early colonial period, there was a shortage of females relative to males in the population of what later became the United States. The sex ratios gradually became more equal in the first part of the eighteenth century, although achieving this balance took longer in some colonies than in others. The Table A.1 shows the sex ratios among white settlers from selected population censuses taken in various colonies prior to the American Revolution. The Table A.2 shows the sex ratios among blacks for the same period.

TABLE A.1 SEX RATIOS IN THE WHITE POPULATION OF SELECTED COLONIES, 1624-1776

DATE	COLONY	WHITE MALE POPULATION	WHITE FEMALE POPULATION	FEMALES PER 100 MALES
1624–5	Virginia*	873	222	25
1698	New York*	5,066	4,677	92
1704	Maryland*	11,026	7,163	65
1726	New Jersey	15,737	14,124	90
1755	Rhode Island	17,860	17,979	101
1764–5	Massachusetts	106,611	110,089	103
1771	Vermont	2,503	2,147	86
1774	Connecticut	96,182	94,296	98

TABLE A.2 SEX RATIOS IN THE BLACK POPULATION OF SELECTED COLONIES, 1624-1776

DATE	COLONY	BLACK MALE POPULATION	BLACK FEMALE POPULATION	FEMALES PER 100 MALES
1624–5	Virginia*	11	10	91
1703	New York	1,174	1,084	92
1726	New Jersey	1,435	1,146	80
1755	Maryland*	10,947	8,007	73
1755	Rhode Island	2,387	2,310	97
1764–5	Massachusetts	2,824	2,067	73
1774	Connecticut	2,883	2,218	77

Source: U.S. Bureau of the Census, *Historical Statistics of the United States, Colonial Times to 1970* (Washington: GPO, 1975), 1169-71.

---

*These figures include adults only. Children were counted separately and not distinguished by gender.

In the nineteenth century, sex ratios in the native-born white population were fairly stable, with a slight male surplus. In contrast, there was a slight surplus of women among free blacks during slavery and among blacks generally after emancipation, and a substantial surplus of men among foreign-born whites in the second half of the century. (See Figure A.1.)

FIGURE A.1 POPULATION OF THE UNITED STATES BY SEX, RACE, AND NATIVITY

A. Whites (Native and Foreign-Born) 1800–1880
(millions)

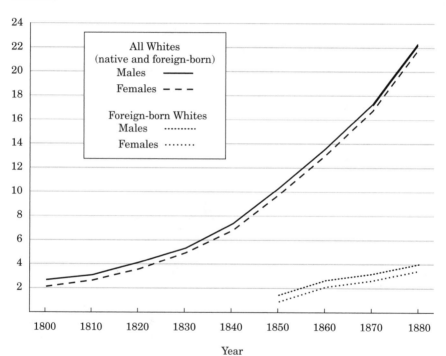

B. Black Slaves 1820–1860
(100,000's)

C. Free Blacks 1820–1860 and Blacks 1870–1880
(100,000's)

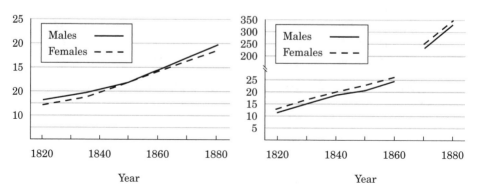

SOURCE: U.S. Bureau of the Census, *Historical Statistics of the United States, Colonial Times to 1970* (Washington: GPO, 1975), 14, 18.

Life expectancy was very low in the nineteenth century, by today's standards. Those who survived the first twenty years of life, however, were likely to be quite long-lived. Life expectancy was slightly higher for women than for men in the nineteenth century, and for both sexes it increased somewhat over time. Figure A.2 summarizes the fragmentary data on life expectancy available for this period, which are from Massachusetts only. No data are available by race or national origin, but twentieth-century sources suggest that life expectancy for blacks and the foreign-born was considerably poorer than that for native-born whites, and there is good reason to think this was the case in the nineteenth century (and earlier) as well.

FIGURE A.2 LIFE EXPECTANCY AT SPECIFIED AGES, BY SEX, FOR MASSACHUSETTS, 1850–1882

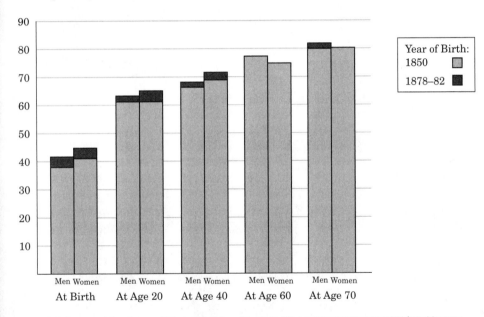

SOURCE: U.S. Bureau of the Census, *Historical Statistics of the United States, Colonial Times to 1970* (Washington: GPO, 1975), 56.

Women typically married at around age twenty in the nineteenth century, and much of their lives thereafter was spent bearing and rearing children. In 1800, the average white woman bore seven children. Of course, given the high infant and child mortality rates, not all of these children survived into adulthood. Fertility rates fell significantly over the course of the nineteenth century for whites, as Figure A.3 shows. Data for black women for this period are fragmentary, but their fertility rates declined later, probably starting around 1880, than those of white women.

FIGURE A.3 FERTILITY RATES (BIRTHS PER WOMAN) FOR WHITE WOMEN IN THE UNITED STATES, 1800–1880

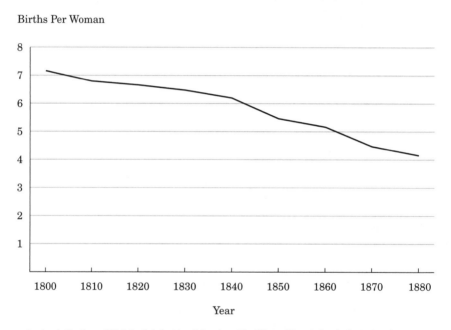

SOURCE: Ansley J. Coale and Melvin Zelnik, *New Estimates of Fertility and Population in the United States* (Princeton: Princeton University Press, 1963),36.

The extent of women's involvement in wage labor increased slowly in the nineteenth century. (No figures are available prior to 1800.) The figures in Figure A.4 do not include the bulk of the female population, who labored at home without receiving a wage. And for 1800 to 1860, these figures include only free women, both black and white. An estimated 90 percent of female slaves aged ten and over were in the labor supply in this period, although very few were paid wages.[*]

FIGURE A.4 WOMEN'S PARTICIPATION IN THE U.S. LABOR FORCE, 1800–1880

Percentage of All Women Who Were Employed

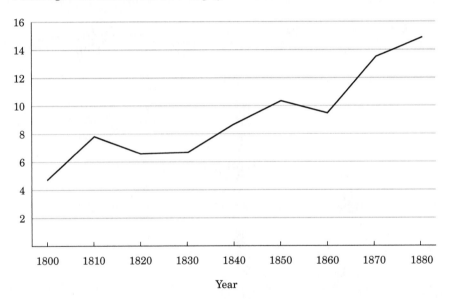

Year

SOURCE: W. Elliott Brownlee and Mary M. Brownlee, *Women in the American Economy* (New Haven: Yale University Press, 1976), 3.

---

[*]Stanley Lebergott, *Manpower in Economic Growth* (New York: McGraw-Hill, 1964), 59.

Before 1850, there are no national records of the distribution of women workers among the various occupations making up the wage labor market. In 1850, the U.S. Census Bureau began collecting such statistics for manufacturing industries only. Figure A.5 shows the distribution of women factory workers in 1850 and 1880 for major industry groups. Women workers in the clothing and textile industries were the overwhelming proportion of the female factory workforce in this period; the textile and clothing industries relied on women for half of their overall workforce. Women's representation was also substantial in the paper and printing, tobacco and cigars, and food industries. The number of women in each of these groups increased between 1850 and 1880, but only in food did they form a greater percentage of the workforce by 1880. Keep in mind, however, that the largest number of women before 1880 were still employed in domestic service and agriculture.

FIGURE A.5 NUMBERS OF WOMEN EMPLOYED AND PERCENT WOMEN FORMED OF TOTAL WAGE EARNERS IN MANUFACTURING, BY INDUSTRY GROUP, 1850 AND 1880

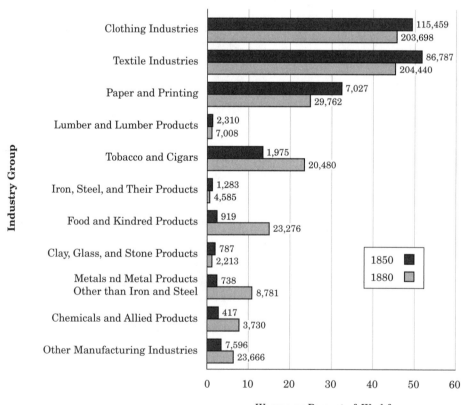

SOURCE: Helen L. Sumner, *History of Women in Industry in the United States* (U.S. Senate Document No.645, 1910), 250.

The 1880 census collected information about women's occupations both within manufacturing and in other fields of employment. Figure A.6 shows the distribution of women by major occupational group, revealing that domestic service was the most common form of employment for women, with nearly twice as many female domestics as factory workers by 1880. There were substantial variations in women's employment, depending on whether they were native-born or immigrant women. Figures in the pie chart refer to the percentage of all women employed in each occupational group.

FIGURE A.6 OCCUPATIONAL DISTRIBUTION OF WOMEN OVER AGE TEN IN PAID LABOR FORCE, FOR NATIVE- AND FOREIGN-BORN WOMEN, 1880

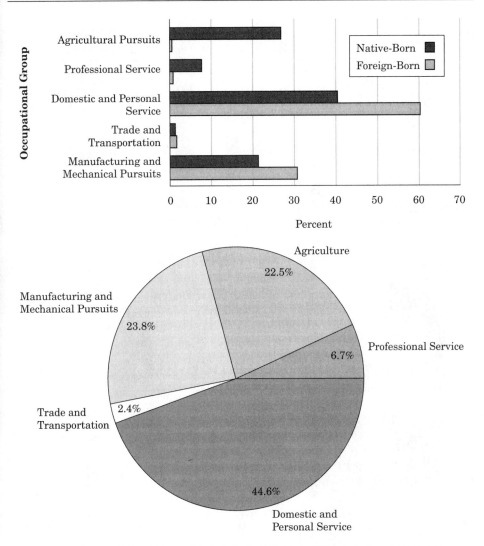

SOURCE: Helen L. Sumner, *History of Women in Industry in the United States* (U.S. Senate Document No.645, 1910), 246.

Patterns of women's employment in the late nineteenth century also varied considerably in different regions of the nation. Figure A.7 provides a regional breakdown for 1880, which reveals that manufacturing employment was especially important in the North and West, whereas in the South agriculture was the major source of women's gainful employment. This pattern partly reflects the large number of black women in the South employed in agriculture. Domestic service was an important source of employment in all regions.

FIGURE A.7 WOMEN'S EMPLOYMENT IN 1880, BY OCCUPATIONAL GROUP AND GEOGRAPHIC REGION

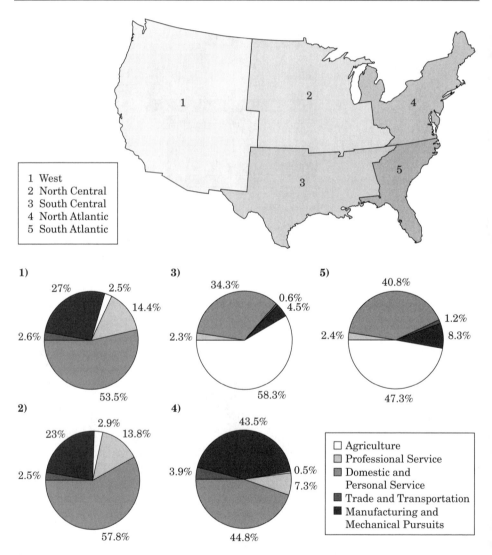

SOURCE: Helen L. Sumner, *History of Women in Industry in the United States* (U.S. Senate Document No.645, 1910), 246.

Text credits   Appendix, "A Statistical Portrait" by Ruth Milkman, copyright 1989 by Ruth Milkman. Reprinted by permission of the author.

Photo Credits   **Page xv** Baby Huestis Cook and Nurse, 1871. Valentine Richmond History Center.; Part I Opener, **page 2** Library of Congress; **page 9** Mary Evans Picture Library/The Image Works; **page 14** The Granger Collection; **page 19** Walt Disney Pictures/Photofest © Walt Disney Productions; **page 28** AKG-Images; **page 38** The Granger Collection, New York; **page 47** Shelburne Museum, Shelburne, Vermont.

Part II Opener, **page 54** "Dance of Native Californians at San Francisco de Assisi Mission, California," 1816. Ludwig Choris. Robert B. Honeyman, Jr. Collection of Early Californian and Western American Pictorial Material. Courtesy of the Bancroft Library; **page 60** Doug Sinclair; **page 75** The Image Works; **page 81** The Edward Lloyd family, painting by Charles Willson Peale, 1771. Courtesy Frances du Pont Winterthur Museum; **page 99** Library of Congress; **page 105** The Granger Collection, New York.

Part III Opener, **page 120** The Granger Collection, New York; **page 138** Porter-Phelps-Huntington Family Papers, Box 132, Folder 2, on deposit at Amherst College Archives and Special Collections, Amherst MA; **page 156** The Granger Collection.

Part IV Opener, **page 164** North Wind Picture Archives; **page 171** John Hay Library, Brown University; **page 177** Library of Congress; **page 192** from *First Peoples: A Documentary Survey of American Indian History*, Second Edition by Colin G. Calloway. Copyright © 2004 by Bedford/St. Martin's. Reproduced by permission of Bedford St. Martin's; **page 184** Courtesy, Charles O. Walker, artist. National Park Service; **page 197** Corbis; **page 206** Courtesy of the North Carolina State Archives; **page 216** "A Live Woman in the Mines" by Alonzo Delano as it appeared in his *Pen Knife Sketches*. California State Library, Sacramento.

Part V Opener, **page 222** Library of Congress; **page 234** Lizzie Scott Neblett Papers, Barker Texas History Collection, Center for American History, The University of Texas at Austin; **page 243** Courtesy of the Robert Langmuir Collection of African-American Photographs. By permission; **page 255** Courtesy, American Social History Project.